Essentials of Public Health

Bernard J. Turnock

Series Editor: Richard Riegelman

Essentials of Public Health

Bernard J. Turnock, MD, MPH

Clinical Professor of Community Health Sciences
Director, Center for Public Health Practice
School of Public Health
University of Illinois at Chicago
Chicago, Illinois

JONES AND BARTLETT PUBLISHERS
Sudbury, Massachusetts
BOSTON   TORONTO   LONDON   SINGAPORE

World Headquarters

Jones and Bartlett Publishers
40 Tall Pine Drive
Sudbury, MA 01776
978-443-5000
info@jbpub.com
www.jbpub.com

Jones and Bartlett Publishers
Canada
6339 Ormindale Way
Mississauga, Ontario
L5V 1J2
CANADA

Jones and Bartlett Publishers
International
Barb House, Barb Mews
London W6 7PA
UK

Jones and Bartlett's books and products are available through most bookstores and online booksellers. To contact Jones and Bartlett Publishers directly, call 800-832-0034, fax 978-443-8000, or visit our website www.jbpub.com.

Substantial discounts on bulk quantities of Jones and Bartlett's publications are available to corporations, professional associations, and other qualified organizations. For details and specific discount information, contact the special sales department at Jones and Bartlett via the above contact information or send an email to specialsales@jbpub.com.

Library of Congress Cataloging-in-Publication Data

Turnock, Bernard J.
    Essentials of public health / Bernard J. Turnock.
      p. ; cm. -- (Essential public health)
    Includes bibliographical references and index.
    ISBN-13: 978-0-7637-4525-7
    ISBN-10: 0-7637-4525-1
    1. Medical care.   2. Public health.   3. Medical policy.   4. Public health administration.
  I. Title.   II. Series.
    [DNLM: 1. Public Health Administration--United States.   2. Public Health Practice--
  United States. WA 540 AA1 T95e 2007]
    RA445.T87 2007
    362.1--dc22
                                                              2006022128

6048

Production Credits
Publisher: Michael Brown
Production Director: Amy Rose
Associate Production Editor: Rachel Rossi
Associate Editor: Katey Birtcher
Associate Marketing Manager: Sophie Fleck
Manufacturing Buyer: Therese Connell
Composition: Graphic World
Cover Design: Kristen E. Ohlin
Photo Research Manager: Kimberly Potvin
Photo Research: Christine McKeen
Printing and Binding: DB Hess
Cover Printing: John P. Pow Company

Printed in the United States of America
11 10 09 08 07   10 9 8 7 6 5 4 3 2

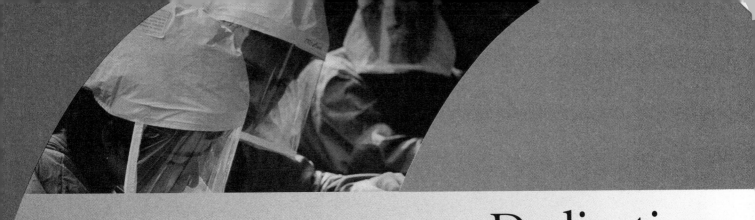

Dedication

To Colleen

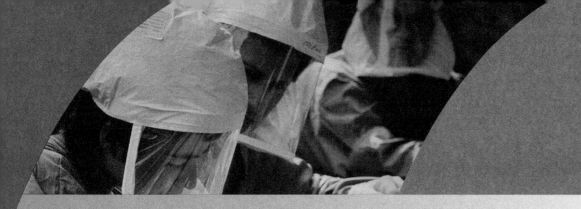

Table of Contents

Prologue   xiii

Series Page   xv

Preface   xvii

Acknowledgments   xix

Chapter 1: What Is Public Health?   1

  Learning Objectives   1

  A Brief History of Public Health in the United States   3

  Images and Definitions of Public Health   5

  Public Health as a System   7

  Unique Features of Public Health   8

  Value of Public Health   13

  Conclusion   15

  Discussion Questions and Exercises   18

Chapter 2: Understanding and Measuring Health   21

  Learning Objectives   21

  Health in the United States   21

  Health, Illness, and Disease   25

  Measuring Health   25

  Influences on Health   29

  Analyzing Health Problems for Causative Factors   36

  Economic Dimensions of Health Outcomes   39

  Healthy People 2010   41

  Conclusion   44

  Discussion Questions and Exercises   46

Chapter 3:   Public Health and the Health System   49
              Learning Objectives   49
              Prevention and Health Services   50
              The Health System in the United States   59
              Changing Roles, Themes, and Paradigms in the Health System   66
              Conclusion   70
              Discussion Questions and Exercises   71

Chapter 4:   Law, Government, and Public Health   73
              Learning Objectives   73
              American Government and Public Health   74
              Public Health Law   76
              Governmental Public Health: Federal Health Agencies   78
              Governmental Public Health: State Health Agencies   83
              Governmental Public Health: Local Public Health Organizations   88
              Intergovernmental Relationships   92
              Conclusion   96
              Discussion Questions and Exercises   97

Chapter 5:   Public Health Emergency Preparedness and Response   99
              Learning Objectives   99
              Public Health Roles in Emergency Preparedness and Response   99
              National Public Health Preparedness and Response Coordination   104
              State and Local Preparedness Coordination   108
              State and Local Bioterrorism Preparedness Grants   113
              Conclusion   117
              Discussion Questions and Exercises   120

Chapter 6:   The Public Health Workforce   123
              Learning Objectives   123
              Public Health Work and Public Health Workers   123
              Size and Distribution of the Public Health Workforce   124
              Composition of the Public Health Workforce   126
              Public Health Worker Ethics, Skills, and Competencies   128
              Characteristics of Public Health Occupations   129
              Conclusion   137
              Discussion Questions and Exercises   138

Chapter 7: Public Health Administration   141
            Learning Objectives   141
            Occupational Classification   141
            Public Health Practice Profile   142
            Important and Essential Duties   142
            Minimum Qualifications   145
            Workplace Considerations   148
            Salary Estimates   148
            Career Prospects   148
            Additional Information   149
            Conclusion   150
            Discussion Questions and Exercises   151

Chapter 8: Environmental and Occupational Health   153
            Learning Objectives   153
            Occupational Classification   153
            Public Health Practice Profile   155
            Important and Essential Duties   155
            Minimum Qualifications   159
            Workplace Considerations   162
            Salary Estimates   162
            Career Prospects   163
            Additional Information   164
            Conclusion   165
            Discussion Questions and Exercises   166

Chapter 9: Public Health Nursing   169
            Learning Objectives   169
            Occupational Classification   170
            Public Health Practice Profile   170
            Important and Essential Duties   171
            Minimum Qualifications   173
            Workplace Considerations   175
            Salary Estimates   175
            Career Prospects   175
            Additional Information   176
            Conclusion   178
            Discussion Questions and Exercises   179

Chapter 10: Epidemiology and Disease Control   181
            Learning Objectives   181
            Occupational Classification   181
            Public Health Practice Profile   182
            Important and Essential Duties   183
            Minimum Qualifications   186
            Workplace Considerations   189
            Salary Estimates   189
            Career Prospects   189
            Additional Information   190
            Conclusion   191
            Discussion Questions and Exercises   192

Chapter 11: Public Health Education and Information   195
            Learning Objectives   195
            Occupational Classification   195
            Public Health Practice Profile   196
            Important and Essential Duties   196
            Minimum Qualifications   199
            Workplace Considerations   201
            Salary Estimates   201
            Career Prospects   201
            Additional Information   202
            Conclusion   203
            Discussion Questions and Exercises   206

Chapter 12: Other Public Health Professional Occupations   209
            Learning Objectives   209
            Nutritionists and Dieticians   210
            Public Health Social, Behavioral, and Mental Health Workers   212
            Public Health Laboratory Workers   214
            Public Health Physicians, Veterinarians, and Pharmacists   217
            Public Health Dental Workers   217
            Administrative Judges and Hearing Officers   217
            Additional Information   218
            Conclusion   218
            Discussion Questions and Exercises   219

Chapter 13:   Public Health Program Occupations   221
                Learning Objectives   221
                Public Health Program Specialists and Coordinators   221
                Public Health Emergency Response Coordinators   225
                Public Health Policy Analysts   226
                Public Health Information Specialists and Analysts   227
                Community Outreach and Other Technical Occupations   227
                Additional Information   228
                Conclusion   228
                Discussion Questions and Exercises   229

Chapter 14:   Public Health Practice: Future Challenges   231
                Learning Objectives   231
                Public Health Workforce Growth   231
                Public Health Workforce Distribution and Composition   233
                Public Health Workforce Skills and Competencies   236
                Public Health Workforce Development   239
                Lessons from a Century of Progress in Public Health   240
                Limitations of 21st-Century Public Health   243
                Conclusion   246
                Discussion Questions and Exercises   247

Glossary   249

Index   261

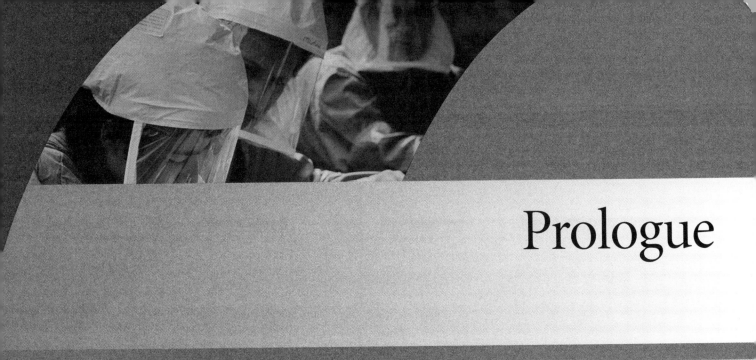

Prologue

The **Essential Public Health** series, an introductory series introduced from Jones and Bartlett Publishers last year, offers texts that will capture the full range of issues that affect the public's health. Robert Friis' *Essentials of Environmental Health* began the series by breaking down the complex subjects of epidemiology, environmental health and research.

Bernard Turnock follows Friis' lead by introducing the new student of public health to its basic elements with this second book in the series, *Essentials of Public Health*. Professor Turnock lays out for the reader a systems approach to public health; that is, public health as a conceptual model characterized by its missions, functions, capacities, processes and outcomes.

Coupled with this systems framework, *Essentials of Public Health* also offers students a nuts and bolts focus on public health jobs and careers. Professor Turnock details, for the aspiring public health worker, specific job duties, qualifications, skills, salary expectations, career ladders and professional networks.

This combination of a concise introduction to the field, and a roadmap of public health career options and opportunities, provide an ideal orientation to students of public health.

As one of the foundation texts in the **Essential Public Health** series, Professor Turnock's *Essentials of Public Health* lays the groundwork for the multiple titles that will follow.

Michael Brown
Publisher—Essential Public Health

Series Page

ESSENTIAL PUBLIC HEALTH

Recently Published:

Essentials of Environmental Health—Robert H. Friis, PhD

Upcoming Texts in the Series:

Essentials of Health Policy and Law—Joel B. Teitelbaum, JD, LLM and Sara E. Wilensky, JD, MPP
With accompanying *Readings*

Essentials of Health Behavior: Social and Behavioral Theory in Public Health—Mark Edberg, PhD
With accompanying *Readings*

Essentials of Global Health—Richard Skolnik, MPA
With accompanying *Case Studies in Global Health: Millions Saved*—Ruth Levine, PhD

Essentials of Infectious Disease Epidemiology—Manya Magnus, PhD, MPH
With accompanying *Readings*

Essentials of Biostatistics—Lisa Sullivan, PhD and Ralph D'Agostino, Sr., PhD
With accompanying *Workbook*

Essentials of Public Health Economics—Diane Dewar, PhD
With accompanying *Workbook*

Essentials of Public Health Biology: A Companion Guide for the Study of Pathophysiology—Constance Battle, MD

Fundamentals of Public Health Management and Leadership—Christopher Cassirer, ScD, MPH and Robert Burke, PhD
With accompanying *Case Studies*

SERIES EDITOR:

Richard Riegelman, MD, MPH, PhD
Professor of Epidemiology–Biostatistics, Medicine, and Health Policy
Founding Dean, George Washington University School of Public Health and Health Services
Washington, DC

Preface

Blending basic public health practice concepts with the nuts and bolts of public health careers is both a unique approach and a real challenge for a public health text. This book addresses that challenge by focusing equally on basic concepts as well as career opportunities, topics that are often of interest for students in their undergraduate years. This approach is especially useful in undergraduate courses that provide an introduction to public health, either as a stand-alone survey course or as an introductory course for an undergraduate concentration or major. Students are exposed to key concepts underlying public health as a system and social enterprise, as well as to careers in the field. As a result, students will take away an understanding of what public health is and how various occupations and professions contribute to its mission and success.

The first five chapters cover important concepts and information on what public health is in 21st-century America. Basic concepts underlying public health are presented in Chapter 1, including definitions, historical highlights, and unique features of public health. This and subsequent chapters focus largely on public health in the United States, although information on global public health and comparisons among nations appear in Chapters 2 and 3. Health and illness and the various factors that influence health and quality of life are discussed in Chapter 2. This chapter also presents data and information on health status and risk factors in the United States and introduces a method for analyzing health problems to identify their precursors. Chapter 3 addresses the overall health system and its intervention strategies, with a special emphasis on trends and developments that are important to public health. It highlights interfaces between public health and a rapidly changing health system. Chapter 4 examines the organization of public health responsibilities in the United States by reviewing its legal basis and the current structure of public health agencies at the federal, state, and local levels. Chapter 5 focuses on the emergency preparedness and response roles of public health, including the opportunities afforded by increased public expectations and a substantial influx of federal funding. Together, these five chapters serve as a primer on what public health is and how it relates to health interests in modern America.

But public health is more than concepts and organizations. Its important work is carried out by a diverse and committed workforce. Chapters 6 through 13 examine key aspects of the work of different public health occupations and professionals in order to provide an understanding of the basic underpinnings of public health jobs and careers. Despite an increasing recognition of its importance, there is little information available on the public health workforce in terms of its size, distribution, composition, skills, and impact on health goals. Chapter 6 examines overall trends affecting the public health workforce. Key characteristics for occupations and careers in public health practice are defined and explained in this chapter. This framework of career characteristics becomes the lens through which the major occupational categories and career pathways available to public health workers are examined. Chapters 7 through 13 provide basic information on many of those occupational categories and disciplines. The concluding chapter focuses on future implications for public health workers and those considering a career in public health.

Each chapter includes a variety of figures and tables that illustrate the concepts and provide useful resources for public health practitioners. A glossary of public health terminology is provided for the benefit of those unfamiliar with some of the commonly used terms, as well as to convey the intended meaning for terms that may have several different connotations in practice.

The story of public health is not a simple one to tell, in part because public health is broadly involved with the biologic, environmental, social, cultural, behavioral, and service utilization factors associated with health. Still, we all share in the successes and failures of our collective decisions and actions, making us all accountable to each other for the results of our efforts. My hope is that this book will present a broad view of the public health system and those who work within it in order to deter current and future public health workers from narrowly defining public health in terms of only what they do. At its core, the purpose of this book is to describe public health simply and clearly in terms of what it is, what it does, and why this work is important to all of us and fulfilling to those who do it on a daily basis.

Internet-based resources for courses based on this text are available at: www.jbpub.com/catalog/0763745251/additional_resources.htm/.

Acknowledgments

Whatever insights and wisdom might be found in this book have filtered through to me from my mentors, colleagues, coworkers, and friends after more than 3 decades in the field. So many people have shaped the concepts and insights provided in this book that it would be foolhardy for me to try to acknowledge them all here. This book blends information and material from two other works published by Jones and Bartlett Publishers—*Public Health: What It Is and How It Works, 3rd edition* (2004) and *Public Health: Career Opportunities That Make a Difference* (2006). Mike Brown at Jones and Bartlett Publishers was instrumental in providing guidance and suggestions for the development of this book. Production editor Rachel Rossi, also at Jones and Bartlett, and copyeditor Julia Catagnus helped make it a reality. I am grateful for their many and varied contributions.

What Is Public Health?

The passing of one century and the arrival of another afford a rare opportunity to look back at where public health has been and forward to the challenges that lie ahead. Imagine a world 100 years from now where life expectancy is 30 years more and infant mortality rates are 95% lower than they are today. The average human life span would be more than 107 years, and less than one of every 2,000 infants would die before their first birthday. These seem like unrealistic expectations and unlikely achievements; yet, they are no greater than the gains realized during the 20th century in the United States. In 1900, few envisioned the century of progress in public health that lay ahead. Yet by 1925 public health leaders such as C.E.A. Winslow were noting a nearly 50% increase in life expectancy (from 36 years to 53

years) for residents of New York City between the years 1880 and 1920.[1] Accomplishments such as these caused Winslow to speculate what might be possible through widespread application of scientific knowledge. With the even more spectacular achievements over the rest of the 20th century, we all should wonder what is possible in the century that has just begun.

The year 2006 will be remembered for many things, but it is unlikely that many people will remember it as a spectacular year for public health in the United States. No major discoveries, innovations, or triumphs set the year 2006 apart from other years in recent memory. Yet, on closer examination, maybe there were! Like the story of the wise man who invented the game of chess for his king and asked for payment by having the king place one grain of wheat on the first square of the chessboard, two on the second, four on the third, eight on the fourth, and so on, the small victories of public health over the past century have resulted in cumulative gains so vast in scope that they are difficult to comprehend.

In the year 2006, there were nearly 900,000 fewer cases of measles reported than in 1941, 200,000 fewer cases of diphtheria than in 1921, more than 250,000 fewer cases of whooping cough than in 1934, and 21,000 fewer cases of polio than in 1951.[2] The early years of the new century witnessed 50 million fewer smokers than would have been expected, given trends in tobacco use through 1965. More than 2 million Americans were alive that otherwise would have died from heart disease and stroke, and nearly 100,000 Americans were alive as a result of automobile seat belt use. Protection of the U.S. blood supply had prevented more than 1.5 million hepatitis B and hepatitis C infections and more than 50,000 human immunodeficiency virus (HIV) infections, as well as more than $5 billion in medical costs associated with these three diseases.[3] Today, average blood lead levels in children are less than one third of what they were a quarter century ago. This catalog of accomplishments could be expanded many times over. Figure 1–1 summarizes this progress, as reflected in two of the most widely followed measures of a population's health status—life expectancy and infant mortality.

These results did not occur by themselves. They came about through decisions and actions that represent the essence of what is public health. It is the story of public health and its immense value and importance in our lives that is the focus of this text. With this impressive litany of accomplishments, it would seem that public health's story would be easily told. For many reasons, however, it is not. As a result, public health remains poorly understood by its prime beneficiary—the public—as well as many of its dedicated practitioners. Although public health's results, as measured in terms of improved health status, diseases prevented, scarce resources saved, and improved quality of life, are more apparent today than ever before, society seldom links the activities of public health with its results. This suggests that the public health community must more

effectively communicate what public health is and what it does, so that its results can be readily traced to their source.

This chapter is an introduction to public health that links basic concepts to practice. It considers three questions:

- What is public health?
- Where did it come from?
- Why is it important in the United States today?

To address these questions, this chapter begins with a sketch of the historical development of public health activities in the United States. It then examines several definitions and characterizations of what public health is and explores some of its unique features. Finally, it offers insights into the value of public health in biologic, economic, and human terms.

Taken together, the topics in this chapter provide a foundation for understanding what public health is and why it is important. A conceptual framework that approaches public health from a systems perspective is introduced to identify the dimensions of the public health system and facilitate an understanding of the various images of public health that coexist in the United States today. We will see that, as in the story of the blind men examining the elephant, various sectors of our

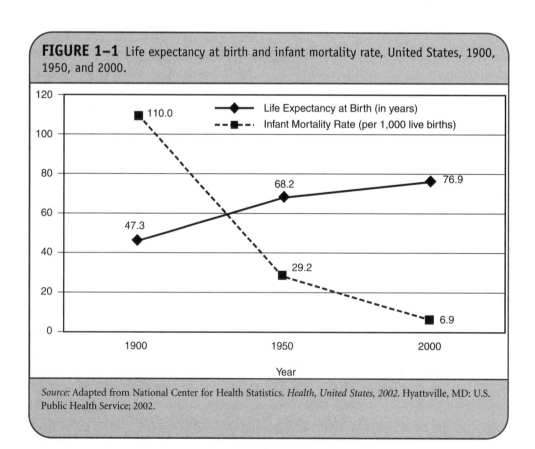

FIGURE 1–1 Life expectancy at birth and infant mortality rate, United States, 1900, 1950, and 2000.

Source: Adapted from National Center for Health Statistics. *Health, United States, 2002.* Hyattsville, MD: U.S. Public Health Service; 2002.

society have mistaken separate components of public health for the entire system. Later chapters will more thoroughly examine and discuss the various components and dimensions of the public health system.

A BRIEF HISTORY OF PUBLIC HEALTH IN THE UNITED STATES

Early Influences on American Public Health

Although the complete history of public health is a fascinating saga in its own right, this section presents only selected highlights. Suffice it to say that when ancient cultures perceived illness as the manifestation of supernatural forces, they also felt that little in the way of either personal or collective action was possible. For many centuries, disease was synonymous with epidemic. Diseases, including horrific epidemics of infectious diseases such as the Black Death (plague), leprosy, and cholera, were phenomena to be accepted. It was not until the so-called Age of Reason and the Enlightenment that scholarly inquiry began to challenge the "givens" or accepted realities of society. Eventually the expansion of the science and knowledge base would reap substantial rewards.

With the advent of industrialism and imperialism, the stage was set for epidemic diseases to increase their terrible toll. As populations shifted to urban centers for purpose of commerce and industry, public health conditions worsened. The mixing of dense populations living in unsanitary conditions and working long hours in unsafe and exploitative industries with wave-after-wave of cholera, smallpox, typhoid, tuberculosis, yellow fever, and other diseases was a formula for disaster. Such disaster struck again and again across the globe, but most seriously and most often at the industrialized seaport cities that provided the portal of entry for diseases transported as stowaways alongside commercial cargo. The experience, and subsequent susceptibility, of different cultures to these diseases partly explains how relatively small bands of Europeans were able to overcome and subjugate vast Native American cultures. Seeing the Europeans unaffected by scourges such as smallpox served to reinforce beliefs that these light-skinned visitors were supernatural figures, unaffected by natural forces.[4]

The British colonies in North America and the fledgling United States certainly bore their share of the burden. American diaries of the 17th and 18th centuries chronicle one infectious disease onslaught after another. These epidemics left their mark on families, communities, and even history. For example, the national capital had to be moved out of Philadelphia due to a devastating yellow fever epidemic in 1793. This epidemic also prompted the city to develop its first board of health in that same year.

The formation of local boards of distinguished citizens, the first boards of health, was one of the earliest organized responses to epidemics. This response was revealing in that it represented an attempt to confront disease collectively. Because science had not yet determined that specific microorganisms were the causes of epidemics, avoidance had long been the primary tactic used. Avoidance meant evacuating the general location of the epidemic until it subsided or isolating diseased individuals or those recently exposed to diseases on the basis of a mix of fear, tradition, and scientific speculation. Several developments, however, were swinging the pendulum ever closer to more effective counteractions.

The work of public health pioneers such as Edward Jenner, John Snow, and Edwin Chadwick illustrates the value of public health, even when its methods are applied amidst scientific uncertainty. Well before Koch's postulates established scientific methods for linking bacteria with specific diseases and before Pasteur's experiments helped to establish the germ theory, both Jenner and Snow used deductive logic and common sense to do battle with smallpox and cholera, respectively. In 1796, Jenner successfully used vaccination for a disease that ran rampant through communities across the globe. This was the initial shot in a long and arduous campaign that, by the year 1977, had totally eradicated smallpox from all of its human hiding places in every country in the world. The potential for its reemergence through the actions of terrorists is a topic left to a later chapter of this text.

Snow's accomplishments even further advanced the art and science of public health. In 1854, Snow traced an outbreak of cholera to the well water drawn from the pump at Broad Street and helped to prevent hundreds, perhaps thousands, of cholera cases. In that same year, he demonstrated that another large outbreak could be traced to one particular water company that drew its water from the Thames River, downstream from London, and that another company that drew its water upstream from London was not linked with cholera cases. In both efforts, Snow's ability to collect and analyze data allowed him to determine causation, which, in turn, allowed him to implement corrective actions that prevented additional cases. All of this occurred without benefit of the knowledge that there was an odd-shaped little bacterium that was carried in water and spread from person to person by hand-to-mouth contact!

England's General Board of Health conducted its own investigations of these outbreaks and concluded that air, rather than contaminated water, was the cause.[5] Its approach, however, was one of collecting a vast amount of information and accepting only that which supported its view of disease causation. Snow, on the other hand, systematically tested his hypothesis by exploring evidence that ran contrary to his initial expectations.

Chadwick was a more official leader of what has become known as the sanitary movement of the latter half of the 19th century. In a variety of official capacities, he played a major part in structuring government's role and responsibilities for protecting the public's health. Due to the growing concern over the social and sanitary conditions in England, a National Vaccination Board was established in 1837. Shortly thereafter, Chadwick's *Report on an Inquiry into the Sanitary Conditions of the Laboring Population of Great Britain* articulated a framework for broad public actions that served as a blueprint for the growing sanitary movement. One result was the establishment in 1848 of a General Board of Health. Interestingly, Chadwick's interest in public health had its roots in Jeremy Bentham's utilitarian movement. For Chadwick, disease was viewed as causing poverty, and poverty was responsible for the great social ills of the time, including societal disorder and high taxation to provide for the general welfare.[6] Public health efforts were necessary to reduce poverty and its wider social effects. This view recognizes a link between poverty and health that differs somewhat from current views. Today, it is more common to consider poor health as a result of poverty, rather than as its cause.

Chadwick was also a key participant in the partly scientific, partly political debate that took place in British government as to whether deaths should be attributed to clinical conditions or to their underlying factors, such as hunger and poverty. It was Chadwick's view that pathologic, as opposed to less proximal social and behavioral, factors should be the basis for classifying deaths.[6] Chadwick's arguments prevailed, although aspects of this debate continue to the present day. William Farr, sometimes called the (father of modern vital statistics), championed the opposing view.

In the latter half of the 19th century, as sanitation and environmental engineering methods evolved, more effective interventions became available against epidemic diseases. Further, the scientific advances of this period paved the way for modern disease control efforts targeting specific microorganisms.

Growth of Local and State Public Health Activities in the United States

In the United States, Lemuel Shattuck's *Report of the Sanitary Commission of Massachusetts* in 1850 outlined existing and future public health needs for that state and became America's blueprint for development of a public health system. Shattuck called for the establishment of state and local health departments to organize public efforts aimed at sanitary inspections, communicable disease control, food sanitation, vital statistics, and services for infants and children. Although Shattuck's report closely paralleled Chadwick's efforts in Great Britain, acceptance of his recommendations did not occur for several decades. In the latter part of the century, his farsighted and far-reaching recommendations came to be widely implemented. With greater understanding of the value of environmental controls for water and sewage and of the role of specific control measures for specific diseases (including quarantine, isolation, and vaccination), the creation of local health agencies to carry out these activities supplemented—and, in some cases, supplanted—local boards of health. These local health departments developed rapidly in the seaports and other industrial urban centers, beginning with a health department in Baltimore in 1798, because these were the settings where the problems were reaching unacceptable levels.

Because infectious and environmental hazards are no respecters of local jurisdictional boundaries, states began to develop their own boards and agencies after 1870. These agencies often had very broad powers to protect the health and lives of state residents, although the clear intent at the time was that these powers be used to battle epidemics of infectious diseases. In later chapters, we will revisit these powers and duties because they serve as both a stimulus and a limitation for what can be done to address many contemporary public health issues and problems.

Federal Public Health Activities in the United States

This sketch of the development of public health in the United States would be incomplete without a brief introduction to the roles and powers of the federal government. Federal health powers, at least as enumerated in the U.S. Constitution, are minimal. It is surprising to some to learn that the word health does not even appear in the Constitution. As a result of not being a power granted to the federal government (such as defense, foreign diplomacy, international and interstate commerce, or printing money), health became a power to be exercised by states or reserved to the people themselves.

Two sections of the Constitution have been interpreted over time to allow for federal roles in health, in concert with the concept of the so-called implied powers necessary to carry out explicit powers. These are the ability to tax in order to provide for the "general welfare" (a phrase appearing in both the preamble and body of the Constitution) and the specific power to regulate commerce, both international and interstate. These opportunities allowed the federal government to establish a beachhead in health, initially through the Marine Hospital Service (eventually to become the Public Health Service). After the ratification of the 16th Amendment in 1916, authorizing a national income tax, the federal government acquired the ability to raise vast sums of money, which could then be directed toward promoting the general welfare. The specific means to this end were a variety of grants-in-aid to state and local governments. Beginning in the 1960s, federal grant-in-aid programs designed to fill gaps in the medical care system nudged state and local governments further and further into the business of medical service provision. Federal grant programs for other social, substance abuse, mental health, and community prevention services soon followed. The expansion of federal involvement into these areas, however, was not accomplished by these means alone.

Prior to 1900, and perhaps not until the Great Depression, Americans did not believe that the federal government should intervene in their social circumstances. Social values shifted dramatically during the Depression, a period of such great social insecurity and need that the federal government was now permitted—indeed, expected—to intervene. Later chapters will expand on the growth of the federal government's influence on public health activities and its impact on the activities of state and local governments.

To explain more easily the broad trends of public health in the United States, it is useful to delineate distinct eras in its history. One simple scheme, illustrated in Table 1–1, uses the years 1850, 1950, and 2000 as approximate dividers. Prior to 1850, the system was characterized by recurrent epidemics of infectious diseases, with little in the way of collective response possible. During the sanitary movement in the second half of the 19th and first half of the 20th century, science-based control measures were organized and deployed through a public health infrastructure that was developing in the form of local and state health departments. After 1950, gaps in the medical care system and federal grant dollars acted together to increase public provision of a wide range of health services. That increase set the stage for the current reexamination of the links between medical and public health practice. Some retrenchment from the direct service provision role has occurred since about 1990. As we will examine in subsequent chapters, a new

era for public health that seeks to balance community-driven public health practice with preparedness and response for public health emergencies lies ahead.

IMAGES AND DEFINITIONS OF PUBLIC HEALTH

The historical development of public health activities in the United States provides a basis for understanding what public health is today. Nonetheless, the term *public health* evokes several different images among the general public and those dedicated to its improvement. To some, the term describes a broad social enterprise or system.

To others, the term describes the professionals and workforce whose job it is to solve certain important health problems. At a meeting in the early 1980s to plan a community-wide education and outreach campaign to encourage early prenatal care in order to reduce infant mortality, a community relations director of a large television station made some comments that reflected this view. When asked whether his station had been involved in infant mortality reduction efforts in the past, he responded, "Yes, but that's not our job. If you people in public health had been doing your job properly, we wouldn't be called on to bail you out!" Obviously, this man viewed public health as an effort of which he was not a part.

Still another image of public health is that of a body of knowledge and techniques that can be applied to health-related problems. Here, public health is seen as what public health does. Snow's investigations exemplify this perspective.

Similarly, many people perceive public health primarily as the activities ascribed to governmental public health agencies. For the majority of the public, this latter image represents public health in the United States, resulting in the common view that public health primarily involves the provision of medical care to indigent populations. Since 2001, however, public health has also emerged as a front line defense against bioterrorism and other threats to personal security and safety.

A final image of public health is that of the intended results of these endeavors. In this image, public health is literally the health of the public, as measured in terms of health and illness in a population.

This chapter will focus primarily on the first of these images, public health as a social enterprise or system. Later chapters will examine each of the other images of public health. It is important to understand what people mean when they speak of public health. As presented in Table 1–2, the profession, the methods, the governmental services, the ultimate outcomes, and even the broad social enterprise itself are all commonly encountered images of what public health is today.

With varying images of what public health is, we would expect no shortage of definitions. There have been many, and

---

TABLE 1–1 Major Eras in Public Health History in the United States

Prior to 1850	Battling epidemics
1850–1949	Building state and local infrastructure
1950–1999	Filling gaps in medical care delivery
After 1999	Preparing for and responding to community health threats

TABLE 1–2 Images of Public Health

- Public health: the system and social enterprise
- Public health: the profession
- Public health: the methods (knowledge and techniques)
- Public health: governmental services (especially medical care for the poor)
- Public health: the health of the public

it serves little purpose to try to catalog all of them here. Three definitions, each separated by a generation, provide important insights into what public health is; these are summarized in Table 1–3.

In 1988 the prestigious Institute of Medicine (IOM) provided a useful definition in its landmark study of public health in the United States, *The Future of Public Health*. The IOM report characterized public health's mission as "fulfilling society's interest in assuring conditions in which people can be healthy."[7] This definition directs our attention to the many conditions that influence health and wellness, underscoring the broad scope of public health and legitimizing its interest in social, economic, political, and medical care factors that affect health and illness. The definition's premise that society has an interest in the health of its members implies that improving conditions and health status for others is acting in our own self-interest. The assertion that improving the health status of others provides benefits to all is a core value of public health.

Another core value of public health is reflected in the IOM definition's use of the term *assuring*. Assuring conditions in

TABLE 1–3 Selected Definitions of Public Health

- "the science and art of preventing disease, prolonging life, and promoting health and efficiency through organized community effort"[8]
- "Successive re-definings of the unacceptable"[9]
- "fulfilling society's interest in assuring conditions in which people can be healthy"[7]

Source: Data from Institute of Medicine, National Academy of Sciences. *The Future of Public Health.* Washington, DC: National Academy Press: 1988; Winslow CEA. The untilled field of public health. *Mod. Med.* 1920; 2:183–191, and Vickers G., What sets the goals of public health? *Lancet.* 1958;1:599–604.

which people can be healthy means vigilantly promoting and protecting everyone's interests in health and well-being. This value echoes the wisdom in the often-quoted African aphorism that "it takes a village to raise a child." Former Surgeon General David Satcher, the first African-American to head this country's most respected federal public health agency, the Centers for Disease Control and Prevention (CDC), once described a visit to Africa in which he met with African teenagers to learn firsthand of their personal health attitudes and behaviors. Satcher was struck by their concerns over the rapid urbanization of the various African nations and the changes that were affecting their culture and sense of community. These young people felt lost and abandoned; they questioned Satcher as to what CDC, the U.S. government, and the world community were willing to do to help them survive these changes. As one young man put it, "Where will we find our village?" Public health's role is one of serving us all as our village, whether we are teens in Africa or adults in the United States. The IOM report's characterization of public health advocated for just such a social enterprise and stands as a bold philosophical statement of mission and purpose.

The IOM report also sought to define the boundaries of public health by identifying three core functions of public health: assessment, policy development, and assurance. In one sense, these functions are comparable to those generally ascribed to the medical care system involving diagnosis and treatment. Assessment is the analogue of diagnosis, except that the diagnosis, or problem identification, is made for a group or population of individuals. Similarly, assurance is analogous to treatment and implies that the necessary remedies or interventions are put into place. Finally, policy development is an intermediate role of collectively deciding which remedies or interventions are most appropriate for the problems identified (the formulation of a treatment plan is the medical system's analogue). These core functions broadly describe what public health does (as opposed to what it is) and will be examined more thoroughly in later chapters.

The concepts embedded in the IOM definition are also reflected in Winslow's definition, developed more than 80 years ago. His definition describes both what public health does and how this gets done. It is a comprehensive definition that has stood the test of time in characterizing public health as

> . . . the science and art of preventing disease, prolonging life, and promoting health and efficiency through organized community effort for the sanitation of the environment, the control of communicable infections, the education of the

individual in personal hygiene, the organization of medical and nursing services for the early diagnosis and preventive treatment of disease, and for the development of the social machinery to insure everyone a standard of living adequate for the maintenance of health, so organizing these benefits as to enable every citizen to realize his birthright of health and longevity.[8]

There is much to consider in Winslow's definition. The phrases, "science and art," "organized community effort," and "birthright of health and longevity" capture the substance and aims of public health. Winslow's catalog of methods illuminates the scope of the endeavor, embracing public health's initial targeting of infectious and environmental risks, as well as current activities related to the organization, financing, and accountability of medical care services. His allusion to the "social machinery necessary to insure everyone a standard of living adequate for the maintenance of health" speaks to the relationship between social conditions and health in all societies.

There have been many other attempts to define public health, although these have received less attention than either the Winslow or IOM definitions. Several build on the observation that, over time, public health activities reflect the interaction of disease with two other phenomena that can be roughly characterized as science and social values: (1) what do we know, and (2) what do we choose to do with that knowledge?

A prominent British industrialist, Geoffrey Vickers, provided an interesting addition to this mix a half century ago while serving as Secretary of the Medical Research Council. In identifying the forces that set the agenda for public health, Vickers noted, "The landmarks of political, economic, and social history are the moments when some condition passed from the category of the given into the category of the intolerable. I believe that the history of public health might well be written as a record of successive re-definings of the unacceptable."[9]

The usefulness of Vickers' formulation lies in its focus on the delicate and shifting interface between science and social values. Through this lens, we can view a tracing of public health over history, facilitating an understanding of why and how different societies have reacted to health risks differently at various points in time and space. In this light, the history of public health is one of blending knowledge with social values to shape responses to problems that require collective action after they have crossed the boundary from the acceptable to the unacceptable.

Each of these definitions offers important insights into what public health is and what it does. Individually and collectively, they describe a social enterprise that is both important and unique, as we will see in the section that follows.

PUBLIC HEALTH AS A SYSTEM

So what is public health? Maybe no single answer will satisfy everyone. There are, in fact, several views of public health that must be considered. One or more of them may be apparent to the inquirer. The public health described in this chapter is a broad social enterprise, more akin to a movement, that seeks to extend the benefits of current knowledge in ways that will have the maximum impact on the health status of a population. It does so by identifying problems that call for collective action to protect, promote, and improve health, primarily through preventive strategies. This public health is unique in its interdisciplinary approach and methods, its emphasis on preventive strategies, its linkage with government and political decision making, and its dynamic adaptation to new problems placed on its agenda. Above all else, it is a collective effort to identify and address the unacceptable realities that result in preventable and avoidable health and quality of life outcomes, and it is the composite of efforts and activities that are carried out by people and organizations committed to these ends.

With this broad view of public health as a social enterprise, the question shifts from what public health is to what these other images of public health represent and how they relate to each other. To understand these separate images of public health, a conceptual model would be useful. Surprisingly, an understandable and useful framework to tie these pieces together has been lacking. Other enterprises have found ways to describe their complex systems, and, from what appears to be an industrial production model, we can begin to look at the various components of our public health system.

This framework brings together the mission and functions of public health in relation to the inputs, processes, outputs, and outcomes of the system. Table 1–4 provides general descriptions for the terms used in this framework. It is sometimes easier to appreciate this model when a more familiar industry, such as the automobile industry, is used as an example. The mission or purpose might be expressed as meeting the personal transportation needs of the population. This industry carries out its mission by providing passenger cars to its customers; this characterizes its function. In this light, we can now examine the inputs, processes, outputs, and outcomes of the system set up to carry out this function. Inputs would include steel, rubber, plastic, and so forth, as well as the workers, know-how, technology, facilities, machinery, and support services necessary to allow the raw materials to become automobiles. The key processes necessary to carry out the primary

---

TABLE 1–4 Dimensions of the Public Health System

Capacity (Inputs):
- The resources and relationships necessary to carry out the core functions and essential services of public health (e.g., human resources, information resources, fiscal and physical resources, appropriate relationships among the system components)

Process (Practices and Outputs):
- Those collective practices or processes that are necessary and sufficient to assure that the core functions and essential services of public health are being carried out effectively, including the key processes that identify and address health problems and their causative factors and the interventions intended to prevent death, disease, and disability, and to promote quality of life

Outcomes (Results):
- Indicators of health status, risk reduction, and quality-of-life enhancement outcomes are long-term objectives that define optimal, measurable future levels of health status; maximum acceptable levels of disease, injury, or dysfunction; or prevalence of risk factors

Source: Adapted from Centers for Disease Control and Prevention, Public Health Program Office, 1990.

---

function might be characterized as designing cars, making or acquiring parts, assembling parts into automobiles, moving cars to dealers, and selling and servicing cars after purchase. No doubt this is an incomplete listing of this industry's processes; it is oversimplified here to make the point. In any event, these processes translate the abstract concept of getting cars to people into the operational steps necessary to carry out this basic function. The outputs of these processes are cars located where people can purchase them. The outcomes include satisfied customers and company profits.

Applying this same general framework to the public health system is also possible but may not be so obvious to the general public. The mission and functions of public health are well described in the IOM report's framework. The core functions of assessment, policy development, and assurance are considerably more abstract functions than making cars but still can be made operational through descriptions of their key steps or practices.[10,11] The inputs of the public health system include its human, organizational, informational, fiscal, and other resources. These resources and relationships are structured to carry out public health's core functions through a variety of processes that can also be termed *essential public health*

practices or services. These processes include a variety of interventions that result from some of the more basic processes of assessing health needs and planning effective strategies.[12] These outputs or interventions are intended to produce the desired results, which, with public health, might well be characterized as health or quality-of-life outcomes. Figure 1–2 illustrates these relationships.

In this model, not all components are as readily understandable and measurable as others. Several of the inputs are easily counted or measured, including human, fiscal, and organizational resources. Outputs are also generally easy to recognize and count (e.g., prenatal care programs, number of immunizations provided, health messages on the dangers of tobacco). Health outcomes are also readily understood in terms of mortality, morbidity, functional disability, time lost from work or school, and even more sophisticated measures, such as years of potential life lost and quality-of-life years lost. The elements that are most difficult to understand and visualize are the processes or essential services of the public health system. Although this is an evolving field, there have been efforts to characterize these operational aspects of public health. By such efforts, we are better able to understand public health practice, to measure it, and to relate it to its outputs and outcomes. A national work group was assembled by the U.S. Public Health Service in 1994 in an attempt to develop a consensus statement of what public health is and does in language understandable to those both inside and outside the field of public health. Table 1–5 presents the result of that process in a statement entitled "Public Health in America."[13] The conceptual framework identified in Figure 1–2 and the narrative representation in the "Public Health in America" statement are useful models for understanding the public health system and how it works, as we will see throughout this text.

This framework attempts to bridge the gap between what public health is, what it does (purpose/mission and functions, Figure 1–2), and how it does what it does (through its capacity, processes, and outcomes). It also allows us to examine the various components of the system so that we can better appreciate how the pieces fit together.

UNIQUE FEATURES OF PUBLIC HEALTH

Several unique features of public health individually and collectively serve to make understanding and appreciation of this enterprise difficult (Table 1–6). These include the underlying social justice philosophy of public health; its inherently political nature; its ever-expanding agenda, with new problems and issues being assigned over time; its link with government; its grounding in a broad base of biologic, physical, quantitative, social, and behavioral sciences; its focus on prevention as a

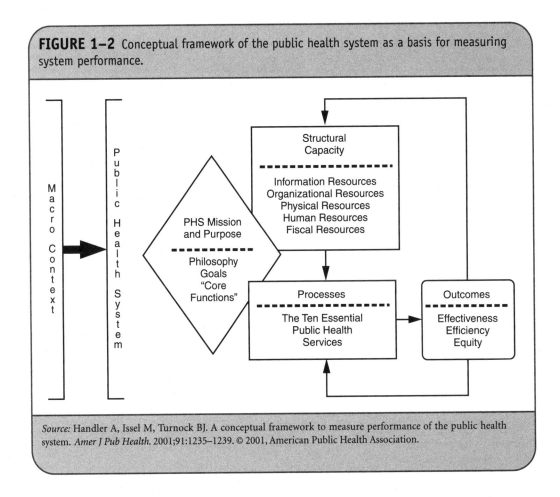

FIGURE 1–2 Conceptual framework of the public health system as a basis for measuring system performance.

Source: Handler A, Issel M, Turnock BJ. A conceptual framework to measure performance of the public health system. *Amer J Pub Health.* 2001;91:1235–1239. © 2001, American Public Health Association.

prime intervention strategy; and the unique bond and sense of mission that links its proponents.

Social Justice Philosophy

It is vital to recognize the social justice orientation of public health and even more critical to understand the potential for conflict and confrontation that it generates. Social justice is said to be the foundation of public health. The concept first emerged around 1848, a time that might be considered the birth of modern public health. Social justice argues that public health is properly a public matter and that its results in terms of death, disease, health, and well-being reflect the decisions and actions that a society makes, for good or for ill.[14] Justice is an abstract concept that determines how each member of a society is allocated his or her fair share of collective burdens and benefits. Societal benefits to be distributed may include happiness, income, or social status. Burdens include restrictions of individual action and taxation. Justice dictates that there is fairness in the distribution of benefits and burdens; injustices occur when persons are denied some benefit to which they are entitled or when some burden is imposed unduly. If

access to health services, or even health itself, is considered to be a societal benefit (or if poor health is considered to be a burden), the links between the concepts of justice and public health become clear. Market justice and social justice represent two forms of modern justice.

Market justice emphasizes personal responsibility as the basis for distributing burdens and benefits. Other than respecting the basic rights of others, individuals are responsible primarily for their own actions and are free from collective obligations. Individual rights are highly valued, whereas collective responsibilities are minimized. In terms of health, individuals assume primary responsibility for their own health. There is little expectation that society should act to protect or promote the health of its members beyond addressing risks that cannot be controlled through individual action.

Social justice argues that significant factors within the society impede the fair distribution of benefits and burdens.[15] Examples of such impediments include social class distinctions, heredity, racism, and ethnism. Collective action, often leading to the assumption of additional burdens, is necessary to neutralize or overcome those impediments. In the case of

TABLE 1–5 Public Health in America

Vision:
Healthy People in Healthy Communities
Mission:
*Promote Physical and Mental Health
and Prevent Disease, Injury, and Disability*

Public Health
- Prevents epidemics and the spread of disease
- Protects against environmental hazards
- Prevents injuries
- Promotes and encourages healthy behaviors
- Responds to disasters and assists communities in recovery
- Assures the quality and accessibility of health services

Essential Public Health Services
- Monitor health status to identify community health problems
- Diagnose and investigate health problems and health hazards in the community
- Inform, educate, and empower people about health issues
- Mobilize community partnerships to identify and solve health problems
- Develop policies and plans that support individual and community health efforts
- Enforce laws and regulations that protect health and ensure safety
- Link people with needed personal health services and assure the provision of health care when otherwise unavailable
- Assure a competent public health and personal health care workforce
- Evaluate effectiveness, accessibility, and quality of personal and population-based health services
- Research for new insights and innovative solutions to health problems

Source: Reprinted from Essential Public Health Services Working Group of the Core Public Health Functions Steering Committee, U.S. Public Health Service, 1994.

TABLE 1–6 Selected Unique Features of Public Health

- Basis in social justice philosophy
- Inherently political nature
- Dynamic, ever-expanding agenda
- Link with government
- Grounding in the sciences
- Use of prevention as a prime strategy
- Uncommon culture and bond

public health, the goal of extending the potential benefits of the physical and behavioral sciences to all groups in the society, especially when the burden of disease and ill health within that society is unequally distributed, is largely based on principles of social justice. It is clear that many modern public health (and other public policy) problems disproportionately affect some groups, usually a minority of the population, more than others. As a result, their resolution requires collective actions in which those less affected take on greater burdens, while not commensurately benefiting from those actions. When the necessary collective actions are not taken, even the most important public policy problems remain unsolved, despite periodically becoming highly visible.[15] This scenario reflects responses to such intractable American problems as inadequate housing, poor public education systems, unemployment, racial discrimination, and poverty. However, it is also true for public health problems such as tobacco-related illnesses, infant mortality, substance abuse, mental health services, long-term care, and environmental pollution. The failure to effect comprehensive national health reform in 1994 is an example of this phenomenon. At that time, middle-class Americans deemed the modest price tag of health reform to be excessive, refusing to pay more out of their own pockets when they perceived that their own access and services were not likely to improve.

These and similar examples suggest that a critical challenge for public health as a social enterprise lies in overcoming the social and ethical barriers that prevent us from doing more with the tools already available to us.[15] Extending the frontiers of science and knowledge may not be as useful for improving public health as shifting the collective values of our society to act on what we already know. Recent public health successes, such as public attitudes toward smoking in both public and private locations and operating motor vehicles after alcohol consumption, provide evidence in support of this assertion. These advances came through changes in social norms, rather than through bigger and better science.

Inherently Political Nature

The social justice underpinnings of public health serve to stimulate political conflict. Public health is both public and political in nature. It serves populations, which are composites of many different communities, cultures, and values. Politics allows for issues to be considered, negotiated, and finally determined for populations. At the core of political processes are differing values and perspectives as to both the ends to be achieved and the means for achieving those ends. Advocating causes and agitating various segments of society to identify and address unacceptable conditions that adversely affect health status often lead to increased expectations and demands on society, generally through government. As a result, public health advocates appear at times as antigovernment and anti-institutional. Governmental public health agencies seeking to serve the interests of both government and public health are frequently caught in the middle. This creates tensions and conflict that can put these agencies at odds with governmental leaders on the one hand and external public health advocates on the other.

Expanding Agenda

A third unique feature of public health is its broad and ever-increasing scope. Traditional domains of public health interest include biology, environment, lifestyle, and health service organization. Within each of these domains are many factors that affect health status; in recent decades, many new public policy problems have been moved onto the public health agenda as their predisposing factors have been identified and found to fall into one or more of these domains.

The assignment of new problems to the public health agenda is an interesting phenomenon. For example, prior to 1900, the primary problems addressed by public health were infectious diseases and related environmental risks. After 1900, the focus expanded to include problems and needs of children and mothers to be addressed through health education and maternal and child health services as public sentiment over the health and safety of children increased. In the middle of the cen-

tury, chronic disease prevention and medical care fell into public health's realm as an epidemiologic revolution began to identify causative agents for chronic diseases and links between use of health services and health outcomes. Later, substance abuse, mental illness, teen pregnancy, long-term care, and other issues fell to public health, as did several emerging problems, most notably the epidemics of violence and HIV infections, including acquired immune deficiency syndrome (AIDS). The public health agenda expanded even further as a result of the recent national dialogue over health reform and how health services will be organized and managed. Bioterrorism preparedness is an even more recent addition to this agenda amidst heightened concerns and expectations after the events of September 11, 2001, and the anthrax attacks the following month.

Link with Government

A fourth unique facet of public health is its link with government. Although public health is far more than the activities of federal, state, and local health departments, many people think only of governmental public health agencies when they think of public health. Government does play a unique role in seeing that the key elements are in place and that public health's mission gets addressed. Only government can exercise the enforcement provisions of our public policies that limit the personal and property rights of individuals and corporations in areas such as retail food establishments, sewage and water systems, occupational health and safety, consumer product safety, infectious disease control, and drug efficacy and safety. Government also can play the convener and facilitator role for identifying and prioritizing health problems that might be addressed through public resources and actions. These roles derive from the underlying principle of beneficence, in that government exists to improve the well-being of its members. Beneficence often involves a balance between maximizing benefits and minimizing harms on the one hand and doing no harm on the other.

Two general strategies are available for governmental efforts to influence public health. At the broadest level, governments can modify public policies that influence health through social and environmental conditions, such as policies for education, employment, housing, public safety, child welfare, pollution control, workplace safety, and family support. In line with the IOM report's definition of public health, these actions seek to ensure conditions in which people can be healthy. Another strategy of government is to directly provide programs and services that are designed to meet the health needs of the population. It is often easier to garner support for relatively small-scale programs directed toward a specific problem (such as tuberculosis or HIV infections) than to achieve consensus around broader health and social issues. This strategy is basically a "command-and-control" approach, in which government attempts to increase access to and utilization of services largely through deployment of its own resources rather than through working with others. A variation of this strategy for government is to ensure access to health care services through public financing approaches (Medicare and Medicaid are prime examples) or through specialized delivery systems (such as the Veterans Administration facilities, the Indian Health Service, and federally funded community health centers).

Whereas the United States has generally opted for the latter of these strategies, other countries have acted to place greater emphasis on broader social policies. Both the overall level of investment for and relative emphasis between these strategies contribute to the widely varying results achieved in terms of health status indicators among different nations (to be discussed in Chapter 2).

Many factors dictate the approaches used by a specific government at any point in time. These factors include history, culture, the structure of the government in question, and current social circumstances. There are also several underlying motivations that support government intervention. For paternalistic reasons, governments may act to control or restrict the liberties of individuals to benefit a group, whether or not that group seeks these benefits. For utilitarian reasons, governments intervene because of the perception that the state as a whole will benefit in some important way. For equality considerations, governments act to ensure that benefits and burdens are equally distributed among individuals. For equity considerations, governments justify interventions in order to distribute the benefits of society in proportion to need. These motivations reflect the views of each society as to whether health itself or merely access to health services is to be considered a right of individuals and populations within that society. Many societies, including the United States, act through government to ensure equal access to a broad array of preventive and treatment services. Equity in health status for all groups within the society may not be an explicit aspiration however, even where efforts are in place to ensure equality in access. Even more important for achieving equity in health status are concerted efforts to improve health status in population groups with the greatest disadvantage, mechanisms to monitor health status and contributing factors across all population groups, and participation of disadvantaged population groups in the key political decision-making processes within the society.[16] To the extent that equity in health status among all population groups does not guide actions of a society's government, these other elements will be only marginally effective.

As noted previously, the link between government and public health makes for a particularly precarious situation for governmental public health agencies. The conflicting value systems of public health and the wider community generally translate into public health agencies having to document their failure in order to make progress. It is said that only the squeaky wheel gets the grease; in public health, it often takes an outbreak, disaster, or other tragedy to demonstrate public health's value. Since 1985, increased funding for basic public health protection programs quickly followed outbreaks related to bacteria-contaminated milk in Illinois, tainted hamburgers in Washington state, and contaminated public water supplies in Milwaukee. Following concerns over preparedness of public health agencies to deal with bioterrorism and other public health threats, a massive infusion of federal funding occurred.

The assumption and delegation of public health responsibilities are quite complex in the United States, with different patterns in each of the 50 states (to be described in Chapter 4). Over recent decades, the concept of a governmental presence in health has emerged and gained widespread acceptance within the public health community. This concept characterizes the role of local government, often, but not necessarily always, operating through its official health agencies, which serve as the residual guarantors that needed services will actually be there when needed. In practice it means that, no matter how duties are assigned locally, there is a presence that ensures that health needs are identified and considered for collective action. We will return to this concept and how it is operationalized in Chapters 4 and 5.

Grounded in Science

One of the most unique aspects of public health—and one that continues to separate public health from many other social movements—is its grounding in science.[17] This relationship is clear for the medical and physical sciences that govern our understanding of the biologic aspects of humans, microorganisms, and vectors, as well as the risks present in our physical environments. However, it is also true for the social sciences of anthropology, sociology, and psychology that affect our understanding of human culture and behaviors influencing health and illness. The quantitative sciences of epidemiology and biostatistics remain essential tools and methods of public health practice. Often five basic sciences of public health are identified: epidemiology, biostatistics, environmental science, management sciences, and behavioral sciences. These constitute the core education of public health professionals.

The importance of a solid and diverse scientific base is both a strength and weakness of public health. Surely there is no substitute for science in the modern world. The public remains curiously attracted to scientific advances, at least in the physical and biologic sciences, and this base is important to market and promote public health interventions. For many years, epidemiology has been touted as the basic science of public health practice, suggesting that public health itself is applied epidemiology. Modern public health thinking views epidemiology less as the basic science of public health than as one of many contributors to a complex undertaking. In recent decades, knowledge from the social sciences has greatly enriched and supplemented the physical and biologic sciences. Yet these are areas less familiar to and perhaps less well appreciated by the public, making it difficult to garner public support for newer, more behaviorally mediated public health interventions. The old image of public health based on the scientific principles of environmental sanitation and communicable disease control is being superseded by a new image of public health approaches more grounded in what the public perceives to be "softer" science. This transition, at least temporarily, threatens public understanding and confidence in public health and its methods.

Focus on Prevention

If public health professionals were pressed to provide a one-word synonym for public health, the most frequent response would probably be prevention. In general, prevention characterizes actions that are taken to reduce the possibility that something will happen or in hopes of minimizing the damage that may occur if it does happen. Prevention is a widely appreciated and valued concept that is best understood when its object is identified. Although prevention is considered by many to be the purpose of public health, the specific intentions of prevention can vary greatly. Prevention can be aimed at deaths, hospital admissions, days lost from school, consumption of human and fiscal resources, and many other ends. There are as many targets for prevention as there are various health outcomes and effects to be avoided.

Prevention efforts often lack a clear constituency because success results in unseen consequences. Because these consequences are unseen, people are less likely to develop an attachment for or support the efforts preventing them. Advocates for such causes as mental health services, care for individuals with developmental disabilities, and organ transplants often make their presence felt. However, few state capitols have seen candlelight demonstrations by thousands of people who did not get diphtheria. This invisible constituency for prevention is partly a result of the interdisciplinary nature of public health. With no predominant discipline, it is even more difficult for people to understand and appreciate the work of public health.

From one perspective, the undervaluation of public health is understandable; the majority of the beneficiaries of recent and current public health prevention efforts have not yet been born! Despite its lack of recognition, prevention as a strategy has been remarkably successful and appears to offer great potential for future success, as well. Later chapters will explore this potential in greater depth.

Uncommon Culture

The final unique feature of public health to be discussed here appears to be both a strength and weakness. The tie that binds public health professionals is neither a common preparation through education and training nor a common set of work experiences and work settings. Public health is unique in that the common link is a set of intended outcomes toward which many different sciences, arts, and methods can contribute. As a result, public health professionals include anthropologists, sociologists, psychologists, physicians, nurses, nutritionists, lawyers, economists, political scientists, social workers, laboratorians, managers, sanitarians, engineers, epidemiologists, biostatisticians, gerontologists, disability specialists, and dozens of other professions and disciplines. All are bound to common ends, and all employ somewhat different perspectives from their diverse education, training, and work experiences. "Whatever it takes to get the job done" is the theme, suggesting that the basic task is one of problem solving around health issues. This aspect of public health is the foundation for strategies and methods that rely heavily on collaborations and partnerships.

This multidisciplinary and interdisciplinary approach is unique among professions, calling into question whether public health is really a profession at all. There are several strong arguments that public health is not a profession. There is no minimum credential or training that distinguishes public health professionals from either other professionals or nonprofessionals. Only a tiny proportion of those who work in organizations dedicated to improving the health of the public possess one of the academic public health degrees (the master's of public health degree and several other master's and doctoral degrees granted by schools of public health and other institutions). With the vast majority of public health workers not formally trained in public health, it is difficult to characterize its workforce as a profession. In many respects it is more reasonable to view public health as a movement than as a profession.

VALUE OF PUBLIC HEALTH

How can we measure the value of public health efforts? This question is addressed both directly and indirectly throughout this text. Later chapters will examine the dimensions of public health's value in terms of lives saved and diseases prevented, as well as in dollars and cents. Nonetheless, some initial information will set the stage for greater detail later.

Public opinion polls conducted in recent years suggest that public health is highly valued in the United States.[18] The overwhelming majority of the public rated a variety of key public health services as "very important." Specifically,

- 91% of all adults believe that prevention of the spread of infectious diseases such as tuberculosis, measles, flu, and AIDS is very important
- 88% also believe that conducting research into the causes and prevention of disease is very important
- 87% believe that immunization to prevent diseases is very important
- 86% believe that ensuring that people are not exposed to unsafe water, air pollution, or toxic waste is very important
- 85% believe that it is very important to work to reduce death and injuries from violence
- 68% believe that it is important to encourage people to live healthier lifestyles, to eat well, and not to smoke
- 66% believe that it is important to work to reduce death and injuries from accidents at work, in the home, and on the streets

In a related poll conducted in 1999, the Pew Charitable Trusts found that 46% of all Americans thought that "public health/protecting populations from disease" was more important than "medicine/treating people who are sick." Almost 30% thought medicine was more important than public health; 22% said both were equally important, and 3% had no opinion. Public opinion surveys suggest that public health's contributions to health and quality of life have not gone unnoticed. Other assessments of the value of public health support this contention.

In 1965, McKeown concluded, "health has advanced significantly only since the late 18th century and until recently owed little to medical advances."[19] This conclusion is bolstered by more recent studies finding that public health's prevention efforts are responsible for 25 years of the nearly 30-year improvement in life expectancy at birth in the United States since 1900. This bold claim is based on evidence that only 5 years of the 30-year improvement are the result of medical care.[20] Of these 5 years, medical treatment accounts for 3.7 years, and clinical preventive services (such as immunizations and screening tests) account for 1.5 years. The remaining 25 years have resulted largely from prevention efforts in the form of social policies, community actions, and personal decisions. Many of these decisions and actions targeted infectious diseases affect-

ing infants and children early in the 20th century. Later in that century, gains in life expectancy have also been achieved through reductions in chronic diseases affecting adults.

Many notable public health achievements occurred during the 20th century (Table 1–7). Several chapters of this text will highlight one or more of these achievements to illustrate the value of public health to American society in the 21st century by telling the story of its accomplishments in the preceding century. The first of these chronicles the prevention and control of infectious diseases in 20th-century America (see "Public Health Achievements in 20th-Century America: Prevention and Control of Infectious Disease," later in this chapter).

The value of public health in our society can be described in human terms as well as by public opinion, statistics of infections prevented, and values in dollars and cents. A poignant example dates from the 1950s, when the United States was in the midst of a terrorizing polio epidemic (Table 1–8). Few communities were spared during the periodic onslaughts of this serious disease during the first half of the 20th century in America. Public fear was so great that public libraries, community swimming pools, and other group activities were closed during the summers when the disease was most feared. Biomedical research had discovered a possible weapon against epidemic polio in the form of the Salk vaccine, however, which was developed in 1954 and licensed for use 1 year later. A massive and unprecedented campaign to immunize the public was quickly undertaken, setting the stage for a triumph of public health. The real triumph came in a way that might not have been expected, however, because soon into the campaign, isolated reports of vaccine-induced polio were identified in

---

TABLE 1–7 Ten Great Public Health Achievements—United States, 1900–1999

- Vaccination
- Motor-vehicle safety
- Safer workplaces
- Control of infectious diseases
- Decline in deaths from coronary heart disease and stroke
- Safer and healthier foods
- Healthier mothers and babies
- Family planning
- Fluoridation of drinking water
- Recognition of tobacco use as a health hazard

Source: Centers for Disease Control and Prevention. Ten great public health achievements—United States, 1900–1999. *MMWR Morb Mortal Wkly Rep.* 1999; 48(12):241–243.

TABLE 1–8 The Value of Public Health: Fear of Polio, United States, 1950s

"I can remember no experience more horrifying than watching by the bedside of my five-year-old stricken with polio. The disease attacked his right leg, and we watched helplessly as his limb steadily weakened. On the third day, the doctor told us that he would survive and that paralysis was the worst he would suffer. I was grateful, although I continued to agonize about whether my wife and unborn child would be affected. What a blessing that no other parent will have to endure the terror that my wife and I and thousands of others shared that August."

—Morton Chapman, Sarasota, Florida

Source: Reprinted from U.S. Public Health Service. *For a Healthy Nation: Returns on Investments in Public Health.* Washington, DC: PHS; 1994.

Chicago and California. Within 2 days of the initial case reports, action by governmental public health organizations at all levels resulted in the determination that these cases could be traced to one particular manufacturer. This determination was made only a few hours before the same vaccine was to be provided to hundreds of thousands of California children. The result was prevention of a disaster and rescue of the credibility of an immunization campaign that has virtually cut this disease off at its knees. The campaign proceeded on schedule and, five decades later, wild poliovirus has been eradicated from the western hemisphere.

Similar examples have occurred throughout history. The battle against diphtheria is a case in point. A major cause of death in 1900, diphtheria infections are virtually unheard of today. This achievement cannot be traced solely to advances in bacteriology and the antitoxins and immunizations that were deployed against this disease. Neither was it defeated by brilliant political and programmatic initiatives led by public health experts. It was the confluence of scientific advances and public perception of the disease itself that resulted in diphtheria's demise as a threat to entire populations. These forces shaped public health policies and the effectiveness of intervention strategies. In the end, diphtheria made some practices and politics possible, while it constrained others.[21] The story is one of science, social values, and public health.

CONCLUSION

Public health evokes different images for different people, and, even to the same people, it can mean different things in different contexts. The intent of this chapter has been to describe some of the common perceptions of public health in the United States. Is it a complex, dynamic, social enterprise, akin to a movement? Or is it best characterized as a goal of the improved health outcomes and health status that can be achieved

EXAMPLE

Public Health Achievements in 20th-Century America: Prevention and Control of Infectious Diseases

Prior to 1900, infectious diseases represented the most serious threat to the health of populations across the globe. The 20th century witnessed a dramatic shift in the balance of power in the centuries-long battle between humans and microorganisms. Changes in both science and social values contributed to the assault on microbes, setting into motion the forces of organized community efforts to improve the health of the public. This approach served as a model for later public health initiatives targeting other major threats to health and well-being. Highlights of this achievement are captured in Figure 1–3 and Table 1–9. The rate of infectious diseases had been reduced to such low levels that the incidence of a few thousand cases of mumps in 2006 was regarded as a significant public health event (see Figure 1–4).

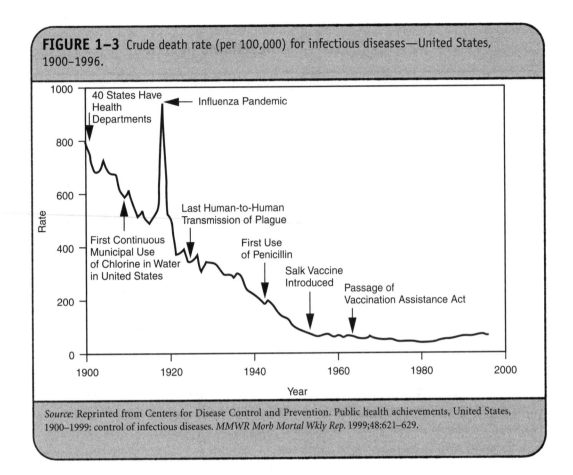

FIGURE 1–3 Crude death rate (per 100,000) for infectious diseases—United States, 1900–1996.

Source: Reprinted from Centers for Disease Control and Prevention. Public health achievements, United States, 1900–1999: control of infectious diseases. *MMWR Morb Mortal Wkly Rep.* 1999;48:621–629.

TABLE 1–9 Baseline 20th-Century Annual Morbidity and 1998 Provisional Morbidity from Nine Diseases with Vaccines Recommended before 1990 for Universal Use for Children, United States

	Baseline 20th-Century Annual Morbidity	1998 Morbidity (provisional)	Percent Decrease
Smallpox	48,164	0	100%
Diphtheria	175,885	1	100%
Pertussis	147,271	6,279	95.7%
Tetanus	1,314	34	97.4%
Poliomyelitis (paralytic)	16,316	0	100%
Measles	503,282	89	100%
Mumps	152,209	606	99.6%
Rubella	47,745	345	99.3%
Congenital rubella syndrome	823	5	99.4%
Haemophilus influenzae type b infection	20,000	54	99.7%

Source: Reprinted from Centers for Disease Control and Prevention. Public health achievements, United States, 1900–1999: impact of vaccines universally recommended for children. *MMWR Morb Mortal Wkly Rep.* 1999;48: 243–248.

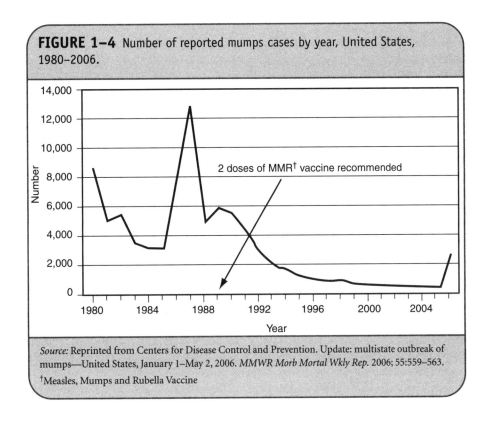

FIGURE 1–4 Number of reported mumps cases by year, United States, 1980–2006.

Source: Reprinted from Centers for Disease Control and Prevention. Update: multistate outbreak of mumps—United States, January 1–May 2, 2006. *MMWR Morb Mortal Wkly Rep.* 2006; 55:559–563.

†Measles, Mumps and Rubella Vaccine

by the work of all of us, individually and collectively? Or is public health some collection of activities that move us ever closer toward our aspirations? Or is it the profession that includes all of those dedicated to its cause? Or is public health merely what we see coming out of our official governmental health agencies—a strange mix of safety-net medical services for the poor and a variety of often-invisible community prevention services?

Although it is tempting to consider expunging the term *public health* from our vocabularies because of the baggage associated with these various images, this would do little to address the obstacles to accomplishing our central task, because public health encompasses all of these images and perhaps more!

Based on principles of social justice, inherently political in its processes, addressing a constantly expanding agenda of problems, inextricably linked with government, grounded in science, emphasizing preventive strategies, and with a workforce bound by common aspirations, public health is unique in many ways. Its value, however, transcends its uniqueness. Public health efforts have been major contributors to recent improvements in health status and can contribute even more as we approach a new century with new challenges.

By carefully examining the various dimensions of the public health system in terms of its inputs, practices, outputs, and outcomes, we can gain insights into what it does, how it works, and how it can be improved. Better results do not come from setting new goals; they come from understanding and improving the processes that will then produce better outputs, in turn leading to better outcomes. This theme of understanding the public health system and public health practice as a necessary step toward its improvement will recur throughout this text.

Discussion Questions and Exercises

1. What definition of public health best describes public health in the 21st century?

2. To what extent has public health contributed to improvement in health status and quality of life over history?

3. What historical phenomena are most responsible for the development of public health responses?

4. Which features of public health make it different from other fields? Which features are most unique and distinctive? Which is most important?

5. Because of your interest in a public health career, a producer working at a local television station has asked you to provide input into the development of a video explaining public health to the general public. What themes or messages would you suggest for this video? How would you propose presenting or packaging these messages?

6. There is little written in history books about public health problems and responses, suggesting that these issues have had little impact on history. Consider the European colonization of the Americas, beginning in the 16th century. How was it possible for Cortez and other European figures to overcome immense Native American cultures with millions of people? What role, if any, did public health themes and issues play?

7. Choose a relatively recent (within the last 3 years) occurrence/event that has drawn significant media attention to a public health issue or problem (e.g., bioterrorism, contaminated meat products, tobacco settlement, hurricane, flooding). Have different understandings of what public health is influenced public, as well as governmental responses to this event? If so, in what ways?

8. Review the history of public health activities in your state or community and describe how public health strategies and interventions have changed over time in the United States. What influences were most responsible for these changes? Does this suggest that public health functions have changed over time, as well?

9. Access the National Library of Medicine Web site <http://www.nlm.nih.gov> and conduct an online literature search of key words related to the definition, development, and current status of public health. Indicate the parameters used in this search and the general contents of the most useful article that you found.

10. Examine each of the Web sites listed below and become familiar with their general contents. Which ones are most useful for providing information and insights related to the question, "What is public health?" Why? Are there other Web sites you would suggest adding to this list?

   - American Public Health Association <http://www.apha.org>
   - Association of State and Territorial Health Officials <http://www.astho.org>
   - National Association of County and City Health Officials <http://www.naccho.org>
   - Public Health Foundation <http://www.phf.org>
   - U.S. Department of Health and Human Services <http://www.dhhs.gov> and its various Public Health Service Agencies (e.g., Centers for Disease Control and Prevention <http://www.cdc.gov>, Food and Drug Administration <http://www.fda.gov>, Health Resources and Services Administration <http://www.hrsa.dhhs.gov>, National Institutes of Health <http://www.nih.gov>, Agency for Healthcare Research and Quality <http://www.ahrq.gov>)
   - U.S. Environmental Protection Agency <http://www.epa.gov>
   - State health departments, available through the ASTHO Web site
   - Local health departments, available through the Web sites of state health departments, NACCHO, and other national public health organizations
   - Association of Schools of Public Health <http://www.asph.org> and individual schools, available through the ASPH Web site

REFERENCES

1. Winslow CEA. Public health at the crossroads. *Am J Public Health.* 1926;16:1075–1085.

2. Hinman A. Eradication of vaccine-preventable diseases. *Ann Rev Public Health.* 1999;20:211–229.

3. U.S. Public Health Service. *For a Healthy Nation: Returns on Investment in Public Health.* Washington, DC: PHS; 1994.

4. McNeil WH. *Plagues and Peoples.* New York: Doubleday; 1977.

5. Paneth N, Vinten-Johansen P, Brody H. A rivalry of foulness: official and unofficial investigations of the London cholera epidemic of 1854. *Am J Public Health.* 1998;88:1545–1553.

6. Hamlin C. Could you starve to death in England in 1839? The Chadwick-Farr controversy and the loss of the "social" in public health. *Am J Public Health.* 1995;85:856–866.

7. Institute of Medicine, National Academy of Sciences. *The Future of Public Health.* Washington, DC: National Academy Press; 1988.

8. Winslow CEA. The untilled field of public health. *Mod Med.* 1920; 2:183–191.

9. Vickers G. What sets the goals of public health? *Lancet.* 1958;1:599–604.

10. Baker EL, Melton RJ, Stange PV, et al. Health reform and the health of the public. *JAMA.* 1994;272:1276–1282.

11. Harrell JA, Baker EL. The essential services of public health. *Leadership Public Health.* 1994;3:27–30.

12. Handler A, Issel LM, Turnock BJ. A conceptual framework to measure performance of the public health system. *Am J Public Health.* 2001;91: 1235–1239.

13. Public Health Functions Steering Committee. *Public Health in America.* Washington, DC: U.S. Public Health Service; 1995.

14. Krieger N, Brin AE. A vision of social justice as the foundation of public health: commemorating 150 years of the spirit of 1848. *Am J Public Health.* 1998;88:1603–1606.

15. Beauchamp DE. Public health as social justice. *Inquiry.* 1976;13:3–14.

16. Susser M. Health as a human right: an epidemiologist's perspective on public health. *Am J Public Health.* 1993;83:418–426.

17. Afifi AA, Breslow L. The maturing paradigm of public health. *Ann Rev Public Health.* 1994;15:223–235.

18. Harris Polls. *Public Opinion about Public Health, United States. 1999.*

19. McKeown T. *Medicine in Modern Society.* London, England: Allen & Unwin; 1965.

20. Bunker JP, Frazier HS, Mosteller F. Improving health: measuring effects of medical care. *Milbank Q.* 1994;72:225–258.

21. Hammonds EM. *Childhood's Deadly Scourge: The Campaign to Control Diphtheria in New York City, 1880–1930.* Baltimore, MD: Johns Hopkins University Press; 1999.

CHAPTER 2

Understanding and Measuring Health

LEARNING OBJECTIVES

After completing Chapter 2, learners will be proficient in applying measures of population health and illness, including risk factors, in community health improvement activities and initiatives. Key aspects of this competency expectation include

- Articulating several different definitions of health
- Identifying four or more categories of factors that influence health
- For each of the these categories, specifying three or more factors that influence health
- Identifying several categories of commonly used measures of health status
- For each of these categories, identifying three or more commonly used measures
- Describing major trends in health status for the United States over the past 100 years
- Accessing and utilizing comprehensive and current national data on health status and factors influencing health in the United States
- Utilizing information on factors that influence health and measures of health to develop community health priorities and effective interventions for improving community health status

The 21st century began much as its predecessor did, with immense opportunities to advance the public's health through actions to assure conditions favorable for health and quality of life. All systems direct their efforts toward certain outcomes; they track progress by ensuring that these outcomes are clearly defined and measurable. In public health, this calls for clear definitions and measures of health and quality of life in populations. That task is the focus of this chapter. Key questions to be addressed are:

- What is health?
- What factors influence health and illness?
- How can health status and quality of life be measured?
- What do current measures tell us about the health status and quality of life of Americans at the beginning of the 21st century?
- How can this information be used to develop effective public health interventions and public policy?

The relevance of these questions resides in their focus on factors that cause or influence particular health outcomes. Efforts to identify and measure key aspects of health and factors influencing health have relied on traditional approaches over the past century, although there are signs that this pattern may be changing. The key questions identified above will be addressed slightly out of order, for reasons that should become apparent as we proceed.

HEALTH IN THE UNITED STATES

Many important indicators of health status in the United States have improved considerably over the past century, although there is evidence that health status could be even better than it is. At the turn of the 20th century, nearly 2% of the U.S. population died each year. The crude mortality rate in 1900 was about 1,700 deaths per 100,000 population. Life expectancy at birth was 47 years. Additional life expectancy at age 65 was another 12 years. Medicine and health care were largely proprietary in 1900 and of questionable benefit to health. More extensive information on the health status of the population at that time would be useful, but very little exists.

Indicators of health status improved in the United States throughout the 20th century.[1] Between 1900 and 2000, the crude mortality rate was cut nearly in half to 872 per 100,000.

By the year 2000, life expectancy at birth was nearly 77 years and life expectancy at age 65 was another 18 years.

The leading causes of death also changed dramatically over the 20th century, as demonstrated in Figure 2–1. In 1900, the 10 leading causes of death were influenza and pneumonia, tuberculosis, diarrhea and related diseases, heart disease, stroke, chronic nephritis, accidents, cancer, perinatal conditions, and diphtheria. By the year 2000, tuberculosis, gastroenteritis, and diphtheria dropped off the list of the top 10 killers, and deaths from influenza and pneumonia fell from first to seventh position on the list. Diseases of aging and other chronic conditions superseded these infectious disease processes as changes in the age structure of the population, especially the increase in persons over age 65, resulted in higher overall crude rates for heart disease and cancer and the appearance of diabetes, Alzheimer's disease, chronic kidney conditions, and septicemia on the modern list of the top 10 killers.

However, changes in crude death rates only partly explain the gains in life expectancy realized for all age groups over the 20th century. On an age-adjusted basis, improvements were even more impressive. Age-adjusted mortality rates fell about 75% between 1900 and 2000. Over the course of the entire 20th century, infant and child mortality rates fell 95%, adolescent and young adult mortality rates dropped 80%, rates for adults aged 25–64 fell 60%, and rates for older adults (older than age 65) declined 35%.

During the second half of the 20th century, overall age-adjusted mortality rates fell about 50% (see Figure 2–2) while infant mortality rates declined more than 75%. During that period, mortality rates among children and young adults (ages 1–24 years) and adults 45–64 years were reduced by more than one half. Mortality rates among adults 25–44 years fell more than 40%, and rates for elderly persons (age 65 and older) fell about one third.

Gains for adult age groups in recent decades have outstripped those for younger age groups, a trend that began about 1960 as progress accelerated toward reduction of mortality from injuries and certain major chronic diseases that largely affected adults (earlier reductions for children also left little room for further improvements). Table 2–1 demonstrates changes in the age-adjusted frequency of selected major causes of death over the second half of the 20th century. Dramatic reductions in the death rates for heart disease, stroke, unintentional injuries, influenza and pneumonia, and infant mortality have been joined by more recent reductions in rates for HIV infections, liver diseases, and suicide. Age-adjusted death rates have increased for diabetes, Alzheimer's disease, and chronic lung and kidney conditions, signaling the new morbidities associated with longer life spans. Homicide rates have improved somewhat over the past decade but reflect a substantial increase since 1950.

Table 2–1 also demonstrates the considerable disparities that exist for many of the major causes of death. Differences among races are notable, but there are also significant differences by gender for the various causes of death. These differences are often dramatic and run from top to bottom through the chain of causation. Disparities are found not only in indicators of poor health outcomes, such as mortality, but also in the levels of risk factors in the population groups most severely affected. A poignant example of these disparities is reflected in the 12-year difference in life expectancy between white females and black males.

There is also evidence that health is improving and that disability levels are declining in the population over time. Disability levels among individuals aged 55–70 years who were offspring of the famous Framingham Heart Study cohort were substantially lower, in comparison with their parents' experience at the same age.[2] In addition, fewer offspring had chronic diseases or perceived their health as fair or poor. Self-reported health status and activity limitations due to chronic conditions changed little during the 1990s, and injuries with lost workdays steadily declined during the 1990s.

In sum, U.S. health indicators tell two very different tales. By many measures, the American population has never been healthier. By others, much more needs to be done for specific racial, ethnic, and gender groups. The gains in health status over the past century have not been shared equally by all subgroups of the population. In fact, relative differences have been increasing. This widening gap in health status creates both a challenge and a dilemma for future health improvement efforts. The greatest gains can be made through closing these gaps and equalizing health status within the population. Yet the burden of greater risk and poorer health status resides in a relatively small part of the total population, calling for efforts that target those minorities with increased resources. An alternative approach is to continue current strategies and resource deployment levels. Although this may continue the steady overall improvement among all groups in the population, it is likely to continue or worsen existing gaps. In the early years of the new century, the major health challenge facing the United States appears to be less related to the need to improve population-wide health outcomes than the need to eliminate or reduce disparities. This challenges the nation's commitment to its principles of equality and social justice. However, addressing inequalities in measures of health and quality of life requires a greater understanding of health and the measures used to describe it than afforded by death rates and life expectancies.

FIGURE 2–1 The 10 leading causes of death as a percentage of all deaths in the United States, 1900 and 2000.

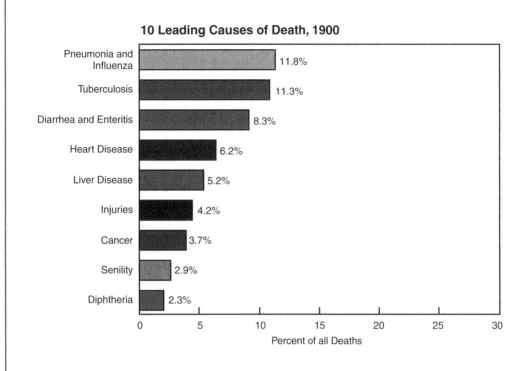

10 Leading Causes of Death, 1900

Cause	Percent
Pneumonia and Influenza	11.8%
Tuberculosis	11.3%
Diarrhea and Enteritis	8.3%
Heart Disease	6.2%
Liver Disease	5.2%
Injuries	4.2%
Cancer	3.7%
Senility	2.9%
Diphtheria	2.3%

Percent of all Deaths

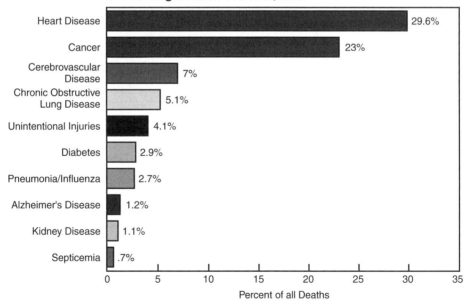

10 Leading Causes of Death, 2000

Cause	Percent
Heart Disease	29.6%
Cancer	23%
Cerebrovascular Disease	7%
Chronic Obstructive Lung Disease	5.1%
Unintentional Injuries	4.1%
Diabetes	2.9%
Pneumonia/Influenza	2.7%
Alzheimer's Disease	1.2%
Kidney Disease	1.1%
Septicemia	.7%

Percent of all Deaths

Source: Adapted from Office of Disease Prevention and Health Promotion. *Healthy People 2010: Understanding and Improving Health.* Rockville, MD: ODPHP; 2000 and National Center for Health Statistics. *Health, United States, 2002.* Hyattsville, MD: NCHS; 2002.

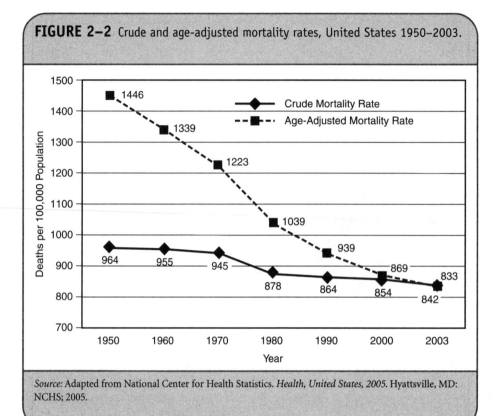

FIGURE 2–2 Crude and age-adjusted mortality rates, United States 1950–2003.

Source: Adapted from National Center for Health Statistics. *Health, United States, 2005.* Hyattsville, MD: NCHS; 2005.

TABLE 2–1 Year 2000 Age-adjusted Death Rates (per 100,000 population) for Selected Leading Causes of Death, Percent of all 2000 Deaths, Percentage Rate Change from 1950–2000, and 2000 Ratio by Sex and Race, United States

Cause of Death	Percent of 2000 Deaths	Year 2000 Rate*	Percent Change in Rates* 1950–2000	Male to Female 2000 Rate* Ratio	Black to White 2000 Rate* Ratio
Diseases of the heart	29.6	257.9	−56.0	1.5	1.3
Malignant neoplasms	23.0	201.0	+3.7	1.5	1.3
Cerebrovascular disease	7.0	60.8	−66.4	1.0	1.4
Chronic lung disease	5.1	44.3	x	1.4	0.7
Accidents & adverse effects	4.1	35.5	−54.5	2.3	1.1
Diabetes	2.9	25.2	+9.1	1.2	2.2
Influenza & pneumonia	2.7	23.7	−50.7	1.3	1.1
Suicide	1.2	10.6	−19.7	4.5	0.5
Chronic liver disease & cirrhosis	1.1	9.6	−15.0	2.2	1.0
Homicide	0.7	6.1	+19.6	3.3	5.7

*Rates age-adjusted to the 2000 U.S. population.

x = 1950 comparison rate not available, although believed to be much lower than 2000 rate.

Source: National Center for Health Statistics. *Health, United States, 2002.* Hyattsville, MD: NCHS; 2002.

HEALTH, ILLNESS, AND DISEASE

The relationship between outcomes and the factors that influence them is complex, often confounded by different understandings of the concepts in question and how they are measured. Health is difficult to define and more difficult yet to measure. For much of history, the notion of health has been negative. This was due in part to the continuous onslaught of epidemic diseases. With disease a frequent visitor, health became the disease-free state. One was healthy by exclusion.

However, as knowledge of disease increased and methods of prevention and control improved, health was more commonly considered from a positive perspective. The World Health Organization (WHO) seized this opportunity in its 1946 constitution, defining health as not merely the absence of disease but a state of complete physical, mental, and social well-being.[3] This definition of health emphasizes that there are different, complexly-related forms of wellness and illness, and suggests that a wide range of factors can influence the health of individuals and groups. It also suggests that health is not an absolute concept.

Although health and well-being may be synonyms, health and disease are not necessarily opposites. Most people view health and illness as existing along a continuum and as opposite and mutually exclusive states. However, this simplistic, one-dimensional model of health and illness does not comport very well with the real world. A person can have a disease or injury and still be healthy or at least feel well. There are many examples, but certainly Olympic wheelchair racers would fit into this category. It is also possible for someone without a specific disease or injury to feel ill or not well. If health and illness are not mutually exclusive, then they exist in separate dimensions, with wellness and illness in one dimension and the presence or absence of disease or injury in another.

These distinctions are important because disease is a relatively objective, pathologic phenomenon, whereas wellness and illness represent subjective experiences. This allows for several different states to exist: wellness without disease or injury, wellness with disease or injury, illness with disease or injury, and illness without physical disease or injury. This multidimensional view of health states is consistent with the WHO delineation of physical, mental, and social dimensions of health or well-being. Health or wellness is more than the absence of disease alone. Furthermore, one can be physically but not mentally and socially well.

With health measurable in several different dimensions, the question arises as to whether there is some maximum or optimal end point of health or well-being or whether health is something that can always be improved through changes in its physical, mental, and social facets. The latter alternative suggests that the goal should be a minimal acceptable level of health, rather than a state of complete and absolute health. Due in part to these considerations, WHO revised its definition in 1978, calling for a level of health that permits people to lead socially and economically productive lives.[4] This shifts the focus of health from an end in itself to a resource for everyday life, linking physical to personal and social capacities. It also suggests that it will be easier to identify measures of illness than of health.

Disease and injury are often viewed as phenomena that may lead to significant loss or disability in social functioning, making one unable to carry out one's main personal or social functions in life, such as parenting, schooling, or employment. In this perspective, health is equivalent to the absence of disability; individuals able to carry out their basic functions in life are healthy. This characterization of health as the absence of significant functional disabilities is perhaps the most common one for this highly sought state. Still, this definition is negative in that it defines health as the absence of disability.

In attempting to measure health, both quantity and quality become important considerations. However, it is not always easy to answer the questions: How much? Compared with what? For example, physical health for a 10-year-old child carries a much different expectation than physical health for an 80-year-old. It is reasonable to conclude that the natural processes of aging lead to gradual diminution of functional reserve capacity and that this is normal and not easily prevented. Thus, our perceptions of normal functioning are influenced by social and cultural factors.

The concept of well-being advanced in the WHO definition goes beyond the physical aspects of health that are the usual focus of measurements and comparisons. Including the mental and social aspects of well-being or health legitimizes the examination of factors that affect mental and social health. Together, these themes suggest that we need to consider carefully what we are measuring in order to understand what these measures are telling us about health, illness, and disease states in a population and the factors that influence these outcomes.

MEASURING HEALTH

The availability of information on health outcomes suggests that measuring the health status of populations is a simple task. However, although often interesting and sometimes even dramatic, the commonly used measures of health status fail to paint a complete picture of health. Many of the reasons are obvious. The commonly used measures actually reflect disease and mortality, rather than health itself. The longstanding misperception that health is the absence of disease is reinforced by the relative ease of measuring disease states, in comparison with states of health. Actually, the most commonly used indicators focus on a state that is neither health nor disease—namely, death.

Despite the many problems with using mortality as a proxy for health, mortality data are generally available and widely used to describe the health status of populations. This is ironic because such data only indirectly describe the health status of living populations. Unfortunately, data on morbidity (illnesses, injuries, and functional limitations of the population) are neither as available nor as readily understood as are mortality data. This situation is improving, however, as new forms and sources of information on health conditions become more readily available. Sources for information on morbidities and disabilities now include medical records from hospitals, managed care organizations, and other providers, as well as information derived from surveys, businesses, schools, and other sources. Assessments of the health status of populations are increasingly utilizing measures from these sources. An excellent compilation of data and information on both health status and health services, *Health United States*,[1] is published annually by the National Center for Health Statistics. Much of the data used in this chapter is derived from this source.

Mortality-Based Measures

Although mortality-based indicators of health status are both widely used and useful, there are some important differences in their use and interpretation. The most commonly used are crude mortality, age-specific and age-adjusted mortality, life expectancy, and years of potential life lost (YPLL). Although all are based on the same events, each provides somewhat different information as to the health status of a population.

Crude mortality rates count deaths within the entire population and are not sensitive to differences in the age distribution of different populations. The mortality comparisons presented in Figure 2–2 illustrate the limitations of using crude death rates to compare the mortality experience of the U.S. population late in the 20th century with that of the year 1950. On the basis of these data, we might conclude that mortality rates in the United States had declined about 20% since 1950. However, because there was a greater proportion of the late 20th century population in the higher age categories, these are not truly comparable populations. The 20% reduction actually understates the differences in mortality experience over the 20th century. Because differences in the age characteristics of the two populations are a primary concern, we look for methods to correct or adjust for the age factor. Age-specific and age-adjusted rates do just that.

Age-specific mortality rates relate the number of deaths to the number of persons in a specific age group. The infant mor-

tality rate is probably the best-known example, describing the number of deaths of live-born infants occurring in the first year of life per 1,000 live births. Public health studies often use age-adjusted mortality rates to compensate for different mixes of age groups within a population (e.g., a high proportion of children or elderly). Age-adjusted rates are calculated by applying age-specific rates to a standard population (we now use the 2000 U.S. population). This adjustment permits more meaningful comparisons of mortality experience between populations with different age distribution patterns. Differences between crude and age-adjusted mortality rates can be substantial, such as those in Figure 2–2. The explanation is simply that the population at the end of the 20th century had a greater proportion of persons in older age groups than the 1900 or 1950 populations. Using crude rates, the improvement between 1950 and 2000 was about 20%; age-adjusted rates showed a 40% improvement.

Life expectancy, also based on the mortality experience of a population, is a computation of the number of years between any given age (e.g., birth or age 45) and the average age of death for that population. Together with infant mortality rates, life expectancies are commonly used in comparisons of health status among nations. These two mortality-based indicators are often perceived as general indicators of the overall health status of a population. Infant mortality and life expectancy measures for the United States are mediocre, in comparison with those of other developed nations. Figure 2–3 presents international comparisons of life expectancy by gender for the United States and selected other countries for 2001.

Years of potential life lost (YPLL) is a mortality-based indicator that places greater weight on deaths that occur at younger ages. Years of life lost before some arbitrary age (often age 65 or 75) are computed and used to measure the relative impact on society of different causes of death. If age 65 is used as the threshold for calculating YPLL, an infant death would contribute 65 YPLL, and a homicide at age 25 would contribute 40 YPLL. A death due to stroke at age 70 would contribute no years of life lost before age 65, and so on. Until relatively recently, age 65 was widely used as the threshold age. With life expectancies now exceeding 75 years at birth, YPLL calculations using age 75 as the threshold have become more common. Table 2–2 presents data on YPLL before age 75, illustrating the usefulness of this approach in providing a somewhat different perspective as to which problems are most important in terms of their magnitude and impact. The use of YPLL ranks cancer, HIV/AIDS, and various forms of injury-related deaths higher than does the use of crude numbers or rates. Conversely, the use of crude rates ranks heart disease, stroke, pneumonia, diabetes, and chronic lung and liver diseases higher than does

Morbidity, Disability, and Quality Measures

Mortality indicators can also be combined with other health indicators that describe quality considerations to provide a measure of the span of healthy life. These indicators can be an especially meaningful measure of health status in a population because they also consider morbidity and disability from conditions that impact on functioning but do not cause death (e.g., cerebral palsy, schizophrenia, arthritis). A commonly used measure of aggregate disease burden is the disability-adjusted life year or DALY. Other variants on this theme are span-of-healthy-life indicators (called years of healthy life [YHL]) that combine mortality data with self-reported health status and activity limitation data acquired through the National Health Interview Survey. In 1998, an average of 11.5 years of life (when life expectancy was 76.7 years at birth) involved limitations of major life activities, such as self-care (e.g., bathing, grooming, cooking), recreation, work, and school. The 65-year span of healthy life presents a better, although not precise, picture of health status and quality of life. This indicator is illustrated in Figure 2–4, with 1998 data identifying disparities among blacks, whites, and Hispanics in both the number of healthy years of life and the percentage of healthy years in comparison

FIGURE 2–3 Life expectancy at birth by gender and ranked by selected countries, 2001.

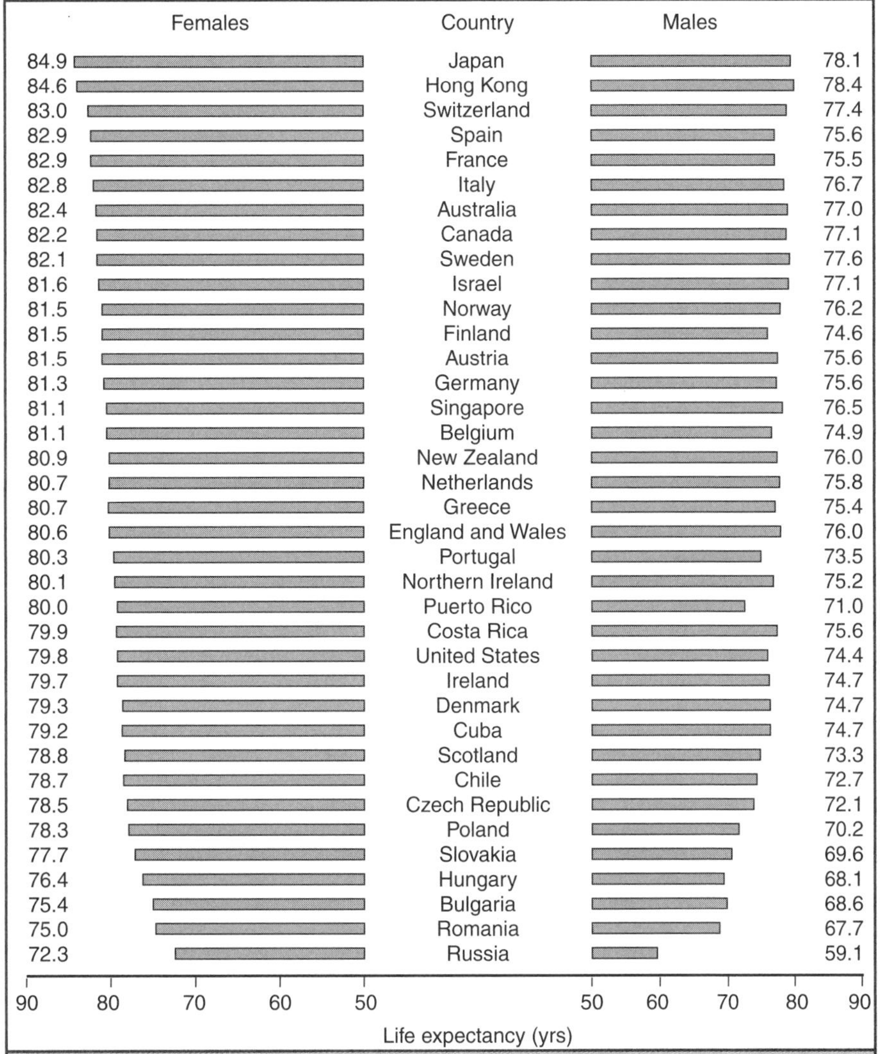

Females	Country	Males
84.9	Japan	78.1
84.6	Hong Kong	78.4
83.0	Switzerland	77.4
82.9	Spain	75.6
82.9	France	75.5
82.8	Italy	76.7
82.4	Australia	77.0
82.2	Canada	77.1
82.1	Sweden	77.6
81.6	Israel	77.1
81.5	Norway	76.2
81.5	Finland	74.6
81.5	Austria	75.6
81.3	Germany	75.6
81.1	Singapore	76.5
81.1	Belgium	74.9
80.9	New Zealand	76.0
80.7	Netherlands	75.8
80.7	Greece	75.4
80.6	England and Wales	76.0
80.3	Portugal	73.5
80.1	Northern Ireland	75.2
80.0	Puerto Rico	71.0
79.9	Costa Rica	75.6
79.8	United States	74.4
79.7	Ireland	74.7
79.3	Denmark	74.7
79.2	Cuba	74.7
78.8	Scotland	73.3
78.7	Chile	72.7
78.5	Czech Republic	72.1
78.3	Poland	70.2
77.7	Slovakia	69.6
76.4	Hungary	68.1
75.4	Bulgaria	68.6
75.0	Romania	67.7
72.3	Russia	59.1

Life expectancy (yrs)

Source: Adapted from National Center for Health Statistics. *Health, United States, 2005.* Hyattsville, MD: NCHS; 2005.

the use of YPLL. Four of the top 10 causes of death, as determined by the number of deaths, do not appear in the list of the top 10 causes of YPLL.

Each of these different mortality indicators can be examined for various racial and ethnic subpopulations to identify disparities among these groups. For example, age-adjusted rates of YPLL before age 75 for 2000 ranged from 6,284 per 100,000 population for Hispanics to 7,029 for whites and 13,177 for blacks. The rate for all groups was 7,694 per 100,000. The large disparity for blacks is attributable primarily to differences in infant mortality, homicide, and HIV infection deaths.

with life expectancy. Hispanics had the greatest life expectancy at 82.1 years, of which 66.3 (81%) were years of healthy life. In contrast, blacks had 11 fewer years in life expectancy (71.3 years), but the same proportion (81%) were healthy years. Life expectancy for whites was 77.3 years, with a higher percentage of healthy years (86%) than Hispanics or blacks. These differences illustrate different forms of disparities among these groups, with blacks experiencing higher mortality (lower life expectancy) and Hispanics carrying a greater burden of disease prevalence (higher number of unhealthy life years) than the white population. Among the mortality-related measures

TABLE 2–2 Age-Adjusted Years of Potential Life Lost (YPLL) before Age 75 by Cause of Death and Ranks for YPLL and Number of Deaths, United States, 2000

Causes of Death	YPLL	Rank by YPLL	Rank by Number of Deaths
Cancer	1,698,500	1	2
Heart Disease	1,270,700	2	1
Unintentional injuries	1,052,500	3	5
Suicide	343,300	4	11
Homicide	274,200	5	14
Cerebrovascular diseases	226,500	6	3
Chronic obstructive lung disease	190,700	7	4
Diabetes mellitus	181,200	8	6
HIV infections	178,900	9	18
Chronic liver disease and cirrhosis	141,700	10	12

Note: Years lost before age 75 per 100,000 population younger than 75 years of age.
Source: Adapted from National Center for Health Statistics. *Health, United States, 2002.* Hyattsville, MD: NCHS; 2002.

FIGURE 2–4 Total life expectancy and years of healthy life by race and Hispanic origin, United States, 1998.

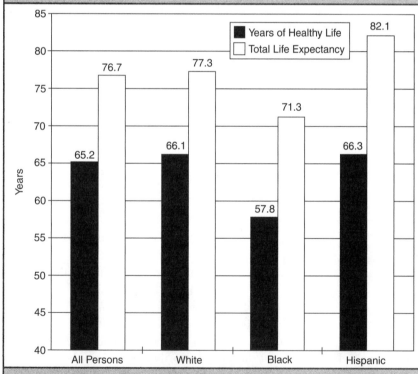

Source: CDC/NCHS National Vital Statistics System and National Health Interview Survey.[29]

status. Figure 2–5 presents information on both morbidity and disability for children in terms of the prevalence of specific childhood diseases (here, the percentage of children 0–17 years old who have ever had these conditions) and the relationship between these conditions and self-reported health and activity status (a measure of disability).

Both prevalence (the number or rate of cases at a specific point or period in time) and incidence (the number or rate of new cases occurring during a specific period) are widely used measures of morbidity. One of the earliest systems for reporting on diseases of public health significance is the national notifiable disease-reporting system for specific diseases. This system operates through the collaboration of local, state, and federal health agencies. Although initially developed to track the incidence of communicable diseases, this system has steadily moved toward collecting information on noninfectious conditions, as well as important risk factors.

Increasingly, information on self-reported health status and on days lost from work or school due to acute or chronic conditions is collected through surveys of the general population. The National Center for Health Statistics also conducts ongoing surveys of

discussed here, span of healthy life comes closest to measuring health in terms of the ability to function normally.

Although less frequently encountered, indicators of morbidity and disability are also quite useful in measuring health

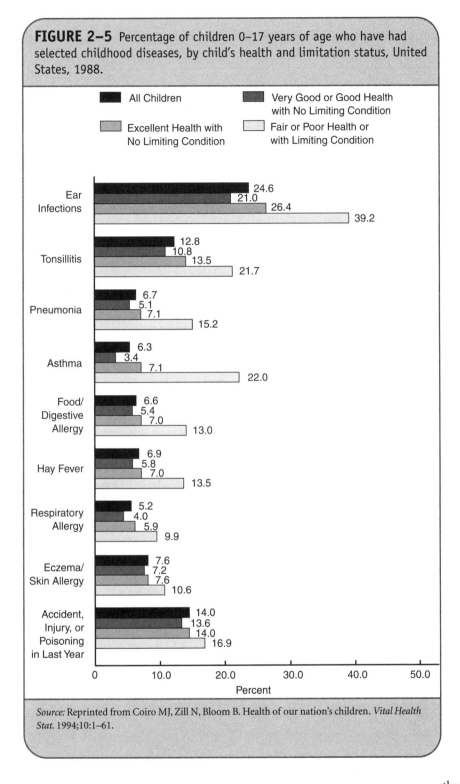

FIGURE 2–5 Percentage of children 0–17 years of age who have had selected childhood diseases, by child's health and limitation status, United States, 1988.

Legend:
- All Children
- Excellent Health with No Limiting Condition
- Very Good or Good Health with No Limiting Condition
- Fair or Poor Health or with Limiting Condition

Ear Infections: 24.6, 21.0, 26.4, 39.2
Tonsillitis: 12.8, 10.8, 13.5, 21.7
Pneumonia: 6.7, 5.1, 7.1, 15.2
Asthma: 6.3, 3.4, 7.1, 22.0
Food/Digestive Allergy: 6.6, 5.4, 7.0, 13.0
Hay Fever: 6.9, 5.8, 7.0, 13.5
Respiratory Allergy: 5.2, 4.0, 5.9, 9.9
Eczema/Skin Allergy: 7.6, 7.2, 7.6, 10.6
Accident, Injury, or Poisoning in Last Year: 14.0, 13.6, 14.0, 16.9

Percent (0, 10.0, 20.0, 30.0, 40.0, 50.0)

Source: Reprinted from Coiro MJ, Zill N, Bloom B. Health of our nation's children. *Vital Health Stat.* 1994;10:1–61.

INFLUENCES ON HEALTH

In 1996, public health surveillance in the United States took a historic step, reflecting changes in national morbidity and mortality patterns as well as in the ability to identify specific factors that result in disease and injury. At that time, the Centers for Disease Control and Prevention (CDC) added prevalence of cigarette smoking to the list of diseases and conditions to be reported by states to CDC.[5] This action marked the first time that a health behavior, rather than an illness or disease, was considered nationally reportable—a groundbreaking step for surveillance efforts. How the focus of public health efforts shifted from conventional disease outcomes to reporting on underlying causes amenable to public health intervention is an important story. That story is closely linked to one of the most important and most bitterly contested public health achievements of the 20th century, the recognition of tobacco use as a major health hazard. "Public Health Achievements in Twentieth-Century America: Tobacco Use," chronicles this story, providing important lessons for public health efforts in the 21st century seeking to improve measures of health status and quality of life.

Risk Factors

The recognition of tobacco use as a major health hazard was no simple achievement, partly because many factors directly or indirectly influence the level of a health outcome in a given population. For example, greater per capita tobacco use in a population is associated with higher rates of heart disease and lung cancer, and lower rates of early prenatal care are associated with higher infant mortality rates. Because these factors are part of the chain of causation for health outcomes, tracking their levels provides an early indication as to the direction in which the health outcome is likely to change. These factors increase the likelihood or risk of particular health outcomes occurring and can be characterized broadly as risk factors.

health providers on complaints and conditions requiring medical care in outpatient settings. These surveys provide direct information on self-reported health status and illuminate some of the factors, such as household income levels depicted in Figure 2–6, that are associated with health status.

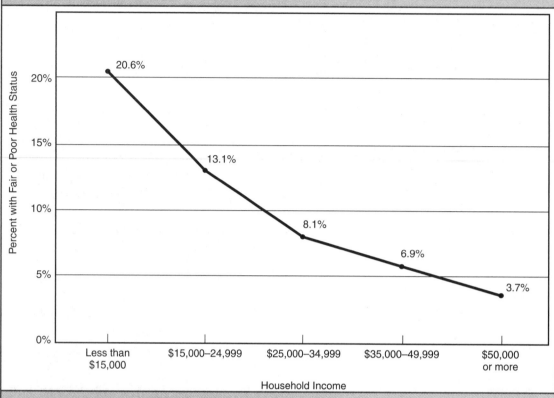

FIGURE 2–6 Percentage of persons with fair or poor perceived health status by household income, United States, 1995.

Source: Reprinted from Office of Disease Prevention and Health Promotion. *Healthy People 2010; Understanding and Improving Health.* Rockville, MD: ODPHP; 2000.

The types and number of risk factors are as varied as the influences themselves. Depending on how these factors are lumped or split, traditional categories include biologic factors (from genetic endowment to aging), environmental factors (from food, air, and water to communicable diseases), lifestyle factors (from diet to injury avoidance and sexual behaviors), psychosocial factors (from poverty to stress, personality, and cultural factors), and use of and access to health-related services. Some recent refinements of this framework differentiate several outcomes of interest, including disease, functional capacity, prosperity, and well-being that can be influenced by various risk factors (Figure 2–9). These various components are often interrelated (e.g., stress, a social environmental factor, may stimulate individual responses, such as tobacco or il-

EXAMPLE

Public Health Achievements in 20th-Century America: Tobacco Use

Initial suspicions that tobacco use was harmful for humans were confirmed by epidemiologic studies in the mid-20th century, stimulating new interest in measures of health, illness, and their related factors. By the time the prevalence of tobacco use, a risk behavior, became a reportable condition in the 1990s, the use of a wide variety of measures of health had become commonplace in public health practice. Figures 2–7 and 2–8 trace key aspects of this important achievement.

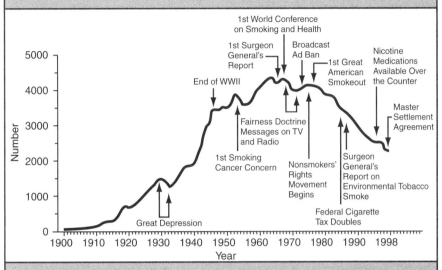

FIGURE 2-7 Annual adult per capita cigarette consumption and major smoking and health events—United States, 1900–1998.

Source: Reprinted from Centers for Disease Control and Prevention. Achievements in public health, United States, 1900–1999: tobacco use. *MMWR Morb Mortal Wkly Rep.* 1999;48:986–993.

overnutrition, and diabetes are well-known risk factors for heart disease. Epidemiologic research and studies over the past 50 years have identified behavioral risk factors for many common diseases and conditions,[6] as shown in Table 2–3. In recent decades, the prevalence of obesity has doubled in virtually all gender, age, racial, and ethnic groups. Ongoing behavioral risk factor surveys (often through telephone interviews) are conducted by governmental public health agencies to track trends in the prevalence of many important risk behaviors within the population. These surveys document that the health-related behaviors of tens of millions of Americans place them at risk for developing chronic disease and injuries.

Despite the recent emphasis on behavioral factors, risk factors in the physical environment remain important influences on health. Air pollution, for example, is directly related to a wide range of diseases, including lung cancer, pulmonary emphysema, chronic bronchitis, and bronchial asthma. National standards exist for many of the most

licit drug use, which, in turn, influence the likelihood of disease, functional capacity, and well-being). In addition, variations in one outcome, such as disease, may influence changes in others, such as well-being, depending on the mix of other factors present. This complex set of interactions draws attention to general factors that can result in many diseases, rather than focusing on specific factors that contribute little to population-wide health outcomes.

Although many factors are causally related to health outcomes, some are more direct and proximal causes than others. Specific risk factors have been clearly linked to specific adverse health states through epidemiologic studies. For example, numerous studies have linked unintentional injuries with a variety of risk factors, including the accessibility to firearms and the use of alcohol, tobacco, and seat belts. Tobacco, hypertension,

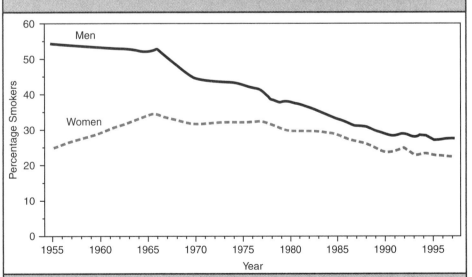

FIGURE 2-8 Trends in cigarette smoking among persons ≥18 years, by sex—United States, 1955–1997.

Source: Reprinted from Centers for Disease Control and Prevention. Achievements in public health, United States, 1900–1999: tobacco use. *MMWR Morb Mortal Wkly Report.* 1999;48:986–993.

FIGURE 2–9 Determinants of health.

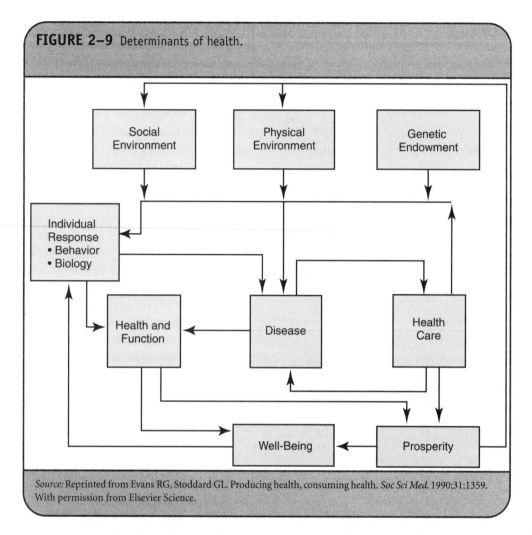

Source: Reprinted from Evans RG, Stoddard GL. Producing health, consuming health. *Soc Sci Med.* 1990;31:1359. With permission from Elsevier Science.

comes under study and measures used. For example, a study using 1980 data found tobacco, hypertension, and overnutrition responsible for about three fourths of deaths before age 65 and injury risks, alcohol, tobacco, and gaps in primary prevention accountable for about three fourths of all YPLL before age 65.[8] Further complicating these analyses is the finding that individual risk factors may result in several different health outcomes. For example, alcohol use is linked with motor vehicle injuries, other injuries, cancer, and cirrhosis; tobacco use can result in heart disease, stroke, ulcers, fire and burn injuries, and low birth weight, as well as cancer.[6,8]

Despite problems with their measurement, the identification of antecedent causes is important for public health policy and in-

important air pollutants and are tracked to determine the extent of these risks in the general population. The proportion of the U.S. population residing in counties that have exceeded national standards for these pollutants suggests that air pollution risks, like behavioral risks, affect tens of millions of Americans.[7] Environmental risks are ubiquitous and growing in the United States. Estimates from CDC are that 22–30 million people drink water from private wells; 40–45 million people are exposed to extreme heat; 150 million people are exposed to environmental tobacco smoke; and 65 million people reside in homes built before 1950, when lead paint was banned for residential use.

Behavioral and environmental risk factors are clearly germane to public health interest and efforts. Focusing on these factors provides a different perspective of the enemies of personal and public health than that conveyed by disease-specific incidence or mortality data. Such a focus also promotes rational policy development and interventions. Unfortunately, determining which underlying factors are most important is more difficult than it appears due to differences in the out-

terventions. Table 2–4 provides a comparison of 2000 deaths by their listed causes of death, and their actual causes (major risk factors).[9] The two lists provide contrasting views as to the major health problems and needs of the U.S. population. Although this debate has continued since the days of Chadwick and Farr (see Chapter 1), it is by no means settled.

Coroners and medical examiners view immediate and underlying causes of death somewhat differently from the perspective offered in Table 2–4. Death certificates have two parts, one for entering the immediate and underlying conditions that caused the death and a second for identifying conditions or injuries that contributed to death but did not cause death. For example, a death attributed to cardiovascular disease might list cardiac tamponade as the immediate cause, due to or a consequence of a ruptured myocardial infarction, which itself was due to or a consequence of coronary arteriosclerosis. For this death, hypertensive cardiovascular disease might be listed as a significant condition contributing to, but not causing, the immediate and underlying causes. So where

TABLE 2–3 Selected Behavioral Risk Factors Related to Leading Causes of Deaths in the United States, 2000

Cause of Death and Percent of all Deaths	Smoking	High Fat/Low Fiber	Sedentary Lifestyle	High Blood Pressure	Elevated Cholesterol	Obesity	Alcohol Use
Heart disease (30%)	X	X	X	X	X	X	X
Cancer (23%)	X	X	X			X	X
Stroke (7%)	X	X		X	X	X	
Chronic lung disease (5%)	X						
Unintentional injuries (4%)	X						X
Pneumonia & influenza (3%)	X						
Diabetes (3%)		X	X			X	
HIV infection (1%)							
Suicide (1%)							X
Chronic liver disease (1%)							X
Atherosclerosis (1%)	X	X	X		X		

Source: Causes and percent deaths adapted from National Center for Health Statistics. *Health United States 2002.* Hyattsville, MD: NCHS; 2002. Risk factors related to causes adapted from Brownson RC, Remington PL, Davis JR, et al. *Chronic Disease Epidemiology and Control.* 2nd ed. Washington DC; American Public Health Association; 1998 and U.S. Public Health Service. *The Surgeon General's Report on Nutrition and Health.* Washington, DC: PHS; 1988.

TABLE 2–4 Listed and Actual Causes of Death, United States, 2000

10 Leading Causes of Death	Number	Actual Causes of Death	Number
Heart disease	710,760	Tobacco	435,000
Malignant neoplasm	553,091	Poor diet and physical inactivity	400,000
Cerbrovascular disease	167,661	Alcohol consumption	85,000
Chronic lower respiratory tract diseases	122,009	Microbial agents	75,000
Unintentional injuries	97,900	Toxic agents	55,000
Diabetes mellitus	69,301	Motor vehicle	43,000
Influenza and pneumonia	65,313	Firearms	29,000
Alzheimer disease	49,558	Sexual behavior	20,000
Nephritis, nephrotic syndrome, and nephrosis	37,251	Illicit drug use	17,000
Septicemia	31,224		
Other	499,283		
Total	2,403,351	Total	1,159,000

Source: Mokdad AM, Marks JS, Stoup DF, Gerberding JL. Actual causes of death in the United States, 2000. JAMA. 2004;291:1238–1245.

do smoking, obesity, diet, and physical inactivity get identified as the real causes of such deaths? Perhaps the Chadwick-Farr debate continues into the 21st century in terms of whether deaths in the year 2000 should be attributed to tobacco use, just as many of those in England in 1839 should have been attributed to starvation.

Social and Cultural Influences

Understanding the health effects of biologic, behavioral, and environmental risk factors is straightforward in comparison with understanding the effects of social, economic, and cultural factors on the health of populations. This is due in part to a lack of agreement as to what is being measured.

Socioeconomic status and poverty are two factors that generally reflect position in society. There is considerable evidence that social position is an overarching determinant of health status, even though the indicators used to measure social standing are imprecise, at best.

Social class affects lifestyle, environment, and the utilization of services; it remains an important predictor of good and poor health in our society. Social class differences in mortality have long been recognized around the world. In 1842, Chadwick reported that the average ages at death for occupationally stratified groups in England were as follows: "gentlemen and persons engaged in the professions, 45 years; tradesmen and their families, 26 years; mechanics, servants and laborers, and their families, 16 years."[10] Life expectancies and other health indicators have improved considerably in England and elsewhere since 1842, but differences in mortality rates among the various social classes persist to the present day.

Some countries (such as Great Britain and the United States) have identifiable social strata that permit comparisons of health status by social class. Britain conducts ongoing analyses of socioeconomic differences according to official categorizations based on general social standing within the community. For the United States, educational status, race, and family income are often used as indirect or proxy measures of social class. Despite the differences in approaches and indicators, there is little evidence of any real difference between Britain and the United States in terms of what is being measured. In both countries, explanations for the differences in mortality appear to relate primarily to inequalities in social position and material resources.[11,12] This effect operates all up and down the hierarchy of social standing; at each step improvements in social status are linked with improvements in measures of health status. For example, a study based on 1971 British census follow-up data found that a relatively affluent, home-owning group with two cars had a lower mortality risk than did a similar relatively privileged group with only one car.[11]

In the United States, epidemiologists have studied socioeconomic differences in mortality risk since the early 1900s. Infant mortality has been the subject of many studies that have consistently documented the effects of poverty. Findings from the 1988 National Maternal and Infant Health Survey, for example, demonstrated that the effects of poverty were greater for infants born to mothers with no other risk factors than for infants born to high-risk mothers.[13] Poverty status was associated with a 60% higher rate of neonatal mortality and a 200% higher rate for postneonatal mortality than for those infants of higher-income mothers.

Poverty affects many health outcomes, as illustrated in Figure 2–6 and Table 2–5. Low-income families in the United States have an increased likelihood (or relative risk) of a variety of adverse health outcomes, often two to five times greater than that of higher-income families. The percentage of persons reporting fair or poor health is about four times as high for persons living below the poverty level as for those with family income at least twice the poverty level (22.2% and 5.5%, age adjusted).[1]

The implications of the consistent relationship between measures of social status and health outcomes suggest that studies need to consider how and how well social class is categorized and measured. Imprecise measures may understate the actual differences that are due to socioeconomic position in society. Importantly, if racial or ethnic differences are simply attributed to social class differences, factors that operate through race and ethnicity, such as racism or ethnism, will be overlooked. These additional factors also affect the difference between the social position one has and the position one would have attained, were it not for one's race or ethnicity. Race in the United States, independent of socioeconomic status, is linked to mortality, although these effects vary across age and disease categories.[14]

Studies of the effect of social factors on health status across nations add some interesting insights. In general, health appears to be closely associated with income differentials within countries, but there is only a weak link between national mortality rates and average income among the developed countries.[15] This pattern suggests that health is affected less by changes in absolute material standards across

TABLE 2–5 Selected Outcomes and Relative Risk for Low-Income Families, as Compared with High-Income Families

Outcome	Relative Risk
Child neglect	9
Child abuse	4.5
Iron-deficiency anemia	3–4
Childhood mortality	>3
Fair or poor health	3
Fatal injuries	2–3
Growth retardation	2.5
Severe asthma	2
Pneumonia	1.6
Infant mortality	1.3–1.5
Low birth weight	1.2–2.2
Extreme behavioral problems	1.3

Source: Data from Geltman PL, Meyers AF, Greenberg J, Zuckerman B. Welfare reform and children's health. *Health Policy and Child Health.* 1996;3:1–5.

affluent populations than by relative income differences and the resulting disadvantage in each country. It is not the richest countries that have the greatest life expectancy. Rather, it is those developed nations with the narrowest income differentials between rich and poor, as illustrated in Figure 2–3. This finding argues that health in the developed world is less a matter of a population's absolute material wealth than of how the population's circumstances compare with those of other members of their society. A similar perspective views income to be related to health through two pathways: a direct effect on the material conditions necessary for survival, and an effect on social participation and the opportunity to control one's own life circumstances.[16] In settings or societies that provide little in the way of material conditions (e.g., clean water, sanitation services, ample food, adequate housing), income is more important for health. Where material conditions are conducive to good health, income acts through social participation.

The effects of culture on health and illness are also becoming better understood. To medical anthropologists, diseases are not purely independent phenomena. Rather, they are to be viewed and understood in relation to ecology and culture. Certainly, the type and severity of disease varies by age, sex, social class, and ethnic group. The different distributions and social patterns of diseases reveal differences in culture-mediated behaviors. Such insights are essential to developing successful prevention and control programs. Culture serves to shape health-related behaviors, as well as human responses to diseases including changes in the environment, which, in turn, affect health. As a mechanism of adapting to the environment, culture has great potential for both positively and negatively affecting health.

There is evidence that different societies shape the ways in which diseases are experienced and that social patterns of disease persist, even after risk factors are identified and effective interventions become available.[17–19] For example, the link between poverty and various outcomes has been well established; yet even after advances in medicine and public health and significant improvement in general living and working conditions, the association persists. One explanation is that as some risks were addressed, others developed, such as health-related behaviors, including violent behavior and alcohol, tobacco, and drug use. In this way, societies create and shape the diseases that they experience. This makes sense, especially if we view the social context in which health and disease reside—the setting and social networks. For problems such as HIV/AIDS, sexually transmitted diseases, and illicit drug use, spread is heavily influenced by the links between those at risk.[20] This also helps to explain why people in disorganized social structures are more

likely to report their own health as poor than are similar persons with more social capital.[21,22]

Societal responses to diseases are also socially constructed. Efforts to prevent the spread of typhoid fever by limiting the rights of carriers (such as Typhoid Mary) differed greatly from those to reduce transmission risks from diphtheria carriers. Because many otherwise normal citizens would have been subjected to extreme measures in order to avoid the risk of transmission, it was not socially acceptable to invoke similar measures for these similar risks.

If these themes of social and cultural influences are on target, they place the study of health disparities at the top of the public health agenda. They also argue that health should be viewed as a social phenomenon. Rather than attempting to identify each and every risk factor that contributes only marginally to disparate health outcomes of the lower social classes, a more effective approach would be to directly address the broader social policies (distribution of wealth, education, employment, and the like) that foster the social disparities that cause the observed differences in health outcomes.[19] This broad view of health and its determinants is critical to understanding and improving health status in the United States, as well as internationally.

Global Health Influences

Considerable variation exists among the world's nations on virtually every measure of health and illness currently in use. The principal factors responsible for observed trends and obvious inequities across the globe fall into the general categories of the social and physical environment, personal behavior, and health services. Given the considerable variation in social, economic, and health status among the developed, developing, and underdeveloped nations, it is naive to make broad generalizations. Countries with favorable health status indicators, however, generally have a well-developed health infrastructure, ample opportunities for education and training, relatively high status for women, and economic development that counterbalances population growth. Nonetheless, countries at all levels of development share some problems, including the escalating costs involved in providing a broad range of health, social, and economic development services to disadvantaged subgroups within the population. Social and cultural upheaval associated with urbanization is another problem common to countries at all levels of development. Over the course of the 20th century, the proportion of the world's population living in urban areas tripled—to about 40%; that trend is expected to continue into the new century.

The principal environmental hazards in the world today appear to be those associated with poverty. This is true for developed as well as developing and underdeveloped countries. Some international epidemiologists predict that, in the 21st century, the effects of overpopulation and production of greenhouse gases will join poverty as major threats to global health. These factors represent human effects on the world's climate and resources and are easily remembered as the "3 Ps" of global health (pollution, population, and poverty):

- Pollution of the atmosphere by greenhouse gases, which will result in significant global warming, affecting both climate and the occurrence of disease
- Worldwide population growth, which will result in a population of 10–12 billion people within the next century
- Poverty, which is always associated with ill health and disease [23,24]

It surprises many Americans that population is a major global health concern. Birth rates vary inversely with the level of economic development and the status of women among the nations of the world. Continuing high birth rates and declining death rates will mean even more rapid growth in population in developing countries. It has taken all of history to reach the world's current population level, but it will take less than half a century to double that. Many factors have influenced this growth, including public health, which has increased the chances of conception by improving the health status of adults, increasing infant and child survival, preventing premature deaths of adults in the most fertile age groups, and reducing the number of marriages dissolved by one partner's death.

In general, public health approaches to dealing with world health problems must overcome formidable obstacles, including the unequal and inefficient distribution of health services, lack of appropriate technology, poor management, poverty, and inadequate or inappropriate government programs to finance needed services. Much of the preventable disease in the world is concentrated in the developing and underdeveloped countries, where the most profound differences exist in terms of social and economic influences. Table 2–6 provides estimates of the preventable toll caused by water-related diseases worldwide.

Although many of these factors appear to stem from low levels of national wealth, the link between national health status and national wealth is not firm, and comparisons across nations are seldom straightforward. Improved health status correlates more closely with changes in standards of living, advances in the politics of human relations, and a nation's literacy, education, and welfare policies than with specific preventive interventions. The complexities involved in identifying and understanding these forces and their interrelationships often confound comparisons of health status between the United States and other nations.

ANALYZING HEALTH PROBLEMS FOR CAUSATIVE FACTORS

The ability to identify risk factors and pathways for causation is essential for rational public health decisions and actions to address important health problems in a population. First, however, it is necessary to define what is meant by *health problem*. Here, health problem means a condition of humans that can be represented in terms of measurable health status or quality-of-life indicators. In later chapters, additional dimensions will be added to this basic definition for the purposes of community problem solving and the development of interventions. This characterization of a health problem as something measured only in terms of outcomes is difficult for some to accept. They point to important factors, such as access to care or poverty itself, and feel that these should rightfully be considered as health problems. Important problems they may be, but if they are truly important in the causation of some unacceptable health outcome, they can be dealt with as related factors rather than health problems.

The factors linked with specific health problems are often generically termed *risk factors* and can exist at one of three levels. Those risk factors most closely associated with the health outcome in question are often termed *determinants*. Risk factors that play a role further back in the chain of causation are called *direct and indirect contributing factors*. Risk factors can be described at either an individual or a population level. For example, tobacco use for an individual increases the chances of developing heart disease or lung cancer, and an increased prevalence of tobacco use in a population increases that population's incidence of (and mortality rates from) these conditions.

Determinants are scientifically established factors that relate directly to the level of a health problem. As the level of the determinant changes, the level of the health outcome changes. Determinants are the most proximal risk factors through which other levels of risk factors act. The link between the determinant and the health outcome should be well established through scientific or epidemiologic studies. For example, for neonatal mortality rates, two well-established determinants are the low-birth-weight rate (the number of infants born weighing less than 2,500 g, or about 5.5 lb, per 100 live births) and weight-specific mortality rates. Improvement in the neonatal mortality rate cannot occur unless one of these determinants improves. Health outcomes can have one or many determinants.

Direct contributing factors are scientifically established factors that directly affect the level of a determinant. Again,

TABLE 2–6 World Health Organization (WHO) Estimates of Morbidity and Mortality of Water-Related Diseases, Worldwide, 1995

Disease	Morbidity (Episodes per Year)	Mortality (Deaths per Year)	Relationship to Water Supply Sanitation
Diarrhea (drinking)	1 billion	3.3 million	Unsanitary excreta disposal, poor personal and domestic hygiene, unsafe water
Infection with intestinal helminths	1.5 billion*	100,000	Unsanitary excreta disposal, poor personal and domestic hygiene
Schistosomiasis	200 million*	200,000	Unsanitary excreta disposal and absence of nearby sources of safe water
Dracunuliasis	100,000*†	—	Unsafe drinking water
Trachoma	150 million‡	—	Lack of face washing, often due to absence of nearby sources of safe water
Malaria	400 million	1.5 million	Poor water management and storage, poor operation of water points and drainage
Dengue fever	1.75 million	20,000	Poor solid wastes management, water storage, and operation of water points and drainage
Poliomyelitis (drinking)	114,000	—	Unsanitary excreta disposal, poor personal and domestic hygiene, unsafe water
Trypanosomiasis	275,000	130,000	Absence of nearby sources of safe water
Bancroftian filariasis	72.8 million*	—	Poor water management and storage, poor operation of water points and drainage
Onchocerciasis	17.7 million*§	40,000	Poor water management and large-scale projects

*People currently infected.
†Excluding Sudan.
‡Case of active disease. Approximately 5.9 million cases of blindness or severe complications of trachoma occur annually.
§Includes an estimated 270,000 blind.
Source: Reprinted from WHO Wams of Inadequate Communicable Disease Prevention, U.S. Public Health Service. *Prevention Health Reports,* 1996;111:296–297.

there should be solid evidence that the level of the direct contributing factor affects the level of the determinant. For the neonatal mortality rate example, the prevalence of tobacco use among pregnant women has been associated with the risk of low birth weight. A determinant can have many direct contributing factors. For low birth weight, other direct contributing factors include low maternal weight gain and inadequate prenatal care.

Indirect contributing factors affect the level of the direct contributing factors. Although several steps distant from the health outcome in question, these factors are often proximal enough to be modified. The indirect contributing factor affects the level of the direct contributing factor, which, in turn, affects the level of the determinant. The level of the determinant then affects the level of the health outcome. Many indirect contributing factors can exist for each direct contributing

factor. For prevalence of tobacco use among pregnant women, indirect contributing factors might include easy access to tobacco products for young women, lack of health education, and lack of smoking cessation programs.

The health problem analysis framework begins with the identification of a health problem (defined in terms of health status indicators) and proceeds to establish one or more determinants; for each determinant, one or more direct contributing factors; and for each direct contributing factor, one or more indirect contributing factors. Intervention strategies at the community level generally involve addressing these indirect contributing factors. When completed, an analysis identifies as many of the causal pathways as possible to determine which contributing factors exist in the setting in which an intervention strategy is planned. The framework for this approach is presented in Table 2–7 and Figure 2–10. This

TABLE 2–7 Risk Factors

Determinant	Scientifically established factor that relates directly to the level of the health problem. A health problem may have any number of determinants identified for it.	Example: Low birth weight is a prime determinant for the health problem of neonatal mortality.
Direct contributing factor	Scientifically established factor that directly affects the level of the determinant.	Example: Use of prenatal care is one factor that affects the low-birth-weight rate.
Indirect contributing factor	Community-specific factor that affects the level of a direct contributing factor. Such factors can vary considerably from one community to another.	Example: Availability of day care or transportation services within the community may affect the use of prenatal care services.

Source: Data from Centers for Disease Control and Prevention, Public Health Practice Program Office. 1991.

FIGURE 2–10 Health problem analysis worksheet.

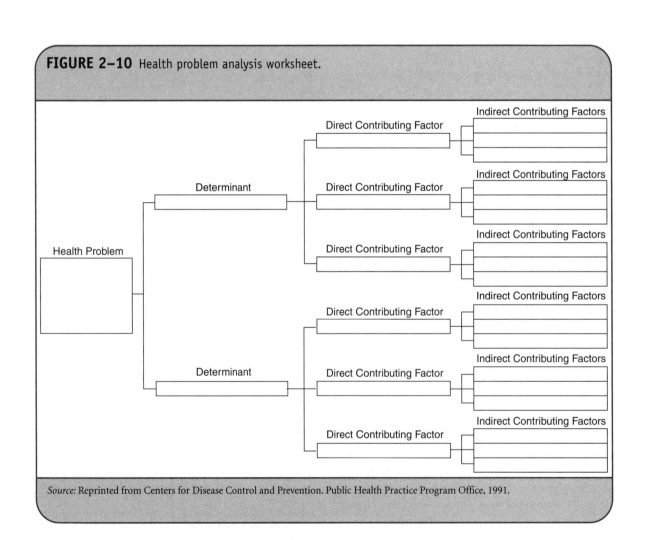

Source: Reprinted from Centers for Disease Control and Prevention. Public Health Practice Program Office, 1991.

framework forms the basis for developing meaningful interventions; it is used in several of the processes and instruments to assess community health needs that are currently in wide use at the local level. Community health improvement processes and tools will be further described in Chapter 5.

Although this framework is useful, it does not fully account for the relationships among the various levels of risk factors. Some direct contributing factors may affect more than one determinant, and some indirect contributing factors may influence more than one direct contributing factor. For example, illicit drug use during pregnancy influences both the likelihood of low birth weight and birth weight-specific survival rates. To account fully for these interactions, some direct and indirect contributing factors may need to be included in several different locations on the worksheet. Despite the advancement of epidemiologic methods, many studies ignore the contributing factors that affect the level of these major risk factors, leading to simplistic formulations of multiple risk factors for health problems that exist at the community level.[25]

ECONOMIC DIMENSIONS OF HEALTH OUTCOMES

The ability to measure and quantify outcomes and risks is essential for rational decisions and actions. Specific indicators, as well as methods of economic analysis, are available to provide both objective and subjective valuations. Several health indicators attempt to value differentially health status; outcomes, including age-adjusted rates; span of healthy life; and YPLL. For example, YPLL represents a method of weighting or valuing health outcomes by placing a higher value on deaths that occur at earlier ages. Years of life lost thus become a common denominator or, in one sense, a common currency. Health outcomes can be translated into this currency or into an actual currency, such as dollars. This translation allows for comparisons to be made among outcomes in terms of which costs more per person, per episode, or per another reference point. Cost comparisons of health outcomes and health events have become common in public health. Approaches include cost-benefit, cost-effectiveness, and cost-utility studies.

Cost-benefit analyses provide comprehensive information on both the costs and the benefits of an intervention. All health outcomes and other relevant impacts are included in the determination of benefits. The results are expressed in terms of net costs, net benefits, and time required to recoup an initial investment. If the benefits are expressed in health outcome terms, years of life gained or quality-adjusted life years (QALYs) may be calculated. This provides a framework for comparing disparate interventions. QALYs are calculated from a particular perspective that determines which costs and consequences are included in the analysis. For public health

analyses, societal perspectives are necessary. When comprehensively performed, cost-benefit analyses are considered the gold standard of economic evaluations.

Cost-effectiveness analyses focus on one outcome to determine the most cost-effective intervention when several options are possible. Cost-effectiveness examines a specific option's costs to achieve a particular outcome. Results are often specified as the cost per case prevented or cost per life saved. For example, screening an entire town for a specific disease might identify cases at a cost of $150 per new case, whereas a screening program directed only at high-risk groups within that town might identify cases at a cost of $50 per new case. Although useful for evaluating different strategies for achieving the same result, cost-effectiveness approaches are not very helpful in evaluating interventions intended for different health conditions.

Cost-utility analyses are similar to cost-effectiveness studies, except that the results are characterized as cost per quality-adjusted life years. These are most useful when the intervention affects both morbidity and mortality, and there are a variety of possible outcomes that include quality of life.

These approaches are especially important for interventions based on preventive strategies. The argument is frequently made that "an ounce of prevention is worth a pound of cure." If this wisdom is true, preventive interventions should result in savings equal to 16 times their actual cost. Not all preventive interventions measure up to this standard, but even crude information on the costs of many health outcomes suggests that prevention has economic as well as human savings. Table 2–8 presents information from *Healthy People 2000*[26] (HP2000) regarding the economics of prevention for a number of common diseases and conditions; for each, the potential savings represents an enormous sum. Figure 2–11 illustrates that the impacts of disease and injuries can be many in terms of medical care costs for treatment in outpatient, emergency department, and hospital settings.[27] The U.S. Public Health Service has estimated that as much as 11% of projected health expenditures for the year 2000 could have been averted through investments in public health for six conditions: motor vehicle injuries, occupationally related injuries, stroke, coronary heart disease, firearms-related injuries, and low-birth-weight infants.[28] Beyond the direct medical effects, there are often nonmedical costs related to lost wages, taxes, and productivity.

Economists assert that the future costs for care and services that result from prevention of mortality must be considered a negative benefit of prevention. For example, the costs of preventing a death due to motor vehicle injuries should include all subsequent medical care costs for that individual over his or her lifetime, because these costs would not have occurred

TABLE 2–8 The Economics of Prevention

Condition	Overall Magnitude	Avoidable Intervention*	Cost/Patient†
Heart disease	7 million with coronary artery disease 500,000 deaths/year 284,000 bypass procedures/year	Coronary bypass surgery	$30,000
Cancer	1 million new cases/year 510,000 deaths/year	Lung cancer treatment Cervical cancer treatment	$29,000 $28,000
Stroke	600,000 strokes/year 150,000 deaths/year	Hemiplegia treatment and rehabilitation	$22,000

Injuries	2.3 million hospitalizations per year
	
	142,500 deaths/year
	177,000 persons with spinal cord injuries
	    in the United States
		Quadriplegia treatment and
		    rehabilitation
		
		Hip fracture treatment and rehabilitation
			$570,000
			(lifetime)
			
			$40,000

HIV infection	1–1.5 million infected 118,000 AIDS cases (as of Jan. 1990)	Severe head injury treatment and rehabilitation AIDS treatment	$310,000 $75,000 (lifetime)
Alcoholism	18.5 million abuse alcohol	Liver transplant	$250,000

Drug abuse	105,000 alcohol-related deaths/year
	Regular users:
	    1–3 million, cocaine
	    900,000, IV drugs
	    500,000, heroin
		Treatment of cocaine-exposed infant	$66,000
			(5 years)

LBW infants	Drug-exposed infants: 375,000 260,000 LBW infants/year	Neonatal intensive care for LBW infant	$10,000

Inadequate immunization	23,000 deaths/year
	Lacking basic immunization series:
	    20–30% aged 2 and younger
	    3% aged 6 and older
		Congenital rubella syndrome treatment	$354,000
			(lifetime)

LBW, low birth weight.
*Interventions represent examples (other interventions may apply).
†Representative first-year costs, except as noted. Not indicated are nonmedical costs, such as lost productivity to society.
Source: Reprinted from National Center for Health Statistics. *Healthy People 2000.* Hyattsville, MD: NCHS; 1990.

otherwise. They also argue that it is unfair to compare future savings to the costs of current prevention programs and that those savings must be discounted to their current value. If a preventive program will save $10 million 20 years from now, that $10 million must be translated into its current value in computing cost benefits, cost-effectiveness, or cost utility. It may be that the value of $10 million 20 years from now is only $4 million now. If the program costs $1 million, its benefit/cost ratio would be 4:1 instead of 10:1 before we even added any additional costs associated with medical care for the lives that were saved. These economic considerations contribute to the difficulty of marketing preventive interventions.

Two additional economic considerations are important for public health policy and practice. The first of these is what

economists term *opportunity costs.* These represent the costs involved in choosing one course of action over another. Resources spent for one purpose are not available to be spent for another. As a result, there is a need to consider the costs of not realizing the benefits or gains from paths not chosen. A second economic consideration important for public health is related to the heavy emphasis of public health on preventive strategies. The savings or gains from successful prevention efforts are generally not reinvested in public health or even other health purposes. These savings or gains from investments in prevention are lost. Maybe this is proper, because the overall benefits accrue more broadly to society, and public health remains, above all else, a social enterprise. However, imagine the situation for American industry and businesses if they could

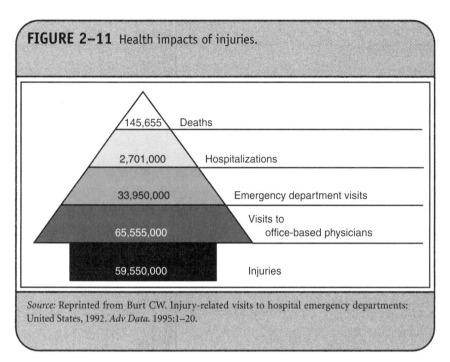

FIGURE 2–11 Health impacts of injuries.

145,655 — Deaths

2,701,000 — Hospitalizations

33,950,000 — Emergency department visits

65,555,000 — Visits to office-based physicians

59,550,000 — Injuries

Source: Reprinted from Burt CW. Injury-related visits to hospital emergency departments: United States, 1992. *Adv Data.* 1995:1–20.

not reinvest their gains to grow their businesses. This is often the situation faced by public health, further exacerbating the difficulty of arguing for and securing needed resources.

HEALTHY PEOPLE 2010

The data and discussion in this chapter only broadly describe health status measures in the United States in the early years of the new century. Several common themes emerge, however, that form the basis for national health objectives focusing on the year 2010.[29] Figure 2–12 (similar to the model illustrated in Figure 2–9) presents a *Healthy People 2010* (HP2010) process grounded in a broad view of the many factors influencing health. The year 2010 objectives build on the nation's experience with panels of health objectives established for the years 1990 and 2000. The Healthy People 1990 effort was initiated in the late 1970s through the efforts of Surgeon General Julius Richmond and coordinated by the Office of Disease Prevention and Health Promotion within the Office of the Assistant Secretary for Health.

Progress toward achievement of the year 2000 national health objectives was assessed in 1998. The status of each of the 319 objectives was reviewed and classified as moving in the right direction, moving in the wrong direction, showing no change, or unable to be tracked. The midcourse review found that 15% had been accomplished, another 44% were moving in the right direction, 18% were moving in the wrong direction, 3% showed no change, 6% showed mixed results, and 14% could not be tracked.[29] A substantially higher proportion of the objectives targeting special populations, especially blacks and American Indians, were found to be moving in the wrong

direction. These findings raise concerns that disparities are persisting, if not increasing, in the United States. Progress toward some of the broader goals of the HP2000 effort was somewhat more positive; age-adjusted mortality targets for all age groups under age 70 were achieved.[29]

The year 2010 national health objectives include 467 specific objectives addressing health status measures, risk factor prevalence, and use of preventive health services. These objectives fall into 28 priority categories (Table 2–9) and focus on two overarching goals: (1) to increase quality and years of healthy life and (2) to eliminate health disparities. Overall success will be gauged in relation to several age-adjusted summary measures for both the general population and racial and ethnic minorities: YPLL before age 75, hospital days per 100,000 population, and reported disability. Figure 2–13 presents data on several HP2010 objectives related to tobacco use. Because tracking 467 national targets is not practical, a list of leading indicators was developed (Table 2–10); these focus on 10 important health issues by incorporating 21 of the HP2010 objectives.

Although the overall goals appear appropriate, they are only arguably linked. From one perspective, they represent two very different approaches to improving outcomes for the population as a whole. If we view the health status of the entire population as a Gaussian curve, one approach would be to shift the entire curve further toward better outcomes, and a second approach would be to change the shape of the curve, reducing the difference between the extremes. These represent quite different strategies that would be associated with quite different policies and interventions. Focusing on the tail end of the distribution of health requires investment in questionably effective attempts that benefit relatively few and fail to promote the health of the majority. On the other hand, even small improvements in overall society-wide health measures have provided greater gains for society than very perceptible improvements in the health of a few.[30] The choice is one that can be viewed as focusing on "epiphenomena," such as risk factors or on the larger context and social environment. *Healthy People 2010* ambitiously seeks to do both.

Monitoring all national health objectives is not considered feasible at the state and local level. Instead, priorities linked to the national health objectives will likely be tracked. An Institute of Medicine (IOM) committee in 1997 identified a basic set of indicators for use in community health

FIGURE 2–12 The *Healthy People 2010* model.

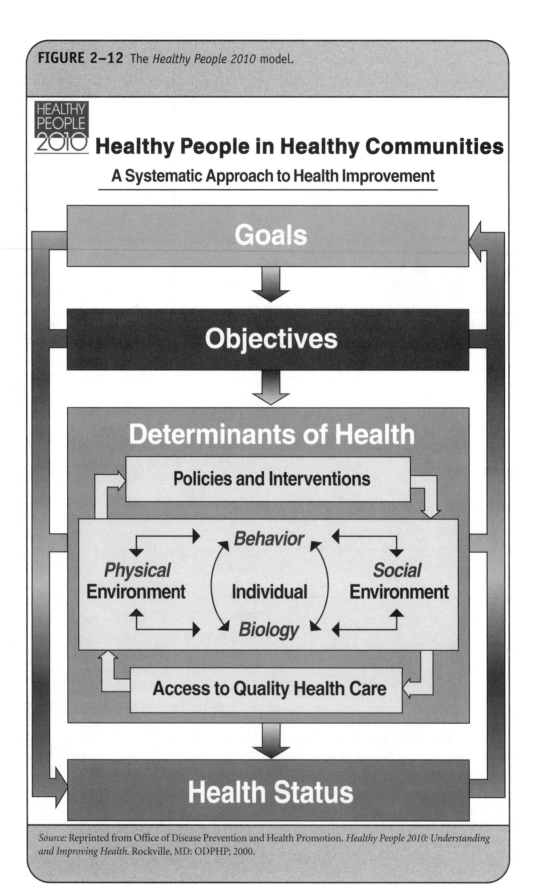

Source: Reprinted from Office of Disease Prevention and Health Promotion. *Healthy People 2010: Understanding and Improving Health.* Rockville, MD: ODPHP; 2000.

TABLE 2–9 *Healthy People 2010* Goals and Focus Areas

Goals
1. Increase Quality and Years of Healthy Life
2. Eliminate Health Disparities

Focus Areas
1. Access to Quality Health Services
2. Arthritis, Osteoporosis, and Chronic Back Conditions
3. Cancer
4. Chronic Kidney Disease
5. Diabetes
6. Disability and Secondary Conditions
7. Educational and Community-Based Programs
8. Environmental Health
9. Family Planning
10. Food Safety
11. Health Communication
12. Heart Disease and Stroke
13. HIV
14. Immunization and Infectious Disease
15. Injury and Violence Prevention
16. Maternal, Infant, and Child Health
17. Medical Product Safety
18. Mental Health and Mental Disorders
19. Nutrition and Overweight
20. Occupational Safety and Health
21. Oral Health
22. Physical Activity and Fitness
23. Public Health Infrastructure
24. Respiratory Diseases
25. Sexually Transmitted Diseases
26. Substance Abuse
27. Tobacco Use
28. Vision and Hearing

Source: Reprinted from Office of Disease Prevention and Health Promotion. *Healthy People 2010: Understanding and Improving Health.* Rockville, MD: ODPHP; 2000.

FIGURE 2–13 Cigarette smoking, United States, 1990–1997.

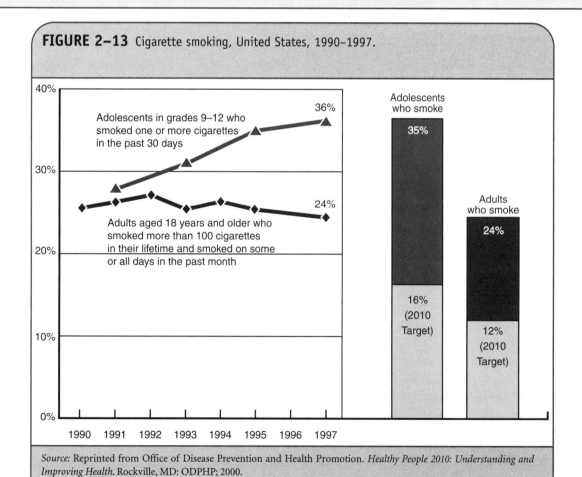

Source: Reprinted from Office of Disease Prevention and Health Promotion. *Healthy People 2010: Understanding and Improving Health.* Rockville, MD: ODPHP; 2000.

TABLE 2–10 *Healthy People 2010* Leading Indicators

Physical Activity
- Proportion of adolescents who engage in vigorous physical activity that promotes cardiorespiratory fitness 3 or more days per week for 20 or more minutes per occasion
- Proportion of adults who engage regularly, preferably daily, in moderate physical activity for at least 30 minutes a day

Overweight and obesity
- Proportion of children and adolescents who are overweight or obese
- Proportion of adults who are obese

Tobacco Use
- Proportion of adolescents who smoke
- Proportion of adults who smoke

Substance Abuse
- Proportion of adolescents not using alcohol or any illicit drugs during the past 30 days
- Proportion of adults using any illicit drug during the past 30 days
- Proportion of adults engaging in binge drinking of alcoholic beverages during the past month

Responsible Sexual Behavior
- Proportion of adolescents who abstain from sexual intercourse or use condoms if sexually active
- Proportion of sexually active persons who use condoms

Mental Health
- Proportion of adults with recognized depression who receive treatment

Injury and Violence
- Death rates due to motor vehicle crashes
- Death rates due to homicides

Environmental Quality
- Proportion of persons exposed to air that does not meet the U.S. Environmental Protection Agency's health-based standards for ozone
- Proportion of nonsmokers exposed to environmental tobacco smoke

Immunization
- Proportion of young children who receive all vaccines that have been recommended for universal administration for at least 5 years
- Proportion of noninstitutionalized adults who are vaccinated annually against influenza and ever vaccinated against pneumococcal disease

Access to Health Care
- Proportion of persons with health insurance
- Proportion of persons who have a specific source of ongoing care
- Proportion of pregnant women who begin prenatal care in the first trimester of pregnancy

Source: Reprinted from Office of Disease Prevention and Health Promotion. *Healthy People 2010: Understanding and Improving Health.* Rockville, MD: ODPHP; 2000.

improvement processes (Table 2–11). This panel is notably more comprehensive than one promoted for use with the HP2000 activities of the 1990s. Together with the catalog of leading health indicators from the HP2010 process, these measures provide a useful starting point for population-based health improvement initiatives.

CONCLUSION

From an ecological perspective, the health status of a population is influenced by many factors drawn from biology, behavior, the environment, and the use of health services. Social and cultural factors also play an important role in the disease patterns experienced by different populations, as well as in

the responses of these populations to disease and illness. Globally, risks associated with population growth, pollution, and poverty result in mortality and morbidity that are still associated with infectious disease processes. In the United States, behaviorally mediated risks, including tobacco, diet, alcohol, and injury risks, rather than infectious disease processes, are the major contributors to health status, and the considerable gap between low-income minority populations and other Americans continues to widen. Reduction of the disparities in health status among population groups has emerged as the most critical national health goal for the year 2010. With the increasing availability of data on health status, as well as on determinants and contributing factors, the

TABLE 2–11 Proposed Indicators for a Community Health Profile

Sociodemographic Characteristics

1. Distribution of the population by age and race/ethnicity
2. Number and proportion of persons in groups such as migrants, homeless, or the non-English speaking for whom access to community services and resources may be a concern
3. Number and proportion of persons aged 25 and older with less than a high school education
4. Ratio of the number of students graduating from high school to the number of students who entered ninth grade 3 years previously
5. Median household income
6. Proportion of children less than 15 years of age living in families at or below the poverty level
7. Unemployment rate
8. Number and proportion of single-parent families
9. Number and proportion of persons without health insurance

Health Status

10. Infant mortality rate by race/ethnicity
11. Numbers of deaths or age-adjusted death rates for motor vehicle crashes, work-related injuries, suicide, homicide, lung cancer, breast cancer, cardiovascular diseases, and all causes, by age, race, and gender, as appropriate
12. Reported incidence of AIDS, measles, tuberculosis, and primary and secondary syphilis, by age, race, and gender, as appropriate
13. Births to adolescents (ages 10–17) as proportion of total live births
14. Number and rate of confirmed abuse and neglect cases among children

Health Risk Factors

15. Proportion of 2-year-old children who have received all age-appropriate vaccines, as recommended by the Advisory Committee on Immunization Practices
16. Proportion of adults aged 65 and older who have ever been immunized for pneumococcal pneumonia; proportion who have been immunized in the past 12 months for influenza
17. Proportion of the population who smoke, by age, race, and gender, as appropriate
18. Proportion of the population aged 18 or older who are obese
19. Number and type of U.S. Environmental Protection Agency air quality standards not met
20. Proportion of assessed rivers, lakes, and estuaries that support beneficial uses (e.g., fishing- and swimming-approved)

Health Care Resource Consumption

21. Per-capita health care spending for Medicare beneficiaries (the Medicaid adjusted average per-capita cost [AAPCC])

Functional Status

22. Proportion of adults reporting that their general health is good to excellent
23. During the past 30 days, average number of days for which adults report that their physical or mental health was not good

Quality of Life

24. Proportion of adults satisfied with the health care system in the community
25. Proportion of persons satisfied with the quality of life in the community

Source: Adapted from the Institute of Medicine. *Using Performance Monitoring to Improve Community Health: A Role for Performance Monitoring.* Washington, DC: National Academy Press; 1997.

potential for more rational policies and interventions has increased. Over the long term, public policies that narrow income disparities and increase access to education, jobs, and housing do far more to improve the health status of populations than do efforts to provide more health care services. Health improvement efforts require more than data on health problems and contributing factors, which view health from a negative perspective. Also needed is information from a positive perspective, in terms of community capacities, assets, and willingness. More important still, there must be recognition and acceptance that the right to health is a basic human right and one inextricably linked to all other human rights, lest quality of life be seriously compromised.[31] It is this right to health that enables the practice of public health and challenges public health workers to measure health and quality of life in ways that promote its improvement.

Discussion Questions and Exercises

1. Is poverty a cause of poor health in a community, or is poor health a cause of poverty? How would different views of this question influence public health policy?

2. You have been asked to review and improve the consensus list of important health status indicators (see Table 2–11). Identify and justify five indicators you would add to this list.

3. Visit the Internet Web site of one of the national print media and use the search features to identify articles on public health for a recent month. Catalog the health problems (both conditions and risks) from that search and compare this with the listing of health problems and issues on Table 2–4. Are the types of conditions and risks you encountered in the print media similar to those on Table 2–4? Were some conditions and risks either overrepresented or underrepresented in the media, in comparison with their relative importance as suggested by Table 2–4? What are the implications for the role of the media in informing and educating the public regarding public health issues?

4. Examine each of these Web sites. Which ones are most useful for the major topics examined in this part of the course? Why?

   - Healthfinder <http://www.healthfinder.gov>, a Department of Health and Human Services (DHHS)-sponsored gateway site that provides links to more than 550 Web sites (including more than 200 federal sites and 350 state, local, not-for-profit, university, and other consumer health sources), nearly 500 selected online documents, frequently asked questions on health issues, and

   databases and Web search engines by topic and agency

   - Fedstats <http://www.fedstats.gov>, a gateway to a variety of federal agency data and information, including health statistics

   - National Center for Health Statistics (NCHS) <http://www.cdc.gov/nchswww>, an invaluable resource for data and information, especially "Health, United States," which can be downloaded from this site

   - Centers for Disease Control and Prevention (CDC) Mortality and Morbidity Weekly Report <http://www2.cdc.gov/mmwr> and MMWR morbidity and mortality data by time and place <http://www2.cdc.gov/mmwr/distrnds.html>

   - U.S. Census data <http://www.census.gov>, the best general denominator data anywhere

5. Compare two "Public Health Achievements in 20th Century America," presented in Chapter 1 (control of infectious diseases) and Chapter 2 (tobacco use). Which of these accomplishments, in your opinion, has had the greatest impact on the health status and quality of life of Americans living in the early 21st century? Justify your selection.

6. After reviewing "Public Health Achievements in 20th Century America: Tobacco Use," select a health outcome related to tobacco use and analyze that problem for its determinants and contributing factors, using the method described in the text. Identify at least two major determinants for the problem that you select. For each determinant, identify at least two direct contributing factors, and for each direct contributing factor, identify at least two indirect contributing factors. At what level of your analysis does tobacco use appear as a risk factor?

7. Figure 2–13 presents data on several Healthy People 2010 objectives related to tobacco use. What are some important factors that must be addressed to achieve these targets in view of trends since 1990?

8. Population, poverty, and pollution are sometimes cited as the three most important factors influencing global health status today. After examining the World

Health Organization (WHO) Web site <http://www.who.ch>, cite reasons for agreeing or disagreeing with this assertion.

9. Great Debate: There are three propositions to be considered. Proposition A: Disease entities should be listed as official causes of death. Proposition B: Underlying factors that result in these diseases should be listed as official causes of death. Proposition C: No causes of death should be listed on death certificates. Select one of these positions and develop a position statement with your rationale.

10. Projections call for a continuing increase in life expectancy through the first half of the 21st century. What effect will increased life expectancy have on the major goals of *Healthy People 2010*—increasing the quality and years of healthy life and eliminating health disparities?

REFERENCES

1. National Center for Health Statistics. *Health, United States, 2005.* Hyattsville, MD: NCHS; 2005.

2. Allaire SH, LaValley MP, Evans SR, et al. Evidence for decline in disability and improved health among persons aged 55 to 70 years: the Framingham heart study. *Am J Public Health.* 1999;89:1678–1683.

3. Constitution of World Health Organization. In: World Health Organization. *Chronicle of World Health Organization.* Geneva, Switzerland: WHO; 1947;1:29–43.

4. Whaley RF, Hashim TJ. *A Textbook of World Health.* New York: Parthenon; 1995.

5. Centers for Disease Control and Prevention. First reportable underlying cause of death. *MMWR Morb Mortal Wkly Rep.* 1996;45:537.

6. Brownson RC, Remington PL, Davis JR, eds. *Chronic Disease Epidemiology and Control.* 2nd ed. Washington, DC: American Public Health Association; 1998.

7. Seitz F, Plepys C. Monitoring air quality in Healthy People 2000. *Healthy People 2000 Statistical Notes.* Hyattsville, MD: National Center for Health Statistics; 1995:No. 9.

8. Amler RW, Eddins DL. Cross-sectional analysis: precursors of premature death in the U.S. In: Amler RW, Dull DL, eds. *Closing the Gap.* Atlanta, GA: Carter Center; 1985:181–187.

9. Mokdad AM, Marks, JS, Stroup DF, Gerberding JL. Actual causes of death in the United States, 2000. *JAMA.* 2004;291:1238–1245.

10. Chadwick E. *Report on the Sanitary Conditions of the Labouring Population of Great Britain 1842.* Edinburgh, Scotland: Edinburgh University Press; 1965.

11. Smith GD, Egger M. Socioeconomic differences in mortality in Britain and the United States. *Am J Public Health.* 1992;82:1079–1081.

12. Schrijvers CTM, Stronks K, van de Mheen HD, Mackenbach JP. Explaining educational differences in mortality: the role of behavioral and material factors. *Am J Public Health.* 1999;89:535–540.

13. Centers for Disease Control and Prevention. Poverty and infant mortality: United States, 1988. *MMWR Morb Mortal Wkly Rep.* 1996;44:922–927.

14. Ng-Mak DS, Dohrenwend BP, Abraido-Lanza AF, Turner JB. A further analysis of race differences in the national longitudinal mortality study. *Am J Public Health.* 1999;89:1748–1751.

15. Wilkenson RG. National mortality rates: the impact of inequality. *Am J Public Health.* 1992;82:1082–1084.

16. Marmot M. The influence of income on health: views of an epidemiologist. *Health Affairs.* 2002;21:31–46.

17. Sargent CF, Johnson TM, eds. *Medical Anthropology: Contemporary Theory and Method.* Rev ed. Westport, CT: Praeger Publishers; 1996.

18. Susser M, Watson W, Hopper K. *Sociology in Medicine.* New York: Oxford University Press; 1985.

19. Link BG, Phelan JC. Understanding sociodemographic differences in health: the role of fundamental social causes. *Am J Public Health.* 1996;86:471–473.

20. Friedman SR, Curtis R, Neaigus A, Jose B, Des Jarlais DC. *Social Networks, Drug Injectors' Lives and HIV/AIDS.* New York: Kluwer Academic Publishers; 1999.

21. Kawachi I, Kennedy BP, Glass R. Social capital and self-rated health: a contextual analysis. *Am J Public Health.* 1999;89:1187–1193.

22. Malmstom M, Sundquist J, Johansson SE. Neighborhood environment and self-reported health status: a multilevel analysis. *Am J Public Health.* 1999;89:1181–1186.

23. Doll R. Health and the environment in the 1990s. *Am J Public Health.* 1992;82:933–941.

24. Winkelstein W. Determinants of worldwide health. *Am J Public Health.* 1992;82:931–932.

25. Fielding JE. Public health in the twentieth century: advances and challenges. *Ann Rev Public Health.* 1999;20:xiii–xxx.

26. National Center for Health Statistics. *Healthy People 2000.* Hyattsville, MD: NCHS; 1990.

27. Burt CW. Injury-related visits to hospital emergency departments: United States, 1992. *Adv Data.* 1995:1–20.

28. U.S. Public Health Service. *For a Healthy Nation: Return on Investments in Public Health.* Washington, DC: PHS; 1994.

29. National Center for Health Statistics. *Healthy People 2000 Final Review.* Hyattsville, MD: NCHS; 2001.

30. McKinlay JB, Marceau LD. A tale of 3 tails. *Am J Public Health.* 1999;89:295–298.

31. Universal Declaration of Human Rights. *GA res* 217 A(iii), UN Doc A/810, art 25(1);1948.

CHAPTER 3

Public Health and the Health System

LEARNING OBJECTIVES

After completing Chapter 3, learners will be proficient in identifying public health and prevention strategies for prevalent health
problems. Key aspects of this competency expectation include

- Describing three or more major issues that make the health system a public health concern

- Identifying five intervention strategies directed toward health
  and illness

- Identifying and describing three levels of preventive interventions

- Describing the approximate level of national expenditures for all
  health and medical services and for the population-based and
  clinical preventive service components of this total

- Citing important economic, demographic, and utilization dimensions of the health sector

- Accessing and utilizing current data and information resources
  available through the Internet's World Wide Web characterizing
  the roles and interests of key stakeholders in the health sector

This chapter picks up where Chapter 2 left off—with influences on health. The influences to be examined in Chapter 3,
however, are the interventions and services available through
the health system.

The relationship between public health and other health-
related activities has never been clear, but in recent years, it has
become even less well defined. Some of the lack of clarity may
be due to the several different images of public health described
in Chapter 1, but certainly not all. In addition to the U.S. health
system remaining poorly understood by the public, there are
different views among health professionals and policymakers as
to whether public health is part of the health system or the
health system is part of the public health enterprise. Most agree
that these components serve the same ends but disagree as to

the balance between the two and the locus for strategic decisions
and actions. The issue of ownership—which component's leadership and strategies will predominate—underlies these different perspectives. In this text, the term *health system* will refer to
all aspects of the organization, financing, and provision of programs and services for the prevention and treatment of illness
and injury. The public health system is a component of this
larger health system. This view conflicts with the image that
most people have of our health system; the public commonly
perceives the health system to include only the medical care
and treatment aspects of the overall system. However, public
health and the overall health sector will be referred to as *systems*,
with the understanding that public health activities are part of
a larger set of activities that focus on health, well-being, disease, and illness.

Although the relationships may not be clear, there is ample
cause for public health interest in the health system. Perhaps
most compelling is the sheer size and scope of the U.S. health
system, characteristics that have made the health system an
ethical issue. Nearly 12 million workers and $2.0 trillion in re-
sources are devoted to health-related purposes.[1] However, this
huge investment in fiscal and human resources may not be accomplishing what it can and should in terms of health outcomes. Lack of access to needed health services for an
increasing number of Americans and inconsistent quality contribute to less than optimal health outcomes. Although access
and quality have long been public health concerns, the excess
capacity of the health system is a relatively new issue for public health.

This chapter examines the U.S. health system from several
perspectives that consider the public health implications of

costs and affordability, as well as several other important public policy and public health questions:

- Does the United States have a rational strategy for investing its resources to maintain and improve people's health?
- Is the current strategy excessive in ways that inequitably limit access to and benefit from needed services?
- Is the health system accountable to its end-users and ultimate payers for the quality and results of its services?

It is these issues of health, excess, access, accountability, and quality that make the health system a public health concern.

Complementary, even synergistic, efforts involving medicine and public health are apparent in many of the important gains in health outcomes achieved during the 20th century. Progress since 1900 in improving pregnancy outcomes and promoting the health of mothers and infants (see "Public Health Achievements in 20th Century America: Improved Maternal and Infant Health" following) tells this story from one perspective. Another perspective will be drawn from a framework for linking various health strategies and activities to their strategic intent, level of prevention, relationship to medical and public health practice, and community or individual focus. Key economic, demographic, and resource trends will then be briefly presented as a prelude to understanding important themes and emerging paradigm shifts. New opportunities afforded by sweeping changes in the health system, many of which relate to managed care strategies, will be apparent in the review of these issues.

PREVENTION AND HEALTH SERVICES

As evidenced in improvements in pregnancy outcome and the health of mothers and children, the health system influences health status through a variety of intervention strategies and services.[2] Key relationships among health, illness, and various interventions intended to maintain or restore health are summarily presented in Table 3–2. As discussed in Chapter 2, health and illness are dynamic states that are influenced by a wide variety of biologic, environmental, behavioral, social, and health service factors. The complex interaction of these factors results in the occurrence or absence of disease or injury, which, in turn, contributes to the health status of individuals and populations. Several different intervention points are possible, including two general strategies that seek to maintain health by intervening prior to the development of disease or injury.[2] These are health promotion and specific protection strategies. Both involve activities that alter the interaction of the various health-influencing factors in ways that contribute to either averting or altering the likelihood of occurrence of disease or injury.

Health Promotion and Specific Protection

Health promotion activities attempt to modify human behaviors to reduce those known to affect adversely the ability to resist disease or injury-inducing factors, thereby eliminating exposures to harmful factors. Examples of health promotion activities include interventions such as nutrition counseling, genetic counseling, family counseling, and the myriad activities that constitute health education. However, health promotion also properly includes the provision of adequate housing, employment, and recreational conditions, as well as other forms of community development activities. What is clear from these examples is that many fall outside the common public understanding of what constitutes health care. Several of these are viewed as the duty or responsibility of other societal institutions, including public safety, housing, education, and even industry. It is somewhat ironic that activities that focus on the state of health and that seek to maintain and promote health are not commonly perceived to be "health services." To some extent,

EXAMPLE

Public Health Achievements in 20th-Century America: Improved Maternal and Infant Health

Both medical and public health strategies have contributed to the impressive improvement in maternal and infant health measures achieved over the 20th century. Reducing infant mortality, for example, calls for either decreasing the proportion of infants born at low birth weight (prevention) or by improving the chances of those infants to survive through more effective medical care. Prevention and treatment should not be considered mutually exclusive strategies. Key aspects of this public health achievement are captured in Table 3–1 and Figures 3–1, 3–2, and 3–3.

TABLE 3–1 Percentage Reduction in Infant, Neonatal, and Postneonatal Mortality, by Year—United States, 1915–1997*

	Percentage Reduction in Mortality		
Year	Infant (aged 0–364 days)	Neonatal (aged 0–27 days)	Postneonatal (aged 28–364 days)
1915–1919	13%	7%	19%
1920–1929	21%	11%	31%
1930–1939	26%	18%	35%
1940–1949	33%	26%	46%
1950–1959	10%	7%	15%
1960–1969	20%	17%	27%
1970–1979	35%	41%	14%
1980–1989	22%	27%	12%
1990–1997	22%	17%	29%
1915–1997	93%	89%	96%

*Percentage reduction is calculated as the reduction from the first year of the time period to the last year of the time period.
Source: Reprinted from Center for Disease Control and Prevention. Achievements in public health, United States, 1900–1999: healthier mothers and babies. *MMWR Morb Mortal Wkly Rep.* 1999;48:849–858.

FIGURE 3–1 Infant mortality rate (per 1,000 live births) by year—United States, 1915–1997.

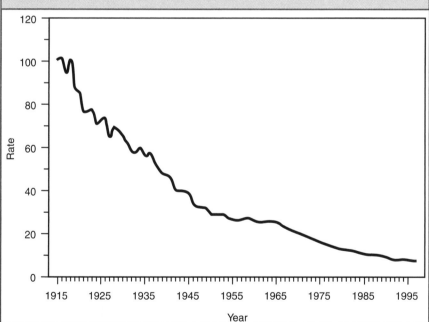

Source: Reprinted from Centers for Disease Control and Prevention. Achievements in public health, United States, 1900–1999: healthier mothers and babies. *MMWR Morb Mortal Wkly Rep.* 1999;48:849–858.

this is also true for the other category of health-maintaining strategies—specific protection activities.

Specific protection activities provide individuals with resistance to factors (such as microorganisms like viruses and bacteria) or modify environments to decrease potentially harmful interactions of health-influencing factors (such as toxic exposures in the workplace). Examples of specific protection include activities directed toward specific risks (e.g., the use of protective equipment for asbestos removal), immunizations, occupational and environmental engineering, and regulatory controls and activities to protect individuals from environmental carcinogens (such as exposure to second-hand or side-stream smoke) and toxins. Several of these are often identified with settings other than traditional health care settings. Many are implemented and enforced through governmental agencies. Table 3–3 presents a catalog of health-related prevention organizations, agencies, and institutions.

FIGURE 3–2 Fertility rates, United States, 1917–1997.

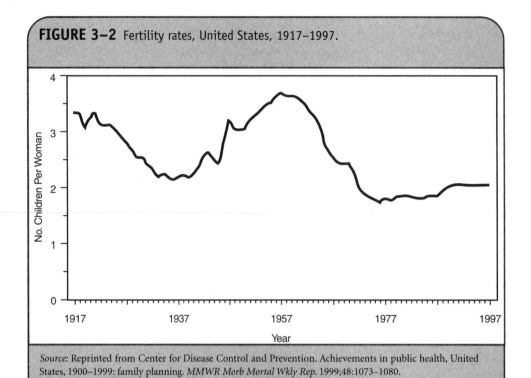

Source: Reprinted from Center for Disease Control and Prevention. Achievements in public health, United States, 1900–1999: family planning. *MMWR Morb Mortal Wkly Rep.* 1999;48:1073–1080.

FIGURE 3–3 Maternal mortality rates (per 100,000 live births) by year, United States, 1900–1997.

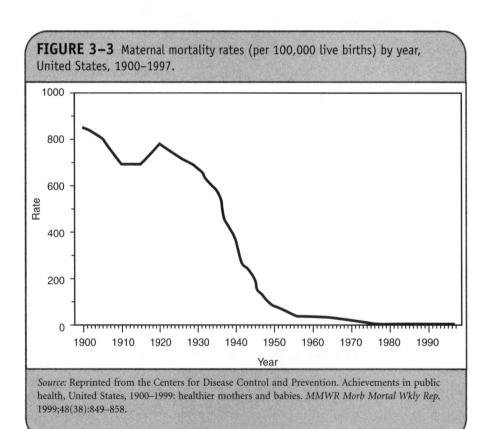

Source: Reprinted from the Centers for Disease Control and Prevention. Achievements in public health, United States, 1900–1999: healthier mothers and babies. *MMWR Morb Mortal Wkly Rep.* 1999;48(38):849–858.

TABLE 3–2 Health Strategies, Prevention Levels, Practice Domains, and Targets

Strategy	State Addressed	Prevention Level	Practice Domain	Target
Health promotion	Health	Primary	Public health	Community
Specific protection	Health	Primary	Public health	Community or risk group
Early case finding and prompt treatment	Illness	Secondary	Public health and primary medical care	Individual
Disability limitation	Illness	Tertiary	Secondary/tertiary medical care	Individual
Rehabilitation	Illness	Tertiary	Long-term care	Individual and group

Source: Data from Leavell HR, Clark EG. *Preventive Medicine for the Doctor in His Community.* 3rd ed. New York: McGraw-Hill; 1965.

TABLE 3–3 Example of Health-Related Prevention Organizations, Agencies, and Institutions

Federal Agencies
Department of Agriculture
Department of Transportation
Department of Energy
Department of Health and Human Services
Department of Homeland Security
Department of Labor
Department of Education
Department of Justice
Department of the Interior
Department of Veterans Administration
Department of Commerce
Department of Treasury
Department of Housing and Urban Development
Environmental Protection Agency
Consumer Product Safety Commission
Federal Mine Safety and Health Review Commission
National Transportation Safety Board
Nuclear Regulatory Commission
Occupational Safety and Health Review Commission
Federal Emergency Management Agency

State Agencies (different agency names in different states)
Aging
Agriculture
Alcoholism and Substance Abuse
Children and Family Services

Council on Health and Fitness
Emergency Services and Disaster Agency
Energy and Natural Resources
Environmental Protection Agency
Guardianship and Advocacy Commission
Health Care Cost Containment Agency
Health Facilities Planning Board and Agency
Mental Health and Developmental Disabilities
Nuclear Safety
Pollution Control Board
Professional Regulation Agency
Public Health
Rehabilitation Services
State Fire Marshall
State Board of Education
State Board of Higher Education
Veterans Affairs

Miscellaneous Organizations and Sites
Foundations
Corporations
Voluntary Health Associations
United Way of America
Physician Office Visits
HMO visits
Dental Visits

Early Case Finding and Prompt Treatment, Disability Limitation, and Rehabilitation

Although health promotion and specific protection both focus on the healthy state and seek to prevent disease, a different set of strategies and activities is necessary if the interaction of factors results in disease or injury. When disease occurs, the strategies that become necessary are those facilitating early detection, rapid control, or rehabilitation, depending on the stage of development of the disease.

In general, early detection and prompt treatment reduce individual pain and suffering and are less costly to both the individual and society than treatment initiated only after a condition has reached a more advanced state. Interventions to achieve early detection and prompt treatment include screening tests, case-finding efforts, and periodic physical exams. Screening tests are increasingly available to detect illnesses before they become symptomatic. Case-finding efforts for both infectious and noninfectious conditions are directed at populations at greater risk for the condition on the basis of criteria appropriate for that condition. Periodic physical exams, such as those mentioned in the age-specific recommendations of the U.S. Preventive Health Services Task Force,[3] incorporate these practices and are best provided through an effective primary medical care system. Primary care providers who are sensitive to disease patterns and predisposing factors can play substantial roles in the early identification and management of most medical conditions.

Another strategy targeting disease is disability limitation through effective and complete treatment. It is this set of activities that most Americans equate with the term *health care*, largely because this strategy constitutes the lion's share of the U.S. health system in terms of resource deployment. Quite appropriately, these efforts largely aim to arrest or eradicate disease or to limit disability and prevent death. The final intervention strategy focusing on disease—rehabilitation—is designed to return individuals who have experienced a condition to the maximum level of function consistent with their capacities.

Links with Prevention

There are several useful aspects of this framework. It emphasizes the potential for prevention inherent in each of the five health service strategies. Prevention can be categorized in several ways. The best-known approach classifies prevention in relation to the stage of the disease or condition.

Preventive intervention strategies are considered primary, secondary, or tertiary. Primary prevention involves prevention of the disease or injury itself, generally through reducing exposure or risk factor levels. Secondary prevention attempts to identify and control disease processes in their early stages, often before signs and symptoms become apparent. In this case, prevention is akin to preemptive treatment. Tertiary prevention seeks to prevent disability through restoring individuals to their optimal level of functioning after damage is done. The selection of an intervention point at the primary, secondary, or tertiary level is a function of knowledge, resources, acceptability, effectiveness, and efficiency, among other considerations.

The relationship of health promotion and specific protection to these levels of prevention is also presented in Table 3–2. Health promotion and specific protection are primary prevention strategies seeking to prevent the development of disease. Early case finding and prompt treatment represent secondary prevention, because they seek to interrupt the disease process before it becomes symptomatic. Both disability limitation and rehabilitation are considered tertiary-level prevention in that they seek to prevent or reduce disability associated with disease or injury. Although these are considered tertiary prevention, they receive primary attention under current policy and resource deployment.

Figure 3–4 illustrates each of the three levels of prevention strategies in relation to population disease status and effect on disease incidence and prevalence. The various potential benefits from the three intervention levels derive from the basic epidemiologic concepts of incidence and prevalence. Prevalence (the number of existing cases of illness, injury, or a health event) is a function of both incidence (the number of new cases) and duration. Reducing either component can reduce prevalence. Primary prevention aims to reduce the incidence of conditions, whereas secondary and tertiary prevention seek to reduce prevalence by shortening duration and minimizing the effects of disease or injury. It should be apparent that there is a finite limit to how much a condition's duration can be reduced. As a result, approaches emphasizing primary prevention have greater potential benefit than do approaches emphasizing other levels of prevention. This basis for understanding the differential impact of prevention and treatment approaches to a particular health problem or condition cannot be overstated.

These same considerations are pertinent to the idea of postponement of morbidity as a prevention strategy, as illustrated in Figure 3–5. As demonstrated in Model I, increased life expectancy without postponement of morbidity may actually increase the burden of illness within a population, as measured by prevalence. However, postponement may result in the development of a condition so late in life that it results in either no or less disability in functioning.

Another approach to classifying prevention efforts groups interventions by the nature of the intervention into clinical,

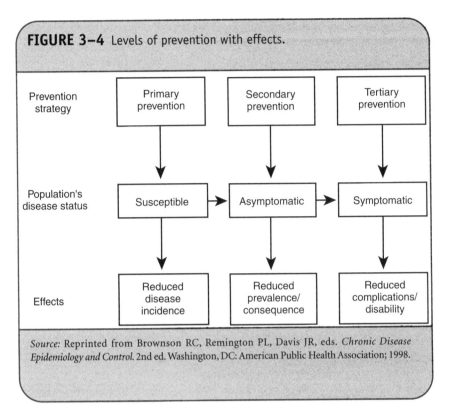

FIGURE 3–4 Levels of prevention with effects.

Source: Reprinted from Brownson RC, Remington PL, Davis JR, eds. *Chronic Disease Epidemiology and Control.* 2nd ed. Washington, DC: American Public Health Association; 1998.

Links with Public Health and Medical Practice

Another useful aspect of this framework is in its allocation of responsibilities for carrying out the various interventions. Three practice domains can be roughly delineated: public health practice, medical practice, and long-term care practice.[2] The framework assigns public health practice primary responsibility for health promotion, specific protection, and a good share of early case finding. It is important to note that the concept of public health practice here is a broad one that accommodates the activities carried out by many different types of health professionals and workers, not only those working in public health agencies. Although many of these activities are carried out in public health agencies of the federal, state, or local government, many are not. Public health practice occurs in voluntary health agencies, as well as in behavioral, or environmental categories. Clinical interventions are provided to individuals, whereas environmental interventions are organized for populations or groups. Behavioral interventions can be provided either for individuals or for populations, including subgroups identified as being at higher risk for a particular condition.

Within this framework for considering intervention strategies aimed at health or illness, the potential for prevention as an element of all strategies is clear. There are substantial opportunities to use primary and secondary prevention strategies to improve health in general and reduce the burden of illness for individuals and for society. As noted in Chapter 2, reducing the burden of illness carries the potential for substantial cost savings. These concepts serve to promote a more rational intervention and investment strategy for the U.S. health system.

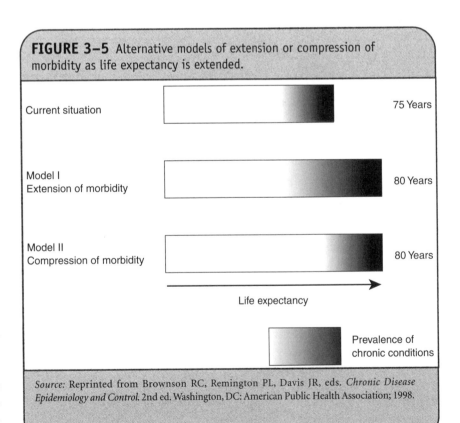

FIGURE 3–5 Alternative models of extension or compression of morbidity as life expectancy is extended.

Source: Reprinted from Brownson RC, Remington PL, Davis JR, eds. *Chronic Disease Epidemiology and Control.* 2nd ed. Washington, DC: American Public Health Association; 1998.

settings such as schools, social service agencies, industry, and even traditional medical care settings. In terms of prevention, public health practice embraces all of the primary prevention activities in the model, as well as some of the activities for early diagnosis and prompt treatment.

The demarcations between public health and medical practice are neither clear nor absolute. In recent decades, public health practice has been extensively involved in screening and has become an important source of primary medical care for populations with diminished access to care. At the same time, medical practice has also been extensively involved with early case finding while traditionally providing the major share of primary care services to most segments of the population.

Medical practice, meaning those services usually provided by or under the supervision of a physician or other traditional health care provider, can be viewed as including three levels (Table 3–4). Primary medical care has been variously defined but generally focuses on the basic health needs of individuals and families. It is first-contact health care in the view of the patient; provides at least 80% of necessary care; includes a comprehensive array of services, on site or through referral, including health promotion and disease prevention, as well as curative services; and is accessible and acceptable to the patient population. This comprehensive description of primary care differs substantially from what is commonly encountered as primary care in the U.S. health system. Often lacking from current so-called primary care services are those relating to health promotion and disease prevention.

The concept of *disease management* has evolved from efforts to provide a more integrated approach to health care delivery in order to improve health outcomes and reduce costs, often for defined populations such as Medicaid enrollees. Disease management focuses on identifying and proactively monitoring high-risk populations, assisting patients and providers to ad-

here to treatment plans that are based on proven interventions, promoting provider coordination, increasing patient education, and preventing avoidable medical complications.

Beyond primary medical care are two more specialized types of care that are often termed *secondary care* and *tertiary care*. Secondary care is specialized care serving the major share of the remaining 20% of the need that lies beyond the scope of primary care. Physicians or hospitals generally provide secondary care, ideally upon referral from a primary care source. Tertiary medical care is even more highly specialized and technologically sophisticated medical and surgical care for those with unusual or complex conditions (generally no more than a few percent of the need in any service category). Tertiary care is frequently provided in large medical centers or academic health centers.

Long-term care is appropriately classified separately because of the special needs of the population requiring such services and the specialized settings where many of these services are offered. This, too, is changing as specialized long-term care services increasingly move out of long-term care facilities and into home settings.

Within the health services pyramid presented in Figure 3–6, primary prevention activities are largely associated with population-based public health services at the base of the pyramid, although some primary prevention in the form of clinical preventative services is also associated with primary medical care services. Secondary prevention activities are split somewhat more evenly between the population-based public health services and primary medical care. Tertiary prevention activities fall largely in the secondary and tertiary medical care components of the pyramid. The use of a pyramid to represent health services implies that each level serves a different proportion of the total population. Everyone should be served by population-wide public health services, and nearly everyone

TABLE 3–4 Health Care Pyramid Levels

- Tertiary Medical Care
    Subspecialty referral care requiring highly specialized personnel and facilities
- Secondary Medical Care
    Specialized attention and ongoing management for common and less frequently encountered medical conditions, including support services for people with special challenges due to chronic or long-term conditions
- Primary Medical Care
    Clinical preventive services, first-contact treatment services, and ongoing care for commonly encountered medical conditions
- Population-Based Public Health Services
    Interventions aimed at disease prevention and health promotion that shape a community's overall health profile

Source: Reprinted from U.S. Public Health Service. *For a Healthy Nation: Return on Investments in Public Health.* Hyattsville, MD: PHS; 1994.

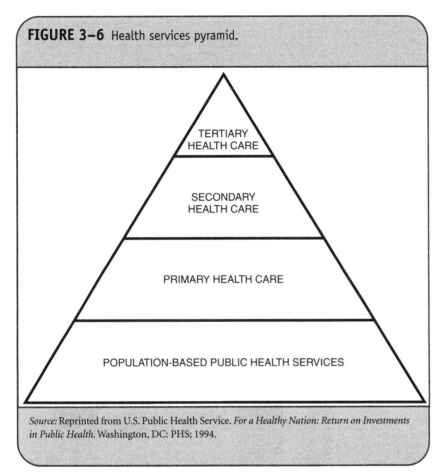

FIGURE 3–6 Health services pyramid.

TERTIARY
HEALTH CARE

SECONDARY
HEALTH CARE

PRIMARY HEALTH CARE

POPULATION-BASED PUBLIC HEALTH SERVICES

Source: Reprinted from U.S. Public Health Service. *For a Healthy Nation: Return on Investments in Public Health.* Washington, DC: PHS; 1994.

should be served by primary medical care. However, increasingly smaller proportions of the total population require secondary- and tertiary-level medical care services. In any event, the system should be built from the bottom up. It would not be rational to build such a system from the top down; there might not be enough resources to address the lower levels that served as the foundation for the system. Nonetheless, there is evidence in later sections of this chapter that this is exactly what has occurred with the U.S. health system.

Targets of Health Service Strategies

A final facet of this model characterizes the targets for the strategies and activities. Generally, primary preventive services are community-based and are targeted toward populations or groups rather than individuals. Early case-finding activities can be directed toward groups or toward individuals. For example, many screening activities target groups at higher risk when these are provided through public health agencies. The same screening activities can also be provided for individuals through physicians' offices and hospital outpatient departments. Much of primary and virtually all of secondary and

tertiary medical care is appropriately individually oriented. It should be noted that there is a concept, termed *community-oriented primary care,* in which primary care providers assume responsibility for all of the individuals in a community, rather than only those who seek out care from the provider. Even in this model, however, care is provided on an individual basis. Long-term care involves elements of both community-based service and individually oriented service. These services are tailored for individuals but often in a group setting or as part of a package of services for a defined number of recipients, as in a long-term care facility.

Public Health and Medical Practice Interfaces

This framework also sheds light on the potential conflicts between public health and medical practice. Although the two are presented as separate domains of practice, there are many interfaces that provide a template for either collaboration or conflict. Both paths have been taken over the past century. Public health practitioners have traditionally deferred to medical practitioners for providing the broad spectrum of services for disease and injuries in individuals. Medical practitioners have generally acknowledged the need for public health practice for health promotion and specific protection strategies. The interfaces raise difficult issues. For example, for one specific protection activity—childhood immunizations—it can be argued that the extensive role of public health practice has served to fragment health services for children. It would be logical to provide these services within a well-functioning primary care system, where they could be better integrated with other services for this population. Despite occasional differences as to roles, in most circumstances, medical practice has supported the role of public health to serve as the provider of last resort in ensuring medical care for persons who lack financial access to private health care. This, too, has varied over time and from place to place.

Advances in bacteriologic diagnoses in public health laboratories, for example, fostered friction between medical practitioners and public health professionals for diseases such as tuberculosis and diphtheria that were often difficult to identify from other common but less serious maladies. Clinicians feared that laboratory diagnoses would replace clinical diagnoses and that, in highly competitive medical markets, paying patients would abandon private physicians for public health agencies. Issues of turf and scope of practice persist in many communities.

Some of the most serious conflicts have come in the area of primary care services, including early case-finding activities. Because of the increased yield of screening tests when these are applied to groups at higher risk, public health practice has sought to deploy more widely risk group or community case-finding methods (including outreach and linkage activities). This has, at times, been perceived by medical practitioners as encroachment on their practice domain for certain primary care services, such as prenatal care. Although there has been no rule that public health practice could not be provided within the medical practice domain and vice versa, the perception that these are separate, but perhaps unequal, territories has been widely held by both groups.

It is important to note that this territoriality is not based only on turf issues. There are significant differences in the world views and approaches of these two domains. Medical practice quite properly seeks to produce the best possible outcome through the development and execution of individualized treatment plans. Seeking the best possible outcome for an individual suggests that decisions are made primarily for the benefit of that individual. Costs and resource availability are secondary considerations. Public health practice, on the other hand, seeks to deploy its limited resources to avoid the worst outcomes (at the level of the group). Some level of risk is tolerated at the collective level to prevent an unacceptable level of adverse outcomes from occurring. These are quite different approaches to practice: maximizing individual positive outcomes, as opposed to minimizing adverse collective outcomes. As a result, differences in perspective and philosophy often underlie differences in approaches that initially appear to be concerns over territoriality.

An example that illustrates these differences is apparent in approaches to widespread use of human immunodeficiency virus (HIV) antibody testing in the mid- and late 1980s. Medical practitioners perceived that HIV antibody testing would be very useful in clinical practice and that its widespread use would enhance case finding. As a result, medical practitioners generally opposed restrictions on use of these tests, such as specific written informed consent and additional confidentiality provisions. Public health practitioners perceived that widespread use of the test without safeguards and protections would actually result in fewer persons at risk being tested and decreased case finding in the community. With both groups focusing on the same science in terms of the accuracy of the specific testing regimen, these differences in practice approaches may be difficult to understand. However, in view of their ultimate aims and concerns as to individual versus collective outcomes, the conflict is more understandable.

Perspectives and roles may differ for public health and medical practice, but both are important and necessary. The real question is what blending of these approaches will be most successful in improving health status throughout the population. There is sufficient cause to question current policy and investment strategies. Table 3–5 examines the potential contributions of various strategies (personal responsibility, health care services, community action, and social policies) toward reducing the impact of the actual causes of death identified in Chapter 2. This table suggests that more medical care services are not as likely to reduce the toll from these causes as are public health approaches (community action and social policies). Yet, there are opportunities available through the current system and perhaps even greater opportunities in the near term as the system seeks to address the serious problems that have brought it to the brink of major reform.

Medicine and Public Health Collaborations

The need for a renewed partnership between medicine and public health generated several promising initiatives in the final years of the 20th century. Just as bacteriology brought together public health professionals and practicing physicians at the turn of the 20th century to battle diphtheria and other infectious diseases, technology and economics may become the driving forces for a renewed partnership at the dawn of the 21st century. In pursuit of this vision, the American Medical Association and the American Public Health Association established the Medicine/Public Health Initiative in 1994 to provide an ongoing forum to define mutual interests and promote models for successful collaborations. Regional and state meetings followed a National Congress in 1996. A variety of collaborative structures were identified and promoted through the widely circulated monograph, *Medicine and Public Health: The Power of Collaboration*.[4] More than 400 examples of collaborations are highlighted in the monograph. General categories of collaboration include coalitions, contracts, administrative/management systems, advisory bodies, and intraorganizational platforms. This initiative represents a major breakthrough for public health interests, one long overdue and welcome; in fact, it represents the first time that these two major professional organizations have met around mutual interests.

Collaborations between public health and hospitals have also gained momentum. Increasingly, hospitals and managed care organizations have begun to pursue community health goals, at times in concert with public health organizations and

TABLE 3–5 Actual Causes of Death in the United States and Potential Contribution to Reduction

Causes	Deaths		Potential Contribution to Reduction[*]			
	Estimated No.	%	Personal	Health Care System	Community Action	Social Policy
Tobacco	435,000	19	++++	+	+	++
Diet/activity patterns	400,000	14	+++	+	+	++
Alcohol	85,000	5	+++	+	+	+
Microbial agents	75,000	4	+	++	++	++
Toxic agents	55,000	3	+	+	++	++++
Motor vehicles	43,000	1	++	+	+	++
Firearms	29,000	2	++	+	+++	+++
Sexual behavior	20,000	1	++++	+	+	+
Illicit use of drugs	20,000	<1	+++	+	++	++

[*]Plus sign indicates relative magnitude (4+ scale).
Source: Data from Fielding J, Halfon L. Where is the health in health system reform? *JAMA.* 1994;272:1292–1296 and Mokdad AH, Marks JS, Stroup DF, Gerberding JL. Actual causes of death in the United States, 2000. *JAMA.* 2004:291:1238–1245.

at other times filling voids that exist at the community level. In many parts of the United States, hospitals have taken the lead in organizing community health planning activities. More frequently, however, they participate as major community stakeholders in health planning efforts organized through the local public health agency. A variety of positive interfaces with managed care organizations have been documented.[5] Hospital boards and executives now commonly include community benefit objectives in their annual performance evaluations. Examples of community health strategies include:

- Establishing "boundary spanner" positions that report to the chief executive officer but focus on community-wide, rather than institutional, interests
- Changing reward systems in terms of salaries and bonuses that executives and board members linked to the achievement of community health goals
- Educating staff on the mission, vision, and values of the institution, and linking these with community health outcomes
- Exposing board to the work of community partners
- Engaging board members with the staff and community
- Reporting on community health performance (report cards)[6]

THE HEALTH SYSTEM IN THE UNITED STATES

There are many sources of more complete information on the health system in the United States than will be provided in this chapter. Here, the intent is to examine those aspects of the health industry and health system that interface with public health or raise issues of public health significance. There is no shortage of either. This section will examine some of the issues facing the health system in the United States, with a special focus on the problems of the system that are fueling reform and change. Interfaces with public health will be identified and discussed, as will possible effects of these changes on the various images of public health. Throughout these sections, data from the *Health, United States* series, published annually by the National Center for Health Statistics, will be used to describe the economic, demographic, and resources aspects of the American health system.

Economic Dimensions

The health system in the United States is immense and growing rapidly, as shown in Figure 3–7. Total national health expenditures in the United States nearly doubled during the 1990s to nearly $1.4 trillion by 2000, more than four times the sum expended in 1980 and nearly 50 times more than in 1960. In 2005, health expenditures exceeded $2.0 billion. It is naive to consider the possible public health interfaces with the health system in the United States without understanding the context in which they take place—the health sector of modern America. In the early years of the new century, economic growth and employment in the United States weakened after nearly two decades of prosperity and improved productivity. The health care sector is now a powerful component in the overall U.S. economy. By the year 2005, the health care sector represented nearly one sixth of the total

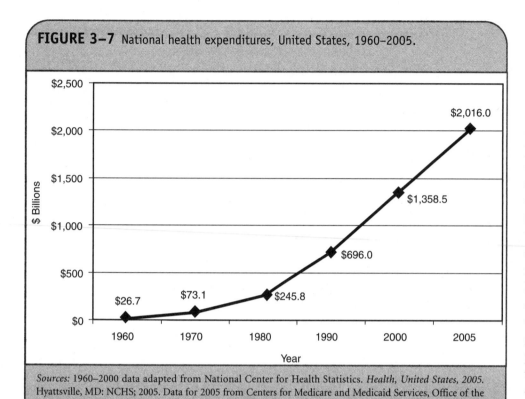

FIGURE 3–7 National health expenditures, United States, 1960–2005.

Sources: 1960–2000 data adapted from National Center for Health Statistics. *Health, United States, 2005.* Hyattsville, MD: NCHS; 2005. Data for 2005 from Centers for Medicare and Medicaid Services, Office of the Actuary.

far less; and the opportunity costs are considerable.

Expenditures for personal health care services comprise 87% of all health expenditures. Administrative costs in both the public and private sector account for 6.4% and investments (research and construction) comprise another 3.4%. The remaining 3.4% is devoted to government public health activities (about $8.3 billion in 2000), including personal health care services provided directly by the government.[1] Chapter 4 further examines governmental health and public health expenditure trends for the various levels of government in the United States.

national gross domestic product (GDP); Figure 3–8 traces the growth in health expenditures as a proportion of GDP.

The United States spends a greater share of the GDP on health care services than any other industrialized nation. Health expenditures in the United Kingdom and Japan are about one half and in Germany and Canada about three fourths the U.S. figure (16.2%). Per capita expenditures on health show the same pattern, with more than $4,600 per capita spent on health in the United States in 2000, compared with about $2,500 per capita in Germany and Canada, and only $1,600–1,800 per capita in Japan and the United Kingdom.[1] Several factors suggest that this is too much: the current system is reaching the point of no longer being affordable; the U.S. population is no healthier than other nations that spend

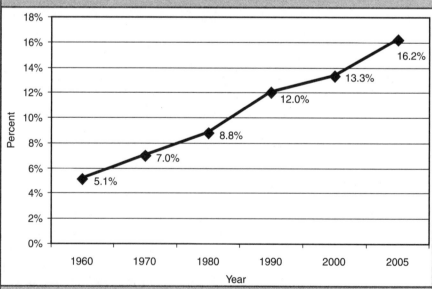

FIGURE 3–8 Percent of national gross domestic expenditures spent for health-related purposes, U.S. 1960–2005.

Sources: 1960–2000 data adapted from National Center for Health Statistics. *Health, United States, 2005.* Hyattsville, MD: NCHS; 2005. Data for 2005 from Centers for Medicare and Medicaid Services, Office of the Actuary.

There are three general sources for personal health care expenditures: government at all levels pays 44%; private health insurance covers 36%; individuals pay about 16% out of pocket; and the remaining 4% is covered by other private funds.[1] The rapidly increasing costs for health services have hit all these sources in their pocketbooks, and each is reaching the point at which further increases may not be affordable. The largest single purchaser of health care in the United States remains the federal government, but the ultimate payers are individuals. Even those individuals covered by health insurance plans are experiencing a steady increase in the triple burden of higher premiums, increased cost sharing, and reduced benefits.

Only limited information is available on expenditures for prevention and population-based public health services. A study using 1988 data estimated that total national expenditures for all forms of health-related prevention (including clinical preventive services provided to individuals and population-based public health programs, such as communicable disease control and environmental protection) amounted to $33 billion.[7] The analysis sought to include all activities directed toward health promotion, health protection, disease screening, and counseling. As a result, the $33 billion figure approximates expenditures for primary and secondary prevention efforts. Included in this total, however, was $14 billion for activities not included in the calculation of national health expenditures (such as sewage systems, water purification, and air traffic safety). The remaining $18 billion in prevention-related health expenditures was included in the calculation of total national health expenditures but represented only 3.4% of all national health expenditures for that year.

Nearly one half (48%) of the health-related prevention resources identified in this analysis came from the federal government; another 31% represented expenditures for clinical preventive services, often paid out of pocket by individuals.[7] Preventive health services were the largest category of health-related prevention expenditures (36%), although health protection (30%) and health promotion services (23%) were also significant targets of prevention-related expenditures. The share of these expenditures that represents population-based preventive services cannot be directly determined from this study. However, it appears that population-based services constituted about $6–7 billion in 1988, in view of the prominence of health protection and health promotion services.

As part of the development of a national health reform proposal in 1994, federal officials developed an estimate of national health expenditures for population-based services.[8] On the basis of expenditures in 1993, this analysis concluded that about 1% of all national health expenditures ($8.4 billion) supported population-based programs and services. Based on

data available, this analysis found that the proportion of all health expenditures attributed to population-based services declined slightly during the 1980s from 1.2% in 1980 to 0.9% a decade later. U.S. Public Health Service (PHS) agencies spent $4.3 billion for population-based services in 1993, and state and local health agencies expended another $4.1 billion. PHS officials estimated that achieving an "essential" level of population-based services nationwide would require doubling 1993 expenditure levels and that achieving a "fully effective" level would require tripling the 1993 levels.

Consistent with these earlier analyses, data from the National Health Accounts identify levels of population-based health expenditures by federal, state, and local governments to have been $7.8 billion in 1990, $12.3 billion in 1995, and $17.1 billion in 2000 (see Figure 3–9).[9,10] On a per capita basis, governmental expenditures for population-based public health activities increased more than 1,200% between 1960 and 2000 (Figure 3–10), but governmental public health agencies continue to spend more of their resources on providing personal health care series than on population-based public health activities, as Figure 3–9 illustrates.

The implications of these expenditure patterns will be discussed in Chapter 4. Here, however, these gross figures are presented in order to demonstrate the very small slice of the national health expenditure pie devoted to population-based preventive services and the public health system. As shown in Figure 3–11, governmental public health spending as a percent of total national health expenditures grew from 1960 through 1975, then declined from 1975 to 1985, and has been increasing steadily since 1985. The availability of resources from the 1998 settlement between states and the major tobacco companies, together with bioterrorism preparedness funding from Congress beginning in 2002, presented an opportunity to achieve the doubling of expenditures for population-based prevention deemed necessary to achieve an essential level of services by the PHS in 1994. Although such a doubling would require only a small shift in resource allocation strategies within a $2.0 trillion dollar enterprise, there was little hope for increased resources for population-based public health activities until the tobacco settlement and bioterrorism preparedness funds appeared. Subsequent chapters will provide additional information as to the effect these additional resources are having on the public health system.

But macro-economic trends tell only part of the story. The disparities between rich and poor in the United States are also growing, leaving an increasing number of Americans without financial access to many health care services. These and other important aspects will be examined as we review the demands on and resources of the U.S. health system.

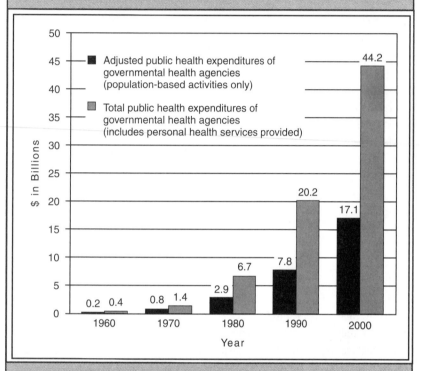

FIGURE 3–9 Total expenditures (in $ billions) of governmental health agencies (including personal health services) and adjusted total governmental public health spending (population-based services only), United States, 1960–2000.

Sources and Notes: Data compiled from National Center for Health Statistics. *Health, United States, 2002.* Hyattsville, MD: NCHS; 2002 and Centers for Medicare and Medicaid Services, National Health Accounts (NHA) 1960–2000. The NHA breaks down health spending by source of funding and by activity and type of service provided. Adjusted total public health expenditures include expenditures at both the federal and state/local level. State/local public health expenditures are adjusted in an attempt to include only funding for essential (i.e., population-based) public health services and to exclude personal health care services.

Demographic and Utilization Trends

Several important demographic trends affect the U.S. health care system. These include the slowing population growth rate, the shift toward an older population, the increasing diversity of the population, changes in family structure, and persistent lack of access to needed health services for too many Americans. The relative prevalence of particular diseases is another demographic phenomenon but will not be addressed here, although recent history with diseases such as HIV infections illustrates how specific conditions can place increasing demands on fragile health care systems.

Census studies document that the growth of the U.S. population has been slowing, a trend that would be expected to restrain future growth in demand for health care services. However, this must be viewed in light of projected changes in the age distribution of the U.S. population. Between 2000 and 2030, the population older than age 65 will double, whereas the younger age groups will grow little, if at all.

Utilization of health care services, in general, is closely correlated with the age distribution of the population. For example, adults age 75 years and older visit physicians three to four times as frequently as do children younger than age 17. Because older persons utilize more health care services than do younger people, their expenditures are higher. Obvious reasons for the higher utilization of health care resources by the elderly include the high prevalence of chronic conditions, such as arteriosclerosis, cerebrovascular disease, diabetes, senility, arthritis, and mental disorders. As the population ages, it is expected that the prevalence of chronic disorders and the treatment costs associated with them will also increase. This could be minimized through prevention efforts that either avert or postpone the onset of these chronic diseases. Nonetheless, these important demographic shifts portend greater use of health care services in the future.

Another important demographic trend is the increasing diversity of the population. The nonwhite population is growing three times faster than the white population, and the Hispanic population is increasing at five times the rate for the entire U.S. population. Between 1980 and 2000, Hispanics increased from 6.4% to 12.5% of the U.S. population. African Americans increased from 11.5% to 14.5% of the total population, while the number of Asian/Pacific Islanders more than doubled from 1.6% to 3.7%. The white population declined from 79.7% to 69.1% of the total population over these two decades. Figure 3–12 projects these trends through the years 2025 and 2050. These trends reflect differences in fertility and immigration patterns and disproportionately affect the younger age groups, suggesting that services for mothers and children will face considerable challenges in their ability to provide culturally sensitive and acceptable services. At the same time, the considerably less diverse baby boom generation will be increasing its ability to affect public policy decisions and resource allocations in the early years of the 21st century. These trends also underscore the importance of cultural competence for health professionals. Cultural competence is a set of be-

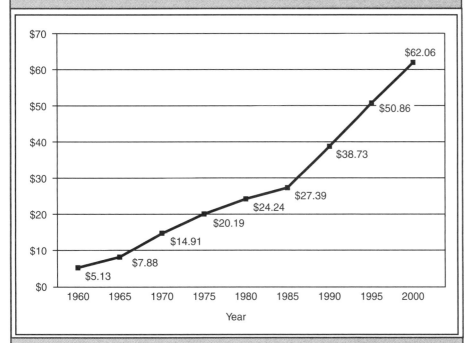

FIGURE 3-10 Per capita adjusted total governmental public health expenditures, United States, 1960–2000.

Sources and Notes: Data compiled from National Centers for Health Statistics. *Health, United States, 2002.* Hyattsville, MD: NCHS; 2002 and Centers for Medicare and Medicaid Services, National Health Accounts (NHA) 1960–2000. The NHA breaks down health spending by source of funding and by activity and type of service provided. Adjusted total public health expenditures include expenditures at both the federal and state/local level. State/local public health expenditures are adjusted in an attempt to include only funding for essential (i.e., population-based) public health services and to exclude personal health care services.

haviors and attitudes, as well as a culture within an institution or system that respects and takes into account the cultural background, cultural beliefs, and values of those served and incorporates this into the way services are delivered.

Changes in family structure also represent a significant demographic trend in the United States. There is only a 50% chance that married partners will reach their 25th anniversary. One in three children live part of their lives in a one-parent household; for black children, the chances are two in three. Labor force participation for women more than doubled from under 25% in 1950 to 54% by 1985. Even more indicative of gender changes in the labor market, the proportion of married women in the work force with children under age five grew from 44% in 1975 to 64% in 1987. Many American households have maintained their economic status over the past 2 decades with the second paychecks from women in the work force. As the nature of families changes, so do their needs for access, availability, and even types of services (such as substance abuse, family violence, and child welfare services).

Intermingled with many of these trends are the persistent inequalities in access to services for low-income populations, including blacks and Hispanics. For example, despite higher rates of self-reported fair or poor health and greater utilization of hospital inpatient services, low-income persons are 50% more likely to report no physician contacts within the past 2 years than are persons in high-income households. Utilization rates for prenatal care and childhood immunizations are also lower for low-income populations.

Despite outspending other developed countries on health services, the United States leads other industrialized nations by a wide margin in the rate of its citizens who lack health insurance coverage. Various studies since 1998 place the figure at approximately 45 million Americans and rising. Health insurance coverage of the population has been declining since 1980 for all age groups except those younger than age five, whose access was improved through Medicaid eligibility changes. The age-adjusted percentage of persons who were not covered by health insurance increased from 14% in 1984 to almost 17% in 2000. Young adults 18–24 years of age were most likely (30%) to be uninsured in 2000.[1]

Blacks were two thirds more likely than whites, and Hispanics were almost three times as likely as whites to be uninsured in 2000. Individuals in households at 150% or less of the poverty level were more than four times more likely to be uninsured than were persons living in households at 200% or more of the poverty level (Figure 3–13). Still, of the 41 million uninsured people younger than age 65, about two thirds are 15–44 years of age, three fourths are white, and one third live in families earning $25,000 or more. Lack of insurance coverage may disproportionately affect minority low-income individuals, but its growth in recent years has affected individuals in almost all groups. About two thirds of uninsured individuals in the United States are either employed or are dependents of an employed family member. Part-time workers

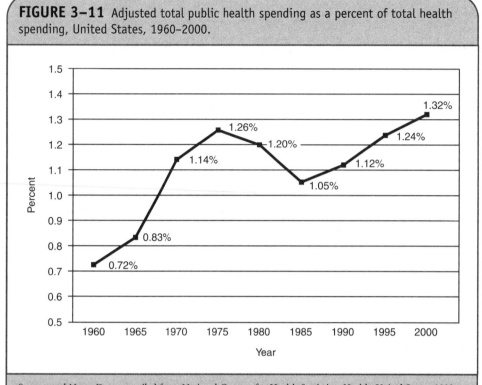

FIGURE 3–11 Adjusted total public health spending as a percent of total health spending, United States, 1960–2000.

Sources and Notes: Data compiled from National Centers for Health Statistics. *Health, United States, 2002.* Hyattsville, MD: NCHS; 2002 and Centers for Medicare and Medicaid Services, National Health Accounts (NHA) 1960–2000. The NHA breaks down health spending by source of funding and by activity and type of service provided. Adjusted total public health expenditures include expenditures at both the federal and state/local level. State/local public health expenditures are adjusted in an attempt to include only funding for essential (i.e., population-based) public health services and to exclude personal health care services.

and the self-employed are as likely as the unemployed to be uninsured. Access to health services is one of the 10 leading indicators of the health status of the United States; Figure 3–14 illustrates targets set for the nation as part of the *Healthy People 2010* initiative.

Health Care Resources

The supply of health care resources is another key dimension of the health care system. During the past quarter-century, the number of active U.S. physicians increased by more than two thirds, with even greater increases among women physicians and international medical graduates. The specialty composition of the physician population also changed during this period, as a result of many factors, including changing employment opportunities, advances in medical technology, and the availability of residency positions. Suffice it to say that medical and surgical subspecialties grew more rapidly than did the primary care specialties. Recent projections suggest that the early 21st century will see a substantial surplus of

physicians, primarily those trained in the surgical and medical specialties.

Health care delivery models have also experienced major changes in recent years. For example, hospital-based resources have changed dramatically. Since the mid-1970s, the number of community hospitals has decreased, and the numbers of admissions, days of care, average occupancy rates, and average length of stay have all declined, as well. On the other hand, the number of hospital employees per 100 average daily patients has continued to increase. Hospital outpatient visits have also been increasing since the mid-1970s.

The growth in the number and types of health care delivery systems in recent years is another reflection of a rapidly changing health care environment. Figure 3–15 traces changes in the types of health plan options available to workers with health insurance coverage between 1988 and 2001. Increasing competition, combined with cost containment initiatives, has led to the proliferation of group medical practices, health maintenance organizations (HMOs), preferred provider organizations, ambu-

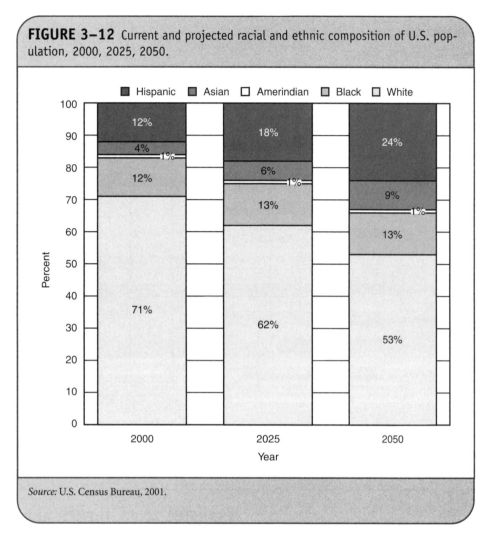

FIGURE 3–12 Current and projected racial and ethnic composition of U.S. population, 2000, 2025, 2050.

Source: U.S. Census Bureau, 2001.

latory surgery centers, and emergency centers. Common to many of these delivery systems since the early 1990s have been managed care strategies and methods that seek to control the utilization of services. Managed care represents a system of administrative controls intended to reduce costs through managing the utilization of services. Elements of managed care strategies generally include some combination of the following:

- Risk sharing with providers to discourage the provision of unnecessary diagnostic and treatment services and, to some degree, to encourage preventive measures
- To attract specific groups, designing of tailored benefit packages that include the most important (but not necessarily all) services for that group; cost sharing for some services through deductibles and copayments can be built into these packages
- Case management, especially for high-cost conditions, to encourage seeking out of less expensive treatments or settings

- Primary care gatekeepers, generally the enrollee's primary care physician, who control referrals to specialists
- Second opinions as to the need for expensive diagnostic or elective invasive procedures
- Review and certification for hospitalizations, in general, and hospital admissions through the emergency department, in particular
- Continued-stay review for hospitalized patients as they reach the expected number of days for their illness (as determined by diagnostic related groupings)
- Discharge planning to move patients out of hospitals to less expensive care settings as quickly as possible

The growth and expansion of these delivery systems has significant implications for the cost of, access to, and quality of health services. These, in turn, have substantial impact on public health organizations and their programs and services.[5] By the year 2000, more than one half of the U.S. population was served through a managed care organization. Within the next

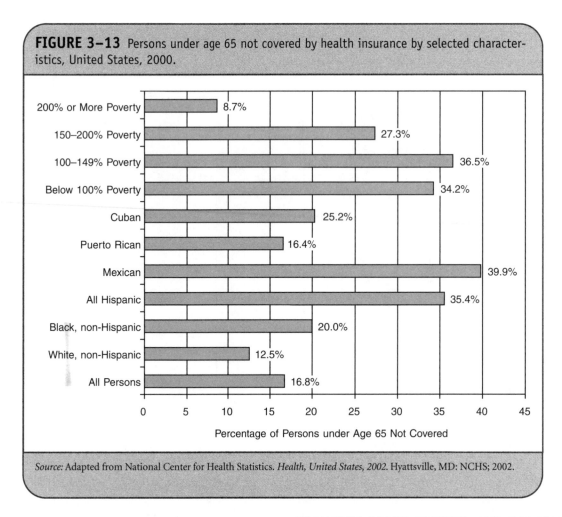

FIGURE 3–13 Persons under age 65 not covered by health insurance by selected characteristics, United States, 2000.

Percentage of Persons under Age 65 Not Covered

Source: Adapted from National Center for Health Statistics. *Health, United States, 2002.* Hyattsville, MD: NCHS; 2002.

decade, managed care will capture 80–90% of the market. The growth of managed care also has significant implications for both the population-based services of governmental public health agencies and the clinical services that have been provided in the public sector.

The dramatic growth in the number of HMOs during the early and mid-1980s was followed by a period of slower growth and consolidations and mergers. Rapid growth resumed in the 1990s, with more than one third of the population (about 80 million Americans) enrolled in HMOs in 2001, up from only 4% in 1980. Considerable variation is apparent across regions of the country, ranging from 35–40% in the West and Northeast to 21–22% in the Midwest and South. The structure of HMOs varies as well, with about 80% of enrollees found in independent practice and mixed-model HMOs; only about 20% are served by group-model HMOs. Recent growth has come largely in the form of the mixed-model HMOs, which include aspects of both the staff and independent models. In general, cost-control measures are more effectively implemented through group-model HMOs.

CHANGING ROLES, THEMES, AND PARADIGMS IN THE HEALTH SYSTEM

Even a cursory review of the health sector requires an examination of the key participants or key players in the health industry. The list of major stakeholders has been expanding as the system has grown and now includes government, business, third-party payers, health care providers, drug companies, and labor, as well as consumers. The federal government has grown to become the largest purchaser of health care and, along with business, has attempted to become a more prudent buyer by exerting more control over payments for services. Government seeks to reduce rising costs by altering the economic performance of the health sector through stimulation of a more competitive health care market. Still, budget problems at all levels make it increasingly difficult for government to fulfill commitments to provide health care services to the poor, the disadvantaged, and the elderly. Over recent years, new and expensive medical technology, inflation, and unexpected increases in utilization forced third parties to pay out more for health care than they anticipated when premiums were deter-

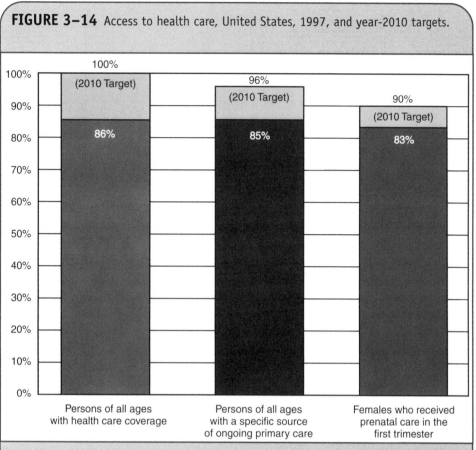

FIGURE 3–14 Access to health care, United States, 1997, and year-2010 targets.

Source: Reprinted from Office of Disease Prevention and Health Promotion. *Healthy People 2010: Understanding and Improving Health.* Rockville, MD: ODPHP; 2000.

mined. As a result, insurers have joined government in becoming more aggressive in efforts to contain health care costs. Many commercial carriers are exploring methods to anticipate utilization more accurately and to control outlays through managed care strategies. Business, labor, patients, hospitals, and professional organizations are all trying to restrain costs while maintaining access to health services.

Reducing the national deficit and balancing the federal budget will look in part to proposals that will control costs within Medicare and Medicaid, as well as in discretionary federal health programs. Except for Medicare, these recommendations are likely to be politically popular, even though the public has little understanding of the federal budget. For example, a 1994 poll[11] found that Americans believe health care costs constitute 5% of the federal budget, although these costs actually constitute 16%. At the same time, Americans believed that foreign aid and welfare constitute 27% and 19%, respectively, of the federal budget when, in fact, they constituted only 2% and 3%, respectively. When the time comes to balance the

federal budget and reduce the national deficit, the American public will face difficult choices as to which programs can be reduced. Public health programs, largely discretionary spending, may not fare well in this scenario.

As these stakeholders search for methods to reduce costs and as competition intensifies, efforts to preserve the quality of health care will become increasingly important. An Institute of Medicine study concluded that medical errors account for as many deaths each year as motor vehicle crashes and breast cancer (Figure 3–16).[12] Public debate will continue to focus on how to define and measure quality. Despite the difficulty in measuring quality of medical care, it is likely that quality measurement systems will increase substantially. Dialogue and debate among the major stakeholders in the health system will be influenced by the tension between cost containment and regulation; the interdependence of access, quality, and costs; the call for greater accountability; and the slow but steady acceptance of the need for health reform.

Almost certainly, health policy issues will become increasingly politicized. The debate on health care issues will continue to expand beyond the health care community. Many health policy issues may no longer be determined by sound science and practice considerations, but rather by political factors. Changes in the health sector may lead to unexpected divisions and alliances on health policy issues. The intensity of economic competition in the health sector is likely to continue to increase because of the increasing supply of health care personnel and because of the changes in the financing of care. Increased competition is likely to cause realignments among key participants in the health care sector, often depending on the particular issue involved.

The failure of health reform at the national policy level in 1994 did not preclude the implementation of significant

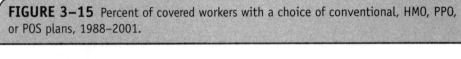

FIGURE 3–15 Percent of covered workers with a choice of conventional, HMO, PPO, or POS plans, 1988–2001.

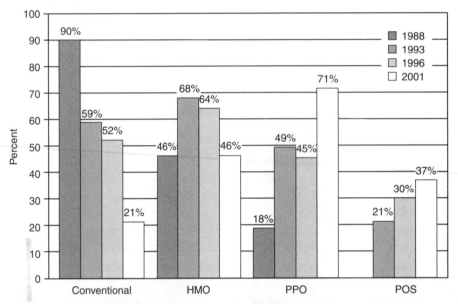

Sources: Data from Kaiser Family Foundation/Health Research and Education Trust Survey of Employer-Sponsored Health Benefits: 2001; KPMG Survey of Employer-Sponsored Health Benefits: 1988, 1993, 1996. Information was not obtained for POS plans in 1988. HMO refers to health maintenance organizations; PPO refers to preferred provider organizations; and POS refers to point-of-service plans.

FIGURE 3–16 Selected causes of death in the United States, 1998.

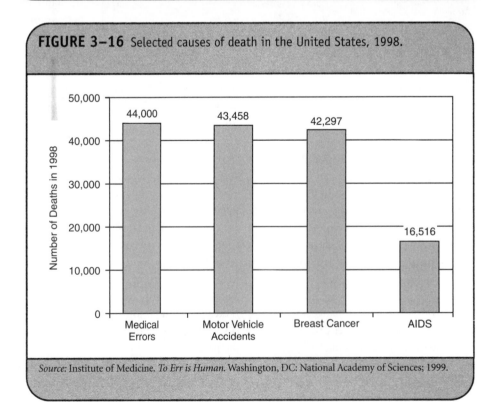

Source: Institute of Medicine. *To Err is Human.* Washington, DC: National Academy of Sciences; 1999.

improvements in either the public or the private components of the health sector. With or without changes in national health policies, the health system in the United States is clearly reforming itself. With the persistence of cost and access as the system's twin critical problems, new approaches and models were both needed and expected. The federal, as well as state, governments have moved to control the costs of Medicaid services, primarily through attempts to enroll nondisabled Medicaid populations (largely, mothers and children) into capitated managed care programs. The rapid conversion of Medicaid services to managed care operations and the growth of private managed care organizations pose new issues for the delivery of clinical preventive and public health services.[5] Although it is anticipated that these changes will result in fewer clinical preventive and treatment services being provided through public health agencies, both the extent and impact of these shifts remain unclear. In any event, the underlying investment strategy of the U.S. health system appears to remain unchanged, with 97% of the available resources allocated for treatment services, approximately 2% for clinical preventive services, and 1% for population-based public health services. Without at least some additional investment in prevention and public health approaches, the long-term prospects for controlling costs within the U.S. health system are bleak. In the meantime, some 40–45 million Americans remain outside the system and will continue to incur excessive costs when they inappropriately access needed services. Universal access is a prerequisite for eventual control of costs. However, it is not clear how true reform can be effected without reform of both our medical care and public health subsystems.

Although progress along this road has been painfully slow, there is evidence that a paradigm shift is already under way. The Pew Health Professions Commission argues that the American health care system of the 21st century will be quite different from its 1990s counterpart.[13] The health system of the 21st century will be

- More managed, with better integration of services and financing
- More accountable to those who purchase and use health services
- More aware of and responsive to the needs of enrolled populations
- More able to use fewer resources more effectively
- More innovative and diverse in how it provides for health
- More inclusive in how it defines health
- Less focused on treatment and more concerned with education, prevention, and care management

- More oriented to improving the health of the entire population
- More reliant on outcomes data and evidence

These gains, however, are likely to be accompanied by pain. The number of hospitals may decline by as much as 50% and the number of hospital beds by even more than that. There will be continued expansion of primary care in community and other ambulatory settings; this will foster replication of services in different settings, a development likely to confuse consumers. These forces also suggest major traumas for the health professions, with projected deficits of some professions, such as nurses and dentists, and surpluses of others, such as physicians and pharmacists.[13] An estimated 100,000–150,000 excess physicians, mainly specialists, could be joined by 200,000–300,000 excess nurses as the hospital sector consolidates and by as many as 40,000 excess pharmacists as drug dispensing is automated and centralized. The massive fragmentation among 200 or more allied health fields will cause consolidation into multiskilled professions to meet the changing needs of hospitals and other care settings. One of the few professions likely to flourish in this environment will be public health, with its focus on populations, information-driven planning, collaborative responses, and broad definition of health and health services.

Where these forces will move the health system is not yet known. To blend better the contributions of preventive and treatment-based approaches, several important changes are needed. There must be a new and more rational understanding of what is meant by "health services." This understanding must include a broad view of health promotion and health protection strategies, and must afford these equal standing with treatment-based strategies. Once and for all, health services must be seen to include services that focus on health, as well as those that focus on ill health. This should result in support for a more comprehensive approach to defining a basic benefit package that would be provided to all Americans. A second and companion change needed is to finance this enhanced basic benefit package from the same source, rather than funding public health and most prevention from one source (government resources) and treatment and the remaining prevention activities from private sources (business, individuals, insurance). With these changes, a gradual reallocation of resources can move the system toward a more rational and effective investment strategy.

The sheer size and scope of the American health system make it a force to be reckoned with, engendering comparisons with a similar force that existed in the United States in the 1950s and 1960s. At that time, and as he left office, President Eisenhower warned the nation of the potentially dangerous influence of the nation's "military industrial complex." His ob-servations were both ominous and insightful as he decried a powerful industry whose self-interest was coloring the nation's view of other countries and their people. The plight of the American health system raises the specter of a modern ana-logue in a "medical industrial complex." One danger posed by these complexes is their ability to influence the way we address (or even think about) a major public policy problem or issue. This occurs through interpreting and recasting the issues in-volved, sometimes even to the extent of altering public per-ceptions as to what is occurring and why.

Public understanding of the meaning of the terms *health reform* and *health care* is a case in point. Although, as a society, we have come to substitute the term health care for what is re-ally medical or treatment care, these are simply not the same. The health status of a population is largely determined by a dif-ferent set of considerations, as discussed in Chapter 2. Those considerations are very much the focus of the public health system. If the ultimate goal is a healthier population and, more specifically, the prevention of disease and disability, the na-tional health system must aggressively balance treatment with population- and community-based prevention strategies.

There is a term for when an organization finds that it is unable to achieve its primary objectives and outcomes (bottom line), then justifies its existence in terms of how well it does the things it is doing. *Outcome displacement* is that term; it means that the original outcome (here, improved health status) has been displaced by a focus on how well the means to that end (the organization, provision, and financing of services) are being addressed. These, then, become the new purpose or mis-sion for that system. Instead of "doing the right things" to af-fect health status, the system focuses on "doing things right" (regardless of whether they maximally affect health). It is pos-sible to have the best medical care services in the world but still have an inadequate health system.

CONCLUSION

Every day in America, decisions are made that influence the health status of individuals and groups of individuals. The ag-gregate of these decisions and the activities necessary to carry them out constitute our health system. It is important to view interventions as linked with health and illness states, as well as with the dynamic processes and multiple factors that move an individual from one state to another. Preventive interventions act at various points and through various means to prevent the development of a disease state or, if it occurs, to minimize its effects to the extent possible. These interventions differ in

their linkages with public health practice, medical practice, and long-term care, as well as in their focus on individuals or groups. The framework represents a rational one, reflecting known facts concerning each of its aspects and their relation-ships with each other.

As this chapter has described, current health policy in the United States reflects a different view of the factors incorpo-rated in the model. Current policy focuses unduly on disease states and strategies for restoring, as opposed to promoting or protecting, health. It directs the vast majority of human, phys-ical, and financial resources to tertiary prevention, particu-larly to acute treatment. It focuses disproportionately on individually-oriented secondary and tertiary medical care. In so doing, it raises questions as to whether these policies are effective and ethical.

Characterized in the past largely by federalism, pluralism, and incrementalism, the health sector in the United States is undergoing fundamental change, primarily in response to eco-nomic realities that have invested a trillion dollars in a model that equates medical care with health care. We are now realiz-ing that this investment strategy is not producing results com-mensurate with its resource consumption. Health indicators, including those characterizing large disparities in outcomes and access among important minority groups, are not re-sponding to more resources being deployed in the usual ways. The major problems have been widely characterized as cost and access, with the former being considered a cause of the latter. How to fix the cost question without aggravating the ac-cess issue has yet to be addressed, although managed care ap-proaches are serving to place some controls on the utilization of specific services. A better representation of the twin prob-lems facing the U.S. health sector might be excess and access, suggesting a return to the strategic drawing boards for ap-proaches that reduce and redeploy resources, rather than only reducing them. Within this reexamination of purpose and strategies for the health sector, the need to address health, as well as disease and prevention, as well as treatment, should be apparent. To accomplish these aims, there must be consensus that basic health services include population-based public health services and clinical preventive services, as well as diag-nostic and treatment services. To facilitate rational policy mak-ing and investment decisions, these services should be funded from a common source. This may require that health insurance premiums replace governmental appropriations as the source of funding for public sector activities. It is to be hoped that these realizations will take place before the health sector reaches its meltdown point.

Discussion Questions and Exercises

1. What are the most critical issues facing the health care system in the United States today? Before answering this question, see what insights you can find at the Web sites of these major health organizations: American Medical Association <http://www.ama-assn.org>, American Hospital Association <http://www.aha.org>, American Nurses Association <http://www.ana.org>, and the American Association of Medical Colleges <http://www.aamc.org>.

2. What forces are most likely to fuel further movement toward major health care reform in America?

3. Why is there less concern over national policy solutions (or "health reform") today than there was in 1994?

4. Select an important health problem (disease or condition) related to maternal and infant health (see "Public Health Achievements in 20th-Century America: Improved Maternal and Infant Health") and describe interventions for this problem across the five strategies of health-related and illness-related interventions (health promotion, specific protection, early detection, disability limitation, rehabilitation) presented in Chapter 3.

5. For the same health problem related to maternal and infant health (see "Public Health Achievements in 20th-Century America: Improved Maternal and Infant Health") selected in Question 4, describe interventions for this problem across the three levels of preventive interventions (primary, secondary, tertiary) presented in Chapter 3.

6. Table 3–3 lists organizations, agencies, and institutions that might be considered part of an overall national prevention effort. Identify those elements that should be included in a compilation of health-related prevention efforts. On the basis of what you know of these agencies, which of their programs or services should be included? Explain the reasons for your choices in terms of categories of preventive activities (e.g., health promotion, health protection, clinical preventive services). Identify those that you would include if you had the task of quantifying the scope and cost of all health-related prevention activities and expenditures in the United States. Which would you choose to leave off this list? Why?

7. Examine the data on the health system in a city or county of interest that is available through a state or local health agency. What elements from this site are most useful?

8. Great Debate: This debate examines contributors to improvement in health status in the United States since 1900. There are two propositions to be considered. Proposition A: Public health interventions are responsible for these improvements. Proposition B: Medical care interventions are responsible for these improvements. Select one of these positions to argue and submit a summary of arguments.

9. Is an ounce of prevention still worth a pound of cure in the United States? If not, what is the relative value of prevention in comparison with treatment?

10. Has the recent growth of managed care strategies within the health sector had a positive or a negative impact on the public's health? How? Why?

REFERENCES

1. National Center for Health Statistics. *Health, United States, 2005.* Hyattsville, MD: NCHS; 2005.

2. Leavell HR, Clark EG. *Preventive Medicine for the Doctor in His Community.* 3rd ed. New York: McGraw-Hill; 1965.

3. U.S. Preventive Services Task Force. *Guide to Clinical Preventive Services.* 2nd ed. Washington, DC: U.S. Department of Health and Human Services; 1995.

4. Lasker RD. *Medicine & Public Health: The Power of Collaboration.* New York: New York Academy of Medicine; 1997.

5. Halverson PK, Kaluzny AD, McLaughlin CP. *Managed Care & Public Health.* Gaithersburg, MD: Aspen Publishers; 1998.

6. Weil PA, Bogue RJ. Motivating community health improvement: leading practices you can use. *Healthc Exec.* 1999;14:18–24.

7. Brown RE, Elixhauser A, Corea J, Luce BR, Sheingold S. *National Expenditures for Health Promotion and Disease Prevention Activities in the United States.* Washington, DC: Medical Technology Assessment and Policy Research Center; 1991.

8. Core Functions Project, Public Health Service, Office of Disease Prevention and Health Promotion. *Health Care Reform and Public Health: A Paper Based on Population-Based Core Functions.* Washington, DC: PHS; 1993.

9. Centers for Medicare and Medicaid Services, National Health Accounts, 1960–2000.

10. Frist B. Public health and national security: the critical role of increased federal support. *Health Aff (Millwood).* 2002;21:117–130.

11. Blendon RJ. *Kaiser/Harvard/KRC National Election Night Survey.* Menlo Park, CA: Henry J. Kaiser Family Foundation; 1994.

12. Institute of Medicine. *To Err is Human.* Washington DC: National Academy of Sciences; 1999.

13. Pew Health Professions Commission. *Critical Challenges: Revitalizing the Health Professions for the Twenty-First Century.* San Francisco: University of California Center for Health Professions; 1995.

Law, Government, and Public Health

Public health is not limited to what governmental public health agencies do, although this is a widely held misperception among those inside and outside the field. Still, particular aspects of public health rely on government. For example, the enforcement of laws remains one of those governmental responsibilities important to the public's health and public health practice. Yet, law and the legal system are important for public health purposes above and beyond the enforcement of laws and regulations. Laws at all levels of government bestow the basic powers of government and distribute these powers among various agencies, including public health agencies. Law represents governmental decisions and their underlying collective social values; it provides the basis for actions that influence the health of the public.

Decisions and actions that take place outside the sphere of government also influence the health of the public, perhaps even more than those made by our elected officials and administrative agencies. Private sector and voluntary organizations play key roles in identifying factors important for health and advancing actions to promote and protect health for individuals and groups. Public health involves collective decisions and actions, rather than purely personal ones; however, it is often governmental forums that raise issues, make decisions, and establish priorities for action. Many governmental actions reflect the dual roles of government often portrayed on official governmental seals and vehicles of local public safety agencies—to protect and to serve. As they relate to health, the genesis of these two roles lies in separate, often conflicting, philosophies and legacies of government. This chapter will examine how these roles are organized in the United States. This examination particularly emphasizes the relationships among law, government, and public health, seeking answers to the following questions:

- What are the various roles for government in serving the public's health?
- What is the legal basis for public health in the United States?
- How are public health responsibilities and roles structured at the federal, state, and local levels?

To review the organization and structure of governmental public health, this chapter, unlike the history briefly traced in Chapter 1, will begin with federal public health roles and activities, to be followed, in turn, by those at the state and local levels. The focus is primarily on form and structure, rather than function. In most circumstances, it is logical for form to follow function. Here, however, it is necessary to understand the legal and organizational framework of governmental public health as part of the context for public health practice. The framework established through law and governmental agencies is a key element of the public health's infrastructure and one of the basic building blocks of the public health system. This structure is a product of our uniquely American approach to government.

AMERICAN GOVERNMENT AND PUBLIC HEALTH

Former Speaker of the U.S. House of Representatives, Tip O'Neil, frequently observed, "all politics is local." If this is so, public health must be considered primarily a local phenomenon, as well, because politics are embedded in public health processes. After all, public health represents collective decisions as to which health outcomes are unacceptable, which factors contribute to those outcomes, which unacceptable problems will be addressed in view of resource limitations, and which participants need to be involved in addressing the problems. These are political processes, with different viewpoints and values being brought together to determine which collective decisions will be made. All too often, the term politics carries a very different connotation, one frequently associated with overtones of partisan politics. However, political processes are necessary and productive, and perhaps the best means devised by humans to meet our collective needs.

The public health system in the United States is a product of many forces that have shaped governmental roles in health. The framers of the U.S. Constitution did not plan for the federal government to deal directly with health or, for that matter, many other important issues. The word *health* does not even appear in that famous document, relegating health to the group of powers reserved to the states or the people. The Constitution explicitly authorized the federal government to promote and provide for the general welfare (in the Preamble and Article I, Section 8) and to regulate commerce (also in Article I, Section 8). Federal powers evolved slowly in the area of health on the basis of these explicit powers and subsequent U.S. Supreme Court decisions that broadened federal authority by determining that additional powers are implied in the explicit language of the Constitution.

The initial duties to regulate international affairs and interstate commerce led the federal government to concentrate its efforts on preventing the importation of epidemics and assisting states and localities, upon request, with their episodic needs for communicable disease control. The earliest federal health unit, the Marine Hospital Service, was established in 1798, partly to serve merchant seamen and partly to prevent

importation of epidemic diseases; it evolved over time into what is now the U.S. Public Health Service.

However, the power to promote health and welfare did not always translate into the ability to act. The federal government acquired the ability to raise significant financial resources only with the authority to levy a federal tax on income, provided by the 16th Amendment in the early 20th century. The ability to raise vast sums generated the capacity to address health problems and needs through transferring resources to state and local governments in various forms of grants-in-aid. Despite its powers to provide for the general welfare and regulate commerce, the federal government could not act directly in health matters; it could act only through states as its primary delivery system. After 1935, the power and influence of the federal government grew rapidly through its financial influence over state and local programs, such as the Hospital Services and Construction (Hill-Burton) Act of 1946 and, after 1965, through its emergence as a major purchaser of health care through Medicare and Medicaid. As for a public health presence at the federal level, the best-known and most widely respected federal public health agency, now known as the Centers for Disease Control and Prevention (CDC), was not established until 1946.[1]

The emergence of the federal government as a major influence in the health system displaced states from a position they had held since before the birth of the American republic. States were sovereign powers before agreeing to share their powers with the newly established federal government; their sovereignty included powers over matters related to health emanating from two general sources. First, they derived from the so-called police powers of states, which provide the basis for government to limit the actions of individuals in order to control and abate hazards and nuisances. A second source for state health powers lay in the expectation for government to serve those individuals unable to provide for themselves. This expectation had its roots in the Elizabethan Poor Laws and carried over to states in the new American form of government. Despite this common heritage, states assumed these roles quite differently and at different points in time because the evolution of states themselves during the 19th century took place unevenly.

States developed structures and organizations needed to use their police powers to protect citizens from communicable diseases and environmental hazards, primarily from wastes, water, and food. State health agencies developed first in Massachusetts, then across the country, during the latter half of the 19th century. When federal grants became available, especially after 1935, states eagerly sought out federal funding for maternal and child health services, public health laboratories, and other basic public health programs. In so doing, states surrendered some of their autonomy over health issues. Priorities were increasingly dictated by federal grants tied to specific programs and services. It is fair to say that the grantor-grantee arrangement has never been fully satisfactory to either party, and the results in terms of health, welfare, education, and environmental policy suggest that better frameworks may be possible.

States possess the ultimate authority to create the political subunits that provide various services to the residents of a particular jurisdiction. In this manner, counties, cities, and other forms of municipalities, townships, boroughs, parishes, and the like are established. Special-purpose districts for every conceivable purpose—from library services and mosquito control to emergency medical services and education—have also abounded. The powers delegated to or authorized for all of these local jurisdictions are established by state legislatures for health and other purposes. Although many big-city health departments were established prior to the establishment of their respective state health agencies, states are free to use a variety of approaches to structuring public health roles at the local level. Because most states use the county form of subdividing the state, counties became the primary local governmental jurisdictions with health roles after 1900.

State constitutions and statutes impart the authority for local governments to influence health. This authority comes in two forms: those responsibilities of the state specifically delegated to local governments and additional authorities allowed through home rule powers. Home rule options permit local jurisdictions to enact a local constitution or charter and to take on additional authority and powers, such as the ability to levy taxes for local public health services and activities.

Counties generally carry out duties delegated by the state. More than two thirds of U.S. counties have a county commission form of government, with anywhere from 2 to 50 elected county commissioners (supervisors, judges, and other titles are also used).[2] These commissions carry out both legislative and executive branch functions, although they share administrative authority with other local elected officials, such as county clerks, assessors, treasurers, prosecuting attorneys, sheriffs, and coroners. Some counties—generally, the more populous ones—have a county administrator accountable to elected commissioners, and a small number of counties (less than 5%) have an elected county executive. Elected county executives often have veto power over the county legislative body; home rule jurisdictions are more likely to have an elected county executive than are other counties.

Local governments in U.S. cities were first on the scene in terms of public health activities, as noted in Chapter 1. Big-city health agencies remain an important force in the public health system in the United States. However, after about 1875 when states became more extensively involved, the relative role of municipal governments began to erode. Both local and state governments were overwhelmed by the availability of federal funding in comparison with their own resources, finding it easier to take what they could get from the federal government rather than generating their own revenue to finance needed services.

Many forces have been at work to alter the initial relationships among the three levels of government for health roles, including:

- Gradual expansion and maturation of the federal government
- Staggered addition of new states and variability in the maturation of state governments
- Population growth and shifts over time
- Ability of the various levels of government to raise revenues commensurate with their expanding needs
- Growth of science and technology as tools for addressing public health and medical care needs
- Rapid growth of the U.S. economy
- Expectations and needs of American society for various services from their government[3,4]

The last of these factors is perhaps the most important. For the first 150 years of U.S. history, there was little expectation that the federal government should intervene in the health and welfare needs of its citizenry. The massive need and economic turmoil of the Great Depression years drastically altered this longstanding value as Americans began to turn to government to help deal with current needs and future uncertainties.

The complex public health network that exists today evolved slowly, with many different shifts in relative roles and influence. Economic considerations and societal expectations, both reaching a critical point in the 1930s, set the tone for the rest of the 20th century. In general, power and influence were initially greatest at the local level, residing there until states began to develop their own machinery to carry out their police power and welfare roles. States then served as the primary locus for these health roles until the federal government began to use its vast resource potential to meet changing public expectations in the 1930s. Federal grant programs for public health and, eventually, personal health care service programs soon drove state actions, especially after the 1960s. It was then that several new federal health and social service programs were targeted directly to local governments, bypassing states. At the same time, a new federal-state partnership for the medically indigent (Medicaid) was established to address the national policy concern over the plight of the medically indigent.

Political and philosophical shifts since about 1980 are altering roles once again.[3] Debates over federal versus state roles continued throughout the 1980s and 1990s, although current indications suggest that some diminution of federal influence and enhancement of state influence is likely to persist for the near term. Still, the federal government has considerable ability to influence the health system through its fiscal muscle power, as well as its research, regulatory, technical assistance, and training roles.

PUBLIC HEALTH LAW

One of the chief organizing forces for public health lies in the system of law. Law has many purposes in the modern world, and many of these are evident in public health laws. Unfortunately, there is no one repository where the entire body of law, even the body of public health law, can be found. This has occurred because laws are products of the legal system, which, in the United States, includes a federal system and 50 separate state legal systems. These developed at different times in response to somewhat different circumstances and issues. Common to each is some form of a state constitution, a considerable amount of legislation, and a substantial body of judicial decisions. If there is any road map through this maze, it lies in the federal and state constitutions, which establish the basic framework dividing governmental powers among the various branches of government in ways that allow each to create its own laws.

As a result, four different types of law can be distinguished by virtue of their form or authority:

- Constitutionally based law
- Legislatively based law
- Administratively based law
- Judicially based law

This framework still allows latitude for judicial interpretation and oversight. A brief description of each of these forms of law follows.

Types of Law

Constitutional law is ultimately derived from the U.S. Constitution, the legal foundation of the nation, in which the powers, duties, and limits of the federal government are established. States basically gave up certain powers (e.g., defense, foreign diplomacy, printing money), ceding these to the federal government while retaining all other powers and duties. Health is not one of those powers explicitly bestowed upon the federal government. The federal constitution also included a Bill of Rights intended to protect the rights of individuals from abuses by their government. States, in turn, have developed their own state constitutions, often patterned after the federal framework, although state constitutions tend to be more clear and specific in their language, leaving less room and need for judicial interpretation. State constitutions provide the broad framework from which states determine which activities will be undertaken and how those activities will be organized and funded. These decisions and actions come in the form of state statutes.

Statutory (legislatively-based) law includes all of the acts and statutes enacted by Congress and the various state and local legislative bodies. This collection of law represents a wide range of governmental policy choices, including

- Simple expressions of preferences in favor of a particular policy or service (such as the value of home visits by public health nurses)
- Authorizations for specific programs (such as the authority for local governments to license restaurants)
- Mandates or requirements for an activity to occur or, alternatively, to be prohibited (such as requiring all newborns to be screened for specific metabolic diseases or prohibiting smoking in public places)
- Providing resources for specific purposes (such as the distribution of medications to patients with acquired immune deficiency syndrome [AIDS])

If the legislative intent is for something to occur, the most effective approaches are generally to require or prohibit an activity.

The basic requirement for statutory-based laws is that they must be consistent with the U.S. Constitution and, for state and local statutes, with state constitutions as well. State laws also establish the various subunits of the state and delineate their responsibilities for carrying out state mandates, as well as the limits of what they can do. At the local level, the legislative bodies of these subunits (e.g., city councils and county commissions) enact ordinances and statutes setting forth the duties and authorizations of local government and its agencies. Laws affecting public health are created at all levels in this hierarchy, but especially at the state and local levels. Among other purposes, these laws establish state and local boards of health and health departments, delineate the responsibilities of these agencies, including their programs and budgets, and establish health-related laws and requirements. Many of these laws are enforced by governmental agencies.

Administrative law is law promulgated by administrative agencies within the executive branch of government. Rather than enact statutes that include extensive details of a professional or technical nature and to allow greater flexibility in their design and subsequent revision, administrative agencies are provided with the authority to establish law through rule-making processes. These rules, administrative law, carry the force of law and represent a unique situation in which legislative, judicial, and executive powers are carried out by one agency. Administrative agencies include cabinet-level departments, as well as other boards, commissions, and the like that are granted this power through an enactment of the legislative body.

The fourth type of law is judicial law, also known as common law. This includes a wide range of tradition, legal custom, and previous decisions of federal and state courts. To ensure fairness and consistency, previous decisions are used to guide judgments on similar disputes. This form of law becomes especially important in areas in which laws have not been codified by legislative bodies. In public health, nuisances (unsanitary, noxious, or otherwise potentially dangerous circumstances) are one such area in which few legislative bodies have specified exactly what does and what does not constitute a public health nuisance. In this situation, the common law for nuisances is derived from previous judicial decisions. These determine under what circumstances and for what specific conditions a public health official can take action, as well as the actions that can be taken.

Purposes of Public Health Law

Two broad purposes for public health law can be described: protecting and promoting health and ensuring the protection of rights of individuals in the processes used to protect and promote health. Public health powers ultimately derive from the U.S. Constitution, which bestows the authority to regulate commerce and provide for the general welfare, and from the various state constitutions, which often provide clear but broad authorities, based largely on the police power of the state. States often have reasonably well-defined public health codes. However, there is considerable diversity in their content and scope, despite similarities in their basic sources of power and authority.

Many public health laws are enacted and enforced under what is known as the state's "police power." This is a broad concept that encompasses the functions historically undertaken by governments in protecting the health, safety, welfare, and general well-being of their citizens. A wide variety of laws derive from the police power of the state, a power that is considered one of the least limitable of all governmental powers. The police power of the state can be vested in an administrative agency, such as a state health agency, which becomes accountable for the manner in which these responsibilities are executed. In these circumstances, its use is a duty, rather than a matter of choice, although its form is left to the discretion of the user.

The courts have upheld laws that appear to limit severely or restrict the rights of individuals where these were found to be reasonable, rather than arbitrary and capricious attempts to accomplish government's ends. The state's police power is not unlimited, however. Interference with individual liberties and the taking of personal property are considerations that must be balanced on a case-by-case basis. At issue is whether the public interest in achieving a public health goal outweighs the public interest in protecting civil liberties. Public health laws requiring vaccinations or immunizations to protect the community have generally withstood legal challenges claiming that they infringed upon the rights of individuals to make their own health decisions. A precedent-setting judicial opinion upheld a Massachusetts ordinance authorizing local boards of health to require vaccinations for smallpox to be administered to residents if deemed necessary by the local boards.[5] Such decisions argue that laws that place the common good ahead of the competing rights of individuals should govern society. Similarly, courts have weighed the power of the state to appropriate an individual's property or limit the individual's use of it if the best interests of the community make such an action desirable. In some circumstances, equitable compensation must be provided. Issues of community interest and fair compensation are commonly encountered in dealing with public health nuisances in which an individual's private property can be found to be harmful to others.

The various forms of law and the changing nature of the relationships among the three levels of government have created a patchwork of public health laws. Despite its relatively limited constitutionally based powers, the federal government can preempt state and local government action in key areas of public health regulation involving commerce and aspects of communicable disease control. States also have authority to preempt local government actions in virtually all areas of public health activity. Although this legal framework allows for a clear and rational delineation of authorities and responsibilities, a quite variable set of arrangements has arisen. Often, the higher level of government chooses not to exercise its full authority and shifts that authority to a lower level of government. This can be accomplished in some instances by delegating or requiring, and in other instances by authorizing (with incentives), the lower level of government to exercise authorities of the higher level. This has made for a complex set of relationships among the three levels of government and for 50 variations of the theme to be played in the 50 states. These relationships and their impact on the form and structure of governmental public health agencies will be evident in subsequent sections of this chapter.

There have been many critiques of the statutory basis of public health in the United States. A common one is that public health law, not unlike law affecting other areas of society, simply has not kept pace with the rapid and extensive changes in science and technology. Laws have been enacted at different points in time in response to different conditions and circumstances. These laws have often been enacted with little consideration as to their consistency with previous statutes and their overall impact on the body of public health law. For example, many states have different statutes and legal frameworks for similar risks, such as general communicable diseases, sexually transmitted diseases (STDs), and human immunodeficiency virus (HIV) infections. Confidentiality and privacy provisions, which trace their origins to the vow in the Hippocratic oath not to reveal patient's secrets, are often inconsistent from law-to-law, and enforcement provisions vary as well. Beyond these concerns, public health laws often lack clear statements of purpose or mission and are not linked to public health core functions and essential public health services.

In view of these criticisms, recommendations have been advanced calling for a complete overhaul and recodification of public health law. Recommendations for improvement of the public health codes often call for

- Stronger links with the overall mission and core functions of public health
- Uniform structures for similar programs and services
- Confidentiality provisions to be reviewed and made more consistent
- Clarification of police power responsibilities to deal with unusual health risks and threats
- Greater emphasis on the least restrictive means necessary to achieve the law's intent through use of intermediate sanctions and compulsive measures, based on proven effectiveness
- Fairer and more consistent enforcement and administrative practices

Although these recommendations have been advanced for several decades, little progress has been made at either the federal or state level. At times, states have sought to recodify public health statutes by relocating their placement in the statute books, rather than dealing with the more basic issues of reviewing the scope and allocation of their public health responsibilities so that these are clearly presented and assigned among the various levels of government. The intricacies of public health law often help drive the inner workings of federal, state, and local public health agencies. We will now turn to the form and structure of these agencies.

GOVERNMENTAL PUBLIC HEALTH

Federal Health Agencies

The U.S. Public Health Service (PHS) serves as the focal point for health concerns at the federal level. Although there have been frequent reorganizations affecting the structure of PHS and its placement within the massive Department of Health and Human Services (DHHS), the restructuring completed in 1996 was the most significant in recent decades. The changes were undertaken as part of the federal Reinvention of Government Initiative to bring expertise in public health and science closer to the Secretary of DHHS. In the restructuring, the line authority of the Assistant Secretary for Health over the various agencies within PHS was abolished, with those agencies now reporting directly to the Secretary of DHHS, as illustrated in Figure 4–1. The Assistant Secretary for Health became the head of the Office of Public Health and Science (OPHS), a new division reporting to the Secretary that also includes the Office of the Surgeon General. Each of the former PHS agencies became a full DHHS operating division. These eight operating agencies, the OPHS, and the regional health administrators for the 10 federal regions of the country now constitute the PHS. In effect, PHS has become a functional rather than an organizational unit of DHHS. In 2003, several activities related to emergency preparedness and response were moved into the newly established Department of Homeland Security (see Chapter 5). An Office of Public Health Emergency Preparedness and Response remained at DHHS to coordinate bioterrorism and other public health emergency activities managed by various PHS agencies.

The PHS agencies address a wide range of public health activities, from research and training to primary care and health protection, as described in Table 4–1. The key PHS agencies are

- Health Resources and Services Administration (HRSA)
- Indian Health Service (IHS)
- Centers for Disease Control and Prevention (CDC)
- National Institutes of Health (NIH)
- Food and Drug Administration (FDA)
- Substance Abuse and Mental Health Services Administration (SAMHSA)
- Agency for Toxic Substances and Disease Registry (ATSDR)
- Agency for Health Care Research and Quality (AHRQ)

PHS agencies actually represent only a small part of DHHS. Other important operating divisions within DHHS include the Administration for Children and Families, the Health Care Financing Administration, and the Office of

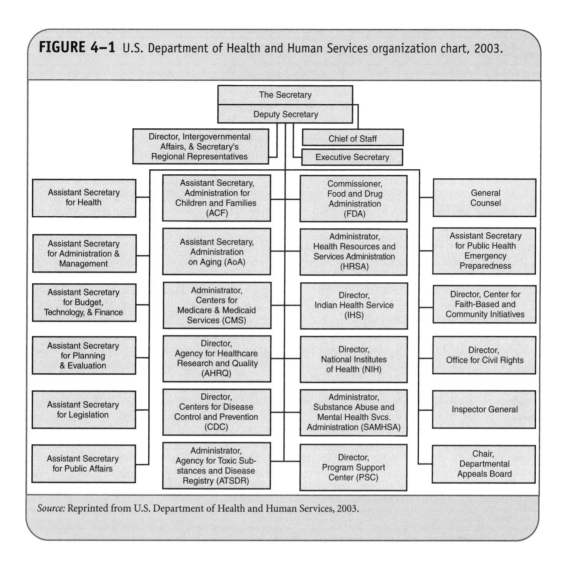

FIGURE 4–1 U.S. Department of Health and Human Services organization chart, 2003.

Source: Reprinted from U.S. Department of Health and Human Services, 2003.

the Assistant Secretary for Aging. In addition, there are several administrative and support units within DHHS for management and the budget, intergovernmental affairs, legal counsel, civil rights, the inspector general, departmental appeals, public affairs, legislation, and planning and evaluation.

Beyond DHHS, health responsibilities have been assigned to several other federal agencies, including the federal Environmental Protection Agency (EPA) and the Departments of Homeland Security, Education, Agriculture, Defense, Transportation, and Veterans Affairs, just to name a few. The importance of some of these other federal agencies should not be underestimated in terms of the level and proportion of their resources devoted to health purposes. Health-specific agencies at the federal level are a relatively new phenomenon. PHS itself remained a unit of the Treasury Department until 1944, and the first cabinet-level federal human services agency of any kind

was the Federal Security Agency in 1939. This historical trivia demonstrates that federal powers and authority in health and public health are a relatively recent phenomenon in U.S. history.

The federal government is the largest purchaser of health-related services, although spending on health purposes represents only a fraction of the total federal budget. Figure 4–2 compares total national health expenditures with health expenditures attributed to the federal government and to state local governments. Health expenditures constituted nearly 25% of total federal expenditures in 2003, up from 12% in 1980, and only 3% in 1960 (Figure 4–3). Escalating costs for health care services seriously constrain efforts to reduce the federal budget deficit, and there is little public or political support for additional taxes for health purposes.

It is no simple task to describe the federal budget development and approval process that determines funding levels

TABLE 4-1 U.S. Public Health Service Agencies

Health Resources and Services Administration (HRSA)	HRSA helps provide health resources for medically underserved populations. The main operating units of HRSA are the Bureau of Primary Health Care, Bureau of Health Professions, Maternal and Child Bureau, and the HIV/AIDS Bureau. A nationwide network of 643 community and migrant health centers, plus 144 primary care programs for the homeless and residents of public housing, serve 8.1 million Americans each year. HRSA also works to build the health care workforce and maintains the National Health Service Corps. The agency provides services to people with AIDS through the Ryan White Care Act programs. It oversees the organ transplantation system and works to decrease infant mortality and improve maternal and child health. HRSA was established in 1982 by brining together several existing programs. HRSA has more than 1,300 employees at its headquarters in Rockville, MD, and another 750 employees in 10 regional offices throughout the United States.
Indian Health Service (IHS)	IHS is responsible for providing federal health services to American Indians and Alaska Natives. The provision of health services to members of federally recognized tribes grew out of the special government-to-government relationship between the federal government and Indian tribes. This relationship, established in 1787, is based on Article I, Section 8 of the Constitution, and has been given form and substance by numerous treaties, laws, Supreme Court decisions, and Executive Orders. IHS is the principal federal health care provider and health advocate for Indian people, and its goal is to raise their health status to the highest possible level. IHS currently provides health services to approximately 1.5 million American Indians and Alaska Natives who belong to more than 557 federally recognized tribes in 35 states. IHS was established in 1924; its mission was transferred from the Interior Department in 1955. Agency headquarters are in Rockville, MD.
Centers for Disease Control and Prevention (CDC)	Working with states and other partners, CDC provides a system of health surveillance to monitor and prevent disease outbreaks, including bioterrorism events and threats, and maintains national health statistics. CDC also provides for immunization services, supports research into disease and injury prevention, and guards against international disease transmission, with personnel stationed in more than 25 foreign countries. CDC was established in 1946; its headquarters are in Atlanta, GA. CDC has 8,500 employees.
National Institutes of Health (NIH)	Begun as a one-room Laboratory of Hygiene in 1887, NIH today is one of the world's foremost medical research centers and the federal focal point for health research. NIH is the steward of medical and behavioral research for the nation. Its mission is science in pursuit of fundamental knowledge about the nature and behavior of living systems and the application of that knowledge to extend healthy life and reduce the burdens of illness and disability. In realizing its goals, NIH provides leadership and direction to programs designed to improve the health of the nation by conducting and supporting research in the causes, diagnosis, prevention, and cure of human diseases; in the processes of human growth and development; in the biological effects of environmental contaminants; in the understanding of mental, addictive and physical disorders; and in directing programs for the collection, dissemination, and exchange of information in medicine and health,

for federal health programs. Although nearly one fourth of the federal budget supports health activities, the major share is spent on Medicare and Medicaid. These and other entitlement programs constitute two thirds of the federal budget; this spending is mandatory and cannot be easily controlled. The remaining one third represents discretionary spending; half of this is related to national defense purposes. Spending for discretionary programs is more readily controlled. Non-defense discretionary spending for health purposes competes with a wide array of programs, including education, training, science, technology, housing, transportation, and foreign aid. Despite a small increase due to national terrorism preparedness ini-

tiatives, it has declined as a proportion of all federal spending, from 23% in 1966 to 19% in 2003.

Decisions authorizing and funding health programs are made in an annual budget approval process. The current process is a complex one that establishes ceilings for broad categories of expenditures and then reconciles individual programs and funding levels within those ceilings in omnibus budget reconciliation acts. For discretionary programs, Congress must act each year to provide spending authority. For mandatory programs, Congress may act to change the spending that current laws require. The result is a mixture of substantive decisions as to which programs will be authorized and

TABLE 4–1 U.S. Public Health Service Agencies (*continued*)

National Institutes of Health (NIH) (*continued*)	including the development and support of medical libraries and the training of medical librarians and other health information specialists. Alhough the majority of NIH resources sponsor external research, there is also a large in-house research program. NIH includes 27 separate health institutes and centers; its headquarters are in Bethesda, MD. NIH has more than 16,000 employees.
Food and Drug Administration (FDA)	FDA ensures that the food we eat is safe and wholesome, that the cosmetics we use won't harm us, and that medicines, medical devices, and radiation-transmitting products such as microwave ovens are safe and effective. FDA also oversees feed and drugs for pets and farm animals. Authorized by Congress to enforce the Federal Food, Drug, and Cosmetic Act and several other public health laws, the agency monitors the manufacture, import, transport, storage, and sale of $1 trillion worth of goods annually, at a cost to taxpayers of about $3 a person. FDA has over 9,000 employees, located in 167 U.S. cities. Among its staff, FDA has chemists, microbiologists, and other scientists, as well as investigators and inspectors who visit 16,000 facilities a year as part of their oversight of the businesses that FDA regulates. FDA, established in 1906, has its headquarters in Rockville, MD.
Substance Abuse and Mental Health Services Administration (SAMHSA)	SAMHSA was established by Congress under Public Law 102-321 on October 1, 1992, to strengthen the nation's health care capacity to provide prevention, diagnosis, and treatment services for substance abuse and mental illnesses. SAMHSA works in partnership with states, communities, and private organizations to address the needs of people with substance abuse and mental illnesses as well as the community risk factors that contribute to these illnesses. SAMHSA serves as the umbrella under which substance abuse and mental health service centers are housed, including the Center for Mental Health Services (CMHS), the Center for Substance Abuse Prevention (CSAP), and the Center for Substance Abuse Treatment (CSAT). SAMHSA also houses the Office of the Administrator, the Office of Applied Studies, and the Office of Program Services. In fiscal year 2000, SAMHSA's budget is approximately $2.6 billion. The agency employs approximately 550 staff members. SAMHSA headquarters are in Rockville, MD; the agency has about 600 employees.
Agency for Toxic Substances and Disease Registry (ATSDR)	Working with states and other federal agencies, ATSDR seeks to prevent exposure to hazardous substances from waste sites. The agency conducts public health assessments, health studies, surveillance activities, and health education training in communities around waste sites on the U.S. Environmental Protection Agency's National Priorities List. ATSDR also has developed toxicologic profiles of hazardous chemicals found at these sites. The agency is closely associated administratively with CDC; its headquarters are also in Atlanta, GA. ATSDR has more than 400 employees.
Agency for Health Care Research and Quality (AHRQ)	AHRQ supports cross-cutting research on health care systems, health care quality and cost issues, and effectiveness of medical treatments. Formerly known as the Agency for Health Care Policy and Research, AHRQ was established in 1989, assuming broadened responsibilities of its predecessor agency, the National Center for Health Services Research and Health Care Technology Assessment. The agency has about 300 employees: its headquarters are in Rockville, MD.

what they will be authorized to do, together with budget decisions as to the level of resources to be made available through 13 annual appropriations bills. In recent years federal law has imposed a cap on total annual discretionary spending and requires that spending cuts must offset increased mandatory spending or new discretionary programs. This budgetary environment presents major challenges for new public health programs and, not infrequently, threatens continued funding for programs that have been operating for decades.

The organization of federal health responsibilities within DHHS is quite complex fiscally and operationally. In federal fiscal year 2007, the overall DHHS budget is about $700 bil-

lion.[6] DHHS has nearly 65,000 employees and is the largest grant-making agency in the federal government, with some 60,000 grants each year. DHHS manages more than 300 programs through its 11 operating divisions. The major share of the DHHS budget supports the Medicare and Medicaid programs within Health Care Financing Administration (HCFA). PHS activities account for less than one tenth of the fiscal year 2007 DHHS budget. In addition to HCFA and the PHS agencies, DHHS also includes the Administration for Children and Families and the Administration on Aging.

Budgets for PHS operating divisions in federal fiscal year 2007 range from $29 billion for NIH to $300 million for AHRQ

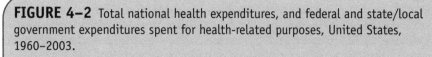

FIGURE 4–2 Total national health expenditures, and federal and state/local government expenditures spent for health-related purposes, United States, 1960–2003.

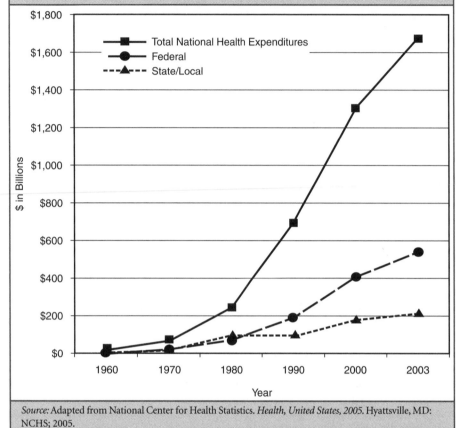

Source: Adapted from National Center for Health Statistics. *Health, United States, 2005.* Hyattsville, MD: NCHS; 2005.

an LPHA functioning at some level of capability. Baseline data on how many local agencies were effectively carrying out the core functions were not available when this objective was established in 1990. Several studies of core function-related perform-ance in the 1990s suggest that the nation fell far short of achieving its year 2000 target.

PHS agencies have promoted greater use of performance mea-sures in key federal health programs, including immunizations, tuber-culosis control, STDs, substance abuse, and mental health services. As previously described, federal grants-in-aid have long been the prime strategy and mechanism by which the federal government gen-erates state and local action toward important health problems. A vari-ety of approaches to grant making have been used over recent decades. These can be categorized by the ex-tent of restrictions or flexibility im-parted to grantees. The greatest flexibility and lack of requirements are associated with revenue-sharing grants. Block grants, including those initiated in the early 1980s, consolidate previously categor-

(Figure 4–4). Sixty percent of all PHS funds support NIH re-search activities, and another $20 billion support the remain-ing PHS agencies with HRSA and CDC together accounting for about $12 billion, which represents about 2% of total DHHS resources and about 0.5% of all federal spending.

Since the late 1970s, the Office of Health Promotion and Disease Prevention within the Office of the Assistant Secretary for Health has coordinated the development of the national agenda for public health and prevention efforts. Results of these efforts are apparent in the establishment of national health objectives that targeted the years 1990, 2000, and 2010 (see Chapter 2). Only one of more than 500 objectives from the 1990 and 2000 processes related to the public health system; that objective called for 90% of the population to be served by a local public health agency (LPHA) that was effectively carry-ing out public health's core functions by the year 2000.[7] Current estimates are that about 95% of the U.S. population is served by

ical grant programs into a block that generally comes with fewer restrictions than the previous collection of categorical grants. Formula grants are awarded on the basis of some pre-determined formula, often based at least partly on need, which determines the level of funding for each grantee. Project grants are more limited in availability and are generally intended for a specific demonstration program or project.

In the 1990s, DHHS proposed a series of federal part-nership performance grants to address some of the short-comings attributed to block grants implemented in the early 1980s. At that time, restrictions were relaxed for the categor-ical programs folded into the block grants, including the Maternal and Child Health (MCH) Block Grant and the Prevention Block Grant. Lessons learned from the previous experience suggest the need for a cautious approach to new federal block grant proposals. In the 1980s, the new block grants indeed came with fewer strings attached. However,

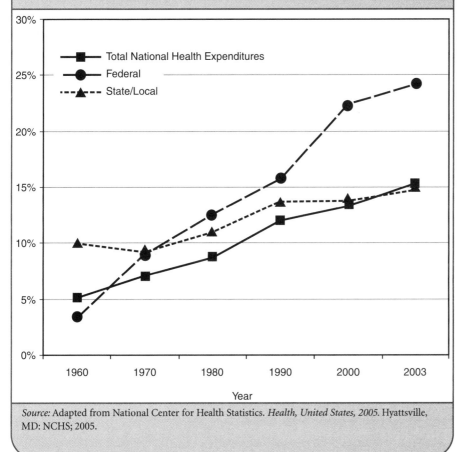

FIGURE 4–3 Percentage of national gross domestic expenditures, and federal and state/local government expenditures spent for health-related purposes, United States, 1960–2003.

Source: Adapted from National Center for Health Statistics. *Health, United States, 2005.* Hyattsville, MD: NCHS; 2005.

for maternal and child health promoted personnel standards in state and local agencies that fostered the growth of civil service systems across the country. Other effects on state and local health agencies will be apparent as these are examined in the following sections.

State Health Agencies

Several factors place states at center stage when it comes to health. The U.S. Constitution gives states primacy in safeguarding the health of their citizens. From the mid-19th century until the 1930s, states largely exercised that leadership role with little competition from the federal government and only occasional conflict with the larger cities. Federal funding turned the tables on states after 1935, reaching its peak influence in the 1960s and 1970s. At that time, numerous federal health and human service initiatives (such as model cities, community health centers, and community mental health services) were funded directly to local governments and even to community-based organizations. This practice greatly concerned state capitals and served to damage tenu-

they also came at funding levels that were reduced about 25% from the previous arrangement. The blocking of several categorical programs into one mega grant also served to dissipate the constituencies for the categorical programs. Without active and visible constituencies advocating for programs, restoration or even maintenance of previous funding levels proved difficult. In addition, the reduction in reporting requirements made it more difficult to justify budget requests. Any new federal approaches to overcome these obstacles will be watched closely by advocates, as well as by state and local public health officials.

In addition to being a prime strategy to influence services at the state and local level, federal grants also serve to redistribute resources to compensate for differences in the ability of states to fund and operate basic health services. They have also served as a useful approach to promoting minimum standards for specific programs and services. For example, federal grants

ous relationships among the three levels of government. The relative influence of states began to grow once again after 1980, with both increasing rhetoric and federal actions restoring some powers and resources to states and their state health agencies. Although states were finding it increasingly difficult to finance public health and medical service programs, they demanded more autonomy and control over the programs they managed, including those operated in partnership with the federal government. At the same time, local governments were making demands on state governments similar to those that states were making on the federal government. States have found themselves uncomfortably in the middle between the two other levels of government. At the same time, states are one step removed from both the resources needed to address the needs of their citizens and the demands and expectations of the local citizenry. For health issues, especially those affecting oversight and regulation of health services and

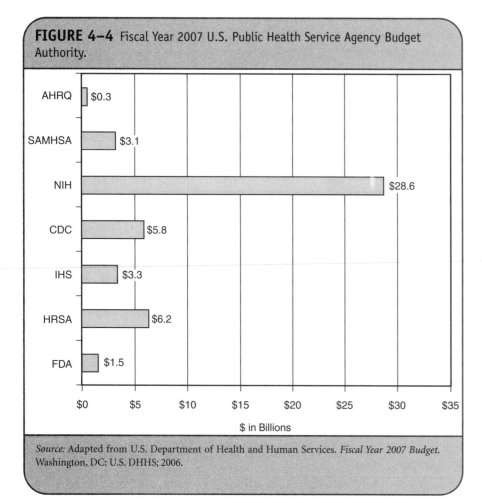

FIGURE 4–4 Fiscal Year 2007 U.S. Public Health Service Agency Budget Authority.

Source: Adapted from U.S. Department of Health and Human Services. *Fiscal Year 2007 Budget.* Washington, DC: U.S. DHHS; 2006.

social services. State health agencies are freestanding agencies in about 30 states and are part of multipurpose health and/or human services agencies in the others.

The range of responsibilities for the official state health agency varies considerably in terms of specific programs and services. Staffing levels and patterns also show a wide range, reflecting the diversity in agency responsibilities. Comprehensive information on the resources and programs of state health agencies has not been available since the early 1990s, due to the demise of a national reporting system coordinated by the Association of State and Territorial Health Officials (ASTHO) and the Public Health Foundation. The data presented on state health agencies in this chapter are derived from the most recent compilation available[8]; this information was collected as part of a salary survey of state health officials in 2002. Figure 4–5 illustrates the variability in state health agencies' responsibilities for programs. In 2002, for example, 90% of the official state health agencies administered the Supplemental Food Program for Women, Infants, and Children (WIC), vital statistics systems, public health laboratories, and tobacco prevention and control programs. Less than one half of the state health agencies administered the state Medicaid Program, mental health and substance abuse services, and health professional licensing. Most state health agencies administered programs for environmental health services, most frequently involving food and drinking water safety. However, only 25% of the state health agencies served as the environmental regulatory agency within their state, which often includes responsibility for clean air, resource conservation, clean water, superfund sites, toxic substance control, and hazardous substances.

providers, states often appear unduly influenced by large, politically active lobbies representing various aspects of the health system.

States carry out their health responsibilities through many different state agencies, although the overall constellation of health programs and services within all of state government is similar across states. Table 4–2 outlines more than 20 state agencies that carry out health responsibilities or activities in a typical state. Somewhere in the maze of state agencies is an identifiable lead agency for health. These official health agencies are often freestanding departments reporting to the governor of the state. In about two thirds of the states, the state health agency reports to a state board of health, although the prevalence of this reporting relationship is declining. Another approach to the organizational placement of state health agencies finds them within a multipurpose human service agency, often with the state's social services and substance abuse responsibilities. This approach has waxed and waned in popularity, although its popularity increased in the 1990s with the hopes of fostering better integration of community services across the spectrum of health and

As illustrated in Figure 4–2, state and local governments spent nearly $200 billion on health-related purposes in 2003. Health expenditures have comprised 13–15% of state and local government expenditures since 1990 (Figure 4–3). Before the advent of Medicaid and Medicare in 1965, state and local governments actually spent more for health purposes than did the federal government.

TABLE 4–2 Typical State Agencies with Health Roles (Names Vary from State to State)

- Official State Health Agency (Department of Health/Public Health)
- Department of Aging
- Department of Agriculture
- Department of Alcoholism and Substance Abuse
- Asbestos Abatement Authority
- Department of Children and Family Services
- Department of Emergency and Disaster Services
- Department of Energy and Natural Resources
- Environmental Protection Agencies
- Guardianship and Advocacy Commissions
- Health and Fitness Council
- Health Care Cost Containment Council
- Health Facilities Authority
- Health Facilities Planning Board

- Department of Homeland Security
- Department of Mental Health and Developmental Disabilities
- Department of Mines and Minerals
- Department of Nuclear Safety
- Pollution Control Board
- Department of Professional Regulation
- Department of Public Aid
- Department of Rehabilitation Services
- Rural Affairs Council
- State Board of Education
- State Fire Marshall
- Department of Transportation
- State University System
- Department of Veterans Affairs

FIGURE 4–5 Selected organizational responsibilities of state health agencies, 2002.

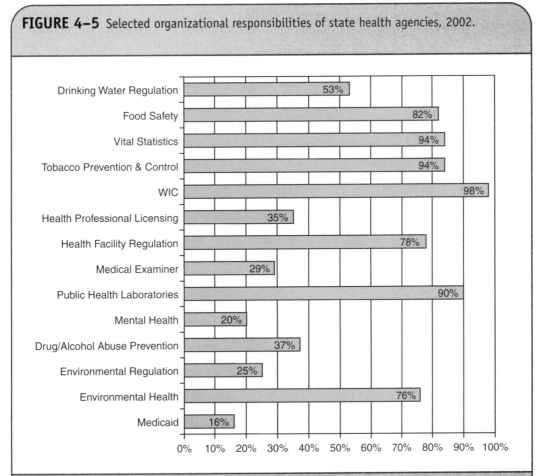

Source: Adapted from Association of State and Territorial Health Officials. *2002 Salary Survey of State and Territorial Health Officials.* Washington, DC: ASTHO; 2003.

With public health responsibilities allocated differently across the various states, data on state health agency expenditures are both difficult to interpret and incomplete in several important respects. These data do not allow for meaningful comparison across states because of the variation in responsibilities assigned to the official state health agency and those assigned to other state agencies. More importantly, these data do not differentiate between population-based public health activities and personal health services. Also lacking is a composite picture of resource allocations for important public health purposes across all state and local agencies with health roles, including substance abuse, mental health, and environmental protection agencies. This limitation is especially apparent for environmental health and protection roles.

The organizational placement and specific responsibilities of state health agencies largely determine the size of their budgets and workforce. Figure 4–6 provides information on four groups of state health agencies as determined by the number of employees. Just over 50% of the state health agencies have 1,500 or fewer employees; these agencies have budgets approximating $250 million. This group includes many freestanding agencies that have responsibility for traditional public health services but not for Medicaid, mental health, substance abuse, and environmental regulation. As these other responsibilities are added, the budgets and workforce of state health agencies increase substantially. Nine state health agencies have more than 4,500 employees and average expenditures of almost $6 billion.

State health agency expenditures include grants and contracts to local public health agencies, although the current level of these intergovernmental transfers is not known. In 1991, an estimated

$2 billion was transferred from state to local public health agencies.[9] As indicated in Figure 4–7, sources of the combined expenditures of state and local health agencies in 1991 were

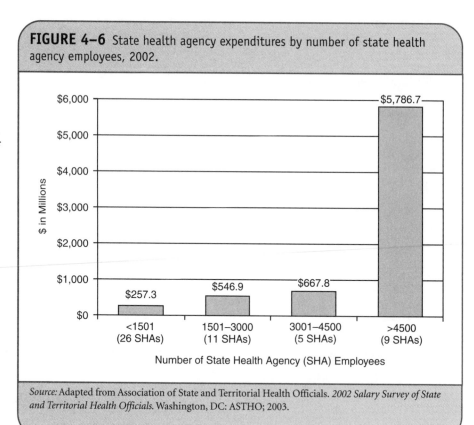

FIGURE 4–6 State health agency expenditures by number of state health agency employees, 2002.

Source: Adapted from Association of State and Territorial Health Officials. *2002 Salary Survey of State and Territorial Health Officials.* Washington, DC: ASTHO; 2003.

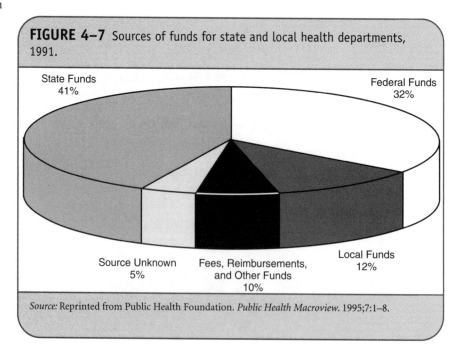

FIGURE 4–7 Sources of funds for state and local health departments, 1991.

Source: Reprinted from Public Health Foundation. *Public Health Macroview.* 1995;7:1–8.

state funds (41%), federal funds (32%), local funds (12%), and fees and reimbursements (10%). For state health agencies alone, sources were state funds (55%), federal funds for WIC (20%), federal MCH Block Grant funds (5%), and other federal sources (5%). Excluding WIC funding, the remaining resources are 69% state, 6% MCH, and 13% other federal funds.

At the federal level, more than a dozen federal departments, agencies, and commissions (Transportation, Labor, Health and Human Services, Commerce, Energy, Defense, EPA, Homeland Security, Interior, Consumer Product Safety Commission, Agriculture, Nuclear Regulatory Commission, and Housing and Urban Development) have environmental health roles. State and local governments have largely replicated this web of environmental responsibility, creating a complex system often poorly understood by the private sector and general public. Federal statutes have driven the organization of state responsibilities. Key federal environmental statutes include

- Clean Air Act (CAA)
- Clean Water Act (CWA)
- Comprehensive Environmental Response, Competition, and Liability Act (CERCLA) and Superfund Amendments and Reauthorization Act (SARA)
- Federal Insecticide, Fungicide, and Rodenticide Act (FIFRA)
- Resource Conservation and Recovery Act (RCRA)
- Safe Drinking Water Act (SDWA)
- Toxic Substance Control Act (TSCA)
- Food, Drug, and Cosmetic Act (FDCA)

- Federal Mine Safety and Health Act (MSHA)
- Occupational Safety and Health Act (OSHA)

States, however, have responded in no consistent manner in assigning implementation of federal statutes among various state agencies. The focus of federal statutes on specific environmental media (water, air, waste) has fostered the assignment of environmental responsibilities to state agencies other than official state health agencies, as demonstrated in Table 4–3. The implications of this diversification are important for public health agencies. State health agencies are becoming less involved in environmental health programs; only a handful of states utilize their state health agency as the state's lead agency for environmental concerns. This role has shifted to state environmental agencies, although many other state agencies are also involved. Still, the primary strategy has shifted from a health-oriented approach to a regulatory approach. Despite their diminished role in environmental concerns, state health agencies continue to address a very diverse set of environmental health issues and maintain epidemiologic and quantitative risk assessment capabilities not available in other state agencies. Linking this important expertise to the workings of other state agencies is a particularly challenging task, and there are other implications of this scenario, as well.

The shift toward regulatory strategies is clearly reflected in resource allocation at the state level. In the mid-1990s, about $6 billion was spent on environmental health and regulation by states, with only about $1 billion of that total for environmental health (as opposed to environmental regulation) activities.[10] Public health considerations often take a back seat

TABLE 4–3 Number and Type of State Agencies Responsible for Implementation of Federal Environmental Statutes

Statute	Agriculture	Environment	Health	Labor	Total
Clean Air Act	0	41	10	1	52
Clean Water Act	1	41	11	1	54
CERCLA (Superfund) Act	3	38	25	1	67
Federal Insecticide, Fungicide, and Rodenticide Act	0	41	11	2	54
Resource Conservation and Recovery Act	0	36	33	3	72
Safe Drinking Water Act	0	12	23	3	38
Toxic Substance Control Act	37	4	5	0	46
Food, Drug, and Cosmetic Act	1	1	15	39	56
Federal Mine Safety and Health Act	0	0	0	12	12
Occupational Safety and Health Act	15	1	13	0	29

Source: Reprinted from Health Resources and Services Administration. *Environmental Web: Impact of Federal Statutes on State Environmental Health and Protection—Services, Structure and Funding.* Rockville, MD: HRSA; 1995.

to regulatory concerns when budget decisions are made. In addition, the fact that many environmental health specialists are working in nonhealth agencies poses special problems for both their training and their practice performance.

The wide variation in organization and structure of state health responsibilities suggests that there is no standard or consistent pattern to public health practice among the various states. An examination of enabling statutes and state public agency mission statements provides further support for this conclusion. Only 11 of 43 state agency mission statements address the majority of the concepts related to public health purpose and mission in the Public Health in America document.[11,12] When state public health enabling statutes are examined for references to the essential public health services (also found in the Public Health in America document), the majority of the essential public health services can be identified in only one fifth of the states. The most frequently identified essential public health services reflect traditional public health activities, such as enforcement of laws, monitoring of health status, diagnosing and investigating health hazards, and informing and educating the public. The essential public health services least frequently referenced in these enabling statutes reflect more modern concepts of public health practice, including mobilizing community partnerships, evaluating the effects of health services, and research for innovative solutions. Only three states had both enabling statutes and state health agency mission statements highly congruent with the concepts advanced in the Public Health in America document.[11]

In sum, state health agencies face many challenges related to the fragmentation of public health roles and responsibilities among various state agencies. Central to these are two related challenges: how to coordinate public health's core functions and essential services effectively and how to leverage changes within the health system to instill greater emphasis on clinical prevention and population-based services. As the various chapters of this text suggest, these are related aims.

Local Public Health Organizations

In the overall structuring of governmental public health responsibilities, local public health agencies (LPHAs) are where the "rubber meets the road." These agencies are established to carry out the critical public health responsibilities embodied in state laws and local ordinances and to meet other needs and expectations of their communities. Although some cities had local public health boards and agencies prior to 1900, the first county health department was not established until 1911. At that time, Yakima County, Washington, created a permanent county health unit, based on the success of a county sanitation campaign to control a serious typhoid epidemic. The Rockefeller Sanitary Commission, through its support for county hookworm eradication efforts, also stimulated the development of county-based LPHAs. The number of LPHAs grew rapidly during the 20th century, although in recent decades, expansion has been tempered by closures and consolidations.

LPHAs should not be considered separately from the state network in which they operate. It is important to remember that states, through their state legislative and executive branches, establish the types and powers of local governmental units that can exist in that state. In this arrangement, the state and its local subunits, however defined, share responsibilities for health and other state functions. How health duties are shared in any given state depends on a complex set of factors that include state and local statutes, history, need, and expectations.

Local health agencies relate to their state public health systems in one of three general patterns.[4] In most states, LPHAs are formed and managed by local government, reporting directly to some office of local government, such as a local Board of Health, county commission, or city or county executive officer. In this decentralized arrangement, LPHAs often have considerable autonomy although they may be required to carry out specific state public health statutes. Also, there are some states that share oversight of LPHAs with local government through the power to appoint local health officers or to approve an annual budget. In some states with decentralized LPHAs, some areas of the state lack coverage because the local government chooses not to form a local health agency and the state must provide services in those uncovered areas.[13] This mixed arrangement occurs in about 20% of the states. Another 30% of the states use a more centralized approach, in which local health agencies are directly operated by the state or there are no LPHAs and the state provides local health services.

LPHAs are established by governmental units, including counties, cities, towns, townships, and special districts, by one of two general methods. The legislative body may create an LPHA through enactment of a resolution, or the citizens of the jurisdiction may create a local board and agency through a referendum. Both patterns are common. Resolution health agencies are often funded from the general funds of the jurisdiction, whereas referendum health agencies often have a specific tax levy available to them. There are advantages and disadvantages to either approach. Resolution health agencies are simpler to establish and may develop close working relationships with the local legislative bodies that create them. Referendum agencies reflect the support of the local electorate and may have access to specific tax levies that avoid the need to compete with other local government funding sources.

Counties represent the most common form of subdividing states. In general, counties are geopolitical subunits of states that carry out various state responsibilities, such as law enforcement (sheriffs and state's attorneys) and public health. Counties largely function as agents of the state and carry out responsibilities delegated or assigned to them. In contrast, cities are generally not established as agents of the state. Instead, they have considerable discretion through home rule powers to take on functions that are not prohibited to them by state law. Cities can choose to have a health department or to rely on the state or their county for public health services. City health departments often have a wider array of programs and services because of this autonomy. As described previously, the earliest public health agencies developed in large urban centers, prior to the development of either state health agencies or county-based LPHAs. This status also contributes to their sense of autonomy. These considerations, as well as the increased demands and expectations to meet the needs of those who lack adequate health insurance, have made many city-based, especially big city-based, LPHAs qualitatively different from other LPHAs.

Both cities and counties have resource and political bases. Both rely heavily on property and sales taxes to finance health and other services, and both are struggling with the limitations of these funding sources. Political concerns over increasing property taxes are the major limitation for both. Relatively few counties and cities have imposed income taxes, the form of taxation relied upon by federal and state governments. However, both generally have strong political bases, although cities are generally more likely than counties to be at odds with state government on key issues.

Counties play a critical role in the public sector, the extent and importance of which is often overlooked. Three fourths of all LPHAs are organized at the county level, serving a single county, a city-county, or several counties. As a result, counties provide a substantial portion of the community prevention and clinical preventive services offered in the United States. Counties provide care for about 40 million persons who access LPHAs and other facilities; they spend more than $30 billion of their local tax revenues on health and hospital services annually through some 4,500 sites that include hospitals, nursing homes, clinics, health departments, and mental health facilities. Counties play an explicit role in treatment, are legally responsible for indigent health care in over 30 states, and pay a portion of the nonfederal share of Medicaid in about 20 states. In addition, counties purchase health care for more than 2 million employees.[14]

The National Association of County and City Health Officials (NACCHO) tracks public health activities of LPHAs; the most recent survey of LPHAs took place in 1999.[15] Data provided in this chapter are derived from this 1999 survey, as well as from two other NACCHO profiles of LPHAs completed earlier in the 1990s.[13,16]

One limitation of information on LPHAs is that there is neither a clear nor a functional definition of what constitutes an LPHA. The most widely used definitions call for an administrative and service unit of local government, concerned with health, employing at least one full-time person, and carrying responsibility for health of a jurisdiction smaller than the state. By this definition, more than 3,200 local health agencies operate in 3,042 U.S. counties.[13] The number of local public health agencies varies widely from state to state; Rhode Island has none, whereas neighboring Connecticut and Massachusetts report more than 100 LPHAs.

Nearly 60% of LPHAs are single-county health agencies, and over 80% operate out of a county base (single county, multicounty, or city-county).[15] Other LPHAs function at the city, town, or township levels; some state-operated units also serve local jurisdictions. Although the precise number is uncertain, it appears that the total number of LPHAs has been increasing, from about 1,300 in 1947 to about 2,000 in the mid-1970s to somewhere over 3,000 today.

Several reports going back more than 50 years have proposed extensive consolidation of small LPHAs because of perceived lack of efficiency and coordination of services, inconsistent administration of public health laws, and inability of small LPHAs to raise adequate resources to carry out their prime functions effectively. Consolidations at the county level would appear to be the most rational approach, but only limited progress has been achieved in recent decades.

Most LPHAs are relatively small organizations; as illustrated in Figure 4–8, 62% serve populations of 50,000 or less while 32% of LPHAs serve populations of 50,000–499,999. Only 6% of LPHAs serve populations of 500,000 or more residents.[15]

Some states set qualifications for local health officers or require medical supervision when the administrator is not a physician. About four fifths of LPHAs employ a full-time health officer. Health officers have a mean tenure of about 8 years and a median tenure of about 6 years. Approximately one half of all local health officers are physicians, about 15% are physicians with formal training in public health, and less than one fourth have graduate degrees in public health. LPHAs serving larger populations are more likely to have full-time health officers than are smaller LPHAs.

Local boards of health are associated with most LPHAs; in 2006, 74% of LPHAs reported working with a local board of health. There are an estimated 3,200 local boards of health; about 85% reported an affiliation with an LPHA. However, 15% exist independently of any LPHA; this pattern is most common in Massachusetts, Pennsylvania, New Hampshire,

TABLE 4–4 Vital Statistics for Local Health Departments (LPHAs)

Definition	• An administrative and service unit of state or local government, concerned with health, employing at least one full-time person, and carrying responsibility for health of a jurisdiction smaller than the state
Number	• Approximately 3,200 using the above definition • Functional definition would reduce number considerably • Varies from zero in Rhode Island to more than 100 in seven states
Jurisdiction Type	• 59% — single county • 10% — multi-county • 14% — city-county • 9% — town/township • 7% — city
Jurisdiction Population	• 41% — <25,000 • 21% — 25,000–49,999 • 15% — 50,000–99,999 • 17% — 100,000–499,999 • 6% — 500,000 and greater
Services Most Frequently Provided (% LPHAs)	• 91% — Adult immunizations • 90% — Childhood immunizations • 89% — Communicable disease surveillance • 85% — Tuberculosis screening • 76% — Inspection/Licensing of retail food establishments • 75% — Environmental health surveillance • 75% — Food safety education • 75% — Tuberculosis testament • 72% — High blood pressure screening • 69% — Tobacco use prevention
Budget	• Median — $1,000,000 • 33% — <$500,000 • 20% — >$5,000,000 • Median per capita expenditures: $23 (excluding clinical revenue); $29 (all sources)
Source of Funds	• 29% — local • 23% — state • 13% — federal funds passed through state • 7% — federal direct to local agency • 9% — Medicaid reimbursement • 2% — Medicare reimbursement • 6% — fees • 12% — other

Iowa, and New Jersey. The pattern for size of population, type of jurisdiction, and budget mirrors that for LPHAs. Virtually all local boards of health establish local health policies, fees, ordinances, and regulations. Most also recommend and/or approve budgets, establish community health priorities, and hire the director of the local health agency. Although four fifths of LPHAs relate to a board of health, only 56% report to that board rather than some other office of local government.

Similar to the situation with state health agencies, data on LPHA expenditures lack currency and completeness. Annual LPHA expenditures in 2005 ranged from less than $10,000 to over $1 billion. One half of LPHAs had budgets of $1 million or less and 20% had budgets over $5 million. Total expenditures increase with size of population. LPHAs located in metropolitan areas had substantially higher expenditures than their nonmetropolitan area counterparts. The median per capita

TABLE 4–4 Vital Statistics for Local Health Departments (LPHAs) *(continued)*

Employees
(full time equivalents)

- All LHDs
  - Median — 19 FTE
  - 60% employ <25
  - 14% employ >100
- Median FTEs in Selected Occupational Categories Employed by LHDs

	Population Served				
	<25,000	25,000–49,999	50,000–99,999	100,000–499,999	500,000+
All LHD Staff	6	16	33	88	325
Manager	1	1	1	5	15
Nurse	2	5	10	20	69
Physician	0	0	0	1	3
Environmental Health Specialist	1	2	3	9	24
Other Environmental Health Scientist	0	0	0	1	5
Epidemiologist	0	0	0	1	2
Health Educator	0	0	1	2	6
Nutritionist	0	0	1	3	8
Information Systems Specialist	0	0	0	1	3
Public Information Specialist	0	0	0	0	1
Emergency Preparedness Coordinator	0	0	1	1	1
Administrative/Clerical	2	4	8	23	72

Governance

- 74% of LPHAs relate and/or report to a local board of health
- for 69% of local boards of health, members of the board are appointed to their positions

Leadership

- one half of local health officers are MDs
- one fourth of all local health officers have formal public health training
- median tenure — 6 years

Source: National Association of County and City Health Officials, 2006.

LPHA expenditure level in 2005 was $23 excluding clinical services. Despite concerns as to shrinking public health agencies, 75% of LPHAs reported increased budgets in 2005 as compared with the previous year.

In 2005, LPHAs derived their funding from the following sources: local funds (29%), the state (36%, including 13% that were federal funds passing through the state), direct federal funds (7%), Medicaid and Medicare reimbursements (11%), fees (6%), and other sources (12%). Metropolitan LPHAs and those serving smaller populations are more dependent on local sources of funding, while LPHAs in nonmetropolitan areas and those serving larger populations depend more on state sources.

The number of full-time equivalent employees also increases with the size of the population served. Only 10% of LPHAs employ 125 or more persons, and 50% have 19 or fewer employees. The number of employees and the number

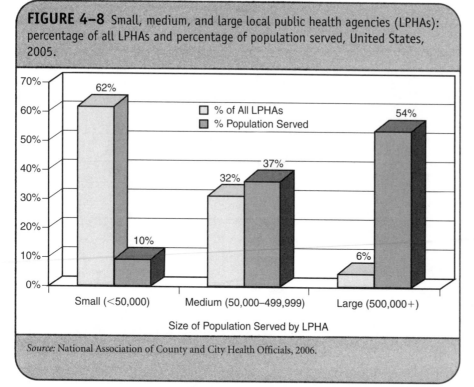

FIGURE 4–8 Small, medium, and large local public health agencies (LPHAs): percentage of all LPHAs and percentage of population served, United States, 2005.

Source: National Association of County and City Health Officials, 2006.

of different disciplines and professions are related to LPHA population size. Clerical staff, nurses, sanitarians, physicians, and nutritionists are the most common disciplines (in that order) and are all found in more than one half of all LPHAs.

There is considerable variety in the services provided by LPHAs. Later chapters will examine in greater detail the functions and services of LPHAs, but several general categories of services are notable. Top priority areas for LPHAs overall are communicable disease control, environmental health, and child health. LPHAs serving both large and small populations report similar priorities, although community outreach replaces environmental health as a top priority for the largest local health jurisdictions (those over 500,000 population). Slight differences in priorities are also apparent between metropolitan and nonmetropolitan area LPHAs. LPHAs in metropolitan areas often include inspections as a high priority, while nonmetropolitan LPHAs are more likely to include family planning and home health care services as priorities.

Many LPHAs provide a common core battery of services that generally includes adult and childhood immunizations, communicable disease control, community assessment, community outreach and education, environmental health services, epidemiology and surveillance programs, food safety and restaurant inspections, health education, and tuberculosis testing. Less commonly, LPHAs provide services related to

primary care and chronic disease, including cardiovascular disease, diabetes, and glaucoma screening; behavioral and mental health services; programs for the homeless; substance abuse services; and veterinary public health.[15]

LPHAs do not always provide these services themselves; increasingly, they contract for these services or contribute resources to other agencies or organizations in the community. Community partners for LPHAs include state health agencies, other LPHAs, hospitals, other units of government, nonprofit and voluntary organizations, academic institutions, community health centers, the faith community, and insurance companies. LPHAs increasingly interact with managed care organizations, although most do not have either formal or informal agreements governing these interactions.[13] Where agreements existed, they were more likely to be formal, to cover clinical and case management services, and to involve the provision (rather than the purchase) of services. More than one fourth of LPHAs had formal agreements for clinical services for Medicaid clients in 1996.

INTERGOVERNMENTAL RELATIONSHIPS

In terms of public health roles, no level of government has complete authority and autonomy. Optimal outcomes result from collaborative and complementary efforts. "Public Health Achievements in 20th-Century America: Motor Vehicle Safety," presented below, tells the story of improved motor vehicle safety in the United States during the 20th century; this achievement relied heavily on effective laws and their enforcement by all levels of government.

The relationships between and among the three levels of government have changed considerably over time in terms of their relative importance and influence in the health sector. This is especially true for the federal and local roles. The federal government had little authority and little ability to influence health priorities and interventions until after 1930. Since that time, it has exercised its influence primarily through financial leverage on both state and local government, as well as on the private medical care system. The massive financing role of the federal government has moved it to a position of preeminence among the various levels of government in

EXAMPLE

Public Health Achievements in 20th-Century America: Motor Vehicle Safety

State and local health agencies are not the only governmental organizations working to reduce the burden of disease and ill health in society. Motor vehicle-related injuries are a prime example. Federal, state, and local government all play important roles through agencies that are better known for other responsibilities, such as law enforcement and transportation. The complexities of government and its various agencies add an important, but not necessarily the most important, dimension to public health practice. Highlights of this achievement are apparent in Figures 4–9 and 4–10.

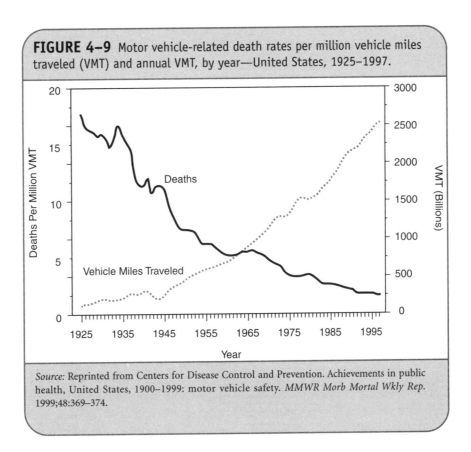

FIGURE 4–9 Motor vehicle-related death rates per million vehicle miles traveled (VMT) and annual VMT, by year—United States, 1925–1997.

Source: Reprinted from Centers for Disease Control and Prevention. Achievements in public health, United States, 1900–1999: motor vehicle safety. *MMWR Morb Mortal Wkly Rep.* 1999;48:369–374.

actual ability to influence health affairs. This is evident in the federal share of total national health expenditures and the federal government's substantial support of prevention activities. However federal public health spending represents only about 1.2% of total federal health spending, nearly 75% less than in 1965 (Figure 4–11). This suggests that the federal commitment to public health has declined over recent decades. The proportion of the federal component of government spending for population-based public health activities shows a similar pattern (Figure 4–12), declining from 72% in 1970

to 29% in 2000. Although federal bioterrorism preparedness funds beginning in 2002 may modify this trend, the financial influence of the federal government on public health activities nationally was lower in 2000 than it had been at any point in the second half of the 20th century.

In recent decades, political initiatives have sought to diminish the powerful federal role and return some of its influence back to the states. However, little in the form of true transfer of authority or resource control has taken place through 2003. It is likely that the federal government's fiscal

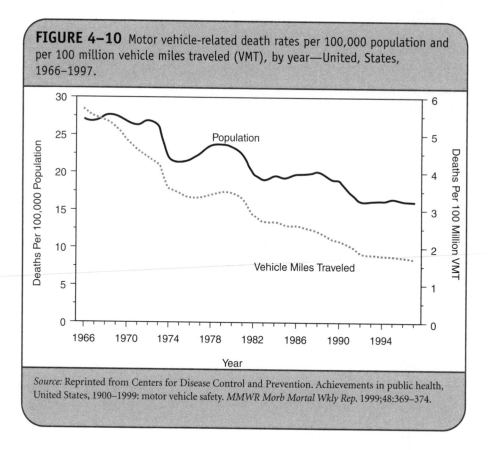

FIGURE 4–10 Motor vehicle-related death rates per 100,000 population and per 100 million vehicle miles traveled (VMT), by year—United, States, 1966–1997.

Source: Reprinted from Centers for Disease Control and Prevention. Achievements in public health, United States, 1900–1999: motor vehicle safety. *MMWR Morb Mortal Wkly Rep.* 1999;48:369–374.

muscle will enable it to continue its current dominant role in its relationships with state and local government.

Local government has experienced the greatest and most disconcerting change in relative influence over the 20th century. Prior to 1900, local government was the primary locus of action, with the development of both population-based interventions for communicable disease control and environmental sanitation and locally provided charity care for the poor. However, the massive problems related to simultaneous urbanization and povertization of the big cities spawned needs that could not be met with local resources alone. Outside the large cities, local government responses generally took the form of LPHAs organized at the county level at the behest of state governments. This was viewed by states as the most efficient manner of executing their broad health powers. States often viewed local governments in general and LPHAs in particular as their delivery system for important programs and services. In any event, the power of states and the growing influence of financial incentives through grant programs of both federal and state government acted to influence local priorities greatly. Priorities were being established by higher levels of government more often than through local determinations of needs. Although the demands and expectations were being directed

at local governments, key decisions were being made in state capitals and in Washington, DC. Unfortunately there are signs that local governments across the country are looking for opportunities to reduce their health roles for both clinical services and population-based interventions where they can. The perception is that the responsibility for clinical services lies with federal and state government or the private sector and that even traditional public health services can be effectively outsourced. How these actions will comport with the widespread belief that services are best provided at the local level raises serious questions regarding new roles of oversight and accountability that are not easily answered. Local governments have lost control over priorities and policies; they bridle under the regulations and grant conditions imposed by state and federal funding sources. As costs increase, grant awards fail to keep pace. However, growing numbers of wholly or partly uninsured individuals now look to local government for services. These rising expectations and increasing costs are occurring at a time when local governments are unable and unwilling to seek additional tax revenues. The complexities of organizing and coordinating community-wide responses to modern public health problems and risks also push local government to look elsewhere for solutions.

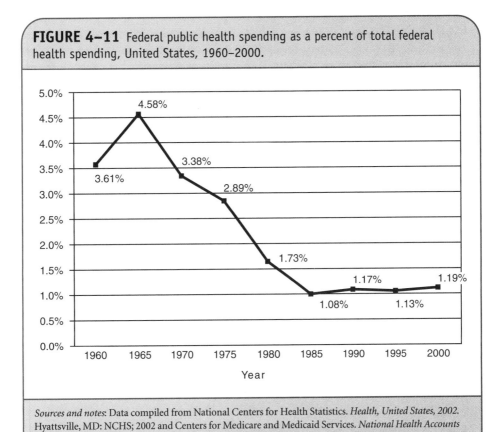

FIGURE 4–11 Federal public health spending as a percent of total federal health spending, United States, 1960–2000.

Sources and notes: Data compiled from National Centers for Health Statistics. *Health, United States, 2002.* Hyattsville, MD: NCHS; 2002 and Centers for Medicare and Medicaid Services. *National Health Accounts (NHA) 1960–2000.* Baltimore, MD: CMS; 2000. The NHA breaks down health spending by source of funding and by activity and type of service provided.

States were slow to assume their extensive powers in the health sector but have been major players since the latter half of the 19th century. Although the growing influence of the federal government since 1930 displaced states as the most important level of government, their relative role has strengthened since about 1980. Still, states have become secondary players in the health sector. Most states lack the means, political as well as statutory, to intervene effectively in the portion of the health sector located within their jurisdictional boundaries. This is further complicated by their tradition of imitating the federal health bureaucracy whenever possible through the decentralization of health roles and responsibilities throughout dozens of administrative agencies. Coordination of programs, policies, and priorities has become exceedingly difficult within state government. Outside of state government, it has become virtually impossible. Still, the widely disparate circumstances from state to state make for laboratories of opportunity in which innovative approaches can be developed and evaluated.

The relationship between state and local government in public health has traditionally been tenuous and difficult. Just as the federal government views the states, states themselves have come to view local governments as just another way to get things done. As a result, states have turned to other parties, such as community-based organizations, and have begun to deal directly with them, leaving local government on the sidelines. This undervaluing of LPHAs, when coupled with the declining appreciation among local governments for their health agencies, presents major challenges for the future of public health services in the United States. Instead of becoming stronger allies, these forces are working to pull apart the fabric of the national public health network.

These ever-changing and evolving relationships call into question whether the governmental public health network can be strengthened through a more centralized approach involving greater federal leadership and direction.[17] In decentralized approaches, some states may truly be laboratories of innovation and provide better services than can be achieved through

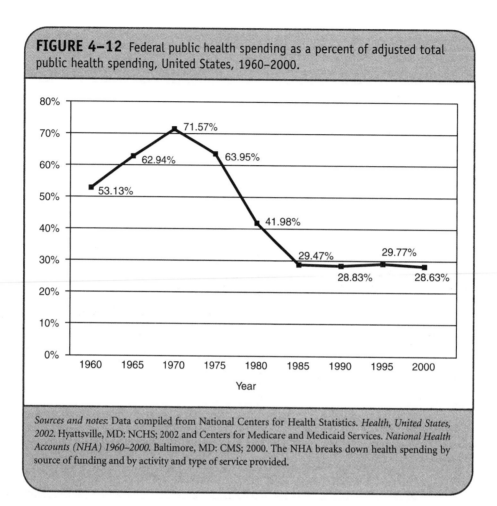

FIGURE 4–12 Federal public health spending as a percent of adjusted total public health spending, United States, 1960–2000.

Sources and notes: Data compiled from National Centers for Health Statistics. *Health, United States, 2002.* Hyattsville, MD: NCHS; 2002 and Centers for Medicare and Medicaid Services. *National Health Accounts (NHA) 1960–2000.* Baltimore, MD: CMS; 2000. The NHA breaks down health spending by source of funding and by activity and type of service provided.

a centralized approach. There are many examples of creative policies and programs at the state level, but there are also many examples of state creativity being stifled by the federal government. The history of state requests for waivers of Medicaid requirements is a case in point. Many states waited 2 or more years for federal approval of the waivers necessary to begin innovative programs, and some of the more creative proposals were actually rejected. Still, it can be argued that state political processes are more reflective of the different political values that must be reconciled for progressive policies to develop.

CONCLUSION

The structural framework for public health in the United States includes a network of state and local public health agencies working in partnership with the federal government. This framework is precariously balanced on a legal foundation that gives primacy for health concerns to states, a financial foundation that allows the federal government to promote equality and minimum standards across 50 diverse states, and a practical foundation of local public health agencies serving as the

point of contact between communities and their three-tiered government. Over time, the relative influence of these partners has shifted dramatically because of changes in needs, resources, and public expectations. The challenges to this organizational structure are many. Those related to the public health emergency preparedness and response are addressed in the next chapter, and those emerging from the rapid changes within the health system and in the expansion of community public health practice are addressed in Chapters 3 and 6 of this text. There are increasing calls for the national government to turn over many public programs to private interests and growing concern over the role of government, in general. These developments make it easy to forget that many of the public health achievements of the past century would not have been possible without a serious commitment of resources and leadership by those in the public sector. In any event, it is clear that the organizational structure of public health—its form—intimately reflects the structure of government in the United States. As a result, the success or failure of these public health organizations will be determined by our success in governing ourselves.

Discussion Questions and Exercises

1. What is the legal basis for public health in the United States, and what impact has that had on the public health powers of federal, state, and local governments?

2. How can the enforcement of nuisance control regulations work for as well as against public health agencies?

3. What is meant by a state's police power, and how is that used in public health?

4. What is the basis for the historic tension between the powers of the federal government and the powers of states in public health matters?

5. How extensive is administrative law in public health, and how does it work? Cite a recent example of important public health rules or regulations in the news media.

6. Describe the basic structure of a typical local public health agency (LPHA) in the United States in terms of type and size of jurisdiction served, budget, staff, and agency head. (The National Association of County and City Health Officials' Web site may be useful here!) How does this compare with the typical LPHA in your own state?

7. For the prevention of motor vehicle injuries (see "Public Health Achievements in 20th-Century America: Motor Vehicle Safety"), how are responsibilities assigned or delegated among the three levels of government (federal, state, local) and among various agencies of those levels of government? Who is responsible for what?

8. What are the primary federal roles and responsibilities for public health in the United States? How do those roles and responsibilities comport with Public Health Service (PHS) agency budget requests for federal fiscal year 2007 (see Figure 4–4)?

9. Has the evolution of both local and federal public health agencies taken parallel pathways? How have their development differed in terms of roles and responsibilities? What are the implications of these similarities and differences for public health problems that require more than one level of government?

10. Access the Web sites of any two U.S. state health departments and compare and contrast the two organizations in terms of their structure, general functions, specific services, resources, and other important features. (The Association of State and Territorial Health Officials' link to state health agency Web sites may be useful here.)

REFERENCES

1. Centers for Disease Control and Prevention. History of CDC. *MMWR Morb Mortal Wkly Rep.* 1996;45:526–528.

2. Centers for Disease Control and Prevention. *Profile of State and Local Public Health Systems 1990.* Atlanta, GA: CDC; 1991.

3. Shonick W. *Government and Health Services: Government's Role in the Development of the U.S. Health Services 1930–1980.* New York: Oxford University Press; 1995.

4. Pickett G, Hanlon JJ. *Public Health Administration and Practice.* 9th ed. St. Louis, MO: Mosby; 1990.

5. *Jacobson v Massachusetts.* 197 US 11 (1905).

6. U.S. Department of Health and Human Services (DHHS). *The Fiscal Year 2007 Budget.* Washington, DC: DHHS; 2006.

7. DHHS. *Healthy People 2000.* Washington, DC: U.S. Public Health Service (PHS); 1990.

8. Association of State and Territorial Health Officials. *2002 Salary Survey of State and Territorial Health Officials.* Washington, DC: ASTHO; 2003.

9. Public Health Foundation. *Public Health Macroview.* 1995;7:1–8.

10. Burke TA, Shalauta NM, Tran NL, Stern BS. The environmental web: a national profile of the state infrastructure for environmental health and protection. *J Public Health Manage Pract.* 1997;3:1–12.

11. Gebbie KM. State public health laws: an expression of constituency expectations. *J Public Health Manage Pract.* 2000;6:46–54.

12. Core Public Health Functions Steering Committee. *Public Health in America.* Washington, DC: DHHS-PHS; 1994.

13. National Association of County and City Health Officials. *Profile of Local Health Departments 1996–1997 Data Set.* Washington, DC: NACCHO; 1997.

14. National Association of County and City Health Officials. Fact Sheet. Washington, DC: NACCHO; 1991.

15. National Association of County and City Health Officials. *Local Public Health Agency Infrastructure: A Chartbook.* Washington, DC: NACCHO; 2001.

16. National Association of County and City Health Officials. *Profile of Local Health Departments 1992–1993.* Washington, DC: NACCHO; 1995.

17. Turnock BJ, Atchison C. Governmental public health in the United States: the implications of federalism. *Health Affairs.* 2002;6:68–78.

CHAPTER 5

Public Health Emergency Preparedness and Response

LEARNING OBJECTIVES

After completing Chapter 5, learners will be proficient in describing the public health role, and their own level of participation, in emergency responses for a range of contingencies that might arise. Key aspects of this competency expectation include

- Differentiating among different types of public health emergencies and disasters, including their definitions and the terminology related to them
- Explaining the concepts of vulnerability, risk, disaster prevention, and the links to longer-term effects
- Describing why emergencies and disasters are problems in which the public health system must be an integral participant across a range of disaster activities
- Describing the role and responsibilities of public health professionals in emergency preparedness and response
- Defining terrorism and bioterrorism, identifying Category A, B, and C biologic agents and their unique characteristics and relevance to bioterrorism events and threats, and
- Describing (in general terms) recent federal public health service initiatives for bioterrorism preparedness

Public health crossed the threshold of a new century as an admittedly important but poorly understood contributor to the American way of life. Despite its contributions to population health status and quality of life throughout the 20th century, the visibility and economic valuation of public health activities remained low. This situation changed rapidly after the terrorist attacks on the World Trade Center and Pentagon on September 11, 2001, and the bioterrorism events spreading anthrax through the U.S. postal system the following month. The nation responded quickly in the aftermath of these events, elevating international terrorism, bioterrorism preparedness, and emergency response to the top of the national agenda.

Within months, more than $2 billion was made available to federal, state, and local public health agencies for emergency preparedness and response activities, with additional funding allocated the following year. This explosion of attention, resources, and expectations typifies the history of public health in America—a dramatic health-related event focusing its spotlight on a largely neglected public health infrastructure followed by rapid infusion of resources to resuscitate the system.

This chapter describes the early years of efforts to enhance public health emergency preparedness, as well as some of the successes, failures, and lessons encountered along the way. The intent is to initiate an examination of whether public health preparedness will become one of the public health achievements in 21st-century America. In the process, this chapter will focus on several key questions:

- What is public health preparedness?
- What are the key components of preparedness?
- Is the public health system currently prepared?
- What can be done to become better prepared?

PUBLIC HEALTH ROLES IN EMERGENCY PREPAREDNESS AND RESPONSE

Chapter 1 introduces and describes a framework for modern public health responses that is organized around six major functions[1]:

- Preventing epidemics and the spread of disease
- Protecting against environmental hazards
- Preventing injuries
- Promoting and encouraging healthy behaviors

- Responding to disasters and assisting communities in recovery, and
- Assuring the quality and accessibility of health services

Although only one of these functions explicitly refers to public health's role in responding to emergencies, all six drive the public health approach to emergency preparedness and response. Public health emergency preparedness and response efforts seek to prevent epidemics and the spread of disease, protect against environmental hazards, prevent injuries, promote healthy behaviors, and assure the quality and accessibility of health services. Each of these is expected by the public and each is evident in effective preparedness and response related to public health emergencies. Together they make preparedness and response a special and particularly critical component of modern public health practice.

For public health emergencies, preparedness and response are inextricably linked.[2] Preparedness is based on lessons learned from both actual and simulated response situations. Effective response is all but impossible without extensive planning and thoughtful preparation. Public health roles in health-related emergencies illustrate both facets.

Public Health Surveillance

Many public health emergencies are readily apparent, but others may not manifest themselves immediately. Effective preparedness and response rely on monitoring disease patterns, investigating individual case reports, and using epidemiologic and laboratory analyses to target public health intervention strategies. For example, foodborne illness outbreaks may involve individuals who remain in the same location after being exposed, making it easier to identify a common exposure pattern when these individuals seek medical care. Alternatively, an exposure at a convention or family reunion is more difficult to detect because individuals may present for medical care far from the location of exposure. Whether within the same community or in distant locations, it is often difficult for individual medical practitioners to recognize that an outbreak or widespread epidemic is occurring. Prompt recognition and reporting of cases to health authorities is a critical link in the public health chain of protection. A relatively new component of public health surveillance involves biosurveillance, the early detection of abnormal disease patterns and nontraditional early disease indicators, such as pharmaceutical sales, school and work absenteeism, and animal disease events.

Epidemiologic Investigation and Analysis

Once a disease is reported, public health agencies can uncover unusual patterns that help identify outbreaks and continuing risks. Public health professionals may use sophisticated analytic tools, such as pattern recognition software and geographic information systems, to determine patterns in disease cases. These surveillance activities help to ensure that disease outbreaks are identified quickly and that appropriate response actions, such as the issuance of health alerts for area providers and communication with response partners, are initiated. Many current disease surveillance systems act in a passive manner (i.e., they rely on providers to initiate disease reports); however, public health agencies are increasingly using active surveillance activities, such as when public health workers proactively seek information from providers and other sources to monitor disease trends. In the event of an actual or threatened public health emergency, active surveillance activities are deployed and/or expanded.

Surveillance activities trigger more extensive and focused epidemiologic investigations in order to determine the identity, source, and modes of transmission of disease agents. Epidemiologic investigations seek to determine what is causing the disease, how the disease is spreading, and who is at risk. Answers to these questions inform efforts to mount rapid and effective interventions. Methods of obtaining epidemiologic information, often characterized as disease detective activities, include contacting patients, obtaining detailed information on location and types of possible exposures, and examining both clinical specimens (such as blood and urine) and environmental samplings (such as food, water, air, and soil). Epidemiologic investigations require trained personnel and, in many cases, are quite human resource intensive in terms of the quantity and quality of manpower needed. Laboratory capacity to support these investigations is critical.

Laboratory Investigation and Analysis

In many situations, laboratories provide the definitive identification of causative agents, both biological and chemical, and through various fingerprinting activities link cases to a common source. Capabilities to identify rare or unusual diseases are often not present in every community, necessitating linkages with higher-level laboratories. Specimens may be sent for analysis and confirmation to a regional or state public health laboratory or possibly even to a Centers for Disease Control and Prevention (CDC) reference laboratory. Some specialized capabilities found at these higher-level laboratories include serotyping to determine the antigenic profile of a microorganism and DNA fingerprinting to not only identify the type of microorganism causing an infectious disease but to also pinpoint the particular strain of bacterium or virus involved. In this way, public health authorities can determine if reported disease cases are part of the same outbreak, and therefore linked to a common source. Public health laboratories must rely on specialized protective laboratory equipment and facilities due to the dangerous agents with which they work. Some agents, such as smallpox, require special biocontainment equipment and procedures; laboratories are rated in terms of the level of safety they can provide.

Intervention

The primary reason for collecting, analyzing, and sharing information on disease is to control that disease. Expending resources for surveillance and analysis makes little sense if actions do not follow. Interventions that protect individuals from risks associated with environmental hazards are many, including setting standards for health and safety, inspecting food production and importation facilities, monitoring environmental conditions, abating conditions that foster infectious disease (e.g., insect and animal control), and enforcing private-sector compliance with established standards. Disease and injury risks associated with these biologic and chemical hazards, whether naturally occurring or initiated by man, are reduced through rigorous monitoring and enforcement activities. Public health agencies also play a substantial role in remediation of environmental hazards by decontaminating sites and facilities after they are identified. The extent of remediation necessary can vary greatly, just as the nature and extent of the contamination varies with different disease agents and their ability to remain viable outside a human host or animal/insect vector.

Risk Communication

Epidemiologic and laboratory investigations drive the initiation of actions intended to limit the spread of disease and to prevent additional cases in the community. The range of possible actions can be quite broad, including restraining the activities of individuals through isolation and quarantine and imposing temporary or permanent barriers around sources of contamination (e.g., sealing buildings, closing restaurants, and cutting off water supplies). In severe and unusual circumstances, special emergency powers may be put into effect limiting human and animal travel and/or restricting certain types of business activity. In these situations, the importance of effective public education and information activities to communicate risk to the public cannot be overstated. Commonly encountered examples include notices to boil drinking water when contaminated water supplies are suspected and product recalls and food safety advisories for potentially contaminated food products. The dissemination of information on mail handling practices during the anthrax attacks in late 2001 served both public education and risk communication purposes.

Promoting and encouraging healthy behaviors during public health emergencies represents another public health intervention strategy. It is not uncommon in the event of a natural disaster or terrorist attack for the most devastating effects to take the form of social disruption and infrastructure damage. The psychological effects of fear and terror, together with disruption of infrastructure components such as electricity, water, and safe housing, may create more casualties than any initial terrorist's biologic or chemical assault. Such conditions can also foster toxicity and infectious disease threats, such as occurred with the mass evacuation of the area around the World Trade Center leading to the abandonment of food supplies in surrounding homes and restaurants. Public health officials in New York City took steps to secure these premises to avoid the proliferation of rodents and other pests that otherwise could have resulted in secondary health threats.

Preparedness Planning

Organizing responses to emergencies is another public health role that assures the availability and accessibility of medical and mental health services. Preparedness and planning cannot eliminate all biologic, chemical, radiation, and mass casualty threats. But coordinated, community-wide planning for emergency medical and public health responses assures that emergency medical services and medical treatment services are deployed in a rapid and effective manner. Such planning foresees the need for public health measures to be activated in order to assure the safety of responders and to prevent secondary effects due to further disease transmission and injury risk. Planning for these coordinated responses includes monitoring available response resources, establishing action protocols, simulating emergency events to improve readiness, training public and private sector personnel, assessing communication capabilities, supplies, and resources, and maintaining relationships with partner organizations to improve coordination.

Community-Wide Response

Public health agencies play an important, but not exclusive, role in community-wide responses to emergencies (Figure 5–1). In many response situations, private sector medical care providers deliver the bulk of the triage and treatment services needed when a mass casualty emergency occurs. Although less involved with direct care, public health agencies play key roles in coordinating and overseeing the delivery of services as well as communicating with providers, the media, and the public. Supervision of decontamination and triage often falls to public health authorities. Countermeasures such as antibiotics, antitoxins, and chemical antidotes as well as prophylactic

Figure 5–1 News media ad in early 2002 promoting public health infrastructure as a front line of defense against bioterrorism.

It's Time to Strengthen Our Front Lines in the Fight Against Bioterrorism

We have learned the critical role of public health in recent weeks. Still today, too many of our communities – the front lines in the fight against bioterrorism – don't have all the resources they need to protect our health.

Congress is now looking for the best way to help local and state officials. The solution must include investments in the fundamentals of our public health defenses, including "early warning" and communications networks, more training for professionals, better equipped public health laboratories, and tracking of diseases.

Investments like these would improve our capacity at the local, state and federal levels to respond to both bioterrorist threats and everyday health concerns like asthma, food safety, birth defects, and cancers.

A bi-partisan group of thirty-three U.S. Senators said it best in Senate Resolution 171: *"Now is the time to strengthen our public health system."*

American College of Preventive Medicine	Association of Public Health Laboratories	National Association of Local Boards of Health
American Medical Association	Health-Track	Physicians for Social Responsibility
American Public Health Association	National Association of County	Public Health Foundation
Association of Schools of Public Health	and City Health Officials	Trust for America's Health

HEALTH-TRACK

SUPPORTED BY THE PEW CHARITABLE TRUSTS THROUGH A GRANT TO GEORGETOWN UNIVERSITY • WWW.HEALTH-TRACK.ORG

Source: Health Track Coalition, 2002.

medications and vaccines must be obtained, deployed, and delivered. Public health plays an active role in situations necessitating deployment of Strategic National Stockpile (SNS) pharmaceuticals, supplies, and equipment. In some situations, public health professionals also provide direct medical care. Public health also contributes through mobilization of regional and national assets and resources when local resources are overwhelmed. Some emergency situations, such as the anthrax attacks of 2001, prompted public fear and overreactions resulting in mountains of unknown powdery substances being tested and thousands of individuals unnecessarily initiating prophylactic antibiotic treatments. That situation and others over recent years argue that the worried well can stress response systems even more than those actually affected.

Unique Aspects of Bioterrorism Emergencies

Across the spectrum of possible public health emergency scenarios, bioterrorism threats represent a particularly challenging form of public health emergency. Bioterrorism is the threatened or intentional release of biologic agents (viruses, bacteria, or their toxins) for the purpose of influencing the conduct of government or intimidating or coercing a civilian population to further political or social objectives. These agents (see Tables 5–1 and 5–2) can be released by way of the air (as aerosols), food, water, or insects. Biologic, chemical, radiation, and mass casualty threats that are intentionally inflicted differ from naturally occurring disease and injury threats in a number of important aspects. Central to these differences, bioterrorism is a criminal act requiring its prevention and response

Table 5–1 Biological Agents with Bioterrorism Potential

Category A
- Variola major (smallpox)
- *Bacillus anthracis* (anthrax)
- *Yersinia pestis* (plague)
- *Clostridium botulinum* (botulism)
- *Francisella tularensis* (tularemia)
- Filoviruses (Ebola and Marburg hemorrhagic fevers)
- Arenaviruses (Lassa fever, Argentine hemorrhagic fever)

Category B
- *Coxiella burnetii* (Q fever)
- *Brucella* species (brucellosis)
- *Burkhoderia mallei* (glanders)
- Alphaviruses (Venezuelan encephalomyelitis, eastern and western equine encephalomyelitis)
- Ricin toxin (*Ricinus communis*)

- Epilson toxin (*Clostridiuym perfringerns*)
- *Staphylococcus* enterotoxin B
- Foodborne and waterborne pathogens
- *Salmonella* species
- *Shigella dysenteria*
- *Escehrichia coli*
- *Vibrio cholerae*
- *Cryptosprodium parvum*

Category C
- Nipah virus
- Hantaviruses
- Tickborne hemorrhagic fever viruses
- Tickborne encephalitis viruses
- Yellow fever
- Multidrug-resistant tuberculosis

Source: Centers for Disease Control and Prevention, 2003.

to include criminal justice, military, and intelligence agencies that are not likely to be familiar with naturally occurring disease outbreaks. Law enforcement agencies, including the Federal Bureau of Investigation, have lead responsibility for responding to a bioterrorism attack. In addition, bioterrorism attacks may involve disease agents that occur infrequently in nature and with which neither public health officials nor clinicians have had much experience. It is increasingly possible to genetically engineer chimeras to create, for example, microorganisms that blend the pathogenic qualities of multiple disease agents. Because such organisms do not exist in nature, they would be completely unknown to public health and medical experts. Attacks related to biologic or chemical threats initiated by a bioterrorist would not likely follow known epidemiologic patterns, diminishing the value of using past experience with disease transmission and manifestation to identify the source or cause.

It is likely that bioterrorists would seek to be covert, expending great energy and attention to assure the delayed discovery of the disease to maximize the population's exposure. Intentional outbreaks may develop in multiple locations simultaneously, thereby straining local, state, and federal response efforts. With many emerging and reemerging infectious disease threats (e.g., Ebola Virus, Sudden Acute Respiratory Syndrome, West Nile Virus, hantavirus), it is increasingly difficult to predict the precise nature of the next public health emergency. It could result from a chance mutation of a mi-

croorganism or it could result from the intentional act of terrorists. Multiple threats are possible, necessitating preparedness and response systems that can address a wide variety of unknown and unanticipated hazards. This concept of multiple threats and unknown hazards has led many experts to advocate for a robust public health infrastructure capable of responding to many different forms of emergencies.

Workplace Preparedness

Public health emergencies, including those related to terrorism, have many different visages and many different venues. Yet most of the direct victims of terrorism in the United States in recent years have been people at work, including the victims of the bombing of the federal building in Oklahoma City, those who died in the World Trade Center and the Pentagon on September 11, 2001, and the victims who contracted anthrax transmitted through the mail later in that same year.

Acts of terrorism intend to make people feel powerless and believe that they cannot take steps to prevent such incidents or mitigate their consequences. But experience to-date in battling other workplace safety risks suggests that there are steps that can be taken by employers and employees. The workplace is, in effect, a key line of defense for homeland security. This is recognized formally in the formation and scope of responsibilities for the new federal Department of Homeland Security as well as in the response of the business community after 2001 in taking tangible steps to enhance security.

Table 5-2 Chemical Agents with Bioterrorism Potential

- Albrin
- Adamsite (DM)
- Agent 15
- Ammonia
- Arsenic
- Arsine (SA)
- Benzene
- Bromobenzylcyanide (CA)
- BZ
- Cannabinoids
- Chlorine (CL)
- Chloroacetophenone (CN)
- Chloropicrin (PS)
- CNB (CN in Benzene and Carbon Tetrachloride)
- CNC (CN in Chloroform)
- CNS (CN and Chloropicrin in Chloroform)
- CR
- CS
- Cyanide
- Cyanogen Chloride (CK)
- Cyclohexyl Sarin (GF)
- Diphenylchloroarsine (DA)
- Diphenylcyanoarsine (DC)
- Diphosgene (DP)
- Distilled Mustard (HD)
- Ethyldichloroarsine (ED)
- Ethylene Glycol
- Fentanyls and Other Opioids
- Hydrafluoric Acid
- Hydrogen Chloride
- Hydrogen Cyanide (AC)
- Lewisite (L, L-1, L-2, L-3)

- LSD
- Mercury
- Methyldichloroarsine (MD)
- Mustard Gas (H) (Sulfur Mustard)
- Mustard/Lewisite (HL)
- Mustard/T
- Nitrogen Mustard (HN-1, HN-2, HN-3)
- Nitrogen Oxide (NO)
- Paraquat
- Perflurorisobutylene (PHIB)
- Phenodichloroarsine (PD)
- Phenothiazines
- Phosgene (CG)
- Phosgene Oxime (CX)
- Phosphine
- Potassium Cyanide (KCN)
- Red Phosphorous (RP)
- Ricin
- Sarin (GB)
- Sesqui Mustard
- Sodium Azide
- Sodium Cyanide (NaCN)
- Soman (GD)
- Strychnine
- Sulfur Trioxide-Chlorosulfonic Acid (FS)
- Tabun (GA)
- Teflon and Perflurorisobutylene (PHIB)
- Thallium
- Titanium Tetrachloride (FM)
- VX
- White Phosphorus
- Zinc Oxide (HC)

Source: Centers for Disease Control and Prevention, 2003.

NATIONAL PUBLIC HEALTH PREPAREDNESS AND RESPONSE COORDINATION

The events of late 2001 resulted in the creation of a new federal Department of Homeland Security (DHS) with extensive authority and powers related to domestic terrorism and security. In accord with the Homeland Security Act of 2002, several important public health functions were transferred into the new DHS in 2003, including the SNS of emergency pharmaceutical supplies and medical equipment. This new federal agency immediately became part of the American everyday experience through activities such as the national homeland security alert system, summarized in Table 5-3, with its color-coded levels of perceived threat.

The establishment of a new federal agency, however, did not substantially alter the configuration of public health responsibilities within the system of operational federalism described in Chapter 4. Federal agencies are significant contributors, but public health remains largely a state responsibility, with the bulk of public health activity taking place at the local level. For public health emergencies, such as bioterrorism events or threats, preparedness and coordinated response across all levels of government are critical. Nonetheless, there are significant issues related to intergovernmental relationships, resource deployment, and financing that make public health emergencies especially difficult challenges for the public health system. The following sections examine key aspects of the structure, operations, and problems in public health emergency preparedness and response at the national, state, and local levels.

Table 5–3 Homeland Security Advisory System

1. *Low Condition (Green)*

   This condition is declared when there is a low risk of terrorist attacks. Federal departments and agencies should consider the following general measures in addition to agency-specific protective measures they develop and implement.
   - Refining and exercising as appropriate preplanned protective measures
   - Ensuring personnel receive proper training on the Homeland Security Advisory System and specific preplanned department or agency protective measures
   - Institutionalizing a process to assure that all facilities and regulated sectors are regularly assessed for vulnerabilities to terrorist attacks and that all reasonable measures are taken to mitigate these vulnerabilities

2. *Guarded Condition (Blue)*

   This condition is declared when there is a general risk of terrorist attacks. In addition to the protective measures taken in the previous threat condition, federal departments and agencies should consider the following general measures in addition to the agency-specific protective measures that they will develop and implement.
   - Checking communications with designated emergency response or command locations
   - Reviewing and updating emergency response procedures
   - Providing the public with any information that would strengthen its ability to act appropriately

3. *Elevated Condition (Yellow)*

   An elevated condition is declared when there is a significant risk of terrorist attacks. In addition to the protective measures taken in the previous threat condition, federal departments and agencies should consider the following general measures in addition to the agency-specific protective measures that they will develop and implement.
   - Increasing surveillance of critical locations
   - Coordinating emergency plans as appropriate with nearby jurisdictions
   - Assessing whether the precise characteristics of the threat require the further refinement of preplanned protective measures
   - Implementing, as appropriate, contingency and emergency response plans

4. *High Condition (Orange)*

   A high condition is declared when there is a high risk of terrorist attacks. In addition to the protective measures taken in the previous threat condition, federal departments and agencies should consider the following general measures in addition to the agency-specific protective measures that they will develop and implement.
   - Coordinating necessary security efforts with federal, state, and local law enforcement agencies or any National Guard or other appropriate armed forces organizations
   - Taking additional precautions at public events and possibly considering alternative venues or even cancellation
   - Preparing to execute contingency procedures, such as moving to an alternate site or dispersing their workforce
   - Restricting threatened facility access to essential personnel only

5. *Severe Condition (Red)*

   A severe condition reflects a severe risk of terrorist attacks. Under most circumstances, the protective measures for a severe condition are not intended to be sustained for substantial periods of time. In addition to the protective measures taken in the previous threat condition, federal departments and agencies should consider the following general measures in addition to the agency-specific protective measures that they will develop and implement.
   - Increasing or redirecting personnel to address critical emergency needs
   - Assigning emergency response personnel and prepositioning and mobilizing specially trained teams or resources
   - Monitoring, redirecting, or constraining transportation systems
   - Closing public and government facilities

Source: U.S. Department of Homeland Security, 2003.

Federal Agencies and Assets

More than 20 separate federal departments and agencies have roles in preparing for or responding to public health emergencies, including bioterrorist attacks. Within this constellation of agencies, the Department of Health and Human Services (DHHS) and DHS play the most important public health roles.

Prior to 2003, DHHS was the primary federal agency responsible for the medical and public health response to emergencies (including major disasters and terrorist events). Beginning in 2003, DHHS now shares center stage with the new DHS. DHHS discharges its responsibilities through several operating agencies, including the following:

- Centers for Disease Control and Prevention (CDC): CDC works with state public health agencies to detect, investigate, and prevent the spread of disease in communities. CDC provides support to state public health agencies in a variety of ways, including financial assistance, training programs, technical assistance and expert consultation, sophisticated laboratory services, research activities, and standards development. The Office of Terrorism Preparedness and Emergency Response coordinates efforts across the various CDC centers, institutes, and offices.
- Health Resources and Services Administration (HRSA): HRSA administers a state grant program to facilitate regional hospital preparedness planning and to upgrade the capacity of hospitals and other health care facilities to respond to public health emergencies. HRSA is also generally responsible for health care workforce development, including grant programs for curriculum development and continuing education for health professionals on bioterrorism preparedness and response.
- Food and Drug Administration (FDA): FDA has responsibilities both for ensuring the safety of the food supply and for assuring the safety and efficacy of pharmaceuticals, biologics, and medical devices. FDA fulfills its food safety responsibilities in partnership with the Department of Agriculture, which is responsible for the safety of meat, poultry, and processed egg products.
- National Institutes of Health (NIH): NIH conducts and supports biomedical research, including research targeted at the development of rapid diagnostics and new and more effective vaccines and antimicrobial therapies.
- Office of Public Health Emergency Preparedness (OPHEP): OPHEP sets policy direction and coordinates public health emergency preparedness and response activities across the various DHHS agencies.

In March 2003, 23 federal agencies, programs, and offices were fashioned into the new federal DHS. The new agency sought to bring a coordinated approach to national security from emergencies and disasters, both natural and man-made. DHS actively promotes an "all-hazards" approach to disasters and homeland security issues. The Federal Emergency Management Agency (FEMA), formerly an independent agency, became one of the major branches of the new DHS responsible for emergency preparedness and response, tasked with responding to, planning for, recovering from, and mitigating against disasters under authority provided by the Stafford Act (Table 5–4).

Within DHS, the Emergency Preparedness and Response Directorate coordinates emergency medical response in the event of a public health emergency, including the National Disaster Medical System and the Metropolitan Medical Response Systems (these are described later in this chapter). Other major directorates (divisions) of the new DHS include Border and Transportation Security, Science and Technology, Information Analysis and Infrastructure Protection, and Management.

A variety of other federal agencies have organizational responsibilities related to bioterrorism and public health emergency preparedness. The Environmental Protection Agency (EPA) responds to emergencies involving chemicals and other

---

Table 5–4 Robert T. Stafford Disaster Relief and Emergency Assistance Act (P.L. 93–288, as amended)

The Congress hereby finds and declares that (1) because disasters often cause loss of life, human suffering, loss of income, and property loss and damage; and (2) because disasters often disrupt the normal functioning of governments and communities, and adversely affect individuals and families with great severity; special measures, designed to assist the efforts of the affected States in expediting the rendering of aid, assistance, and emergency services, and the reconstruction and rehabilitation of devastated areas, are necessary.

It is the intent of Congress, by this Act, to provide an orderly and continuing means of assistance by the Federal Government to State and local governments in carrying out their responsibilities to alleviate the suffering and damage which result from such disasters by—

(1) revising and broadening the scope of existing disaster relief programs;

(2) encouraging the development of comprehensive disaster preparedness and assistance plans, programs, capabilities, and organizations by the States and by local government;

(3) achieving greater coordination and responsiveness of disaster preparedness and relief programs;

(4) encouraging individuals, States, and local governments to protect themselves by obtaining insurance coverage to supplement or replace governmental assistance;

(5) encouraging hazard mitigation measures to reduce losses from disasters, including development of land use and construction regulations; and

(6) providing Federal assistance programs for both public and private losses sustained in disasters.

hazardous substances. The Department of Defense indirectly supports public health preparedness through various research efforts on biologic and chemical weapons, intelligence gathering related to terrorism threats, and civil support functions in the event of an emergency that results in severe social unrest. The Department of Justice has lead responsibility for assessing and investigating terrorist threats, including those related to bioterrorism, and provides funds and assistance to emergency responders (police, fire, ambulance, and rescue personnel) at state and local levels. The Department of Veterans Affairs purchases drugs and other therapeutics for the SNS and operates one of the nation's largest health care systems, which could provide critical surge capacity in the event of a mass casualty event. Several other federal agencies, including the Departments of Transportation, Commerce, and Energy, also have potential roles to play in preparing for and responding to a public health emergency.

National Incident Management System

Prior to the establishment of the new DHS, the management of large-scale health events was complicated by the involvement of so many different federal agencies. States have established a similar web of agencies to manage disasters and other emergencies, with each developing its own form of an incident management system. In order to assure greater consistency across states and for interfaces between the federal government and states, a National Incident Management System (NIMS) was prescribed by a presidential directive in 2003 to cover all incidents (natural and unnatural) for which the federal government deploys emergency response assets. The Secretary of Homeland Security is responsible for the development and implementation of NIMS. Its success depends in large part on the establishment of consistent approaches within the states as to roles and responsibilities for both public health agencies and the hospital community (including their supporting health care systems) in managing emergencies at the state and regional levels and developing and deploying incident management plans at substate levels.

Bioterrorism and other public health incidents fall within the scope of NIMS. To this end, DHHS has the initial lead responsibility for the federal government and deploys assets as needed within the areas of its statutory responsibility (such as the Public Health Service Act and the Federal Food, Drug, and Cosmetic Act) while keeping the Secretary of Homeland Security apprised regarding the course of the incident and nature of the response operations.

DHS assumes responsibility for coordinating federal response operations, including those involving public health components, under certain conditions. DHS coordinates the federal government's resources utilized in response to or recovery from terrorist attacks, major disasters, or other emergencies if and when any of the following four conditions applies[3]:

- A federal department or agency acting under its own authority has requested the assistance
- The resources of state and local authorities are overwhelmed and federal assistance has been formally requested by state and local authorities
- More than one federal department or agency has become substantially involved in responding to the incident
- DHS has been directed to assume responsibility for managing the domestic incident by the President

For states and local governments to gain full benefit from the emergency response assets of the federal government, states must develop incident management systems that are interoperable with NIMS. Beginning in 2004, adherence to and compatibility with NIMS became a condition of all grants and other awards from federal agencies for any aspect of state or local emergency preparedness and response.

Federal Emergency Medical Assets

Several national emergency response assets are available to state and local governments from the new DHS. These include the National Disaster Medical System (NDMS), the Metropolitan Medical Response System (MMRS), and the SNS.

The NDMS now operates within the Emergency Preparedness and Response Directorate of DHS after being transferred from the Office of the Secretary of DHHS. NDMS brings together medical services from DHHS, DHS, Defense, and Veterans Affairs to augment local emergency medical services during a disaster or other large-scale emergency. The NDMS has several operational components, including Disaster Medical Assistance Teams (DMATs), Disaster Mortuary Teams (DMORTs), Federal Coordinating Centers, and Management Support Units.

DMATs are self-sustaining squads of licensed, actively practicing, volunteer professional and paraprofessional medical personnel who provide emergency medical care at the site of a disaster or other emergency. DMAT teams often triage, stabilize, and prepare patients for evacuation in mass casualty situations. They are sent into these situations to supplement, rather than supplant or replace, local capacity. Once activated, these professionals are federalized, allowing them to practice with their current professional licenses in any jurisdiction. DMORTs include mortuary, dental, and forensic specialists who serve to augment the services of local coroners and medical examiners. Portable temporary mortuaries for mass casualty situations are provided when needed. Management support units provide command, coordination, and communication capabilities for DMATs and DMORTs and other federal assets. Federal Coordinating Centers recruit hospitals to participate in the NDMS and recruit health workers for the DMATs and DMORTs.

The MMRS, involving more than 100 metropolitan communities, integrates existing emergency response systems at the local level, including emergency management, medical and mental health providers, public health agencies, law enforcement, fire departments, emergency medical services, and the National Guard. The MMRS seeks to develop a unified regional response to mass casualty events. MMRS was transferred from DHHS when the new DHS was established in 2003.

The SNS (formerly National Pharmaceutical Stockpile) ensures the availability and rapid deployment of life-saving pharmaceuticals, antidotes, other medical supplies, and equipment necessary to counter the effects of nerve agents, biologic pathogens, and chemical agents. The SNS stands ready for immediate deployment to any U.S. location in the event of a terrorist attack using a biologic toxin or chemical agent directed against a civilian population. In the event of possible bioterrorist attack, a 12-hour push package containing 50 tons of stockpile materials can be immediately dispatched to predetermined Receipt, Store, and Storage (RSS) sites identified in state bioterrorism response plans. There are twelve 12-hour push packages centrally located around the United States for immediate deployment. Detailed deployment activities for SNS materials are prescribed in state and local emergency response plans.

Federal Funding for Public Health Infrastructure

Although multiple agencies provide federal funding for emergency preparedness, federal support for the public health infrastructure at the state and local levels is provided largely from grants and cooperative agreements with CDC. In 1999, for the first time, CDC awarded more than $40 million for bioterrorism preparedness to states and cities for enhanced laboratory and electronic communication capacity and another $32 million to establish a national pharmaceutical stockpile to ensure availability of vaccines, prophylactic medicines, chemical antidotes, medical supplies, and equipment needed to support a medical response to a biologic or chemical terrorist incident. At the time, these appeared to be large sums. In the wake of September 11, 2001, and the anthrax attacks the following month, increased concerns regarding homeland security led to a $2.1 billion FY 2002 appropriation for CDC's antiterrorism activities, over a 20-fold increase from FY 1999 levels. The FY 2002 supplemental appropriations provided $917 million for grants to states and localities to upgrade state and local capacity. Similar levels of funding were provided in 2003. The

state and local activities impacted by this funding are described in subsequent sections of this chapter.

STATE AND LOCAL PREPAREDNESS COORDINATION

State Agencies and Assets

Similar to the federal pattern, states rely on a variety of agencies to deliver public health emergency services. Also similar to the federal model, these functions tend to be concentrated within a limited number of agencies at the state level, with the state health department and state emergency management agency playing the most significant roles. As described in Chapter 4, most state health departments are freestanding agencies (not part of a larger human services agency), and most have responsibility for emergency medical service systems within the state. However, most states have an environmental health agency that is separate from the state health agency. Although these states may have a small environmental health section within the health agency, the environmental health agency is charged with monitoring environmental contaminants and remediation of hazardous conditions. Nearly all states have a separate emergency management agency (patterned after FEMA), although some states have established their own Departments of Homeland Security. In responding to a public health emergency, the state health agency works collaboratively with the state emergency management agency as well as with the state environmental protection, law enforcement, public safety, and transportation agencies and, possibly, the National Guard.

States derive their powers and authority to act in public health emergencies from their public health laws as described in Chapter 4. There are concerns that existing public health laws may be inadequate in some states because they are obsolete and fragmented. A Model Public Health Emergency Powers Act has been used to assist states in examining and enhancing their legal framework for public health emergencies. The model act addresses key issues related to preparedness, surveillance, protection of persons, management of property, and public information and communications.[4]

Considerable differences exist among states in the breadth and depth of services provided within their jurisdictions and the degree to which public health service delivery responsibilities are delegated to local governments. In general, however, state governments are ultimately responsible for assuring adequate response to a public health emergency and tend to play certain key roles in preparedness and response, regardless of how decentralized a particular public health system might be. Except in the largest metropolitan local public health departments, local public health officials rely on state personnel and capacity for a number of key functions, including advanced laboratory capacity, epidemiologic expertise, and serving as a conduit for federal assistance.

Incident Command Systems

In order to manage resources effectively and facilitate decision making during emergencies, incident command systems (ICS) are in wide use by police, fire, and emergency management agencies. Initially adopted for the fire service, ICS eliminates many common problems related to communication, terminology, organizational structure, span of control, and other difference across different disciplines and agencies in response to a critical incident. Critical incidents include any natural or man-made event, civil disturbance, or any other occurrence of unusual or severe nature that threatens to cause or actually causes the loss of life or injury to citizens and/or severe damage to property.

In managing critical incidents, clear goals and objectives are established and communicated to responders, response plans are utilized, communications are effective, and resources are utilized in a timely and effective manner. ICS should not be considered an additional set of procedures; rather the system must become part of routine operations, with personnel fully trained in its use and standard operating procedures reflective of the capabilities actually available.

One important key to effective ICS is the ability to size up the incident scene and make the initial call for resources. This allows responders to get control of the incident rather than playing catch-up for the rest of the incident. Appropriate initial size-up prevents unnecessary injury or loss of life, property or environmental damage, and negative perceptions on the responding agencies.

Key components of ICS include

- Common terminology—Major organizational functions and units are named; in multiple incidents, each incident is named. Common names are used for personnel, equipment, and facilities. Clear terms are used in radio transmissions (e.g., codes, such as "10" codes, are not used).
- Modular organization—ICS develops "top down" from the first unit involved based on the specific incident's management needs. Each ICS is staffed with a designated incident commander (responsible for safety, liaison, and information) with other functions (operations, planning, logistics, finance/administration) staffed as needed.
- Integrated communications—ICS uses a common communications plan and redundant two-way communications.

- A unified command structure—This is necessary when the incident is within a single jurisdiction with multiple agencies involved, or the incident is multijurisdictional, or individuals representing different agencies or jurisdictions share common responsibilities. All agencies involved contribute to the unified command process by determining overall goals and objectives, planning jointly for tactical activities, conducting integrated tactical operations, and maximizing the use of assigned resources.
- Consolidated action plans—Written action plans are necessary when the incident is complex and/or when several agencies and/or jurisdictions are involved. Action plans include specific goals, objectives, and support activities.
- A manageable span of control—The number of subordinates one supervisor can manage effectively should be between three and seven, with five being optimal.
- Designated incident facilities—These include the command post from which all incident operations, direction, control, coordination, and resource management are directed. Command posts can be fixed or mobile but need adequate communications capabilities.
- Comprehensive resource management—This maximizes resource use, consolidates control, reduces communications load, provides accountability, and reduces freelancing.

The emergency management team functions at the emergency operations center (EOC), managing strategic decisions through the incident command structure. Ideally, the team should be isolated from the confusion, media, and weather during the incident. EOC participants must have adequate authority and decision-making capability. EOC decisions could include issuing curfews, circumventing normal bidding processes, emergency appointments, permanent or temporary relocation, emergency demolition of unsafe properties, or implementation of prophylaxis to populations. The EOC is supported operationally by incident command posts in the field, which are responsible for tactical decisions as well as oversight and command of responders at the scene.

Effective emergency operations plans and standard operating procedures simplify decision making during incidents. Training makes implementation of decisions easier for subordinates. When the level of preparation and practice exercises is inadequate, emergency operations plans can become overwhelmed by common incidents and unable to deal with those that are not fully anticipated. In such circumstances, decision making becomes complex and challenging. A comprehensively planned and frequently exercised organizational system is necessary to overcome these pitfalls.

As ICS has become increasingly accepted as an effective framework for responding to incidents, its use has extended to other settings. For example, there has been much progress in development and deployment of hospital emergency incident command systems and table-top exercises for hospitals. Several states have expanded on the ICS concept to develop standardized emergency management systems that formally incorporate ICS, mutual aid agreements, and multijurisdictional and interagency cooperation at the substate level, resulting in coordinated and unified decisions throughout the state.

Local Agencies and Assets

The front line of response to public health emergencies is at the local level, where local public health agencies (LPHAs) work collaboratively with other "first responders," such as fire and rescue personnel, emergency medical service providers, law enforcement officers, hazardous materials teams, physicians, and hospitals in preparing for and managing the consequences of health-related emergencies. Although the relationships between state and local public health agencies vary greatly from state to state, and even from local jurisdiction to local jurisdiction within the same state, local government has significant responsibilities for dealing with emergencies in virtually all states. First responders play key roles in

- Recognizing public health emergencies, including those that result from terrorist attacks
- Identifying unique personal safety implications associated with the emergency situation
- Identifying security issues that are unique to the event or to the emergency medical system response
- Understanding basic principles of patient care based upon the type of emergency event encountered

Focusing on the services most directly related to emergency preparedness and response, the vast majority of LPHAs carry out activities related to epidemiology and surveillance, communicable disease control, food safety, and restaurant inspections.[5] LPHAs are somewhat less likely to be directly involved in emergency medical response (61%), and less than one half of LPHAs operate laboratory services (45%), air quality (44%), animal control (40%), or water inspections (44%).[5]

In those cases in which the LPHA is not responsible for these services, they are typically delivered by another local government agency (e.g., a fire department or environmental services agency), a private agency (hospital or ambulance service), or the state. Even when services are offered by an LPHA, they may be quite limited in terms of scope or hours of availability. For example, although nearly one half of LPHAs report providing laboratory services, these services may be quite limited in nature (e.g., to support TB and STD testing). Many LPHAs that report having laboratory services are likely to rely on state public health labs for more specialized diagnostic needs.

The state of readiness among LHPAs has increased since 2001, when only about one fourth of LHPAs had completed a comprehensive emergency response plan with another one fourth indicating their plans were at least 80% complete. LPHAs have tailored the national threat advisory guidelines for public health emergencies. In general, LPHA threat advisory guidelines describe a spectrum of activities that range from planning through implementation. The activities that are undertaken at each threat level are summarized in Table 5–5 and roughly equate to the preparedness and response concepts listed below:

- Low threat (green)—creating, developing, identifying
- General threat (blue)—reviewing, updating, distributing
- Significant threat (yellow)—evaluating, testing, verifying
- High threat (orange)—preparing to implement and implementing partially
- Severe threat (red)—fully implementing

Deployment of LPHA staff to assist in emergencies is limited by the size and qualification of the agency's workforce. More than one half of all LPHAs have 19 or fewer staff members.[5] Larger agencies generally have much higher staffing levels and a more comprehensive range of expertise, as was described in Chapter 4.

The configuration of LHPAs within a state or in a multistate metropolitan area also varies across the country. Several states organize local public health activities at a regional or district level. Other states have virtually hundreds of LHPAs that serve towns or townships, some in counties or districts served by a larger LHPA. Some communities have no LPHA at all. Organizing preparedness and response efforts in these different circumstances present special problems in terms of multijurisdictional response, surge capacity, backup, and mutual aid agreements. Several capacity assessment and enhancement tools are available from NACCHO and CDC to assist local assessment of readiness.[6–8]

Medical Reserve Corps are locally based volunteer response teams that can be deployed in emergency situations. These multidisciplinary teams often have ongoing relationships with local public health agencies and other community medical care providers that may include volunteer work on health promotion and screening projects or assistance with mosquito control activities in communities where West Nile Virus presents a risk. During emergencies, Medical Reserve Corps teams play predetermined roles such as providing local

Table 5–5 Homeland Security Advisory System Guidelines for Local Public Health Agencies

Key Activities for Each Threat Condition

Emergency Planning, Training, Staffing	Green (Low) • Ensure personnel receive proper training on Homeland Security Advisory and agency protective measures/disaster plans • Ensure employee emergency notification system is current • Develop and train staff on staffing modification plans including 24/7 duty assignments • Train staff on local and state disaster plans • Develop and review roles and responsibilities in an emergency situation for each employee in the agency (all-hazards plan, which includes bioterrorism) Blue (Guarded) • Review and update disaster plans specific to the agency (local health department medication distribution plan, smallpox pre- and post-event plans) • Provide training to key personnel on handling inquiries from the media Yellow (Elevated) • Coordinate emergency plans with nearby jurisdictions and review mutual aid agreements • Conduct employee emergency notification system drill • Be aware of large-scale community events (e.g., sports, concerts) and include these in emergency planning • Review technical information on chemical and biologic agents with all staff Orange (High) • Prepare to staff the agency's emergency operations center (EOC) or provide staff at the city/county EOC • Activate the employee emergency notification system and place staff on full alert • Review medication dispensing plans and mass vaccination plans with all staff Red (Severe) • Staff the agency's EOC or provide staff at the city/county EOC • Activate the agency's disaster preparedness plan • Activate the employee emergency notification system and secure as many additional staff as necessary to implement the agency's disaster preparedness plan • Prepare to implement the medication dispensing and mass vaccination plans • Coordinate preparedness and response activities with all public health partners and local jurisdictions (hospitals, physicians, local law enforcement, neighboring local health departments, emergency management agencies, and state health department) • Conduct a comprehensive disaster plan review with all staff to ensure an effective response in the event of a terrorist attack
Communications	Green (Low) • Ensure all emergency communication systems are in operational condition (Health Alert Network, e-mail, fax, and pagers) • Ensure staff have the technical information on chemical and biologic agents necessary to respond to inquiries from the public or the media (fact sheets) • Review procedure/protocol for disseminating information to the community and media during a public health emergency Blue (Guarded) • Alert all agency staff that the threat condition has been raised to Guarded (Blue) • Assign a staff person to routinely monitor for faxes, e-mails, and correspondence from the state health agency • Obtain technical information from the state health agency and the Centers for Disease Control and Prevention on biologic and chemical weapons of mass destruction for possible dissemination to health care providers and the public Yellow (Elevated) • Alert all agency staff that the threat condition has been raised to Elevated (Yellow) • Review media protocols with key personnel • Brief key personnel at least weekly on threat status, changes in security, and potential action plans Orange (High) • Alert all agency staff that the threat condition has been raised to High (Orange)

(continued)

Table 5–5 Homeland Security Advisory System Guidelines for Local Public Health Agencies (*continued*)

	• Ensure that all members of the jurisdiction-wide bioterrorism committee are aware that the threat condition has been raised to High (Orange) • Advise staff of shift modifications if the situation escalates • Test all emergency communication systems Red (Severe) • Alert all agency staff that the threat condition has been raised to Severe (Red) • Ensure that all members of the jurisdiction-wide bioterrorism committee are aware that the threat condition has been raised to Severe (Red) • Issue periodic news releases with factual information on chemical and biologic agents to reduce the potential for public panic • Brief key personnel daily on threat status, changes in security, and potential action plans • Check all emergency communications equipment on a daily basis
Administration	Green (Low) • Maintain routine operations without security stipulations • Continue to include employee safety and common sense practices in daily routines • Report suspicious circumstances and/or individuals to law enforcement agencies • Ensure all staff have issued current security credentials (ID badges) • Build networking relationships with other agencies, inside and outside the health professions Blue (Guarded) • Increase liaison with local and state agencies to monitor the threat • Prohibit casual access by unauthorized personnel • Assess mail handling procedures Yellow (Elevated) • Ensure security of facility operations • Check all essential equipment for operational readiness • Check inventories of critical supplies and reorder if necessary Orange (High) • Ensure security of the agency's critical infrastructure • Have designated staff continuously monitor for emergency communications from state health agency • Have designated staff continuously monitor radio and TV stations for a possible change in threat condition Red (Severe) • Initiate or augment security staffing at department facilities • Control building access and implement positive identification of all persons, include inspection of all incoming packages, brief cases, and deliveries • Maintain continuous monitoring for emergency communications from state health agency, as well as continuous monitoring of radio and TV stations for breaking news concerning terrorist attacks within state or elsewhere in the United States
Public Health Surveillance	Green (Low) • Review agency procedures for handling reportable infectious diseases in the state Blue (Guarded) • Ensure information concerning reportable infectious diseases is coming into the agency from the health care providers within the jurisdiction Yellow (Elevated) • Request that hospitals (infectious control nurses and emergency departments), local laboratories, outpatient clinics, managed care organizations, and physicians report significant increases or clusters of illness of unknown etiology and review mandatory reporting procedures Orange (High) • Contact all hospitals (infectious control nurses and emergency departments), local laboratories, outpatient clinics, managed care organizations, and physicians and emphasize the importance of timely reporting of significant increases or clusters of illness of unknown etiology and review mandatory reporting procedures

Source: Illinois Department of Public Health, 2003.

surge capacity for triage and medical care or assisting with deployment of SNS materials. It is expected that several hundred communities will participate in the Medical Reserve Corps program, either through start-up funding from the HRSA or through local resources.

Private Health-Care Providers and Other Partners

In nearly all communities, government agencies play a central role in preparing for and responding to public health emergencies. Often overlooked, however, is the critical contribution made by private sector health care providers, pharmaceutical manufacturers, agricultural producers, the food industry, and other private sector interests. An important example is the role played by alert health professionals who are trained to recognize potential emergency situations and report these suspicions to public health officials. Clinicians in Florida played a major role in first identifying and then linking anthrax cases with bioterrorism in 2001. Hospital emergency rooms and physicians' offices are where most individuals who have contracted an infectious disease or are exposed to dangerous chemicals encounter their community's emergency response system. That encounter should trigger an appropriate response if the condition is one that represents a threat to others. Every state has incorporated requirements in state statute that call for physicians, laboratories, and other health providers to notify public health officials when specific notifiable diseases or conditions are encountered. Some states include a general provision that physicians should report "unusual" infectious diseases. Despite these laws and regulations, compliance with disease reporting is well documented to be low among physicians for a variety of reasons. The requirements and the reporting procedures may not be understood by some physicians. Others believe reporting is not worth the time and effort. Reporting from laboratories is more complete, but concerns exist as to whether laboratories serving multiple jurisdictions are fully aware of differences in requirements among the jurisdictions served.

In addition to playing an important role in identifying potential public health emergencies, health care providers play a critical role in responding to the medical consequences of those emergencies, especially in mass casualty situations. For the relatively rare disease threats associated with bioterrorism, health care providers often have only limited experience dealing with these conditions and look to public health authority for clinical guidance. Through the development of community-wide emergency response plans, public health agencies, private sector delivery systems, hospitals, physicians, pharmacies, nursing homes, and others are mobilized in the event of an emergency to provide needed treatment to those affected by disease and to provide prophylactic care to those at risk for exposure to disease. State and federal laws that confer tax-exempt status on hospitals typically require those institutions to provide significant community benefit, including the provision of emergency medical services and participation in regional emergency medical service planning. Funds for hospital preparedness, including staff training and preparedness planning, are provided by HRSA and channeled through state health departments.

Other private sector interests also contribute to public health emergency preparedness. Although NIH makes significant investments in the development of new vaccines and antimicrobial agents, pharmaceutical manufacturers represent the primary source of funding for research and development. Efforts to encourage industry interest in the development of vaccines and other countermeasures include incentives such as liability protections, antitrust waivers, patent extensions, and long-term contracts. Similarly, activities to improve the safety and security of the food supply will rely on the agricultural and food production industries to make necessary upgrades to their processes and to seek innovative ways to minimize disease threats.

Public Perceptions

The flurry of activity to improve public health emergency preparedness and response capabilities is understandable. The public is highly concerned over the possibility of terrorist attacks of all types.[9] Fears of possible anthrax or smallpox attacks are nearly as high as concerns of conventional explosives, airline hijacking or bombings, and attacks using radioactive, toxic, or hazardous materials as weapons. Among these potential terrorist weapons, concern is growing that smallpox will be used, related in part to the attention placed on smallpox at the national level with the initiation of smallpox preparedness programs that include vaccinations for key medical and first responder personnel. Although the public believes that the country is better prepared for a biologic or chemical attack than it was prior to 2002, the public perceives that the current level of preparedness is not high enough and more needs to be done. The public is also concerned that the emphasis on bioterrorism will reduce efforts on other public health problems and issues that are important to the public. The public rates bioterrorism preparedness and response high but no higher than health alerts, immunizations, testing and monitoring for diseases, education, and responses to natural epidemics and chronic diseases.[9]

STATE AND LOCAL BIOTERRORISM PREPAREDNESS GRANTS

With the public health infrastructure increasingly viewed as a front-line defense against terrorism and homeland security priority, federal funding for public health purposes increased dramatically beginning in 2002. To put this increase into perspective, total governmental spending in 2000 for population-based public health services was $17.4 billion, with the federal government accounting for 29% of that total, or about $5 billion.[10] The federal share of total governmental public health spending has been under 30% since the mid-1980s, after having been as high as 72% in 1970.

Beginning in 2002, federal funding increased by more than $2 billion, with about one half of that amount directed to state and local governments for public health infrastructure improvements. Similar levels were funded through 2006 and are expected for at least the next few years. The infusion of this magnitude of resources creates the opportunity to address serious and longstanding gaps in public health protection and foster greater consistency and enhanced quality throughout the national network of governmental public health agencies at the federal, state, and local levels.

Public health infrastructure funding, approximately $1 billion annually, is channeled to the states and several large cities (including New York, Chicago, Los Angeles, and Washington, DC) through CDC. Each state receives a minimum award of $5 million plus an additional amount based on a population formula.

State Proposals and Workplans

Activities supported by these funds must be consistent with federal guidance. For funding from CDC for public health preparedness, grantees must undertake activities that increase capacity in state and local public health agencies in order to achieve the preparedness goals identified in Table 5–6.

Key elements of capacity include:

- Preparedness planning and readiness assessment— These activities establish strategic leadership, direction, assessment, and coordination of activities (including SNS response) to ensure statewide readiness, interagency collaboration, local and regional preparedness (both intrastate and interstate) for bioterrorism, other outbreaks of infectious disease, and other public health threats and emergencies.
- Surveillance and epidemiology capacity—Surveillance and epidemiologic capacities enable state and local health departments to enhance, design, and develop systems for rapid detection of unusual outbreaks of illness that may be the result of bioterrorism, other outbreaks of infectious disease, and other public health threats and emergencies. These activities assist state and local health departments in establishing expanded epidemiologic capacity to investigate and mitigate such outbreaks of ill-

ness as part of a National Electronic Disease Surveillance System (NEDSS). NEDSS is an initiative that promotes the use of data and information system standards to advance the development of efficient, integrated, and interoperable surveillance systems at federal, state, and local levels. NEDSS-based systems can be used by states for the surveillance and analysis of notifiable diseases, providing a platform upon which modules can be built to meet state and program area data needs as well as providing a secure, accurate, and efficient way for collecting and processing data.

- Laboratory capacity for biologic agents—These activities ensure that core diagnostic capabilities for bioterrorist agents are available at all state and major city/county public health laboratories in order to conduct rapid and accurate diagnostic and reference testing for select biologic agents likely to be used in a terrorist attack. Given the myriad forms that terrorism might take, emergency preparedness requires not only a variety of different types of analytical laboratories, but also well defined operational relationships among them, especially with respect to routing of samples and sharing of test results. The national Laboratory Referral Network (LRN) provides this connectivity.
- Laboratory capacity for chemical agents—These activities ensure that all state public health laboratories have the capacity to measure chemical threat agents in human specimens (e.g., blood, urine) or to appropriately collect and ship specimens to qualified LRN partner laboratories for analysis and further the establishment of a network of public laboratories for analysis of chemical threat agents.
- Health alert network/communications and information technology—Activities for this focus area enable state and local public health agencies to establish and maintain a network that supports exchange of key information and training over the Internet by linking public health and private partners on a 24/7 basis, provides for rapid dissemination of public health advisories to the news media and the public at large, ensures secure electronic data exchange between public health partners' computer systems, and ensures protection of data, information, and systems, with adequate backup, organization, and surge capacity to respond to bioterrorism and other public health threats and emergencies.
- Health risk communication and health information dissemination—Activities for this focus area ensure that state and local public health organizations develop an effective risk communications capacity that provides for

Table 5–6 CDC 2005–2006 Preparedness Goals

Goal 1	Increase the use and development of interventions known to prevent human illness from chemical, biological, radiological agents, and naturally occurring health threats.
Goal 2	Decrease the time needed to classify health events as terrorism or naturally occurring in partnership with other agencies.
Goal 3	Decrease the time needed to detect and report chemical, biological, radiological agents in tissue, food, or environmental samples that cause threats to the public's health.
Goal 4	Improve the timeliness and accuracy of information regarding threats to the public's health.
Goal 5	Decrease the time to identify causes, risk factors, and appropriate interventions for those affected by threats to the public's health.
Goal 6	Decrease the time needed to provide countermeasures and health guidance to those affected by threats to the public's health.
Goal 7	Decrease the time needed to restore health services and environmental safety to pre-event levels.
Goal 8	Improve the long-term follow-up provided to those affected by threats to the public's health.
Goal 9	Decrease the time needed to implement recommendations from after-action repots following threats to the public's health.

Source: Centers for Disease Control and Prevention, 2005.

timely information dissemination to citizens during a bioterrorist attack, bioterrorism, outbreak of infectious disease, or other public health threat and emergency. This includes training for key individuals in communications skills, the identification of key spokespersons (particularly experts in infectious diseases), the development of printed materials, timely reporting of critical information, and effective interaction with the media.

- Education and training—Activities for this focus area ensure that state and local health agencies have the capacity to assess the training needs of key public health professionals, infectious disease specialists, emergency department personnel, and other health care (including mental health) providers in preparedness for and response to bioterrorism, other outbreaks of infectious disease, and other public health threats and emergencies, and ensure effective provision of needed education and training to key target audiences through multiple channels, including schools of public health, schools of medicine, other academic institutions, health care professionals, CDC, HRSA, and other sources. Emergency preparedness competencies (Table 5–7) for all public health workers serve as the focal point for these assessment, enhancement, and recognition efforts. A more extensive panel of bioterrorism and emergency readiness competencies for various categories of public health workers is also in wide use.[11]

- Hospital preparedness—Although not a focus area funded by CDC, hospital preparedness is the primary category of activity supported by HRSA funding to states and large cities. Activities that are supported include development of regional hospital preparedness and response plans; identification of hospital capacity for isolation, quarantine, and decontamination; procedures for receipt and distribution of materials from the SNS; personal protective equipment; communications capabilities; biological disaster drills; and training.

Several new emphases were injected into guidance for the second and subsequent funding cycles. These included laboratory capacity for chemical agents, integration of mental health services into preparedness planning and response activities, coordination of CDC funding with HRSA-funded hospital preparedness activities, and concurrence of local public health authorities with state spending plans. Finally, the 2003 guidance incorporated specific smallpox preparedness and response capacities and allowed for costs associated with smallpox preparedness to be covered by grant funds. These and several other issues arose in many states during early implementation of bioterrorism preparedness activities.

Early Lessons

Comprehensive preparedness programs require hazard and vulnerability analyses, forecasts of the probable health effects, analyses of the availability of needed resources, identification of vulnerable populations, and development of detailed plans for both preparedness and response. Many factors influence a state's ability to complete these tasks. Public health preparedness is

---

Table 5–7 Emergency Preparedness Core Competencies for All Public Health Workers

All Public Health Workers must be competent to
- Describe the public health role in emergency response in a range of emergencies that might arise (e.g., "The department provides surveillance, investigation, and public information in disease outbreaks and collaborates with other agencies in geological, environmental, and weather emergencies.")
- Describe the chain of command in emergency response.
- Identify and locate the agency emergency response plan (or the pertinent portion of the plan).
- Describe his/her functional role(s) in emergency response and demonstrate his/her role(s) in regular drills.
- Demonstrate correct use of all communication equipment used for emergency communication (e.g., phone, fax, radio).
- Describe communication role(s) in emergency response—within the agency using established communication systems; with the media; with the general public; and personal (with family, neighbors).
- Identify limits to own knowledge/skill/authority and identify key system resources for referring matters that exceed these limits.
- Recognize unusual events that might indicate an emergency and describe appropriate action (e.g., communicate clearly within chain of command).
- Apply creative problem solving and flexible thinking to unusual challenges within his/her functional responsibilities and evaluate effectiveness of all actions taken.

Public Health Leaders/Administrators must also be competent to
- Describe the chain of command and management system ("incident command system") or similar protocol for emergency response in the jurisdiction.
- Communicate the public health information, roles, capacities, and legal authority to all emergency response partners—such as other public health agencies, other health agencies, and other governmental agencies—during planning, drills, and actual emergencies. (This includes contributing to effective community-wide response through leadership, team building, negotiation, and conflict resolution.)
- Maintain regular communication with emergency response partners. (This includes maintaining a current directory of partners and identifying appropriate methods for contacting them in emergencies.)
- Assure that the agency (or the agency unit) has a written, regularly updated plan for major categories of emergencies that respects the culture of the community and provides for continuity of agency operations.
- Assure that the agency (or agency unit) regularly practices all parts of emergency response.
- Evaluate every emergency response drill (or actual response) to identify needed internal and external improvements.
- Assure that knowledge and skill gaps identified through emergency response planning, drills, and evaluation are addressed.

Public Health Professionals must also be competent to
- Demonstrate readiness to apply professional skills to a range of emergency situations during regular drills (e.g., access, use, and interpret surveillance data; access and use lab resources; access and use science-based investigation and risk assessment protocols; identity and use appropriate personal protective equipment).
- Maintain regular communication with partner professionals in other agencies involved in emergency response. (This includes contributing to effective community-wide response through leadership, team building, negotiation, and conflict resolution.)
- Participate in continuing education to maintain up-to-date knowledge in areas relevant to emergency response (e.g., emerging infectious diseases, hazardous materials, and diagnostic tests).

Public Health Technical and Support Staff must also be competent to
- Demonstrate the use of equipment (including personal protective equipment) and skills associated with his/her functional role in emergency response during regular drills.
- Describe at least one resource for backup support in key areas of responsibility.

Source: Bioterrorism & Emergency Readiness Competencies for All Public Health Workers, Centers for Disease Control and Prevention, 2003.

---

particularly challenging because public health and public safety roles differ for federal, state, and local governments. The federal government has primary responsibility for national security, while state and local governments carry the responsibility and financial burden for most other public health responsibilities. Some of the early lessons from the states reflect these themes.

Preparedness, like public health and politics, is primarily local. In that light, careful attention must be paid to identifying and addressing local needs for public health preparedness and response. Local health officials in many states have raised concerns over the distribution of funding, perceiving that local health jurisdictions should have received more than the share allotted to them. In future years, the proportion of funding shared with local health jurisdictions may need to increase as state level needs are addressed. Some local health jurisdictions would prefer that CDC directly fund local jurisdictions in a manner similar to what is now done for only a handful of the largest U.S. cities. They argue that political whims at the state level too often result in poor priorities, state money grabs, and inefficient reimbursement mechanisms. States, on the other hand, argue that state control and decision making promotes interoperable equipment, complementary resources across jurisdictions, and avoidance of gaps in coverage. It is not possible to draw conclusions as to the wisdom of separate grants to states and localities within that state. Some differences in approach are apparent for surveillance systems, hospital relationships, and training. But none appear, as yet, to be major. Strong leadership within state and local health agencies should minimize the potential for problems. Further, strong federal leadership and assurance of consistency across jurisdictions could also serve to avert problems. However, federal guidance for interjurisdictional (city-state), multijurisdictional (multistate) regional preparedness has been minimal to date, at least in comparison to that for state-wide and substate regional preparedness. The impact on local public health practice should ultimately be positive as better systems and workforce development advance. However, preparedness competes with other local priorities and may have suffered in recent years due to the need for West Nile Virus- and smallpox-focused activities. Ongoing community health priorities may have fared even worse.

Notable in recent federal guidance for bioterrorism preparedness grants is the requirement for evidence of consensus, approval, or concurrence between state and local public health officials for the proposed use of the funds. States must provide assurance that both state and local capacity development is to be achieved and local public health officials, especially those serving a significant portion of the state's population, concur with the proposed use of funds. The intent of this guidance is to focus more on the benefit that can be achieved rather than the level of government spending the dollars. Whether it will serve to constructively engage state and local public health interests remains to be seen. In states with a long history of collaboration around public health improvement initiatives, it could serve to upset the delicate balance that has evolved over time.

At the local level, public health preparedness must be well coordinated with hospital preparedness. The experience to date suggests that hospitals feel isolated from much of the community-wide planning that is taking place. Yet hospitals are key players in response to actual events. Lessons from several large-scale national exercises substantiate this concern.

States have identified a need for exercises and drills similar to the TOPOFF 2 exercise (see Figure 5–2) involving Washington State and Illinois in 2003.[12]

Ideally, the infusion of resources to shore up the sagging public health infrastructure would foster positive structural changes in public health systems at the state and local level. The impact on core public health practice activities should be measurable and, ultimately, there is a need to assess this impact as preparedness efforts advance. Preparedness should be viewed as an important quality or attribute of an effective public health system rather than as a categorical end in itself. This is the essence of the philosophy that has become to be known as the "dual use," "multiple use," or "all hazards" strategy. Although this has been the public position of federal officials since late 2001, federal actions have not always been consistent with federal rhetoric.

Indeed, credibility is one theme that constantly reemerges from the early experience of the states with preparedness funding. CDC's emphasis on smallpox preparedness has both helped and hurt its credibility with the state and local public health community. It hurt in several ways, including the lack of information related to the hazard and risk assessment process. States and localities were to accept the risk assessment undertaken by the federal government based on undisclosed intelligence information. Many public health officials questioned whether a terrorist-generated smallpox attack represents enough of a real risk to justify the harm associated with smallpox vaccination strategies. Secondly, federal directives on smallpox undermine the credibility of an all-hazards approach through the enormous emphasis placed on one specific threat at the expense of all others. This nurtures the fear that the federal preparedness program may be little more than another federal categorical program. Countering these concerns is the perception that the implementation steps for smallpox provide useful practical experience that may assist future responses to other threats and actual events. In any event, all sides recognize the need to take full advantage of federal funding increases to leverage overall infrastructure improvements. How this can be done when states and localities are tempted to cut back on their own support of public health infrastructure will require vision, leadership, and follow-through beyond anything seen to date.

CONCLUSION

Preparing for and responding to emergencies is a well-established role for public health agencies and their workers. This role, highlighted in the Public Health in America statement[1] as one of six critical responsibilities, has often been viewed as one of responding to an occasional natural disaster

Figure 5-2 National TOPOFF 2 Exercise, 2003

Terrorism drill unfolds this week

The Department of Homeland Security will stage a weeklong series of simulated disasters in Chicago and Seattle May 10-16 to test the government's ability to respond to terrorist attacks.

THE SCENARIO

A fictional terrorist group releases pneumonic plague in the Chicago area and explodes a "dirty bomb" in Seattle. Local and state agencies in both cities coordinated their responses with federal agencies in Washington, D.C. and the American Red Cross. In Canada, agencies coordinate with U.S. officials after the plague spreads from Chicago to Vancouver.

SATURDAY

The scenario begins in Chicago when pneumonic plague is supposedly released into the environment at three spots, spreading undetected throughout Cook, DuPage, Kane and Lake Counties.

Chicago

☐ *Affected counties*

Sources: Department of Homeland Security, City of Chicago, City of Seattle, Department of the Solicitor General of Canada

Chicago Tribune

MONDAY AND TUESDAY

SEATTLE
MONDAY
• At about noon, a fake radiological dispersion device, or "dirty bomb," is detonated.
TUESDAY
• A public shelter is opened, using high school students as mock victims. Meanwhile, a "safe house" for terrorists is located.

CHICAGO
TUESDAY
• A growing number of mock patients show up at hospitals complaining of flulike symptoms.

WEDNESDAY

CHICAGO
• More mock patients show up at hospitals.
• Five sites are prepared to distribute mock antibiotics.
• Taylor Street from Clinton to Jefferson Streets is scheduled to be closed from 3-7 p.m. A police motorcade is expected to travel the Kennedy Expressway to the downtown area.

THURSDAY

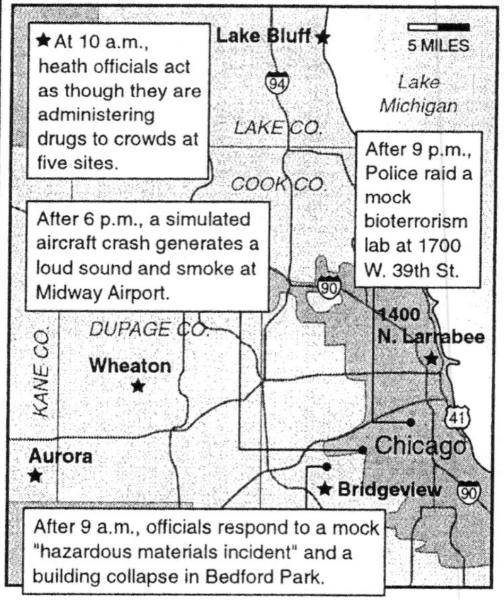

★ At 10 a.m., heath officials act as though they are administering drugs to crowds at five sites.

After 6 p.m., a simulated aircraft crash generates a loud sound and smoke at Midway Airport.

After 9 p.m., Police raid a mock bioterrorism lab at 1700 W. 39th St.

After 9 a.m., officials respond to a mock "hazardous materials incident" and a building collapse in Bedford Park.

Lake Bluff ★
LAKE CO.
COOK CO.
KANE CO.
DUPAGE CO.
Aurora ★
Wheaton ★
Bridgeview
1400 N. Larrabee ★
Chicago
5 MILES
Lake Michigan

WHAT YOU MIGHT SEE

• Traffic delays, emergency vehicles and equipment in southwest Chicago.
• Helicopters, flash grenades and simulated gunshots near 1700 W. 39th St.
• Parking will be prohibited in the 1400 block of North Larrabee Street for several hours beginning at 8 a.m. CTA buses and drill volunteers will be lined up along the street.
• Officials will close 55th Street from Laramie to Central Avenues for several hours starting at about 5 p.m. At Midway Airport, mock victims will wear makeup to resemble injuries. Rescue teams will be present.

Source: Chicago Tribune, May 11, 2003.

such as an earthquake, hurricane, or flood. Large-scale events that threaten public health and safety have seldom been intentionally inflicted, despite recent examples to the contrary, such as the bombing of the federal building in Okalahoma City in the 1990s. Events in the international theater raised the specter of increased risk for terrorist acts, including bioterrorism, directed against the American population and prompted interest in preparedness and response capacities within the federal government in the mid-1990s.

The cycle of progress in public health preparedness has been remarkably consistent over several centuries in the United State. A terrible epidemic or another form of health-related disaster or threat occurs. Public expectations call for such an event to never occur again. Significant new resources are deployed to raise the level of preparedness and protection. The threat seems to dissipate over time. Preparedness, though still important, becomes relatively less important. Eventually, a new threat or event appears, and the cycle repeats itself. This recurring scenario raises the question as to whether current preparedness efforts represent a new and different strategy that could short-circuit this chain of events. Past preparedness efforts focused on a specific threat and diminished as that specific threat diminished. Perhaps a more broadly focused preparedness campaign, one that is valued because it battles many different threats, will fare differently. Although still early in the process, some things are clear.

The price for public health preparedness will be high, regardless of how it is calculated. In crude dollar terms, its costs reflect a 20% increase in the federal investment in governmental public health services provided through governmental public health agencies. This increase will need to be sustained indefinitely, because it primarily supports information, communications, and workforce development systems that are ongoing in nature. And it will require commensurate commitment and investment on the part of state and local governments. Otherwise, supplanting will occur in one form or another, and the opportunity for federal preparedness funds to leverage other resources will be lost.

If the price is to be calculated in terms of federalism and intergovernmental relationships, it will also be high. States will need to encourage and accept stronger federal leadership on the one hand and generate a better understanding of local needs and priorities on the other. These will need to be fashioned into effective local, regional, state, and multistate efforts in ways that will challenge states to live up to their primary responsibility for the health of its citizens. All this must be done while navigating through a treacherous obstacle course laden with political, economic, and bureaucratic impediments to sustained progress.

The federal government must avoid the pitfall of merely throwing money at the problem, without fostering a national vision of public health preparedness and nurturing the state-local public health systems that must carry out that vision. This will require the federal agencies to be accountable for meaningful capacity and performance standards, consistent credibility as to ends and means, integration both across focus areas and across federal agencies, and leadership rather than either regulatory or advisory approaches to dealing with state-local public health system issues.

Although these are formidable challenges, the opportunities (and the opportunity costs) are unprecedented. The boost in federal funding and potential for federal leadership provide a unique opportunity to fashion a more coordinated national public health system. Certainly, the public now expects this,[9] and the price of not being prepared will be high. But progress often comes at a high price. The history of public health preparedness reflects this lesson. Ironically, failure to seize this opportunity will increase the likelihood that another cycle will occur. We can either learn the lessons of the past, the lessons of public health threats and responses, and the lessons of public health operated within a federalist form of government, or we can relive this history over and over again.

Discussion Questions and Exercises

1. What constitutes vulnerability in populations living in disaster-prone areas? Give a concrete example from a disaster that has drawn media attention in recent years (several media Web sites are provided in the Course Resources catalog).

2. Choose a public health discipline or occupational group (either your own or one that you are somewhat familiar with) and describe the range of tasks that group of public health practitioners may be asked to perform in disaster preparedness and response. Why is public health participation important?

3. Why should public health organizations take a leadership role in emergency and disaster planning?

4. Why is the process of planning more important than the written plan itself? Describe the "paper plan" syn-drome and how it can detract from public health emergency preparedness. Identify factors contributing to disaster and other public health emergency planning apathy.

5. What is meant by the term *surge capacity* and how is this addressed in public health emergency response plans?

6. Describe three or more elements of public health statutes that are important elements of public health emergency response plans.

7. Describe the role of your agency and at least four other agencies that work in conjunction with your agency in public health emergencies.

8. Describe your own specific role for several different public health emergency situations.

9. What are the basic functions that a health department should perform in response to an emergency or disaster? When should a health department identify these functions?

10. What public health resources are available at the federal, state, or local level in an emergency or disaster? How would you go about requesting these resources?

REFERENCES

1. Public Health Functions Steering Committee. *Public Health in America.* Washington, DC: Public Health Service; 1995.

2. Landesmann LY. *Public Health Management of Disasters: The Practice Guide.* Washington, DC: American Public Health Association; 2001.

3. Presidential Homeland Security Directive No. 5, February 28, 2003.

4. The Center for Law and the Public's Health. *The Model State Emergency Health Powers Act Emergencies Act.* Georgetown and Johns Hopkins Universities; 2001.

5. National Association of County and City Health Officials. *Local Public Health Infrastructure: A Chartbook.* Washington, DC: NACCHO; 2001.

6. National Association of County and City Health Officials. *Elements of Effective Local Bioterrorism Preparedness: A Planning Primer for Local Public Health Agencies.* Washington, DC: NACCHO; 2001.

7. National Association of County and City Health Officials. *Local Centers for Public Health Preparedness: Models for Strengthening Local Public Health Capacity.* Washington, DC: NACCHO; 2001.

8. Centers for Disease Control and Prevention. *Local Emergency Preparedness and Response Inventory: A Tool for Rapid Assessment of Local Capacity to Respond to Bioterrorism, Outbreaks of Infectious Disease, and Other Public Health Threats and Emergencies.* Atlanta, GA: CDC; 2001.

9. Lake, Snell, Perry & Associates. *Americans Speak Out on Bioterrorism and U.S. Preparedness to Address Risk.* Princeton, NJ: Robert Wood Johnson Foundation; December 2002.

10. Centers for Medicare and Medicaid Services. National Health Accounts, 1960–2000.

11. Columbia University School of Nursing, National Association of County and City Health Officials, and Centers for Disease Control and Prevention. 2003. *Bioterrorism & Emergency Readiness: Competencies for All Public Health Workers.* Available at: http://www.nursing.hs.columbia.edu/institutes-center/chphsr/btcomps.pdf. Accessed August 2, 2006.

12. Dizon NZ. Terrorism drill comes to Chicago. *Chicago Tribune.* Metro Section. May 13, 2003.

CHAPTER 6

The Public Health Workforce

After completing Chapter 6, learners will be proficient in identifying and explaining how various occupations, positions, and roles in the public health workforce contribute to carrying out public health's core functions and essential services. Key aspects of this competency expectation include

- Describing the size, composition, and distribution of the current public health workforce
- Identifying and discussing competency frameworks for routine and emergency public health practice
- Describing approaches to strengthening the public health workforce systems
- Identifying information sources for examining key dimensions of the current and future public health workforce

Public health is important work, and the people who carry out that work contribute substantially to the health status and quality of life of the individuals, families, and communities they serve. Yet public health is not among the best-known or most highly respected careers, in part because when public health efforts are successful, nothing happens. Events that don't occur don't attract attention. For example, the remarkable record of declining mortality rates and ever-increasing spans of healthy life, due in large part to public health efforts, draws little public attention. Indeed, the vast majority of those who will ultimately benefit from the efforts of past and present public health workers are yet to be born. With public health workers not recognized and valued for their accomplishments and contributions, it should not be surprising that careers in public health are among the least understood and appreciated in the health sector.

However, even if the public views public health as poorly defined and abstract, public health workers are real and tangible.

These workers make up a public health workforce that can be defined and described in several important dimensions, including its size, distribution, composition, skills, and career pathways. Unfortunately, there is less information on these vital statistics of the public health workforce than for many other professional and occupational categories working in the health sector today.

Chapters 6 through 13 of this book bring together the information that is available on public health occupations and careers in order to assist individuals seeking to make career decisions. This chapter sets the stage for an appreciation of what public health workers do and how they contribute to societal well-being in the 21st century in examining the following questions:

- What is the public health workforce?
- How large is this workforce and how it is distributed?
- What professions and occupations are included?
- How does the public health workforce impact the health of populations?

PUBLIC HEALTH WORK AND PUBLIC HEALTH WORKERS

From a functional perspective, it is the individuals involved in carrying out the core functions and essential services of public health who constitute the public health workforce. Critical to an understanding of this characterization of the public health workforce are the terms *core functions* and *essential public health services*. Chapter 1 more fully explains these terms with a useful summary of these concepts provided in the "Public Health in America" statement. Table 1–5 in Chapter 1 presents this framework. In it, the practice of public health is described in terms of both its ends (vision, mission, and six broad responsibilities) and how it accomplishes those ends (10 essential public health services). These constitute an aggregate job description for the entire public health workforce, with the workload divided among the many different professional and occupational categories composing the total public health workforce.

This functional perspective clearly links public health workers to public health practice. Unfortunately, this does not simplify the practical task of determining who is, and who is not, part of the public health workforce. There has never been any specific academic degree, even the Master's of Public Health (MPH) degree, or unique set of experiences that distinguish public health's workers from those in other fields. Many public health workers have a primary professional discipline in addition to their attachment to public health. Physicians, nurses, dentists, social workers, nutritionists, health educators, anthropologists, psychologists, architects, sanitarians, economists, political scientists, engineers, epidemiologists, biostatisticians, managers, lawyers, and dozens of other professions and disciplines carry out the work of public health. This multidisciplinary workforce, with somewhat divided loyalties to multiple professions, blurs the distinctiveness of public health as a unified profession. At the same time, however, it facilitates the interdisciplinary approaches to community problem identification and problem solving, which are hallmarks of public health practice.

SIZE AND DISTRIBUTION OF THE PUBLIC HEALTH WORKFORCE

There is little agreement as to the size of the public health workforce in the United States today except that it is only a small subset of the 13 million persons employed in the health sector of the American economy. Enumerations and estimates of public health workers in general, and public health professionals in particular, suffer from several limitations—the definition of a public health worker is unclear; public health workers employed outside governmental public health agencies are difficult to identify; and not all employees of governmental public health agencies have public health responsibilities associated with their jobs. Enumerating specific types of public health workers is also difficult, because many have other professional affiliations.

Due to these limitations, a clear picture of the public health workforce is not available. But it is clear that efforts to identify and categorize public health workers must take into account three important aspects of public health practice:

- Work setting: Public health workers work for organizations actively engaged in promoting, protecting, and preserving the health of a defined population group. The organization may be public or private, and its public health objectives may be secondary or subsidiary to its principal objectives. In addition to governmental public health agencies, other public and private organizations employ public health workers. For example, school health nurses working for the local school district and health educators employed by the local Red Cross chapter are part of the public health workforce.

- Work content: Public health workers perform work addressing one or more of the essential public health services. Many job descriptions for public health workers are tailored from the essential public health services, and the scope of tasks can be very broad. A focus on populations, as opposed to individuals, is often a distinguishing characteristic of these job descriptions. For example, an individual trained as a health educator who works for a community-based teen pregnancy prevention program is clearly a public health worker. But the same can't be said of a health educator working for a commercial advertising firm promoting cosmetics.

- Worker: The individual must occupy a position that conventionally requires at least 1 year of postsecondary specialized public health training and that is (or can be) assigned a professional, administrative, or technical occupational title (to be defined later in this chapter). This distinction may seem artificial but rests on the notion that public health practice relies on a foundation of knowledge, skills, and attitudes that, in most circumstances, cannot be imparted through work experiences alone.

If public health workers cannot be counted from the ground up, maybe they can be approximated from the top down. Various sources estimate that public health activities, including both clinical and population-based services, make up 3–4% of all health expenditures.[1] If public health workers composed a similar percentage of the 13 million health workers in the United States, the number of public health workers would be between 400,000 and 525,000. Because expenditures for some public health activities, such as those for many environmental and occupational health services, are not captured in the total for health expenditures, the actual number of public health workers may range as high as 450,000 to 600,000.

That range is consistent with a crude enumeration of the public health workforce conducted in the year 2000, which identified 450,000 public health workers.[2] The year 2000 enumeration missed most public health workers employed by nongovernmental agencies as well as many public health workers employed by government agencies other than official public health agencies. As a result, the actual total exceeds the 450,000 workers identified in the enumeration.

Data from another source, the ongoing employment census of federal, state, and local health agencies, indicated that there were 552,000 full-time equivalent (FTE) governmental public health workers in 2004.[3] There were nearly 425,000 workers in state and local governments, and another 128,000 were employed by federal agencies (see Table 6–1). Adding in even the admittedly low estimate of 64,000 nongovernmental public health workers from the year 2000 enumeration study, the size of the public health workforce in 2004, using these figures, was nearly 620,000 FTE positions.

The overall workforce in the health sector of the American economy has more than doubled in size since 1975 and has increased by more than 30% since 1990.[4] Table 6–1 indicates that the number of public health workers employed by federal, state, and local health agencies has also been steadily increasing, largely among workers of local public health agencies. Unquestionably, the number of public health workers employed by nongovernmental agencies also grew during this period. The increase in the number of FTE workers in state and local health agencies contrasts sharply with the relatively unchanged number of federal health workers.[3] The number of FTE employees working for governmental health agencies was 487,000 FTEs in 1994 (126,000 federal, 158,000 state, 203,000 local). By 2005, the total was 550,000 (125,000 federal, 178,000 state, 246,000 local). Figure 6–1 demonstrates that the ratio of public health workers to population has also increased during this period, although there is evidence that it may be declining somewhat since reaching its highest level (15.1 per 10,000) in 2001. This is surprising in view of a substantial influx of federal funding for state and local public health agencies since 2002 documented in earlier chapters of this text.

Like most health sector workers, public health workers are more likely to be found in urban and suburban settings rather than rural communities. The public health worker to population ratio, however, is often higher in rural areas than in urban areas. States show significant variation as well, with higher ratios in many of the smaller and less urban states in the East and West and lower ratios in the Central states (see Table 6–2).

In 1980, Health Resources and Services Administration (HRSA) estimated the size of the public health workforce at 500,000 workers including a primary public health workforce of 250,000 professional workers, most working in governmental public health agencies.[5] More than 50,000 occupational health physicians, nurses, and specialists working in the private sector, as well as 20,000 health educators working in schools and 45,000 administrators working in nursing homes, hospitals, and medical group practices were included in the 250,000 professionals characterized by HRSA as the primary public health workforce at the time. If only those working for governmental public health agencies had been included, the number would have been closer to 140,000. The year 2000 public health enumeration identified 40,000 fewer occupational health professionals and did not seek to include health educators working in schools or administrators in nongovernmental clinical settings.

TABLE 6–1 Full Time Equivalent (FTE) Workers of Federal, State, and Local Governmental Health* Agencies, 1994–2005, United States

Year	Federal Health FTE	State Health FTE	Local Health FTE	State + Local FTE	Total (F+S+L) FTE
1994	126,292	157,962	202,732	360,694	486,986
1995	125,048	160,031	208,588	368,619	493,667
1997	119,921	162,605	214,824	377,429	497,350
1998	119,846	166,930	219,655	386,585	506,431
1999	121,033	169,213	223,999	393,212	514,245
2000	120,362	172,678	236,496	409,174	529,536
2001	122,999	172,414	251,399	423,813	546,812
2002	124,979	176,345	252,326	428,671	553,650
2003	124,828	176,868	253,888	430,756	555,584
2004	127,933	174,301	249,857	424,128	552,061
2005	125,163	178,465	246,300	424,765	549,918

*Health: public health services, emergency medical services, mental health, alcohol and drug abuse, outpatient clinics, visiting nurses, food and sanitary inspections, animal control, other environmental health activities (e.g., pollution control), etc.

Source: Data from U.S. Bureau of the Census. Federal, state, and local governments, public employment and payroll data. Available at http://www.census.gov/govs/www/apesstl.html. Accessed June 2006.

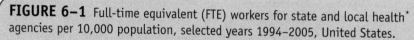

FIGURE 6–1 Full-time equivalent (FTE) workers for state and local health* agencies per 10,000 population, selected years 1994–2005, United States.

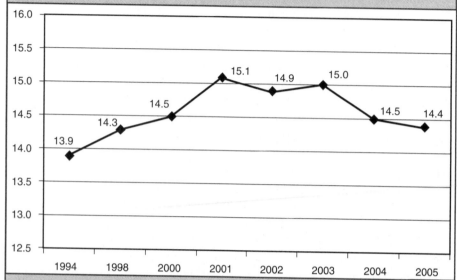

*Health: public health services, emergency medical services, mental health, alcohol and drug abuse, outpatients clinics, visiting nurses, food and sanitary inspections, animal control, other environmental health activities (e.g., pollution control), etc.

Source: Data from U.S. Bureau of the Census. Federal, state, and local governments, public employment and payroll data. Available at: http://www.census.gov/govs/www/apesstl.html. Accessed June 20, 2006.

Comparing the overall 1980 estimate (500,000 workers) with the year 2000 public health workforce enumeration suggests that the public health workforce is shrinking. Comparing the 1980 HRSA estimate with current employment census data, on the other hand, suggests that the public health workforce is growing. As the methods used for the 1980 estimation were considerably different from those in the more recent studies, direct comparison of the results is of questionable value.

The public health workforce enumeration completed in 2000 found one third of public health workers employed by state agencies and another one third employed by agencies of local government, with less than 20% working at the federal level and 14% outside government entirely.[2] Chapter 4 examines key characteristics of the governmental public health agencies that employ these workers. Government employment census data, which excludes nongovernmental workers, also classify one third as state workers but 45% as employees of local government and 22% as working for federal agencies. Some of these differences can be attributed to state public health systems in which state employees work at the local level and may be counted as state employees in the employment census data and as local health department employees in the public health enumeration study. These differences may also be partly attributed

to the inclusion of workers in state and local governmental agencies other than the local public health agency in the government employment census data but not in the year 2000 public health enumeration study. For example, substance abuse and mental health prevention services, school health services, or restaurant inspections may operate from local mental health agencies, school districts, or consumer affairs agencies rather than from the local health department.

Although recent decades have witnessed an increase in the number of public health workers employed by nongovernmental agencies due to expanded partnerships for public health priorities, governmental public health workers are often considered the primary public health workforce. Their number, composition, distribution, and competence are issues of public concern. The government employment census data provide useful insights into overall trends at the national level and among the various levels of government. The year 2000 public health enumeration study, however, provides richer information on the composition of the public health workforce, such as the proportion and types of professional occupational categories within that workforce. Both sources enrich understanding of the size and composition of the public health workforce today.

COMPOSITION OF THE PUBLIC HEALTH WORKFORCE

Public health is multidisciplinary, with many different professions and occupations involved in its work. In recent years, there has been an effort to identify standard occupational classifications for public health workers resulting in nearly 30 different job categories. Because the total number of public health workers is not clear, the precise proportion of the various subgroups cannot be determined. It is clear that nurses and environmental health practitioners constitute the largest subgroups of public health workers. Managers, epidemiologists, health educators, and laboratory workers are also significant subgroups. Professionals comprise more than one half of the overall public health workforce, as will be further described later in this chapter. It is the administrative, professional, and technical positions in the public health workforce that are the focus of this book.

Despite the lack of precise information, it appears that professional occupational categories comprise more than 300,000, or one half, of the estimated 620,000 workers in the public health workforce. For comparison purposes, there were approximately 2.3 million nurses, 800,000 physicians, 200,000 pharmacists, 170,000 dentists, and 90,000 dieticians/nutritionists working in the United States at the turn of the 21st century.[4]

Studies of local public health agencies indicate that three positions are found in more than two thirds of all local public health agencies (LPHAs)—public health nurse, administrator, and sanitarian/environmental health specialist.[6,7] These positions are present in large and small agencies alike. The next most frequent positions (registered nurse, dietitian/nutritionist, licensed practical nurse, nurse practitioner, health educator, and social worker) are found in only 20–33% of LPHAs. There is considerable variation in the proportion of LPHAs with these positions, associated with agency size. For example, health educators are employed in only 10% of LPHAs serving populations under 50,000 persons but in 85% of agencies serving 500,000 or more.

Two general patterns of LPHA staffing exist around a core set of employees. One pattern focuses on clinical services, the other on more population-based programs.[8] The core employees consist of dietitian/nutritionists, sanitarians/environmental specialists, administrators, lab specialists, and health educators. The clinical pattern adds physicians, nurses, and dental health workers. The population-based pattern includes epidemiologists, public health nurses, social workers, and program specialists.

The availability of information on public health workers at the state and local level varies from state to state and is often inconsistent and incomplete. Detailed information from the official state health departments has not been available since the late 1980s and even then did not include public health workers employed by state agencies other than the official state health department. The periodic profiles of LPHAs completed by the National Association of County and City Health Officials (NACCHO) provide only general data on the proportion of responding agencies that employ specific public health job titles, either directly or through contracted services. This information does not allow for aggregation into an actual enumeration of public health workers in the various job categories.

The lack of information on the public health workforce extends to some of the most basic and important characteristics of that workforce. For example, there is very little information available on the racial and ethnic characteristics of the overall public health workforce. Data on cultural competency is also lacking.

TABLE 6–2 FTE Workers for State and Local Health Agencies by State, 2004

State	State + Local FTE	State + Local FTE per 10,000 pop.
AL	10,090	22.3
AK	1,056	16.1
AZ	4,932	8.6
AR	4,932	17.9
CA	54,533	15.2
CO	4,558	9.9
CN	3,425	9.8
DE	2,169	26.1
DC	1,977	34.6
FL	25,501	14.7
GA	16,077	18.2
HI	2,710	21.5
ID	2,095	15.0
IL	9,930	7.8
IN	5,346	8.6
IA	3,171	10.7
KS	3,893	14.2
KY	7,939	19.2
LA	5,621	12.5
ME	1,587	12.1
MD	11,192	20.1
MA	10,035	15.6
MI	13,395	13.3
MN	5,866	11.5
MS	3,214	11.1
MO	7,543	13.1
MT	1,667	18.0
NE	1,455	8.3

(continued)

TABLE 6–2 FTE Workers for State and Local Health Agencies by State, 2004 (*continued*)

State	State + Local FTE	State + Local FTE per 10,000 pop.
NV	2,033	8.7
NH	1,045	8.0
NJ	7,695	8.9
NM	2,617	13.8
NY	27,022	14.1
NC	23,709	27.8
ND	1,829	28.8
OH	21,818	19.0
OK	7,151	20.3
OR	7,081	19.7
PA	7,216	5.8
RI	1,385	12.8
SC	9,214	22.0
SD	893	11.6
TN	7,060	12.0
TX	32,249	15.2
UT	3,326	13.9
VT	776	12.5
VA	11,614	15.6
WA	9,476	15.3
WV	2,445	13.5
WI	7,541	13.7
WY	1,054	20.8
U.S. Total	424,158	14.5

Source: U.S. Bureau of the Census. Federal, state, and local governments, public employment and payroll data. Available at: http://www.census.gov/govs/www/aps.html. Accessed August 20, 2005.

PUBLIC HEALTH WORKER ETHICS, SKILLS, AND COMPETENCIES

Public health workers may come from different academic, professional, and experiential backgrounds, but they share a common bond. All are committed to a common mission and share common ethical principles, as exemplified by the following list advanced by the American Public Health Association[9]:

- Public health should address principally the fundamental causes of disease and requirements for health, aiming to prevent adverse health outcomes.
- Public health should achieve community health in a way that respects the rights of individuals in the community.
- Public health policies, programs, and priorities should be developed and evaluated through processes that ensure an opportunity for input from community members.
- Public health should advocate and work for the empowerment of disenfranchised community members, aiming to ensure that the basic resources and conditions necessary for health are accessible to all.
- Public health should seek the information needed to implement effective policies and programs that protect and promote health.
- Public health institutions should provide communities with the information they have that is needed for decisions on policies or programs and should obtain the community's consent for their implementation.
- Public health institutions should act in a timely manner on the information they have within the resources and the mandate given to them by the public.
- Public health programs and policies should incorporate a variety of approaches that anticipate and respect diverse values, beliefs, and cultures in the community.
- Public health programs and policies should be implemented in a manner that most enhances the physical and social environment.

- Public health institutions should protect the confidentiality of information that can bring harm to an individual or community if made public. Exceptions must be justified on the basis of the high likelihood of significant harm to the individual or others.
- Public health institutions should ensure the professional competence of their employees.
- Public health institutions and their employees should engage in collaborations and affiliations in ways that build the public's trust and the institution's effectiveness.

Information from public health agencies indicates that the majority of public health workers lack formal education and training in public health. In 1980, HRSA determined that only 20% of the 250,000 professionals in the primary public health workforce had formal training in public health.[5] More than 2 decades later, there is little evidence that this situation has improved. While the proportion of those who have formal training varies by category of worker, the lack of formal training is striking in even some of the most critical categories. For example, a NACCHO survey in 1997 found that 78% of local health department leaders had no formal public health education or training.[10] A survey of Illinois local health jurisdictions in the year 2000 yielded similar results, with 79% of local health agency administrators lacking formal preparation in public health.[11]

For many public health workers, formal training focuses only on a specific aspect of public health practice such as environmental health or community or school health nursing. Environmental health practitioners, nurses, administrators, and health educators account for the majority of public health workers with formal training in public health. Even among those with formal training in public health, public health workers with graduate degrees from schools of public health or other graduate public health programs represent only a small fraction of the total. In view of the number of master's-level graduates of schools of public health and other graduate-level public health degree programs—about 7,000 in 2005—this is not surprising.

Evidence of the lack of formal training within this workforce, however, does not necessarily lead to the conclusion that public health workers are unprepared.[12] On the contrary, public health workers enter the field having earned a wide variety of degrees and professional training credentials from academic programs and institutions unrelated to public health. Often overlooked, these institutions produce the bulk of the public health workforce and represent major assets for addressing unmet needs. On-the-job training and work experience contribute substantially to the overall competency and preparedness of the public health workforce. For example, public health workers are frequently involved in responses to earthquakes, floods, and other disasters and have increasingly acquired and demonstrated skills in assessing community health needs and devising community health improvement plans. These are skills that most public health workers acquired through real-world work experience rather than through their formal training.

Continuing education and career development for public health workers has long been a cottage industry involving many different parties. Academic institutions certainly are contributors, but public health agencies at the state and local level, public health associations (national, state, and local), and other voluntary-sector health organizations participate as well. Many different entities offer credits for continuing education, including professional organizations, academic institutions, and hospitals, among others. Public health workers value continuing education credits as a means to satisfy requirements of their core disciplines in order to maintain some level of credentialing status (such as licensed physicians and nurses, certified health education specialists, and so on). A few states, such as New Jersey, enforce continuing education requirements for the public health disciplines licensed by that state. There is no formal system of public health-specific continuing education units (CEUs) and only fledgling efforts toward credentialing public health workers. The final chapter will crystallize current challenges, strategies, and initiatives for public health workforce development.

CHARACTERISTICS OF PUBLIC HEALTH OCCUPATIONS

This remaining sections of this chapter define and describe several key dimensions of public health occupations and organizations that provide the framework for examining specific positions and careers for public health workers in later chapters. Information on the full spectrum of occupations in the public health workforce is available from a variety of sources, including federal health and labor agencies and national public health organizations. Table 6–3 previews the public health titles, occupational categories, and careers examined in Chapters 7 through 13. The first column identifies the public health job titles and careers addressed in each chapter. The second column lists specific Bureau of Labor Statistics standard occupational categories (SOCs) included in each chapter. Standard occupation categories are explained later in this chapter.

There are many aspects of an occupation or career that are important to current and prospective public health workers. The framework used in this book includes

- Occupational classification: these are based on job titles and whether the duties of the job are primarily administrative, professional, technical, or supportive in

TABLE 6–3 Public Health Occupations and Careers Addressed in Chapters 7 Through 13

Chapter Number	Career Category with Specific Public Health Titles Described	Bureau of Labor Statistics Standard Occupational Categories Relevant for Public Health
7	**Public Health Administration** • Health services manager • Public health agency director • Health officer	• Health services manager/administrator
8	**Environmental and Occupational Health** • Environmental engineer • Environmental health specialist (entry level) • Environmental health specialist (midlevel) • Environmental health specialist (senior level) • Occupational health and safety specialist	• Environmental engineer • Environmental engineering technician and technologist • Environmental scientist and specialist • Environmental science technician and technologist • Occupational health and safety specialist • Occupational health and safety technician
9	**Public Health Nursing** • Public health nurse (entry level) • Public health nurse (senior level) • Licensed practical/vocational nurse	• Registered nurse • Licensed practical/vocational nurse
10	**Epidemiology and Disease Control** • Disease investigator • Epidemiologist (entry level) • Epidemiologist (senior level)	• Epidemiologist • Statistician
11	**Public Health Education and Information** • Public health educator (entry level) • Public health educator (senior level) • Public information officer	• Health educator • Public relations/public information/health communications/ media specialist
12	**Other Public Health Professionals** • Public health nutritionist/dietician • Public health social, behavioral, and mental health workers • Public health laboratory workers • Public health physicians • Public health veterinarians • Public health pharmacists • Public health dental workers • Administrative law judge/hearing officer • Dietician/nutritionist • Dietetic technician • Medical and public health social worker • Mental health and substance abuse social worker • Mental health counselor	• Substance abuse and behavioral disorder counselor • Microbiologist • Biochemist/biophysicist • Medical and clinical laboratory technologist • Medical and clinical laboratory technician • Public health physician • Public health veterinarian • Public health pharmacist • Public health dentist • Administrative law judge/hearing officer
13	**Public Health Program Occupations** • Public health program specialist/coordinator • Public health emergency preparedness and response coordinator • Public health policy analyst • Public health information specialists • Community outreach and other technical occupations	

nature. Many positions in public health practice have a variety of job titles associated with them. Similarly, the same job title can have a variety of regular duties and day-to-day responsibilities.

- Public health practice profile: The public health functions and essential public health services addressed by each occupational grouping are presented in a public health practice profile.
- Important and essential duties: These are the defining characteristics of any position describing what the worker does on a daily basis. Examples are derived from a sampling of job and position descriptions from a variety of sources.
- Minimum qualifications: Some positions require a specific academic degree or credential; many do not. Some require previous experience, while others do not. All require some particular minimum level of knowledge, skills, and abilities. Many also require specific physical capabilities. These characteristics will be identified for each public health occupation.
- Workplace considerations: This description will identify levels of government that employ significant numbers of workers in each occupational category as well as important nongovernmental work settings for public health workers. This section will also highlight considerations related to physical demands, work schedules, travel, and general working conditions.
- Salary estimates: Salary levels for public health workers are estimated based on information from current job postings and the May 2004 survey of employment and wages coordinated by the Labor Department's Bureau of Labor Statistics.
- Career prospects: Estimates as to current need and future demand for specific public health occupations and career paths are provided, based on the analyses performed by public health organizations and the Bureau of Labor Statistics' projections for various occupations.
- Additional information: Sources of additional information for each occupation or career are identified, including education and training opportunities.

The following sections briefly describe the type and source of information included for each of these characteristics.

Occupational Classifications

Throughout the economy, including the health sector, occupations are broadly classified as either white collar or blue collar depending on the degree of education and experience normally required. White collar occupations include five major occupational categories (professional, administrative, technical, clerical, and other), based on the subject matter of work, the level of difficulty or responsibility involved, and the educational requirements established for each occupation. Blue collar occupations are composed of the trades, crafts, and manual labor (unskilled, semiskilled, skilled), including foreman and supervisory positions entailing trade, craft, or laboring experience and knowledge as the paramount requirement.

The U.S. Office of Personnel Management tracks occupations in various industries using four general categories—professional, administrative, technical, and support.

- Professional occupations are those that require knowledge in a field of science or learning characteristically acquired through education or training equivalent to a bachelor's or higher degree with major study in or pertinent to the specialized field, as distinguished from general education. The work of a professional occupation requires the exercise of discretion, judgment, and personal responsibility for the application of an organized body of knowledge that is constantly studied to make new discoveries and interpretations, and to improve the data, materials, and methods. Professionals require specialized and theoretical knowledge. Well-known examples of professional job titles include physicians, registered nurses, dieticians, health educators, social workers, psychologists, lawyers, accountants, economists, system analysts, and personnel and labor relations workers. Professionals constitute the majority (56%) of public health workers (see Figure 6–2).
- Administrative occupations are those that involve the exercise of analytical ability, judgment, discretion, personal responsibility, and the application of a substantial body of knowledge of principles, concepts, and practices applicable to one or more fields of administration or management. Although these positions do not require specialized educational majors, they do involve the type of skills (analytical, research, writing, judgment) typically gained through a college-level general education, or through progressively responsible experience. Administrators set broad policies, oversee overall responsibility for the execution of these policies, direct individual departments or special phases of the agency's operations, or provide specialized consultation on a regional, district, or area basis. Common job titles for administrators include department heads, bureau chiefs, division chiefs, directors, deputy directors, and similar titles. Administrators and managers comprise 5% of all public health workers.

• Technical occupations are those that involve work that is not routine in nature and is typically associated with, and supportive of, a professional or administrative field. Such occupations involve extensive practical knowledge gained through on-the-job experience, or specific training less than that represented by college graduation. Work in these occupations may involve substantial elements of the work of the professional or administrative field but requires less than full competence in the field involved. Technical occupations require a combination of basic scientific or technical knowledge and manual skills. Titles include computer specialists, licensed practical nurses, inspectors, programmers, and a variety of technicians (environmental, laboratory, medical, nursing, dental, and so on). The technical occupations category also includes paraprofessionals who perform some of the duties of a professional or technician in a supportive role usually requiring less formal training and experience than that normally required for professional status. Included are outreach workers, research assistants, medical aides, child support workers, home health aides, ambulance drivers and attendants, and so on. Workers in technical occupations account for 20% of all public health workers.

• Administrative support occupations are those that involve structured work in support of office, business, or fiscal operations; duties are performed according to established policies or techniques and require training, experience, or working knowledge related to the tasks to be performed. Clerical titles are often responsible for internal and external communication as well as recording and retrieval of data, information, and other paperwork required in an office. This category includes bookkeepers, messengers, clerk typists, stenographers, court transcribers, hearing reporters, statistical clerks, dispatchers, license distributors, payroll clerks, office machine and computer operators, telephone operators, legal assistants, and so on. In addition, workers in any of the blue-collar occupational categories are considered support workers within the public health workforce. About 19% of public health workers are in the administrative support category.

As indicated in Figure 6–2, 81% of public health workers fall into the professional, administrative, and technical categories. More than one half (56%) are classified as professionals, similar to the proportion of professionals among all 13

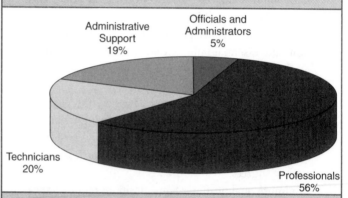

FIGURE 6–2 Percentage of public health workers in selected occupational categories, United States, 2000.

Administrative Support 19%

Officials and Administrators 5%

Technicians 20%

Professionals 56%

Source: Adapted from Health Resources and Services Administration, Bureau of Health Professions, National Center for Health Workforce Information and Analysis and Center for Health Policy, Columbia School of Nursing. *The Public Health Workforce Enumeration 2000.* Washington, DC: HRSA; 2000. Available at: http://www.phppo.cdc.gov/owpp/docs/library/2000/Public%20Health%20Workforce%20Enumeration%202000.pdf. Accessed August 20, 2005.

million health workers. Nursing and environmental health activities employ the largest number of public health workers when both professional and technical occupations are considered. Registered nurses (RNs) represent the largest professional category within the public health workforce.

The U.S. Department of Labor collects information on occupations throughout the economy, including the public sector. An official taxonomy for occupations allows the Department of Labor's Bureau of Labor Statistics (BLS) to track information on hundreds of standard occupational categories in terms of the number and location of jobs, salaries, and duties performed. BLS also develops projections for the number of future positions for these occupational categories based on economic and employment trends. Occupations generally can be found in a variety of industries, making it difficult to pinpoint trends and needs specific to the public health system. For example, registered nurses are the largest occupational category in the overall health workforce, with 2.3 million workers, but only a small percentage of all registered nurses (75,000) work in public health agencies. Many more work in hospitals and other health care organizations. This is also true for physicians, health services administrators, health educators, nutritionists, and many other occupations. Public health agencies, however, are the largest employers of several standard occupational categories, such as environmental health specialists and epidemiologists. For those occupational categories, BLS information is especially useful.

Standard occupational categories relevant for public health are identified in the second column of Table 6–3, with 28 specific categories listed.[13] Each of these categories is addressed in subsequent chapters, with the greatest attention on those with the largest numbers of workers in the public health workforce. These 28 occupational categories clearly do not cover all titles found in public health organizations. Nor do they capture the entire scope of work undertaken by public health workers. For these reasons, each chapter will focus specifically on job titles and job descriptions commonly found in public health organizations (see the first column of Table 6–3), with information on titles, duties, public health roles, and qualifications. Related job titles are addressed in the same chapter in order to demonstrate links and possible career pathways.

Estimates of the number of current workers in each occupational category are synthesized from two sources. The Bureau of Labor Statistics conducts surveys of all standard occupational categories twice yearly, including information on the industries and levels of government that employ workers in each standard occupational category. This source allows for estimates of the total number of workers in a particular standard occupational category who work for federal, state, and local agencies.

A second important source of estimates for public health workers in relevant standard occupational categories is the *Public Health Workforce Enumeration 2000* commissioned by the federal HRSA.[2] This enumeration collected information on workers of federal, state, and local public health agencies in the year 2000 based on existing data, reports, and surveys. As such, it was more of a qualitative and descriptive enumeration than a quantitative one. The year 2000 public health workforce enumeration identified a total of 450,000 public health workers, including 15,000 workers in voluntary sector organizations and 15,000 public health students. Occupational categories could not be established for 112,000 public health workers, making it difficult to project the actual number of workers in specific categories, such as public health nurses or epidemiologists.

To compare information with BLS data, the year 2000 public health enumeration numbers were adjusted to assign an occupational category to all workers. Table 6–4 provides both the actual number of workers identified in specific occupational categories and the adjusted number after those in the "unreported" group are assigned to a category and title. Each chapter then uses information from both sources to estimate the number of existing positions for each occupational category and title.

Public Health Practice Profile

Individual workers, as well as occupational categories, produce work important to achieving public health goals and objectives. As noted in Chapter 1, key public health goals and objectives address preventing disease and injury, promoting healthy behaviors, protecting against health risks and threats, responding to emergencies, and assuring the quality of health services.[14] This overall public health practice framework provides the basis for channeling contributions both by individuals and organizations toward common goals. The specific work tasks of different occupations and individuals generally fall into one or more of the 10 essential public health services. Chapter 1 characterized the essential public health services as the means to achieving public health ends, or how the work of public health is accomplished. It is useful to view these functions and essential public health services as an aggregate job description for the entire public health workforce, with the workload then divided among the many different professional and occupational categories composing the total public health workforce. In that light, Chapters 7 through 13 will each identify several purposes and essential public health services that form the core of the duties and job descriptions for each occupational category and public health career. A summary, in checklist format, appears in each chapter. Chapter 14 provides a composite profile by aggregating the profiles from each of these chapters. An example of this format is provided in Table 6–5.

In this example, the public health occupational category is primarily involved in addressing three public health goals: preventing epidemics, preventing injuries, and promoting healthy behaviors. This public health occupational category works to address these goals largely through performing five essential public health services—monitoring health status, investigating health problems, educating people about health, evaluating effectiveness, and researching new solutions to health problems.

In this example, and in later chapters, the assignment of specific public health purposes and essential public health services may appear somewhat arbitrary. In each case, however, judgments are made as to which purposes and essential services are most closely associated with each occupational category. Some occupational categories may appear to have a relatively limited focus (e.g., public health laboratory workers) in comparison with others (e.g., public health nurses) that may have very broad roles that could conceivably cover all purposes and services. For each occupational category and title, however, the number of purposes and essential services identified for each occupational category is limited to no more than one half the number possible (3 of 6 purposes, 5 of 10 essential public health services).

Characterizing the work of an occupational category in this manner proves a functional view of the work performed.

TABLE 6–4 Number of Public Health Workers in Selected Occupational Categories and Titles, United States, 2000

Gov PH Workers	Reported #	Adjusted #
Administrators	15,920	21,247
Professionals	176,980	236,202
Technicians	61,088	81,530
Other support	59,085	69,283
Unreported	104,763	
TOTAL	417,836	TOTAL 417,836
Occupational Categories		
Health administrators	15,920	21,247
Admin support staff	37,805	62,981
Admin/business prof	4,725	7,306
Attorney/hearing officer	601	929
Biostatistician	1,164	1,800
Environmental engineer	4,549	7,034
Environmental specialist	14,882	23,013
Epidemiologist	927	1,433
Policy analyst/plan/econ	3,678	5,687
Disease investigator	783	1,211
License/inspection spec	13,780	21,309
Social, behavioral, mental	3,762	5,817
Occ. health and safety spec	5,593	8,649
PH dental worker	2,032	3,142
PH educator	2,230	3,448
PH lab professional	14,088	21,785
PH nurse	41,232	63,759
PH nutritionist	6,680	10,330
PH pharmacist	1,496	2,313
PH physician	6,008	9,290
PH program specialist	7,820	12,092
PH veterinarian/animal cont spec	2,037	3,150
Public relations/public info	563	871
Other PH professional	14,119	21,833
Computer specialist	4,326	6,210
Environmental eng technician	414	594
En health technician	501	719
Health info system/data analyst	605	868
Occ health and safety technician	95	136
PH laboratory technician	5,700	8,182
Other PH technician (LPN, etc.)	26,953	38,690
Community outreach/field worker	676	902
Other paraprofessional	18,902	25,227

Source: Reported column adapted from Health Resources and Services Administration, Bureau of Health Professions, National Center for Health Workforce Information and Analysis and Center for Health Policy, Columbia School of Nursing. *The Public Health Workforce Enumeration 2000.* Washington, DC: HRSA; 2000. Available at: http://www.phppo.cdc.gov/owpp/docs/library/2000/Public%20Health%20Workforce%20Enumeration%202000.pdf. Accessed August 20, 2005.

It also facilitates an understanding of how the work of one occupational category relates to the work of another category, and how it relates to the overall work performed across all public health occupational categories (see Chapter 14).

Important and Essential Duties

The most important aspect of any job or career is what workers do day in and day out. It is those basic and routine duties that best define positions in public health or any other field of

TABLE 6–5 Public Health Profile Example

(Example)
**Public Health Practitioners
Make a Difference by:**

Public Health Purposes
  Preventing epidemics and the spread of disease ✓
  Protecting against environmental hazards
  Preventing injuries ✓
  Promoting and encouraging healthy behaviors ✓
  Responding to disasters and assisting communities in recovery
  Assuring the quality and accessibility of health services

Essential Public Health Services
  Monitoring health status to identify community health problems ✓
  Diagnosing and investigating health problems and health hazards in the community ✓
  Informing, educating, and empowering people about health issues ✓
  Mobilizing community partnerships to identify and solve health problems
  Developing policies and plans that support individual and community health efforts
  Enforcing laws and regulations that protect health and ensure safety
  Linking people with needed personal health services and assuring the provision of health care when otherwise unavailable
  Assuring a competent public health and personal health care workforce
  Evaluating effectiveness, accessibility, and quality of personal and population-based health services ✓
  Researching new insights and innovative solutions to health problems ✓

endeavor. This list varies enormously from one position to another and often from one level of the same position to a higher level (e.g., from an entry level environmental health specialist to a midlevel environmental health specialist). Important and essential duties for various titles within Chapters 7 through 13 are based on information from a sampling of job and position descriptions from a variety of public health organizations. Each of these chapters also provides an example of a daily schedule for the occupational category addressed in that chapter.

Minimum Qualifications

Another key dimension of a position is a statement of the minimum qualifications necessary for that job. Often these minimum qualifications must be met in order for a worker to apply for a particular position. Minimum qualifications may emphasize experience or education or both. In any event, there is a battery of skills or competencies that are expected of those applying for and those working in public health positions. Minimum levels of knowledge, skills, and abilities are presented for public health job titles addressed in Chapters 7 through 13. Additional qualifications, such as physical capabilities appropriate for specific jobs or job locations, are also presented. These qualifications are synthesized from a sampling of current position descriptions.

The range of public health occupations and careers extends from those requiring considerable education and training to those that require relatively little. For example, some state and local health officials may hold several degrees, such as a bachelor degree in science, a master's degree in public health, and a doctoral degree in medicine. At the same time, key staff performing investigations of communicable disease or environmental threats may have only an associate or bachelor's degree at the undergraduate level. It is not uncommon for some technical and clerical staff to have no more than a high school diploma with on-the-job training. As this book largely targets undergraduate and graduate-degree students, particular emphasis is on occupations and careers requiring at least an undergraduate degree.

Workplace Considerations

Public health work takes place in many organizations and settings other than governmental public health agencies such as state health agencies or local public health departments. Many community and voluntary organizations collaborate with governmental public health agencies and employ staff whose work parallels that of workers in governmental public health agencies. This is true both for nongovernmental public health efforts here in the United States and those on the international level. Not much is known about public health workers and career opportunities in community and voluntary organizations. There is some information available for local, state, and federal public health agencies on measures such as numbers employed, occupational categories, work locations, salary, and specific duties. This book summarizes work setting information for each public health occupational category or career grouping.

Another important workplace consideration relates to special physical capabilities, travel requirements, and other unique aspects of specific jobs. For example, some positions may require the ability to lift and move items weighing up to 50 pounds. Other jobs may require the ability to walk great distances or to have normal vision or hearing. Others may require the ability to work outside in cold and inclement weather, or to work unusual hours.

Salary Estimates

Detailed and specific salary information is not widely available. Information will be provided based on limited sources, including BLS data and current job postings. This information should not be considered to be definitive or completely accurate. Variations in salary scales are wide from agency to agency depending on a variety of circumstances and conditions. Figure 6–3 indicates that the average salary of a full-time worker employed by a state or local health agency increased by nearly 40% to nearly $43,000 between 1994 and 2005. One trend contributing to this increase is a higher proportion of workers in professional and technical occupational titles in 2005 than a decade earlier.

Career Prospects

Current and future opportunities for public health careers, as do careers in all fields, depend on relationships among the population, the labor force, and the demand for public health programs and services.[15] The size and composition of the population strongly influences both the size of the workforce and the types of services needed by the population.

The U.S. population continues to increase, although at a

slower rate than in recent decades. The average age of the population continues to increase as well, and the proportion of the population in the 55–64 year age category will increase more than 40% over the next 10 years. As this age group nears retirement, replacement of workers will create job opportunities and career advancement possibilities in addition to those created by the continued growth of the overall population.

Among the various sectors of the U.S. economy, the health sector is projected to grow faster and add more jobs than other sectors. About one in every four new jobs will be in the health sector. In the health sector, and in the overall economy, professional and related categories will exhibit the greatest growth and offer the greatest opportunities for new jobs and career advancement. In sum, the overall outlook for professional and technical occupations in public health is very bright for those now in or about to enter the job market.

The optimal number of public health workers is controversial and uncertain. There is widespread concern within the public health community that there will soon be a shortage of public health workers. Several key public health occupational categories are currently in short supply, such as public health nurses and epidemiologists. The information provided

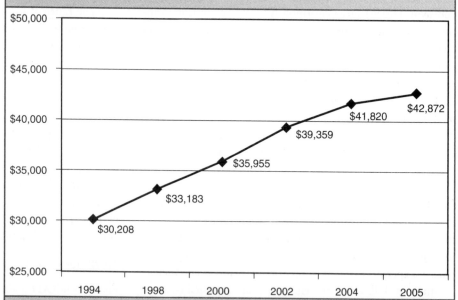

FIGURE 6–3 Mean salary for full-time equivalent workers of state and local health[*] agencies, selected years, 1994–2005, United States.

[*]Health: public health services, emergency medical services, mental health, alcohol and drug abuse, outpatient clinics, visiting nurses, food and sanitary inspections, animal control, other environmental health activities (e.g., pollution control), etc.
Source: Bureau of the Census. Federal, state, and local governments, public employment and payroll data. Available at: http://www.census.gov/govs/www/apesstl.html. Accessed June 20, 2006.

in the career prospect section will identify specific occupational categories that have been identified (rightly or wrongly) as being in greatest need.

Each of Chapters 7 through 13 focuses on a specific public health occupation or career. But careers in public health, like those in many fields, are not always straightforward. Individual workers can begin in one career pathway and then move into another. For example, administrators of public health agencies could come up through the ranks of program and agency management or from one of the public health professional categories, such as environmental health, nursing, or health education. This section will identify some of these paths and career ladders for public health workers.

Additional Information

Only basic information is provided in the chapters that follow. Most public health occupational categories and careers, however, have excellent sources for more detailed information. Several sources, often professional associations or organizations, will be identified in each chapter. Career development opportunities through education, training, and credentialing are also provided for each public health workforce category.

CONCLUSION

Recent decades have witnessed an increase in the number of public health workers employed by both governmental and nongovernmental agencies, caused by expanded public health priorities and partnerships. This expansion of the workforce, however, leaves many questions unanswered as to the number, distribution, training, and preparedness of the public health workforce, making these issues of public concern.[16,17] Some of these concerns have persisted since the late 1800s, as suggested by an editorial appearing in the *Journal of the American Medical Association* more than 110 years ago:

> It is unfortunate that in the absence of epidemics or pestilence, too little attention is paid to the protection of the public health, and as a necessary consequence, to the selection of those whose duties require them to guard the public health.[18(p189)]

This chapter also describes the framework that will be used in later chapters to examine various public health occupations and career pathways and key aspects of the agencies that employ most public health workers. For public health occupations and careers, key characteristics include occupational classification, public health roles, important and essential duties, minimum qualifications, workplace considerations, salary estimates, career prospects, and sources for additional information. For public health organizations, important features include governmental level, range of responsibilities, organizational structure, level and sources of funding, and relationships with nongovernmental organizations.

Discussion Questions and Exercises

1. Choose a recent (within the last 3 years) outbreak or other public health emergency situation that has drawn significant media attention. Describe how specific occupational categories in the public health infrastructure contributed to either the emergency situation or its solution. The *MMWR Morbidity and Mortality Weekly Report* contents for recent weeks would be a good place to look for recent outbreaks; various print and electronic media may also be useful sources of information.

2. What distinguishes a public health professional from a professional working for a public health organization?

3. Are public health professionals viewed as change agents in their communities today? Why or why not? Do you hold the same opinion for public health organizations? Why or why not?

4. What factors determine the optimum size of the public health workforce in your community?

5. How have the needs for different public health occupations changed over the past century? How will the need for various public health occupations change over the next 2 decades?

REFERENCES

1. Turnock BJ. *Public Health: What It Is and How It Works.* 3rd ed. Sudbury, MA: Jones and Bartlett; 2004.

2. Health Resources and Services Administration, Bureau of Health Professions, National Center for Health Workforce Information and Analysis and Center for Health Policy, Columbia School of Nursing. *The Public Health Workforce Enumeration 2000.* Washington, DC: HRSA; 2000. Available at: http://www.phppo.cdc.gov/owpp/docs/library/2000/Public%20Health%20 Workforce%20Enumeration%202000.pdf. Accessed August 20, 2005.

3. U.S. Bureau of the Census. Federal, state, and local governments, public employment and payroll data. Available at: http://www.census.gov/ govs/www/apes.html. Accessed August 20, 2005.

4. U.S. Department of Health and Human Services. *Health, United States, 2004.* Washington, DC: National Center for Health Statistics; 2004.

5. Health Resources and Services Administration, U.S. Department of Health and Human Services. *Public Health Personnel in the United States, 1980: Second Report to Congress.* Washington, DC: U.S. Public Health Service; 1982.

6. National Association of County and City Health Officials. *Profile of Local Health Departments, 1996–1997 Dataset.* Washington, DC: NACCHO; 1997.

7. National Association of County and City Health Officials. *Public Health Infrastructure Chartbook.* Washington, DC: NACCHO; 2001.

8. Gerzoff RB, Baker EL. The use of scaling techniques to analyze U.S. local health department staffing structures, 1992–1993. *1998 Proceedings of the Section on Government Statistics and Section on Social Statistics of the American Statistical Association.* 1998;209–213.

9. American Public Health Association. Public health code of ethics. Available at: http://www.apha.org/codeofethics/ethics.htm. Accessed August 20, 2005.

10. Gerzoff RB, Richards TB. The education of local health department top executives. *J Public Health Manage Pract.* 1997;3:50–56.

11. Turnock BJ, Hutchison KD. *The Local Public Health Workforce: Size, Distribution, Composition, and Influence on Core Function Performance, Illinois 1998–1999.* Chicago, IL: Illinois Center for Health Workforce Studies; 2000.

12. Turnock BJ. Public health workforce preparedness roadmap. *J Public Health Manage Pract.* 2003;9:471–480.

13. Bureau of Labor Statistics, U.S. Department of Labor. May 2004 national, state, and metropolitan area occupational employment and wage estimates. Available at: http://www.bls.gov/oes/current/oes_nat.htm. Accessed August 20, 2005.

14. Essential Public Health Services Working Group, Core Public Health Functions Steering Committee, U.S. Department of Health and Human Services. Public health in America. Available at: http://www.health.gov/ phfunctions/public.htm. Accessed August 20, 2005.

15. Bureau of Labor Statistics, U.S. Department of Labor. *Occupational Outlook Handbook, 2004–2005 Edition.* Available at: http://www.bls.gov/oco/. Accessed August 20, 2005.

16. Tilson H, Gebbie KM. The public health workforce. *Ann Rev Public Health.* 2004;25:341–356. Available at: http://arjournals.annualreviews.org/ doi/full/10.1146/annurev.publhealth.25.102802.124357. Accessed August 20, 2005.

17. Gebbie KM, Turnock BJ. The public health workforce, 2006: new challenges. *Health Aff (Millwood).* 2006;25:923–933.

18. American Medical Association. Editorial. *JAMA.* 1893;20:189.

CHAPTER 7

Public Health Administration

LEARNING OBJECTIVES

After completing Chapter 7, learners will be proficient in describing key features of occupations and careers in public health administration and how these contribute to carrying out public health's core functions and essential services. Key aspects of this competency expectation include

- Describing several different occupational titles in this category
- Identifying several essential public health services that are critical for positions in this category
- Describing important and essential duties for several job titles in this category
- Identifying minimum qualifications and describing general workplace considerations, salary expectations, and career prospects for positions in this category

Public health organizations require leaders, managers, and administrators at various levels throughout the organization to plan, organize, direct, control, and coordinate health services, education, or policy. The people serving in these positions come from a wide variety of educational, professional, and work experience backgrounds. Many lack formal training and previous experience in public health. Nonetheless, they are the third largest occupational category within the public health workforce, behind environmental health professionals and public health nurses, and they represent a force even larger than their numbers. Table 7–1 provides a snapshot of an average day in the life of a public health administrator.

OCCUPATIONAL CLASSIFICATION

There is no standard occupational category specific to public health administrators and managers. There is a more generic standard occupational category *health services administrator*

that encompasses administrative positions in any health care or health services organization. This standard occupational category is one of the administrative occupations within the white collar grouping of occupations.

Public health administrators are health services administrators leading a public health agency, program, or major subunit. Public health administrators plan, analyze, organize, direct, coordinate, and evaluate the use of resources to deliver health services, education, or policy; they often manage or regulate health agencies and facilities. The category includes such job titles as director, administrator, chief, manager, or one of the many titles indicating chief public health official of a jurisdiction (e.g., secretary of health, health officer, health commissioner, health official). Titles that include the term *coordinating* or *senior* are generally not classified as public health administrators but are included with the profession referenced (e.g., coordinating nutritionist with public health nutritionist, senior public health nurse with public health nurse).

Data from the Bureau of Labor Statistics indicate there are 225,000 health services administrators in the United States.[1] There were 25,000 working for federal, state, and local public health agencies in 2004. The *Public Health Workforce Enumeration 2000* identified 21,000 working in governmental public health agencies.[2] Data from these two sources are used throughout this chapter.

In addition to public health administrators and managers, there are several occupational classifications involved with public health administration. These include administrative business professionals and administrative support staff.

Administrative business professionals are trained at a professional level in their field of expertise prior to entry in public

TABLE 7–1 A Typical Day for a Public Health Administrator

7:30 a.m.	Breakfast with local hospital administrator and staff regarding diabetes screening
8:30 a.m.	In office, follow-up call with state epidemiologist regarding recent outbreak of foodborne illness
9:00 a.m.	Weekly meeting with senior staff
10:15 a.m.	Meet with epidemiology, health education, and planning staff regarding completion of community needs assessment
10:45 a.m.	Meet with county commissioner regarding West Nile Virus concerns in her area
11:15 a.m.	Review and update electronic slide presentation for today's lunch meeting
11:45 a.m.	Meet with local Chamber of Commerce leadership before lunch, which includes public health presentation to business community
1:00 p.m.	Discuss budget amendment proposal with fiscal and program staff
1:30 p.m.	Media interview regarding West Nile Virus concerns
2:00 p.m.	Give welcoming remarks and overview for new employee orientation
3:00 p.m.	Conference call for committee of National Association of County and City Health Officials task force on workforce and leadership development
4:00 p.m.	Review information suggested by senior staff for presentation to board of health
4:30 p.m.	Drop by the clinic to see how things went today
5:15 p.m.	Prepare remarks for board of health meeting
7:00 p.m.	Attend monthly meeting of board of health

health and perform work in business, finance, auditing, management, and accounting. The *Public Health Workforce Enumeration 2000* identified 7,500 administrative business professionals working in governmental public health agencies. Administrative business staff, including bookkeepers, accounting clerks, and auditing clerks, perform support work in areas of business and financial operations. In addition, there are another 80,000 administrative support workers (such as receptionists, typists, and stenographers) who perform nontechnical support work in all areas of agency management and program administration. Administrative business professionals and administrative support staff titles fall within the administrative chain of command of an agency but are not classified within the public health administrator category. Nonetheless, these titles can serve as steps along the career development path leading to a public health administrator position.

PUBLIC HEALTH PRACTICE PROFILE

Public health administrators work at a level within an organization that often bears responsibility for achieving organizational goals and objectives. This means they may be involved with addressing any or all six public health responsibilities, although their background and experience may provide greater expertise in some of these roles than others. For example, administrators of local public health agencies who worked their way to the top of the organization through the ranks of environmental health may continue to be directly involved in protecting against environmental hazards or responding to

disasters. An administrator from the ranks of the nursing staff may remain more directly involved in disease prevention and quality assurance of health services. For most public health administrators, managing responses to public health emergencies and assuring the quality of health services require their personal attention. If these administrators also have professional training in epidemiology, disease and injury prevention, environmental health, or health education, they may be directly involved in these duties as well. Otherwise, the professional and program staff of the organization guide activities for these roles.

Similarly, among the 10 essential public health services, administrators may have more personal expertise in some services than others. There are several essential public health services, however, that all administrators must address. These include developing and mobilizing collaborative relationships and partnerships within the community, developing policies and plans, enforcing laws and regulations, assuring a competent workforce, and evaluating the effectiveness, accessibility, and quality of health services. Table 7–2 summarizes public health purposes and essential public health services at the core of positions for public health administrators.

IMPORTANT AND ESSENTIAL DUTIES

There are many possible job titles and positions for public health administrators. The focus in this chapter will be on three positions: (1) health services manager; (2) local public health agency director; and (3) health officer. Each of these

TABLE 7–2 Public Health Practice Profile for Public Health Administration

Public Health Administrators Make a Difference by:

Public Health Purposes

Preventing epidemics and the spread of disease √
Protecting against environmental hazards
Preventing injuries
Promoting and encouraging healthy behaviors
Responding to disasters and assisting communities in recovery √
Assuring the quality and accessibility of health services √

Essential Public Health Services

Monitoring health status to identify community health problems
Diagnosing and investigating health problems and health hazards in the community
Informing, educating, and empowering people about health issues
Mobilizing community partnerships to identify and solve health problems
Developing policies and plans that support individual and community health efforts √
Enforcing laws and regulations that protect health and ensure safety √
Linking people with needed personal health services and assuring the provision of health care when otherwise unavailable
Assuring a competent public health and personal health care workforce
Evaluating effectiveness, accessibility, and quality of personal and population-based health services √
Researching new insights and innovative solutions to health problems

positions and a representative panel of their important and essential duties are described in this section.

Health Services Manager

This is an administrative and management position that directs, plans, analyzes, and coordinates health, public health, and regulatory programs and services. A worker in this or a similar title (such as health administrator) is often responsible for directing or assisting in the overall planning, directing, and coordinating of assigned health, public health, and regulatory programs and services, including the identification of program priorities and the development and implementation of new programs and services. This position could be located at a variety of managerial levels. Responsibilities may be in areas such as chronic disease prevention; environmental health and communicable disease prevention; health standards and licensure; maternal, child, and family health; nutritional health and services; health information; regulation; senior services; health improvement; emergency response; or closely related areas. Positions have program management and decision-making authority, and usually have policy, assessment, planning, budget, and supervisory responsibilities. Direction is received from a designated administrative superior who reviews work through conferences, reports, and evaluation of operational results. The health services manager, however, is expected to ex-

ercise considerable initiative and judgment in planning and carrying out assignments.

Important and essential duties for health services managers may include

- Directs or assists in the overall planning, development, and administration of assigned health, public health, and regulatory programs and services in such areas as chronic disease prevention; maternal, child, and family health; environmental health and communicable disease prevention; nutritional health and services; health standards and licensure; health information; regulations; health improvement; or emergency response
- Develops and coordinates comprehensive public health systems for a specific geographic area, such as a county, city, or district
- Provides consultation to doctors, health care providers, hospitals, local health departments, and other agencies linked with health care in the effective delivery of health, public health, and regulatory programs and services
- Ensures individuals receive program services appropriate to their needs and program eligibility
- Oversees or assists in the development of community-based coalitions and works with coalitions, advocacy groups, and others interested in program issues to develop

plans and outcomes on how to address specific health, public health regulatory, and senior programs and services concerns

- Prepares new or revises existing legislation and develops standards, regulations, and policies to implement the legislation
- Directs or assists administrative personnel in general management aspects of policy development and program planning and coordination as related to assigned responsibilities; assists in the evaluation of the effect of policy and organizational changes and new programs
- Reviews and revises programs in area of responsibility to ensure compliance of operations with laws, regulations, policies, plans, and procedures
- Supervises staff to carry out the strategies of the organization or program
- Participates in meetings with agency administrators to develop, coordinate, implement, and interpret new or revised initiatives
- Participates in conferences and meetings relating to areas of assigned responsibility
- Participates in the development of budget requests and the monitoring of expenditures according to budget allocations and appropriations
- Conducts research, institutes special studies, and prepares or reviews reports and related information to evaluate existing organizations, policies, procedures, and practices as related to the assigned program
- Maintains contact, cooperates with, and addresses local and community organizations and other interested groups pertaining to the assigned programs

Local Public Health Agency Director

Under administrative direction, a local public health agency director plans, organizes, directs, manages, and supervises public health programs for the jurisdiction; directs the enforcement of federal, state, and local health laws and regulations; directs staff providing public health and education programs; represents agency activities, programs, and services with community organizations and other governmental agencies; performs special assignments as directed; and provides administrative support for its governing bodies (such as a board of health or a city or county board of supervisors). Local public health agency directors often serve as department head with general responsibility for the administration of the jurisdiction's public health programs and functions and may serve as the health officer for the jurisdiction. Many of the nonmedical duties of health officers are also performed by local public health agency directors. This position may report to a municipal or county board of health or board of super-

visors (or perhaps a city council) through the municipal or county administrative officer or chief elected official. As agency head, this position often directly supervises positions such as director of nursing, fiscal officer, director of environmental health, director of health education, and sometimes a medical health officer.

Important and essential duties for local public health agency directors may include

- Plans, organizes, directs, coordinates, and administers public health programs for the jurisdiction, such as communicable disease control, immunization, environmental health, health education, maternal and child health, vital statistics, and health programs for adults, children, handicapped children, and schools
- Enforces public health laws and regulations within the jurisdiction
- Develops and recommends agency goals, objectives, and policies
- Provides strategic direction and leadership in identifying community health needs and developing and implementing community health improvement plans that meet identified needs
- Prepares and administers agency budgets recommended by the jurisdiction's executive officer and approved by the governing board or entity
- Controls fiscal expenditures and revenues
- Monitors and evaluates overall agency and program performance and directs change to improve quality and effectiveness
- Hires, supervises, evaluates, and ensures proper training of agency staff in accordance with personnel rules
- Administers a variety of categorical programs
- Provides direction and develops policies for clinical services through protocol development
- Develops policies and protocols for the control and prevention of communicable diseases
- Plans and develops new program efforts
- Develops and administers grants
- Initiates appropriate epidemiologic investigations of communicable disease outbreaks
- Provides health information to the public, community organizations, and other county staff
- Maintains contact with the press and community organizations
- Interprets policies and regulations for the public
- Supervises administration, program development, fiscal management, and provision of direct client services at agency clinic sites
- Represents the agency with other government agencies

Health Officer

Health officers, often physicians, plan, organize, direct, and provide medical oversight over public health programs for the jurisdiction; provide technical consultation to citizens, public officials, staff, and community organizations and agencies on public health and preventive medicine issues; and serve as the designated health officer. A health officer provides medical supervision for the local public health agency by coordinating public health care services with external agencies and health care providers and providing ongoing communication with the local medical community. This position is also responsible for providing medical oversight and enforcement of public health regulations for a variety of public health programs and services including environmental health, vital records, communicable disease control, public health nursing, emergency and disaster medical planning, public health education, and state maternal and child health services. This title is distinguished from the local public health director in that the latter has overall management responsibility for the local public health agency's programs and services, whereas the health officer directs the medical oversight for all public health programs. In some instances, the health officer also serves as local public health director; in others, this position reports to the public health director or to the director of a higher-level health and human services agency. Some states (about one half) require the health officer to be a licensed physician; the other one half allow nonphysicians to act as health officers or set no requirements. Health officers often supervise titles such as the director of public health nursing, the director of environmental health, director of health education, and other professional and program directors.

Important and essential duties for health officers may include

- Plans, organizes, directs, and evaluates the medical oversight of public health programs
- Assures enforcement of applicable public health, environmental health, and sanitation orders, ordinances, and statutes
- Analyzes legislative changes; evaluates and develops medical and public health policies, programs, and procedures; and formulates improvements
- Serves as an advocate to promote statewide public health policies, which also benefit the local jurisdiction
- Disseminates and interprets policies, laws, regulations, and state and federal directives regarding medical and public health issues to physicians, department staff, and representatives of hospitals, nursing homes, medical clinics, and schools by written means and personal contacts; acts as medical epidemiologist for public health diseases

- Consults and coordinates with federal and state officials and representatives of local public and private health agencies in the enforcement of health laws and the development of programs to meet public health needs
- Plans, organizes, directs, coordinates, and administers public health programs for the jurisdiction, such as communicable disease control, immunization, environmental health, health education, maternal and child health, vital statistics, and programs for adults, children, handicapped children, and schools
- Provides direction and advice regarding policies and procedures directed by the state immunization board
- Works closely with the agency director and health services managers to monitor performance and effect changes in practice to improve quality of services
- Confers with members of the public and representatives of federal, state, and local agencies regarding health department programs; cooperates with federal and state public health groups in the enforcement of health and sanitary matters
- Supervises, directs, and evaluates assigned staff, to include assigning work, handling employee concerns and problems, and counseling
- Reviews technical requirements, reports, and procedures generated by the health department
- Prepares public health information materials and news releases
- Consults with physicians, nurses, patients, staff members, other governmental agencies, or other individuals in the diagnosis of, and investigation of, cases of suspected communicable diseases and exchanges information or provides recommendations; takes measures to prevent and control epidemics
- Serves on emergency medical services and public health emergency preparedness committees
- Represents the jurisdiction on committees, boards, at meetings, or otherwise as assigned

MINIMUM QUALIFICATIONS

Public health administrators can emerge from either a professional occupational category or from a career in other management positions. Those arising from the professional ranks may acquire management skills either as part of their education, such as in a master's degree program (such as a master's of public health, master's of public administration, master's of health administration, or master's of business administration degree) or, less commonly, in a doctoral degree program. Schools of public health commonly offer the doctor of public health (DrPH) degree for high-level public health practitioners. PhD and ScD degrees in public health sciences and disciplines are also offered by many institutions.

More commonly, however, public health administrators and managers lack formal training at the master's or doctoral level in public health. For example, only one in five chief administrators of local public health agencies reported formal training in public health in the mid-1990s. This includes administrators whose public health training was in their primary profession (such as nursing, environmental health, medicine, or health education) suggesting that few received public health training in programs preparing administrators. Many public health administrators acquire public health practice management skills on a nondegree basis through a variety of means including management academies and leadership development institutes. Nearly 20 states have developed such institutes for workers in their own and collaborating states. There are also several national public health leadership institutes and a national public health management academy.

Public health administrators represent a significant portion of the public health workforce for which career pathways are particularly unclear. Efforts to establish a greater professional identity for public health administrators are receiving increased attention. Management and leadership development programs are one example. Credentialing of public health administrators is another option under consideration. Several states license public health administrators, and one program credentials public health administrators through an independent review board. Some public health administrators view degrees from programs accredited by the Accrediting Commission on Education for Health Services Administration (ACHESA) or subsequent recognition from the American College of Healthcare Executives as meaningful credentials.

To be considered as qualified for a position as a public health administrator, both experience and education are important. Typical minimum qualifications for health services managers, local public health administrators, and health officers are detailed in the next section.

Typical Minimum Qualifications for Health Services Manager

Knowledge, Skills, and Abilities

A health services manager generally has knowledge of

- Principles and practices involved in the administration of health, public health, and regulatory programs and services
- The organization and operation of public agencies at the national, state, and local levels that are involved in health, public health, and regulatory programs and services

- The philosophy and objectives of state health and public health regulatory programs and services
- Programs and objectives of state and local public health agencies and of the interprofessional relationships in the implementation of their programs
- Current human service issues and theories
- The organization and functions of advocacy groups, voluntary agencies, civic organizations, and similar groups interested in health, public health, and regulatory programs and services and activities
- Managerial techniques and administrative practices

A health services manager generally has the skills and ability to

- Plan, promote, and direct complex public health programs or services at the state level
- Analyze complex health data and formulate plans for coordinating and establishing new or improved health services and programs
- Secure active cooperation from other public and private agencies in developing and guiding health, public health, regulatory, and senior programs and services
- Develop, implement, and administer assigned programs or services to achieve positive program and client outcomes
- Establish and maintain working relationships with departmental officials, legislators, staff associates, the general public, and others
- Analyze and evaluate policies and operations and formulate recommendations
- Communicate effectively
- Provide leadership and supervision to professional, technical, and related program staff
- Manage change, provide program management, and achieve results
- Develop short- and long-range plans that meet established objectives and contribute to the overall goals and mission of the agency

Experience and Education

In many personnel systems, any combination of training and experience that provides the required knowledge and abilities qualifies an individual for this position. A typical career pathway for health services managers is through 3 or more years of professional experience in public health, health care delivery, environmental health or regulation, protective services for adults or the disabled, in-home services, or long-term care. In addition, a qualified applicant would have graduated from an accredited 4-year college or university with specialization in public health;

health care administration; public, personnel, or business administration; biological, physical, environmental, or social sciences; nursing; nutrition/dietetics; social work; human services; gerontology; physical rehabilitation; education; or closely related areas. Graduate work in specified educational areas may sometimes be substituted on a year-for-year basis for 1 or more years of the required experience. Additional qualifying experience in the specified areas may be substituted on a year-for-year basis for any deficiencies in the stated education.

Typical Minimum Qualifications for Local Public Health Agency Director

Knowledge, Skills, and Abilities

The local public health agency director generally has knowledge of

- Basic principles of medical science and their application to local public health programs
- Public health problems and issues and their relationship to the development and operations of public health programs and services
- Federal, state, and local laws, ordinances, and regulations applicable to public health programs and communicable disease control
- Clinical skills and procedures
- Grant development and administration
- Principles, techniques, and practices of business and public health administration
- Budget development and expenditure control
- Principles and techniques of effective employee supervision, training, and development
- Public personnel management

The local public health agency director generally has the skills and ability to

- Plan, organize, supervise, and administer the functions and programs of the local public health agency
- Ensure proper enforcement of public health statues, laws, and regulations
- Provide direction, supervision, and training for agency staff
- Develop and administer budgets and control expenditures
- Develop and administer grants
- Review the work of agency staff and resolve problems
- Oversee the development, maintenance, and preparation of public health statistics, medical records, and reports
- Direct the preparation of and prepare clear, concise reports

- Effectively represent the local public health agency in contact with the public, community organizations, and other government agencies
- Establish and maintain cooperative working relationships
- Coordinate assigned activities with community organizations and other government agencies

Experience and Education

Any combination of training and experience that provides the required knowledge and abilities can qualify an individual for this position. A typical way to obtain the required knowledge and abilities is through broad and extensive experience in the development, analysis, and administration of public health programs and services with 3 years of the background and experience in a management or full supervisory capacity. Ideally this experience includes work in the areas of fiscal management, personnel management, and program development. In addition, a master's degree in public health, public administration, or health care administration is highly desirable.

Typical Minimum Qualifications for Health Officer

Knowledge, Skills, and Abilities

The health officer generally has knowledge of

- Principles, practices, and responsibilities of medicine and of contemporary public health programs and service needs
- Applicable federal and state laws and regulations
- Organization, purpose, and function of federal and state health agencies
- Local medical associations and community health groups
- Principles and methods of public and community relations, and public information practices and techniques
- Principles and methods of determining and servicing public health needs
- Socioeconomic and psychological factors that can impact the effectiveness of health services delivery
- Communicable diseases and methods of control of sexually transmitted diseases
- Basic principles of budgeting
- Principles and practices of management necessary to plan, analyze, develop, evaluate, and direct diverse and complex activities of major health programs

The health officer generally has the skills and ability to

- Plan, organize, and direct public health programs within professional standards, legal requirements, and financial constraints

- Direct and supervise professional and technical personnel
- Analyze situations accurately and take effective actions
- Interpret laws, regulations, and standards pertaining to public health
- Prepare clear and comprehensive records and reports
- Maintain accurate records
- Communicate effectively, both orally and in writing
- Speak effectively in public
- Establish and maintain effective working relationships with staff members, other departments, agencies, public groups, and organizations

Education and Experience

Any combination of training and experience that provides the required knowledge and abilities will qualify an individual for this position. A typical way to obtain the required knowledge and abilities is through 3 years of administrative or supervisory public health medical experience or possession of a master's degree in public health from an accredited school of public health and 1 year of public health medical experience. In some states, health officers must be a graduate of a medical school in good standing and possess a valid license to practice medicine in that state.

WORKPLACE CONSIDERATIONS

Every organization has a management structure with various levels of management positions. Larger and more complex organizations have greater numbers of managers and administrators, although their scope of responsibility is often limited to a specific program or constellation of programs. Smaller organizations are more likely to be dominated by professionals, with administrative positions often filled by workers with professional backgrounds and credentials. For example, more than one half of the directors of the approximately 3,000 local public health agencies in the United States have a health professional degree but no degree in public health. For several decades, there has been a general trend toward more nonprofessional managers rather than elevating professionals into top management positions. This has been occurring at all governmental levels but somewhat more frequently among state and federal health agencies than for local public health agencies. In 2004, there were 25,170 health administrators working for federal (9,530), state (6,420), and local (9,220) governmental agencies (see Table 7–3).

Work settings also influence the typical physical requirement for positions in this occupational category. Similar to administrators and managers throughout the health sector, public health administrators work long and irregular hours.

Most public health administration positions call for workers to be able to sit for extended periods and to frequently stand and walk short distances. Normal manual dexterity and eye-hand coordination, hearing, and vision corrected to within the normal range are also important considerations. Normally, public health administrators will be able to communicate verbally and use office equipment including computers, telephones, calculators, copiers, and fax machines. Although much of the work is performed in an office environment, frequent and/or continuous contact with staff and the public is also necessary. In many situations, administrators may be required to possess a valid driver's license.

SALARY ESTIMATES

The mean annual salary for medical and health administrators working in all settings was $75,000 in 2004, with the middle 50% earning between $53,000 and $89,000. The range between the 10th and 90th percentile was $41,000 and $119,000. Entry-level salaries are likely around $40,000. Mean salaries are higher for administrators working for hospitals and physician practices and lower for those working in the public and voluntary sector.

Salaries for public health administrators vary widely based on the type and size of the organization as well as the credentials and experience of the administrator. Mean salaries for health administrators working for federal agencies were $87,500 in 2004, but salaries for state and local health administrators averaged $72,500 and $69,000 respectively (Table 7–3). Small local public health agencies have notoriously low salary scales (often in the $35,000–$55,000 range), making it difficult to attract administrators with graduate degrees or with extensive previous experience. Larger governmental public health agencies can often offer salaries somewhat competitive of those found in the private and voluntary sector ($65,000–$85,000 range). Administrators with professional credentials, especially physicians, dentists, veterinarians, epidemiologists, and nurses, may be able to attract salaries in the six-figure category.

CAREER PROSPECTS

In 2004, there were nearly 225,000 medical and health services managers in the United States, with 25,000 employed by federal, state, and local public health agencies. This large pool of health managers, in addition to the wide range of qualifications required by potential employers, often results in vacant administrative and management positions being filled even when there are not many applicants with the optimal desired qualifications. This is easy to appreciate, as organizations must have people in leadership and management positions.

TABLE 7–3 Number and Mean Salary for Health Administrators Working in Federal, State, and Local Governmental Agencies, May 2004

Occupational Category	Federal Workers	Federal Worker Mean Salary	State Workers	State Worker Mean Salary	Local Workers	Local Worker Mean Salary	Total Federal, State, and Local Workers	Adjusted PH Enum. 2000 Workers
Administrators	9,530	$86,470	6,420	$72,650	9,220	$69,150	25,170	21,247
Administrative Business Professionals	NA	NA	NA	NA	NA	NA	NA	7,306
Administrative, Business, and Other Support	NA	NA	NA	NA	NA	NA	NA	77,162

Source: Data for federal, state, and local governmental agency workers from Bureau of Labor Statistics. May 2004 national, state, and metropolitan area occupational employment and wage estimates. Available at: http://www.bls.gov. Accessed August 20, 2005. See Chapter 6 for adjusted number of public health workers from *Year 2000 Public Health Workforce Enumeration.*

It is not uncommon to hear public health officials express concerns over difficulties in filling administrative positions with qualified candidates. It is not clear, however, whether this is a supply and demand issue or whether there are not adequate systems in place to recognize, reward, and value competent performance. Because administration and management require fairly nonspecific and generic skills, these positions are many times filled with individuals who are new to the field of public health. Public health professionals within such organizations often view such administrators as not necessarily committed to the same values and ethics as the professional staff. In any event, overall demand for public health administrators appears to be relatively steady and stable.

Public health administrators often have a general academic degree at the bachelor's or associate degree level and rise through the ranks of public service in the governmental sector. It is also common for an experienced public health professional such as an environmental health practitioner or public health nurse to be promoted into an agency leadership position. In sum, career pathways are many and varied for public health administration positions.

ADDITIONAL INFORMATION

There are many good sources of information on public health administration as a career. Several sources are available for information on educational programs for health administration as well as for continuing education and leadership development for practicing public health administrators.

The Association of University Programs in Health Administration (AUPHA) Web site (http://www.aupha.org/index.php) provides information on approximately 150 undergraduate and graduate degree programs in health administration in the United States. AUPHA works closely with the Commission on Accreditation of Healthcare Management Education (http://www.cahmeweb.org) and ACHESA, the organization that accredits master's-level programs. Only ACHESA-accredited programs can become a full member of AUPHA.

Both AUPHA and ACHESA are linked with the American College of Healthcare Executives (http://www.ache.org/career.cfm), which credentials health administrators. A similar, but considerably smaller, program that certifies public health administrators is operated by the Public Health Practitioner Certification Board (http://www.phpcb.org).

Schools of public health are among the institutions offering graduate degrees in health administration. The Association of Schools of Public Health (http://www.asph.org) has identified a battery of core health administration competencies appropriate for all students receiving the master's of public health (MPH) degree (Table 7–4). These competencies provide a useful baseline for professional public health administration and indicate what, upon graduation, a student with an MPH should be able to do.

The American Public Health Association's (APHA) Health Administration Section is another good source of information for public health administration. Its Web site can be accessed

TABLE 7–4 Health Administration Competency Expectations for Graduates of MPH Degree Programs

1. Identify the main components and issues of the organization, financing, and delivery of health services and public health systems in the United States.
2. Discuss the policy process for improving the health status of populations.
3. Describe the legal and ethical bases for public health and health services.
4. Apply quality and performance improvement concepts to address organizational performance issues.
5. Demonstrate leadership skills for building partnerships.
6. Apply principles of strategic planning and marketing to public health.
7. Communicate health policy and management issues using appropriate channels and technologies.
8. Apply the principles of program planning, development, budgeting, management, and evaluation in organizational and community initiatives.
9. Explain methods of ensuring community health safety and preparedness.
10. Apply "systems thinking" for resolving organizational problems.

Source: Association of Schools of Public Health (ASPH). MPH Core Competency Development Process, Version 2. Available at: http://www.asph.org. Accessed June 20, 2006.

through the main APHA site (http://www.apha.org). The Health Administration Section has a nearly 100-year history, beginning as a section for medical health officers but expanding to include a broader spectrum of public health administrators.

The Public Health Leadership Society (http://www.phls.org/) includes graduates of the National Public Health Leadership Institute (http://www.phli.org/), operating from the University of North Carolina School of Public Health, as well as alumni of approximately 20 state and regional public health leadership development institutes (http://www.heartlandcenters.slu.edu/nln/). These programs serve public health practitioners through an intensive leadership development curriculum undertaken on a continuing education basis. The University of North Carolina also offers a Management Academy for Public Health serving public health managers and administrators from states in the southeast region of the United States.

CONCLUSION

Public health administrators are one of the largest and most important of the professional occupational categories in the public health workforce. There are more than 20,000 health administrators working in public health settings. This group is also one of the most diverse in terms of academic credentials and previous work experiences. Public health administration offers a variety of work settings, especially at the local level, and a broad range of career pathways that are open to both individuals trained in public health and those new to the field. Because of the diverse backgrounds and skill levels, ongoing education and training are especially relevant issues for this occupational category. Demand for these positions is steady to slightly increasing and likely to remain so over the near term.

Discussion Questions and Exercises

4. What do you think are the most important new or expanded roles for public health administrators in the 21st century?

5. In which organizations and geographic regions will the need for public health administrators expand most rapidly in the next 2 decades?

1. What are the most important contributions to improving the health of the public that public health administration makes today?

2. What features make public health administration a career worth pursuing?

3. Using a scale from 1 to 10, how important to the effectiveness of the overall public health system is the need for more and better prepared public health administrators? How did you arrive at this rating?

REFERENCES

1. Bureau of Labor Statistics, U.S. Department of Labor. May 2004 national, state, and metropolitan area occupational employment and wage estimates. Available at: http://www.bls.gov/oes/current/oes_nat.htm. Accessed August 20, 2005.

2. Health Resources and Services Administration, Bureau of Health Professions, National Center for Health Workforce Information and Analysis and Center for Health Policy, Columbia School of Nursing. *The Public Health Workforce Enumeration 2000.* Washington, DC: HRSA; 2000.

Environmental and Occupational Health

Environmental health is an expansive field that has been an important part of public health practice for more than 150 years. The exploits of John Snow in battling cholera in England in the 1850s demonstrated the link between communicable disease and sanitary conditions. As briefly described in Chapter 1, the pioneering efforts of Chadwick in England and Shattuck in the United States resulted in blueprints for early public health responses and systems. Many public health successes in the latter part of the 1800s and the early years of the 1900s were the direct result of environmental engineering and sanitation advances. The people carrying out these duties have been an integral part of the public health workforce and remain so. These workers are employed in public health and environmental protection agencies at all levels of government and throughout the private sector as well. Although an accurate count of their numbers is not available, the Bureau of Labor Statistics reported 163,000 workers in environmental engi-

neering, specialist, and technician positions and another 47,000 in occupational health and safety positions.[1] There were 75,000 environmental and occupational health workers employed by federal, state, and local governmental agencies in 2004. The *Public Health Workforce Enumeration 2000* identified 40,000 working for federal, state, and local public health agencies.[2] Data from these two sources are used throughout this chapter. The difference between these two sources indicates that many environmental and occupational health personnel work in nonhealth agencies at all levels of government, such as environmental protection agencies, departments of natural resources, and sanitation agencies. In any event, environmental health workers are one of the largest occupational groupings within the public health workforce today. Environmental public health workers, for many decades working primarily in local and state public health agencies, are increasingly finding positions in private sector organizations that offer a wide variety of environmental and occupational health services. Table 8–1 provides a snapshot of an average day in the life of an environmental health practitioner.

OCCUPATIONAL CLASSIFICATION

There are six specific standard occupational categories for environmental health workers. These include environmental engineer, environmental engineering technician, environmental scientist/specialist, environmental science and protection technician, occupational health and safety specialist, and occupational health and safety technician. Three of these titles are professional occupations (environmental engineer, environmental scientist/specialist, and occupational health and safety specialist). The others are technical occupations.

TABLE 8–1 A Typical Day for an Environmental Health Practitioner

7:30 a.m.	Visit septic field inspection site to assist environmental health specialists on site
8:30 a.m.	Office time for paperwork and information sharing with staff
9:00 a.m.	Staff meeting to review priorities for week
10:15 a.m.	Interview candidates for vacant entry-level environmental health specialist position
10:45 a.m.	Meet with communicable disease control, epidemiology, and public health nursing staff regarding community concerns over West Nile Virus threat
11:45 a.m.	Brown bag lunch with other environmental health staff; today's guest is a professor from a state university undergraduate degree program in environmental health
1:00 p.m.	Brief agency director regarding status of West Nile Virus threat
1:30 p.m.	Supervise inspection of food services, swimming pools, and septic systems at county fair site
3:00 p.m.	Conference call meeting with epidemiology and environmental health staff of neighboring jurisdictions and state health department regarding current status of West Nile Virus
4:00 p.m.	Review information suggested by staff for tonight's community meeting
4:30 p.m.	More paperwork related to permit approvals
5:15 p.m.	Prepare remarks for tonight's community meeting
7:00 p.m.	Represent agency at community meeting regarding West Nile Virus concerns

- Environmental engineers (e.g., water supply or waste water engineers, solid waste engineers, air pollution engineers, sanitary engineers) apply engineering principles to control, eliminate, ameliorate, and/or prevent environmental health hazards. There are 48,000 environmental engineers in the United States. Private-sector companies (architectural and engineering companies, management and technical consulting firms) employ the largest numbers of environmental engineers. Federal, state, and local government agencies employ 13,000 environmental engineers. The *Public Health Workforce Enumeration 2000* identified 7,000 in governmental public health agencies.

- Environmental engineering technicians (e.g., water or waste water plant operators, water or waste water testing technicians, air pollution technicians) assist environmental engineers and other environmental health professions in controlling, eliminating, ameliorating, and/or preventing environmental health hazards. There are 20,000 environmental engineering technicians working in the United States. Architectural and engineering companies employ the largest number of environmental engineering technicians, followed by local government and scientific research and development companies. Governmental agencies employ only 3,000 environmental engineering technicians, 600 of which were identified in the *Public Health Workforce Enumeration 2000*.

- Environmental scientists or specialists (e.g., environmental researchers, environmental health specialists, food scientists, soil and plant scientists, air pollution specialists, hazardous materials specialists, toxicologists, water or waste water or solid waste specialists, sanitarians, entomologists) apply biological, chemical, and public health principles to control, eliminate, ameliorate, and/or prevent environmental health hazards. There are 67,000 environmental specialists working in the United States. State governments are the leading source of employment for environmental specialists. Local government and private-sector companies also employ large numbers of environmental specialists. Governmental agencies employ 32,000 environmental specialists; the *Public Health Workforce Enumeration 2000* identified 23,000 in federal, state, and local public health agencies.

- Environmental science and protection technicians (e.g., air pollution technicians, vector control workers) assist environmental scientists and specialists and other environmental health professionals in the control, elimination, and/or prevention of environmental health hazards. There are 28,000 workers in the United States in environmental science and engineering technician positions. Local governments are the largest employer of environmental science technicians. Private companies and state governments are other important employment sources. Nearly 11,000 environmental science and protection technicians work for government agencies. The *Public Health Workforce Enumeration 2000* identified 700 working in governmental public health agencies.

- Occupational health and safety specialists (e.g., industrial hygienists, occupational health specialists, radiologic health inspectors, safety inspectors) review, evaluate, and analyze workplace environments and exposures. They design programs and procedures to control, eliminate, ameliorate, and/or prevent disease and injury caused by chemical, physical, biological, and ergonomic risks to workers. There are 37,000 occupational health and safety specialists in the United States. Local and state governments are the largest employment sources for occupational safety and health specialists; hospitals are another large employer. Government agencies employ 14,000 occupational health and safety specialists. The *Public Health Workforce Enumeration 2000* identified nearly 9,000 working in governmental public health agencies.

- Occupational health and safety technicians collect data on workplace environments and exposures for analysis by occupational safety and health specialists; they also implement programs and conduct evaluation of programs designed to limit chemical, physical, biological, and ergonomic risks to workers. There are 11,000 occupational health and safety technicians in the United States, with 3,000 working for federal, state, and local governmental agencies. The *Public Health Workforce Enumeration 2000* identified only 150 working in governmental public health agencies.

As is apparent from these occupational categories, both professional and technical positions are common in the environmental health component of the public health workforce. Among the 40,000 positions identified in the *Public Health Workforce Enumeration 2000*, more than one half were professional titles. Among professional positions, environmental health ranks second only to nursing within the public health workforce. Professional titles include engineers, scientists, and specialists. Technical titles include technicians and technologists.

PUBLIC HEALTH PRACTICE PROFILE

Environmental and occupational health workers generally function at a program or unit level within public health agencies at all levels of government, but especially those at the local and state level. They are most frequently involved in public health responsibilities that focus on protecting against environmental hazards, preventing injuries, and preventing epidemics and the spread of disease. Environmental and occupational health

workers may also be key components of efforts to prepare and respond to public health emergencies, especially natural disasters for which protection of water and food supplies can be critical.

Among the 10 essential public health services, environmental and occupational health workers are most likely to be involved in diagnosing and investigating health problems and health hazards in the community, enforcing laws and regulations that protect health and ensure safety, monitoring health status to identify community health status, and evaluating the effectiveness and quality of environmental and occupational health services in the community. With much of their work done in community settings, environmental and occupational health workers also inform, educate, and empower people about important health issues. Table 8–2 summarizes public health purposes and essential public health services at the core of positions for environmental and occupational health workers.

IMPORTANT AND ESSENTIAL DUTIES

There are many different job titles and positions used for environmental and occupational health workers. The focus in this chapter will be on five representative positions: (1) environmental engineer; (2) entry-level environmental health specialist; (3) midlevel environmental health specialist; (4) senior-level environmental health specialist; and (5) midlevel occupational health and safety specialist. Each of these positions and a representative panel of their important and essential duties are described in this section.

Environmental Engineer

This is a professional environmental engineering position with duties within an assigned environmental program involving the protection of public health and/or the protection or restoration of the environment. There are often several grades for this position. Entry-level titles generally do not have any supervisory responsibilities. Higher-level environmental engineer titles may supervise or lead assigned engineers and/or other staff. Workers in this title are responsible for the performance of professional engineering duties in performing field surveys and investigations of water supplies, sewage systems, streams, industrial waste facilities, solid and hazardous waste facilities, air pollution control systems, and/or dams and reservoirs. Work includes preparing reports of findings, and making recommendations to improve the public health, safety, and the environment. Environmental engineers work under general technical supervision and receive work assignments from a designated superior. There may be several levels of positions with this title.

TABLE 8-2 Public Health Practice Profile for Environmental Health

Environmental and Occupational Health Workers Make a Difference by:

Public Health Purposes

Preventing epidemics and the spread of disease √
Protecting against environmental hazards √
Preventing injuries √
Promoting and encouraging healthy behaviors
Responding to disasters and assisting communities in recovery
Assuring the quality and accessibility of health services

Essential Public Health Services

Monitoring health status to identify community health problems √
Diagnosing and investigating health problems and health hazards in the community √
Informing, educating, and empowering people about health issues √
Mobilizing community partnerships to identify and solve health problems
Developing policies and plans that support individual and community health efforts
Enforcing laws and regulations that protect health and ensure safety √
Linking people with needed personal health services and assuring the provision of health care when otherwise unavailable
Assuring a competent public health and personal health care workforce
Evaluating effectiveness, accessibility, and quality of personal and population-based health services √
Researching new insights and innovative solutions to health problems

Important and essential duties for environmental engineers include

- Participates in the engineering review of the hydraulics and details of water supply systems and plants, industrial and domestic waste treatment systems, solid and hazardous waste management systems, air pollution control systems, dams and reservoirs, and so on
- Gathers and interprets data on pollution, contamination, and construction and design features relevant for environmental engineering projects
- Reviews engineering plans and specifications for sewage and industrial waste treatment plants, water supply systems, solid and hazardous waste disposal areas, air pollution control systems, and dams and reservoirs for compliance with approved standards
- Confers with officials and owners/operators of plants and establishments with regard to laws, regulations, and engineering requirements of appropriate state and local agencies
- Collects samples of water and sewage for bacteriologic, chemical, or biologic analysis
- Examines and prepares charts, tables, and maps for the interpretation of engineering data, and prepares reports of findings and analysis
- Prepares papers and lectures on subjects relating to the environment and/or dam safety

- Prepares technical and detailed reports of engineering surveys
- Participates in special investigations of fish kills and unusual stream conditions with representatives of other agencies
- Supervises, assigns, and assists in the work of a unit composed of a small group of professional personnel
- Trains subordinate engineers and other technical staff

Environmental Specialist (Entry Level)

This position serves as an entry-level environmental specialist performing one or more of the following functions under close direction and supervision: conducting routine compliance and enforcement activities; assisting in the development of draft legislation, policies, and regulations; conducting routine scientific analyses and technical services on assigned office or field projects; providing regulatory assistance; providing project administration and environmental technical assistance for grants, contracts, or loans; interpreting policy and technical assistance; conducting less complex surveys and analyses; recording field conditions; gathering and analyzing information to assist in developing recommendations and decision making; and assisting in permit development. The number of levels for this position varies from one personnel system to another. In many systems there are three to five levels of environmental health specialist positions that allow for career advancement.

Important and essential duties for entry-level environmental health specialists include

- Assists in the installation, operation, and maintenance of environmental monitoring/sampling equipment; assists in performing field and office surveys and studies; performs surveillance and other special projects
- Assists in routine repairs and calibrations of environmental monitoring/sampling equipment, in accordance with specifications and standard operating procedures; performs basic sampling data review for precision and accuracy
- Assists in responding to complaints, routine inspections/surveillance, and permit review to meet compliance requirements
- Assists in the research and compilation of basic information for use in regulation or policy development
- Enters and maintains basic databases or inventories
- Assists in preparing for public meetings, hearings, and workshops
- Assists with routine inspections or investigations of facilities or project sites that require specialized knowledge of industry processes, pollutant sources, or natural processes
- Responds to routine inquiries or requests for technical assistance regarding the scientific background and technical implementation of agency programs
- Reviews plans for technical accuracy and makes recommendations to higher-level staff
- Conducts routine sampling and testing; analyzes, evaluates, and interprets data; writes reports; and assists higher-level staff
- Maintains and utilizes computerized environmental databases in support of technical projects
- Reviews routine permit applications for technical accuracy and makes recommendations regarding the scientific merit of proposals
- Provides technical and administrative assistance to grant, contract, or loan recipients in the planning, design, construction, and implementation of environmental protection projects

Environmental Specialist (Midlevel)

This position serves as a staff environmental specialist performing one or more of the following functions independently with little direction and supervision: conducting compliance and enforcement activities; developing draft legislation; developing, performing, coordinating, implementing, and evaluating scientific analyses, plans, or services involving office or field projects; conducting surveys, analyses, and recording field conditions; providing project administration and environmental technical assistance for grants, contracts, and loans; gathering and analyzing information to develop recommendations for decision making and permit development, review, and oversight. This position may lead or supervise assigned staff.

Important and essential duties for midlevel environmental specialists include

- Independently performs the installation, operation, and maintenance of environmental monitoring/sampling equipment; on an area or site list basis performs and/or provides guidance for surveys, field studies, or other special data-gathering activities
- Performs complex equipment repair and calibrations; reviews monitored data for evaluation of equipment performance
- Responds to and investigates complex or highly technical complaints or violations; performs complex inspections or field investigations; coordinates complaint and enforcement priorities, schedules, and assists in negotiating agreements and settlements; prepares final permit evaluation or report for approval; may impose on-site enforcement action; performs follow-up inspections to ensure corrective action is implemented
- Plans, develops, researches, and conducts or oversees technical data collection and analyzes, evaluates, and interprets data; analyzes or interprets information requirements and coordinates information gathering for a team or other assignment outside of a team; writes reports and reviews draft reports
- Determines database or inventory requirements; works with agency and nonagency sources on data submittals; evaluates databases or inventories for analysis, reporting, or compliance purposes; may design and/or develop databases or inventories to be utilized in support of technical projects
- Reviews permit applications for technical accuracy, negotiates permit conditions, conducts conflict resolution, and makes decisions regarding the scientific merit of proposals; serves as a senior permit writer or historical/institutional memory for geographic area or complex site
- Develops and/or implements project plans, consent decrees, orders, or scientific studies for cleanups, resource management, or policy/regulation development; conducts research for technical projects; reviews project plans for technical accuracy and makes decisions on the scientific merit of proposals
- Oversees contractor or consultant services for compliance and certifies performance; provides assistance to other staff, agencies, and the public

- Makes recommendations to senior staff regarding new or modified sampling and analytical testing methods, best management practices, and technical operating procedures
- Makes technical and scientific recommendations regarding the development, coordination, and implementation of environmental technical assistance programs involving pollution prevention, pollution control, or natural resource management
- Evaluates data to determine technical compliance with regulatory requirements
- Plans, facilitates, and represents the program or agency in public meetings, hearings, and workshops
- Conducts literature evaluations to assess evidence-based practice; formulates grant proposals; proposes and designs assessment and research projects
- Develops evidence-based protocols for specific program interventions and services
- Independently provides technical and administrative assistance to grant, contract, or loan recipients in the planning, design, construction, or implementation of environmental protection projects
- Coordinates the development of policies, procedures, statutes, and regulations of a high degree of complexity
- Directs or coordinates nonagency employees at large spills or complex sites

Environmental Specialist (Senior Level)

This position serves as a senior program expert in one or more program subject areas as designated in writing by a program manager, agency director, or higher. A senior environmental specialist performs, directs, implements, and evaluates activities that are of critical agency, regional, statewide, or national interest, sensitivity, or complexity. Such activities may include planning and directing surveys and analyses of projects that are a high priority for the agency or involve participation in the resolution of major environmental questions. In most circumstances, this position supervises five or more professional environmental staff.

Important and essential duties for senior-level environmental specialists include

- Advises program management on monitoring and sampling policies, priorities, effectiveness, and cross-media or agency issues and requirements
- Evaluates equipment inventories for material readiness, amortization, and technology transfer; management of contracted services and equipment utilization; conducts equipment needs assessments

- Advises program management on violations of critical or controversial agency interest; evaluates rule effectiveness and recommends enforcement/compliance rule making; may represent the program on multimedia or highly complex or controversial enforcement/compliance actions involving other programs or agencies
- Works with other programs and agencies in identifying information required for policy development, legislation, regulations, and recommended priorities, scheduling requirements, and information parameters for program management
- Evaluates databases and inventories for policy or regulation development; determines new, changing, or emerging requirements for databases and inventories; may work with other programs or agencies on database/inventory requirements
- Conducts literature evaluations to assess evidence-based practice; formulates grant proposals; proposes and designs assessment and research projects
- Develops evidence-based protocols for specific program interventions and services
- Coordinates controversial or critical plans for resource management, policy or regulation development, or statewide cleanup priorities
- Advises program or agency management on the need for contractor or consultant services versus agency staff and expertise
- Identifies critical or emerging issues and recommends preventative or corrective measures
- Represents agency and testifies at legal or public hearings or conferences and before Congress
- Provides expertise or historical background not otherwise available to the agency that is used as a basis for agency management decisions
- Serves as an agency representative to regional and national commissions and environmental or professional organizations relevant to assigned responsibilities with the agency

Occupational Health and Safety Specialist

This is midlevel professional scientific work in evaluating work and indoor environments for safety and health hazards. Occupational health and safety specialists make comprehensive safety and health hazard evaluations, including the more difficult evaluations, of all general industry and indoor environments, involving office buildings and factories. A comprehensive safety and health hazard evaluation may consist of the following: conducting a physical survey; establishing appropriate sampling techniques; collecting samples as necessary to assess the presence of chemical, physical, and microbial agents in accordance with the requirements of the Occupational Safety and Health Act; analyzing the data generated by sampling and making a professional judgment using accepted industrial hygiene practices and federal standards to determine the degree of hazard present; interviewing employers and employees and other potentially exposed individuals to determine possible sources of safety and health hazards; preparing a technical report of the safety and health hazard evaluation that can be understood and followed by lay personnel; and making recommendations within this report that will reduce or correct the health hazard. Occupational health and safety specialists receive minimal supervision from an administrative superior.

Important and essential duties for midlevel occupational health and safety specialists include

- Conducts initial conferences with employers to introduce the services offered by the agency
- Consults with employers on the existence, utilization, and operating condition of powered mechanical ventilation devices, personal safety equipment and procedures, noise abatement equipment and procedures, material safety data sheets, hazardous chemical correction, and safety and health programs
- Performs difficult safety and health hazard evaluations requiring literature research, analysis, and scientific design
- Determines the magnitude of exposure or nuisance to workers and the public; selects or devises methods and instruments suitable for measurements; studies and tests materials associated with the work operation
- Collects samples from office buildings and other workplaces to determine the presence of toxic substances and other potential hazards; evaluates building ventilation systems for possible deficiencies; and provides technical advice on remedial action
- Interprets results of the examination of the work environment in terms of the potential of causing a community nuisance or damage or impairing worker safety, health, and efficiency; and presents specific conclusions to appropriate interested parties by means of a technical report
- Determines the need for, or effectiveness of, control measures, and when necessary, recommends procedures that will be suitable and effective in achieving those measures
- Interprets occupational safety and health laws, rules, and regulations; determines compliance with safety and health laws; holds conferences with management to discuss identified violations and deficiencies and recommends corrections
- Reviews facility safety and health programs required by the federal Occupational Safety and Health Administration (OSHA)

MINIMUM QUALIFICATIONS

Environmental and occupational health includes a mix of professional and technical occupations, both of which generally have several levels of positions. This provides a natural career pathway and allows environmental and occupational health workers to remain in this field for many years. Comparable positions exist in local public agencies of all sizes, making career advancement from a small to larger employer a common story for these workers.

Although environmental and occupational health professionals are produced by schools of public health, there are many undergraduate and graduate degree programs specializing in environmental sciences. It is these programs that are even larger producers of environmental and occupational health practitioners. Many workers in technical positions have less than a bachelor degree; some have no more than a high school degree.

As with virtually all public health positions, both experience and education are important considerations for hiring and promotion. Experience and education both contribute to necessary knowledge, skills, and abilities required for workers in this field. Typical minimum qualifications for environmental engineers, three levels of environmental health specialists, and occupational health and safety specialists are detailed below.

Typical Minimum Qualifications for Environmental Engineer
Knowledge, Skills, and Abilities

An environmental engineer will generally have knowledge of

- Principles and practices of environmental engineering and/or environmental sanitation
- Design, construction, and operation of air quality control, water supply and treatment, and sewage and industrial waste disposal systems
- Laws and regulations governing sanitation
- Physical and biologic sciences, including chemistry, bacteriology, and physical properties of ambient air, water, sewage, and liquid waste as related to environmental engineering
- Mathematics, geometry, calculus, and engineering formulas

An environmental engineer will generally have the skills and ability to

- Develop designs involving environmental engineering theory and judgment
- Establish and maintain cooperative working relationships with public officials and community groups
- Perform investigations involving the application of professional theory and interpretation of laws, regulations, and requirements
- Plan, promote, and conduct engineering projects
- Analyze significant environmental engineering and sanitation data
- Consult with and advise plant owners and operators on proper design, construction, and operation of plants
- Prepare engineering reports and papers and lectures related to the environment

Experience and Education

Any combination of training and experience that provides the requisite knowledge and abilities will qualify an individual for this position. A typical way to obtain the required knowledge and abilities is through acquisition of a master's degree with major study in one of the engineering fields (such as sanitary, water resource, civil, geotechnical, environmental, chemical, or mechanical engineering) and 1 year of experience in environmental engineering. Another path is through acquisition of an engineer-in-training certificate or a bachelor degree with a major study in one of the engineering fields listed above and 2 years of environmental engineering experience. Some jurisdictions may require registration as a professional engineer within the state or another state with equivalent requirements for registration or an engineer-in-training certificate. In some instances, a PhD degree in an engineering field may substitute for 1 or more years of environmental engineering experience. Requirements for professional registration as an engineer in some states may require up to 8 years of professional experience (which may include up to 4 years of college-level engineering education) and successful completion of professional licensing exams.

Typical Minimum Requirements for Entry-Level Environmental Specialist

Knowledge, Skills, and Abilities

An entry-level environmental health specialist will generally have knowledge of

- Field investigative techniques, including data gathering and basic research

- Practices and methods of environmental problem solving
- Soil, water, or air sampling methods and techniques
- Characteristics of pollutants
- Principles, practices, and methods of environmental science, natural resource management, pollution prevention, and pollution control
- Applicable federal, state, and local environmental regulations

An entry-level environmental health specialist will generally have the skills and ability to

- Use sound judgment in performing assigned tasks
- Understand and apply environmental regulations and related laws
- Write clearly and concisely, and prepare maps, plans, charts, and graphs
- Communicate effectively with agency staff, other agencies, industry, and the general public

Experience and Education

Entry-level environmental health specialists come from a wide range of educational levels and previous work experiences, which generally include

- A bachelor degree involving major study in environmental, physical, or one of the natural sciences; environmental planning; or other allied field
- Experience at or above the environmental technician level, or equivalent will substitute, year for year, for education

Typical Minimum Requirements for Midlevel Environmental Specialist

Knowledge, Skills, and Abilities

A midlevel environmental health specialist will generally have knowledge of

- Principles, practices, and methods of environmental or resource management and environmental pollution prevention and pollution control
- Methods and techniques of field sampling, testing, data gathering, basic research, and field investigations
- Soil science, geology, hydrology, hydrogeology, metrology, and toxicology
- Applicable federal, state, and local environmental regulations and policies
- Characteristics and health effects of pollutants
- Technical report writing methods

A midlevel environmental health specialist will generally have the skills and ability to

- Use sound, independent judgment in making decisions on environmental problems and completing assigned tasks
- Understand and interpret plans, maps, and equipment specifications
- Prepare clear and concise written reports and make oral presentations
- Analyze and prepare plans and reports
- Understand and communicate complex environmental regulations and statutes
- Communicate effectively with agency staff, other agencies, industry, and the general public

Experience and Education

Any combination of training and experience that provides the requisite knowledge and abilities will qualify an individual for this position. A typical way to obtain the required knowledge and abilities is through acquisition of a bachelor degree involving major study in environmental, physical, or one of the natural sciences; environmental planning; or other allied field; and 2 years of professional-level experience in environmental analysis, control, or planning. Additional qualifying experience may substitute, year for year, for education. A master's degree in one of the above fields may also substitute for 1 year of the required experience. Another way to meet these qualifications is through acquisition of a PhD degree in one of the above fields or through 1 year of experience in the next lower-level environmental specialist position.

Typical Minimum Qualifications for Senior-Level Environmental Specialist

Knowledge, Skills, and Abilities

A senior-level environmental specialist will generally have knowledge of

- Applicable federal, state, and local environmental regulations and policies
- Soil science, geology, hydrology, hydrogeology, metrology, and toxicology
- Methods for the development of an environmental program or complex study
- Multimedia environmental principles and practices

A senior-level environmental specialist will generally have the skills and ability to

- Identify and assess program or agency service delivery needs and requirements

- Recognize emerging issues and conduct advanced planning to address those issues
- Represent program or agency management on complex or controversial issues with other agencies, jurisdictions, or interest groups
- Effectively negotiate and resolve conflict
- Effectively communicate technical information clearly, both orally and in writing
- Demonstrate a high degree of technical expertise in a particular field or specialty as shown through the publication of papers in peer-reviewed, scientific, or technical journals or the presentation of papers at professional conferences

Experience and Education

Any combination of training and experience that provides the requisite knowledge and abilities will qualify an individual for this position. A typical way to obtain the required knowledge and abilities is through a bachelor degree involving major study in environmental, physical, or one of the natural sciences; environmental planning; or other allied field; and 6 years of professional-level experience in environmental analysis, control, or planning, which includes 2 years equal to the midlevel environmental specialist position. Additional qualifying experience may substitute, year for year, for education. Another pathway to satisfy these qualifications is through acquisition of a master's degree in one of the preceding fields and 4 years of professional-level experience that include 2 years equal to a midlevel environmental specialist. Yet another way to satisfy these requirements is through acquisition of a PhD degree in one of the preceding fields and 3 years of professional-level experience that include 2 years equal to a midlevel environmental specialist.

Typical Minimum Qualifications for Occupational Health and Safety Specialist

Knowledge, Skills, and Abilities

An occupational health and safety specialist generally has knowledge of

- Sampling and direct measuring techniques for gas, vapor, dust, noise, and radiation
- Microbiology, radiology, physiology, and chemistry
- Common diseases and health hazards related to indoor environments and industrial occupations and of their possible sources
- The standard types of machinery and equipment used in industrial and commercial establishments
- The Occupational Safety and Health Act and the applicable regulations of the U.S. Environmental Protection Agency (USEPA) that relate to workplace safety and health

An occupational health and safety specialist generally has the skills and ability to

- Analyze complex problems of environmental hazard reduction and arrive at sound decisions regarding actions to be taken
- Develop, organize, and present training through a comprehensive company-specific safety program
- Analyze and interpret technical reports and criteria documents on exposure limits
- Operate and maintain detection and measurement apparatus
- Communicate thoughts and ideas clearly and concisely
- Establish and maintain effective working relationships with plant managers, safety directors, employees, and the public

Experience and Education

Any combination of training and experience that provides the requisite knowledge and abilities will qualify an individual for this position. A typical way to obtain the required knowledge and abilities is through 1 year of experience as an entry-level occupational safety and health specialist or 1 year of professional experience in safety and health consultation in a governmental agency or program or in private industry as an industrial hygienist, industrial safety professional, safety manager, or other closely related position in the occupational safety or health field, and graduation from an accredited 4-year college or university with specialization in industrial hygiene or safety or a closely related area. In some instances, graduate work in industrial hygiene or safety may be substituted on a year-for-year basis for the stated experience. Certification as a certified industrial hygienist (CIH) by the American Board of Industrial Hygiene or as a certified safety professional (CSP) by the Board of Certified Safety Professionals may be substituted for 6 months of the stated experience. Some states may require specific certifications and licensing.

WORKPLACE CONSIDERATIONS

State and local governmental agencies employ more than 60,000 environmental and occupational health workers (both professional and technical titles). Federal agencies employ another 12,000 workers, making governmental agencies the largest sources of jobs for environmental and occupational health workers.

Work settings and working conditions influence the typical physical requirement for positions in environmental and occupational health categories. For example, entry-level and midlevel environmental and occupational health specialists spend considerable time outside the office. Environmental health specialists often find themselves at various environmental sites; occupational health specialists often do their work at business sites. Environmental engineers and higher-level environmental and occupational health specialists spend somewhat more time in an office setting.

Most positions call for workers to be able to sit for extended periods and to frequently stand and walk extended distances. Normal manual dexterity and eye-hand coordination, hearing, and vision corrected to within the normal range are also important considerations. This work requires good vision to peruse and review correspondence, statutes, and related material and to perform visual inspections required for work activities conducted on site. Also important are the ability to stand, walk, and have full use of upper and lower extremities to effect investigations and collection efforts in business establishments and in the field. At times, this work may require climbing ladders and entering confined areas for investigations.

Normally, environmental and occupational health workers can communicate verbally and use office equipment including computers, telephones, calculators, copiers, and fax machines. For work performed in an office environment, frequent or continuous contact with staff and the public is also necessary. In many situations, environmental and occupational health workers must be mobile and may be required to possess a valid driver's license. Important attributes are verbal and reasoning ability in order to read and understand a variety of written matter; to process directives, reports, and correspondence; and to initiate action required. These positions require emotional stability and good judgment to deal with the public and personnel whose business activities are being inspected or investigated.

SALARY ESTIMATES

Salaries vary considerably across environmental and occupational health positions, depending on whether they are professional or technical titles as well as on educational attainment and experience. Salaries for environmental engineers average $68,000, with the middle 50% ranging from $51,000 to $84,000. The mean salary for environmental engineers employed by federal agencies was $80,000 in 2004. Average salaries are lower for environmental engineers working in state ($57,000) and local ($63,500) governmental agencies (see Table 8–3). Mean salaries are somewhat higher for environmental engineers working in the private sector (architectural and engineering companies, and management and technical consulting companies).

Environmental engineering technicians have mean salaries of $41,000, with the middle 50% ranging from $30,000 to $51,000. Salaries are generally higher for those working in

TABLE 8–3 Number and Mean Salary for Environmental and Occupational Health Workers in Federal, State, and Local Governmental Agencies, May 2004

Occupational Category	Federal Workers	Federal Worker Mean Salary	State Workers	State Worker Mean Salary	Local Workers	Local Worker Mean Salary	Total Federal, State, and Local Workers	Adjusted PH Enum. 2000 Workers
Environmental Engineers	4,160	$79,930	5,440	$57,040	3,670	$63,530	13,270	7,034
Environmental Engineering Technicians	NA	NA	590	$39,550	2,010	$43,720	2,600	594
Environmental Health Specialists	5,210	$73,320	17,130	$48,420	10,010	$51,310	32,350	23,013
Environmental Health Technicians	310	$39,200	4,180	$40,540	6,440	$40,390	10,930	719
Occupational Health and Safety Specialists	1,260	$72,670	5,490	$44,890	7,010	$49,910	13,760	8,649
Occupational Health and Safety Technicians	1,010	$68,120	460	$39,190	1,320	$41,330	2,790	136

Source: Data for federal, state, and local governmental agency workers from Bureau of Labor Statistics. May 2004 national, state, and metropolitan area occupational employment and wage estimates. Available at: http://www.bls.gov. Accessed August 20, 2005. See Chapter 6 for adjusted number of public health workers from *The Public Health Workforce Enumeration 2000*.

private-sector companies, although environmental engineering technicians employed by local governmental agencies have mean salaries nearing $44,000. Salaries for environmental engineering technicians working for state governmental agencies averaged $40,000 in 2004.

For environmental health specialists, salaries average $56,000, with the middle 50% ranging from $39,000 to $68,000. Average salaries are well above the mean for environmental health specialists employed by the federal government ($73,500) and lower for those working in state ($48,500) and local ($32,500) governmental agencies.

The average annual salary for environmental technicians is $38,000, with the middle 50% earning between $28,000 and $46,000. Average salaries are similar (at $40,000) for those employed by federal, state, and local governmental agencies.

Occupational health and safety specialists have an average salary of $54,000, with the middle 50% ranging between $40,000 and $66,000. State and local governments are the leading employers for this category. Mean salaries for occupational health and safety specialists employed by federal agencies are well above those of workers at state and local agencies ($72,500 federal, $45,000 state, $50,000 local).

Occupational health and safety technicians average $45,000 per year with the middle 50% ranging between $30,000 and $57,000. Mean salaries for occupational health and safety technicians employed by federal agencies are well above those of workers at state and local agencies ($68,000 federal, $39,000 state, $41,500 local).

CAREER PROSPECTS

Over the next 10 years, the Bureau of Labor Statistics projects that job growth will be greater than average for environmental engineers, environmental health specialists, occupational health and safety specialists, and environmental technicians. There are several reasons for these projections. There is increasing recognition of environmental engineering as a specialty distinct from civil and other engineering fields of endeavor. In addition, there has been a steady increase in recognition of the importance of regulatory compliance for industries and businesses in order to protect and maintain the environment and assure the safety of workers. An increasing emphasis on prevention as an overall strategy to safeguard environmental and human resources also fosters new job opportunities for these occupations. Finally, as many of these positions are in the public sector, they are somewhat insulated from economic shifts and downturns.

Although environmental and occupational health is a broad category, career pathways are somewhat limited. Specific academic preparation and experience are necessary for environmental engineers. For example, there is little opportunity for a technician in this field to advance to engineer status without completing the academic degrees required for the field. The academic requirements for environmental and occupational health and safety specialists are somewhat less restrictive. It is possible for technicians to advance into some of these professional positions through continuing education and work experience.

Technicians often begin work as trainees in routine positions under the direct supervision of a professional title or a more experienced senior technician. Technicians with previous hands-on experience with equipment used in that field usually require shorter periods of on-the-job training. As they become more experienced and proficient, technicians progress to become more independent in carrying out their duties. Their ability to move beyond technical titles, however, may be limited unless they acquire additional education or secure specific professional certifications.

Most of these occupational categories do provide their own job ladder with several levels of titles for entry-level to midlevel to senior-level positions. Over a span of several decades, these can comprise a satisfactory framework for a career. At higher levels, professional titles can lead to appointments into management and leadership positions. A substantial number of local public health agency directors, for example, come from the ranks of environmental health professionals.

ADDITIONAL INFORMATION

There are many good sources of information on environmental and occupational health as a career. Several sources are available for information on educational programs for environmental and occupational health as well as for continuing education and leadership development for practitioners.

The National Environmental Health Association (NEHA) (http://www.neha.org) offers several nationally recognized credentials within the environmental health profession. Each credential signifies a level of expertise and competence based on education and experience. Eligibility to sit for these credentialing exams is determined by the NEHA. Certifications and credentials available through NEHA include

- Onsite wastewater system installers: This credential is being developed through a cooperative agreement with the USEPA and will be completed by early 2006. Credentialing and licensing is one of the goals of the USEPA Voluntary Management Guidelines and is also recommended by the National Onsite Wastewater Recycling Association (NOWRA) Model Code.

- Registered environmental health specialist/registered sanitarian (REHS/RS): The REHS/RS is the premiere NEHA credential. It is available to a wide range of environmental health professionals. Individuals holding the REHS/RS credential show competency in environmental health issues, direct and train personnel to respond to routine or emergency environmental situations, and frequently provide education to their communities on environmental health concerns. The advantages of NEHA's REHS/RS registration program are: (1) the nationwide recognition of the REHS/RS credential, (2) the continual update of the REHS/RS examination and study guide based on an ongoing assessment of the environmental health field, and (3) the tracking of an individual's continuing education by NEHA.

- Certified food safety professional (CFSP): NEHA has created a credential especially for food safety professionals. The CFSP is designed for individuals within the public and private sectors whose primary responsibility is the protection and safety of food. The exam for this prestigious credential integrates food microbiology, Hazard Analysis and Critical Control Point (HACCP) principles, and regulatory requirements into questions that test problem-solving skills and knowledge.

- Certified environmental health technician (CEHT): The CEHT is for individuals who are interested in field-intensive environmental health activities (e.g., testing, sampling, and inspections) and who are required to provide information on safe environmental health practices and to eliminate environmental health hazards.

- Registered environmental technician (RET): NEHA's RET is a baseline credential for entry-level hazardous materials professionals. The credential is an excellent way for recent, 2-year graduates (Associate of Arts [AA]) or career-changing professionals to demonstrate competency in the core requirements of hazardous materials handling and management.

- Registered hazardous substances professional (RHSP): The RHSP provides technically qualified professionals with national recognition for proven expertise in hazardous materials and toxic substances management.

- Registered hazardous substances specialist (RHSS): The RHSS credential is for individuals who follow protocols for field-intensive hazardous materials activities (e.g., testing, sampling, and handling) and who ensure personal, public, and site safety.

- Board of Certified Safety Professionals (BCSP) offers the Certified Safety Professional (CSP) credential.

TABLE 8–4 Environmental Health Competency Expectations for Graduates of MPH Degree Programs

1. Specify approaches for assessing, preventing, and controlling environmental hazards that pose risks to human health and safety.
2. Describe the direct and indirect human, ecological, and safety effects of major environmental and occupational agents.
3. Specify current environmental risk assessment methods.
4. Describe genetic, physiologic, and psychomotor factors that affect susceptibility to adverse health outcomes following exposure to environmental hazards.
5. Discuss various risk management and risk communication approaches in relation to issues of environmental justice and equity.
6. Explain the general mechanisms of toxicity in eliciting a toxic response to various environmental exposures.
7. Develop a testable model of environmental injury.
8. Describe federal and state regulatory programs, guidelines, and authorities that control environmental health issues.

Source: Association of Schools of Public Health (ASPH) MPH Core Competency Development Process, Version 2. Available at: http://www.asph.org. Accessed June 20, 2006.

• American Board of Industrial Hygiene (ABIH) offers the Certified Industrial Hygienist (CIH) and Certified Associate Industrial Hygienist (CAIH) credentials.
• Council on Certification of Health, Environmental, and Safety Technologists (CCHEST) offers the Occupational Health and Safety Technologist (OHST) certification, which has requirements that are less stringent than for CSP, CIH, or CAIH credentials. This remains a voluntary credential, although many employers encourage or require certification.

In addition to NEHA, the Web site of the American Academy of Environmental Engineers (http://www.aaee.net) is a useful resource for environmental engineers. The Environmental Health Section of the American Public Health Association's Web site (http://www.apha.org) is another good source of information for environmental health. Schools of public health are among the institutions that offer graduate degrees in environmental and occupational health. The Association of Schools of Public Health (http://www.asph.org) has identified a battery of core environmental health competencies appropriate for all students receiving the master's of public health (MPH) degree. These competencies provide a useful baseline for professional practice and summarize what an MPH graduate should be able to do (Table 8–4).

CONCLUSION

Environmental and occupational health covers a wide range of duties and roles at a variety of levels. Career development opportunities in this area of public health practice are plentiful. A mix of education and experience prepares environmental health workers for increasing responsibility in public-sector agencies as well as the private sector. The field is increasingly moving toward competency-based credentials and certifications. Ongoing education and training are especially relevant concerns for this occupational category. Demand for these positions is steady, and prospects will likely increase over the near term.

Discussion Questions and Exercises

1. What are the most important contributions to improving the health of the public that environmental and occupational health workers make today?

2. What features make environmental and occupational health a career worth pursuing?

3. Using a scale from 1 to 10, how important to the effectiveness of the overall public health system is the need for more and better prepared environmental and occupational health workers? How did you arrive at this rating?

4. What do you think are the most important new or expanded roles for environmental and occupational health workers in the 21st century?

5. In which organizations and geographic regions will the need for environmental and occupational health workers expand most rapidly in the next 2 decades?

REFERENCES

1. Bureau of Labor Statistics, U.S. Department of Labor. May 2004 national, state, and metropolitan area occupational employment and wage estimates. Available at: http://www.bls.gov/oes/current/oes_nat.htm. Accessed August 20, 2005.

2. Health Resources and Services Administration (HRSA), Bureau of Health Professions, National Center for Health Workforce Information and Analysis and Center for Health Policy, Columbia School of Nursing. *The Public Health Workforce Enumeration 2000.* Washington, DC: HRSA; 2000.

CHAPTER 9

Public Health Nursing

LEARNING OBJECTIVES

After completing Chapter 9, learners will be proficient in describing key features of occupations and careers in public health nursing and how these contribute to carrying out public health's core functions and essential services. Key aspects of this competency expectation include

- Describing several different occupational titles in this category
- Identifying several essential public health services that are critical for positions in this category
- Describing important and essential duties for several job titles in this category
- Identifying minimum qualifications and describing general workplace considerations, salary expectations, and career prospects for positions in this category

The title *public health nurse* designates a nursing professional with educational preparation in public health and nursing science with a primary focus on population-level outcomes. The primary aim of public health nursing is to promote health and prevent disease for entire population groups. This may include assisting and providing care to individual members of the population. It also includes the identification of individuals who may not request care but who have health problems that put themselves and others in the community at risk, such as those with infectious diseases.

The focus of public health nursing is not on providing direct care to individuals in community settings. Public health nurses support the provision of direct care through a process of evaluation and assessment of the needs of individuals in the context of their population group. Public health nurses work with other providers of care to plan, develop, and support systems and programs in the community to prevent problems and provide access to care.

As defined by the Public Health Nursing section of the American Public Health Association (APHA), public health nursing is the practice of promoting and protecting the health of populations using knowledge from nursing, social, and public health sciences. Public health nursing practice is a systematic process by which

- The health and health care needs of a population are assessed in order to identify subpopulations, families, and individuals who would benefit from health promotion or who are at risk of illness, injury, disability, or premature death.
- A plan for intervention is developed with the community to meet identified needs that takes into account available resources, the range of activities that contribute to health, and the prevention of illness, injury, disability, and premature death.
- The plan is implemented effectively, efficiently, and equitably.
- Evaluations are conducted to determine the extent to which the interventions have an impact on the health status of individuals and the population.
- The results of the process are used to influence and direct the delivery of care, deployment of health resources, and the development of local, regional, state, and national health policy and research to promote health and prevent disease.

Table 9–1 provides a snapshot of an average day in the life of a public health nurse.

OCCUPATIONAL CLASSIFICATION

There is no standard occupational category specific to public health nurses. There is a more generic standard occupational category *registered nurse* that encompasses professional nursing positions in any health care or health services organization. This standard occupational category is one of the administrative occupations within the white collar grouping of occupations.

Public health nurses plan, develop, implement, and evaluate nursing and public health interventions for individuals, families, and populations at risk of illness or disability. This category covers all positions identified at the registered nurse level, unless specified as performing work defined under some other professional occupational category (such as epidemiologist or occupational health and safety specialist) and includes graduates of diploma and associate degree programs with the RN license. Common job titles for public health nurses include community health nurse, nurse consultant, school nurse, public health nurse, occupational health nurse, home health nurse, and RN case manager. Public health nurses holding administrative positions have titles such as supervising nurse, nursing coordinator, program director, and director of nursing. Public health nurses who provide clinical services often function with titles such as staff nurse, nurse clinician, or nurse practitioner. Licensed practical (or vocational) nurses (LPNs/LVNs) are considered as technical rather than professional workers in this classification.

There are 2.3 million registered nurses and 700,000 licensed vocational/practical nurses in the United States. Only 13% of registered nurses (300,000) work in community or public health settings. Bureau of Labor Statistics data indicated that in 2004 more than 175,000 nurses (135,000 registered nurses and 42,000 licensed practical nurses) worked for federal, state, and local governmental agencies.[1] The *Public Health Workforce Enumeration 2000* identified 64,000 public health nurses and an estimated 15,000–20,000 licensed vocational/practical nurses working for governmental public health organizations, with another 8,000 registered nurses working for voluntary-sector agencies.[2] Data from these two sources are used throughout this chapter.

PUBLIC HEALTH PRACTICE PROFILE

Nurses have long been the professional core of the public health workforce. Nurses provide both clinical and community health services in a wide variety of public and private organizations. Services are provided within maternal and child health programs, communicable disease prevention and control, immunization, and school health programs, to name just a few. Many nurses trained in public health take on supervisory and management roles and serve as chief administrator or as part of the senior management team for many local public health agencies. Nurses also serve as program coordinators and consultants for state and federal health agencies. Their broad expertise and professional credibility assists in advocacy and coalition-building activities and in the evaluation of programs within the community. Public health nurses are also active in community health planning and community health improve-

---

TABLE 9–1 A Typical Day for a Public Health Nurse

7:30 a.m.	Breakfast meeting with visiting nursing agency to discuss interagency coordination
8:30 a.m.	Consult with clinic staff on issues requiring follow-up, such as missed appointments
9:00 a.m.	Visit home of family missing recent appointments
10:15 a.m.	Back in office for meeting to update director of nursing
10:45 a.m.	Meeting with communicable disease control and epidemiology staff regarding community concerns over West Nile Virus threat
11:45 a.m.	Informal lunch meeting with community college faculty and students to promote interest in public health nursing careers
1:00 p.m.	Back in office to discuss referrals from clinic and communicable disease staff
1:30 p.m.	Visit patient receiving directly supervised therapy for tuberculosis; identify need for job training assistance and assist with referral
3:00 p.m.	Back in office, assist clinic staff with back-to-school physicals and immunizations
4:30 p.m.	Time to complete paperwork and follow-up phone calls for today's activities
5:15 p.m.	Review and plan tomorrow's schedule
7:00 p.m.	Attend community meeting regarding West Nile Virus concerns to assist epidemiology and environmental health staff

ment initiatives across the United States. Nurses are directly involved in a wide variety of health promotion and disease and injury prevention efforts. Their skills are critical to achieving community health objectives and broader public health goals through performing one or more of the essential public health services. As a result, public health nurses are involved in a wider array of public health purposes and essential public health services than most other public health occupational categories. It is somewhat misleading to highlight only a few public health purposes and essential public health services that are most closely associated with public health nursing. Virtually all fit within the scope of their professional expertise. For the sake of consistency with other public health occupations and titles addressed in this book, three public health purposes and five essential public health services are identified for public health nurses in Table 9–2.

IMPORTANT AND ESSENTIAL DUTIES

Nursing positions within public health organizations have many different titles. In some organizations, all registered nurses are covered by one series usually called public health nurse. In other organizations, registered nurses performing clinical duties may be distinguished from those performing community and public health nursing duties. Some organizations employ nurse practitioners to provide primary medical care. In addition to registered nurses, some public health or-

ganizations employ licensed practical nurses or licensed vocational nurses to provide supportive nursing services for clinical care programs. The focus in this chapter will be on three nursing positions: entry-level public health nurse, senior-level public health nurse, and licensed vocational nurse.

Public Health Nurse (Entry Level)

Under direction, entry-level public health nurses provide public health nursing services, including health education, the promotion of health awareness, and the prevention and control of diseases. This is the entry and first working level in the public health nurse class series. Incumbents must have requisite public health nursing certification but have limited public health nursing work experience. As experience is gained, incumbents learn to perform the full scope of public health nursing duties. Entry-level public health nurses are distinguished from midlevel public health nurses who independently perform a larger scope of public health nursing duties and activities. Midlevel public health nurses perform a larger range of duties and activities on a more independent basis and are distinguished from senior public health nurses in that senior public health nurses perform more complex, specialized assignments, as well as provide lead direction, work coordination, and training for other professional nursing and support staff. Entry-level and midlevel public health nurses generally report to a senior public health nurse or the

---

TABLE 9–2 Public Health Practice Profile for Public Health Nurses

Public Health Nurses Make a Difference by:

Public Health Purposes
- Preventing epidemics and the spread of disease √
- Protecting against environmental hazards
- Preventing injuries
- Promoting and encouraging healthy behaviors √
- Responding to disasters and assisting communities in recovery
- Assuring the quality and accessibility of health services √

Essential Public Health Services
- Monitoring health status to identify community health problems √
- Diagnosing and investigating health problems and health hazards in the community
- Informing, educating, and empowering people about health issues √
- Mobilizing community partnerships to identify and solve health problems
- Developing policies and plans that support individual and community health efforts
- Enforcing laws and regulations that protect health and ensure safety
- Linking people with needed personal health services and assuring the provision of health care when otherwise unavailable √
- Assuring a competent public health and personal health care workforce
- Evaluating effectiveness, accessibility, and quality of personal and population-based health services √
- Researching new insights and innovative solutions to health problems √

director of nursing services. Entry-level positions do not supervise other staff.

Important and essential duties for entry-level public health nursing positions may include

- Participate in planning, organizing, and providing public health nursing services, health instruction, counseling, and guidance for individuals, families, and groups regarding disease control, health awareness, health maintenance, and rehabilitation in a clinic setting
- Identify and interact with local care providers in the coordination of health care
- Provide referrals to other community-based health and social services
- Teach and demonstrate health practices to individuals and groups
- Instruct clients in immunization procedures, family planning, and sexually transmitted disease prevention and follow-up
- Identify individual and family problems that are detrimental to good health
- Make home visits to assess a patent's progress and intervene accordingly
- Work with families to alleviate health problems and promote good health habits
- Refer and coordinate the care of individuals and families with other public and private agencies
- Identify special health needs for assigned cases, recommending and implementing services to meet those needs
- Assist individuals and families with implementing physician recommendations
- Participate in planning, directing, and performing epidemiologic investigations in homes, schools, workplaces, the community, and public health clinics
- Prepare appropriate records and case documentation, arranging follow-up services based on findings
- Confer with physicians, nursing staff, and other staff regarding public health programs, patient reports, evaluations, medical tests, and related items
- Participate in multidisciplinary teams for the purpose of creating a plan of service for at-risk families
- Participate and collaborate with community groups to identify public health needs, develop needed public health services, and improve existing public health services
- Prepare reports and maintain records
- Compile statistical information for appraisal and planning purposes

Public Health Nurse (Senior Level)

Under direction, senior public health nurses provide lead direction and work coordination for other professional nursing and support staff. Senior public health nurses plan and conduct a variety of public health nursing clinics and services and provide complex, specialized, and general nursing, health education, and health consulting services, including the prevention and control of diseases and the promotion of health awareness. This is the advanced level and lead class in the public health nurse series. Incumbents provide the more complex public health nursing services in a specialized public health program, as well as provide lead direction and coordination for other professional nursing staff. This class is distinguished from the midlevel public health nurse by assignment of a higher level of public health program responsibilities and the performance of lead responsibilities for other professional nursing staff. Senior public health nurses report to the director of nursing services and, in turn, provide lead direction and work coordination for entry-level and midlevel public health nurses.

Important and essential duties for senior-level public health nurses may include

- Investigate outbreaks of communicable diseases
- Plan and implement programs for the prevention and control of communicable disease, including tuberculosis, sexually transmitted diseases, and AIDS
- Develop procedures to control the spread of communicable diseases and identify people needing public health services
- Provide interpretations of public health laws and regulations for others
- Assess individuals and families, using health histories, observations of physical condition, and a variety of evaluative methods to identify health problems, health deficiencies, and health service needs
- Identify psychosocial, cultural background, and environmental factors that may hinder the use of or access to health care services
- Assist with determining funding needs for specific programs, and monitor budget expenditures within those programs
- Plan and coordinate services for special programs such as family planning, or perinatal, maternal, child, or adolescent programs
- Perform public health nursing activities to promote perinatal, child, and adolescent health
- Provide local case management and coordination within specific programs

- Participate in programs to enhance school children health
- Work with community groups to identify needs, develop and facilitate a variety of health services, and improve existing programs
- Refer individuals and families to appropriate agencies and clinics for health services
- Participate in programs to enhance community health services and education
- Attend conferences and workshops related to community health issues
- Assist with the preparation of program and service policies and procedures
- Supervise paraprofessional staff and volunteers
- Prepare reports and maintain records
- Compile and analyze statistical information for appraisal and planning purposes
- Provide lead direction, training, and work coordination for other professional nurses

Licensed Vocational/Practical Nurse

Under general supervision, licensed vocational (or practical) nurses perform a variety of health-related activities in the provision of basic nursing care, including administering immunizations and vaccinations, hearing and vision screening, basic skin and blood tests, and blood pressure monitoring. Licensed vocational nurses assist with a variety of activities related to implementation of various agency health programs. Workers in this title do not have the necessary education, experience, or license requirements to qualify as either a registered nurse or a public health nurse. Workers perform a variety of clinical and basic nursing duties consistent with their license and experience. Licensed vocational nurses report to a midlevel or senior-level public health nurse or to the director of nursing. These positions do not carry supervisory responsibility.

Important and essential duties for licensed vocational nursing positions may include

- Perform, read, and evaluate skin, hearing, vision, and blood tests
- Perform and evaluate blood pressure readings
- Provide health education sessions
- Administer immunizations and vaccinations
- Participate in health care clinics, coordinating activities as assigned
- Maintain a current inventory of clinic supplies
- Operate a mobile health van
- Evaluate medical records and determine the need for immunization or vaccination

- Prepare patients for physical examinations
- Weigh and measure patients
- Assist with examinations
- Refer clients to other health care providers
- Prepare specimens for mailing
- Provide basic health information and instruction to individuals and families
- Answer health-related questions from the public
- Sterilize equipment
- Maintain safety requirements in a clinical setting
- Triage requests for information

MINIMUM QUALIFICATIONS

Nurses working in public health come from a wide variety of backgrounds and academic preparation. The number of registered nurses (RNs) produced by 4-year baccalaureate programs is increasing, but there are many RNs from diploma programs in the public health workforce as well. Many nursing schools offer master's-level preparation in community health nursing, school health, and other public health specializations. As described later in this chapter, there is a highly respected, competency-based credential that is offered for community health nurses. Nonetheless, many of those working as nurses in public health settings, including those holding public health nursing titles, do not qualify for this credential because of inadequate educational attainment.

Typical Minimum Qualifications for Entry-Level Public Health Nurse

Knowledge, Skills, and Abilities

The typical entry-level public health nurse generally has knowledge of

- Principles, methods, practices, and current trends of general and public health nursing and preventive medicine
- Community aspects of public nursing including community resources and demography
- Federal, state, and local laws and regulations governing communicable disease, public health, and disabling conditions
- Environmental, sociological, and psychological problems related to public health nursing programs
- Child growth and development
- Causes, means of transmission, and methods of control of communicable disease
- Methods of promoting child and maternal health and public health programs
- Principles of health education

A typical entry-level public health nurse has the skills and ability to

- Learn to organize and carry out public health nursing activities in an assigned program
- Collect, analyze, and interpret technical, statistical, and health data
- Analyze and evaluate health problems of individuals and families, and take appropriate action
- Provide instruction in the prevention of diseases
- Develop and maintain health records, and prepare clear and concise reports
- Communicate effectively orally and in writing
- Interact tactfully and courteously with the public, community organizations, and other staff when explaining public health issues and providing public health services
- Establish and maintain cooperative working relationships
- Effectively represent the agency and nursing division in contacts with public, other staff, and other governmental agencies

Experience and Education

Any combination of training and experience that provides the required knowledge and abilities will qualify an individual for this position. A typical way to obtain the required knowledge and abilities is to complete a bachelor degree and have adequate work experience to meet existing state certification requirements. These often call for 1 year of previous public health nursing experience comparable to an entry-level public health nurse with the hiring organization. Special requirements include possession of a valid state license as a registered nurse. A state-issued certificate as a public health nurse and possession of a valid state driver's license may also be required by some agencies.

Typical Minimum Qualifications for Senior-Level Public Health Nurse

Knowledge, Skills, and Abilities

In addition to those required for entry-level public health nurses, senior-level public health nurses generally have knowledge of

- Unique psychosocial and cultural issues encountered in a rural health program
- Principles of health education
- Program planning, evaluations, and development principles
- Principles of lead direction, program and work coordination, and training

- Community health assessment principles, strategies, and tools

A senior-level public health nurse generally has the skills and ability to

- Plan, organize, and carry out public health nursing activities and services for an assigned service area or program
- Develop and maintain effective working relationships with clients, staff, community groups, and other government organizations
- Collect, analyze, and interpret technical, statistical, and health data
- Analyze and evaluate health problems of individuals and families, and take appropriate action
- Provide work direction and coordination for other staff
- Provide instruction in the prevention and control of diseases
- Communicate effectively in writing and orally
- Develop and maintain health records and prepare clear and concise reports

Experience and Education

Any combination of training and experience that provides the required knowledge and abilities will qualify an individual for this position. A typical way to obtain the required knowledge and abilities is to complete sufficient education and experience to meet state certification requirements. This may require 1 year of public health nursing experience comparable to a midlevel public health nurse. In addition, special requirements may include possession of a valid state license as a registered nurse, state certification as a public health nurse, and a valid state driver's license.

Typical Minimum Qualifications for Licensed Practical/Vocational Nurses

Knowledge, Skills, and Abilities

A licensed practical/vocational nurse generally has knowledge of

- Principles, methods, and procedures of general nursing
- Causes, means of transmission, and methods of controlling communicable diseases
- Basic medical terminology
- Principles and procedures of medical record keeping
- Health problems and requirements of infants, children, adolescents, and the elderly
- State laws relating to reporting child abuse and neglect

A licensed practical/vocational nurse generally has the skills and ability to

- Operate a variety of standard medical testing equipment
- Communicate effectively in writing and orally
- Follow oral and written instructions
- Provide responsible nursing care and services
- Maintain confidentiality of material
- Interview patients and families to gather medical history
- Perform skin tests and interpret results
- Prepare medical forms and records
- Work responsibly with physicians and other members of the health care team
- Effectively represent the agency in contacts with the public, community organizations, and other government agencies
- Establish and maintain cooperative working relationships with patients and others

Experience and Education

Any combination of training and experience that provides the required knowledge and abilities will qualify an individual for this position. A typical way to obtain the required knowledge and abilities is through 1 year of vocational nursing experience and completion of nursing studies and curriculum sufficient to obtain requisite state licenses. In addition, special requirements may include possession of a valid state license as a licensed vocational nurse and a valid state driver's license.

WORKPLACE CONSIDERATIONS

Public health nurses have long been one of the most important, and most numerous, categories within the professional public health workforce. Public health nurses are especially prominent in local public health agencies, where they are involved in a wide range of disease prevention, health promotion, and health service programs. They are also found in state and federal health agencies, although not as frequently today as in past decades. Public health nurses play key roles in maternal and child health services, WIC programs, immunization and communicable disease control programs, and in the clinical operations of local public health agencies. Their professional background also makes them effective links with other community health organizations and agencies, especially local hospitals and schools. Public health nurses need to know medical terminology and how to perform various medical screening tests and basic nursing procedures.

Work is performed in clinics and health care offices, at work site, and in home environments with occasional exposure to communicable diseases and bloodborne pathogens as well as saliva, urine, and feces. Nurses are expected to understand and follow recommended practices and precautions for prevention of disease transmission. Ongoing contact with other staff and the public is part of the daily routine for public health nurses. Public health nurses may need to travel to various locations within the community, including to remote or unsafe areas in all weather conditions in order to perform their duties. Personal safety is enhanced through safety training, use of cell phones and identification badges, and not traveling alone to neighborhoods with high crime rates.

Typical physical requirements for nurses at all levels include the ability to sit and stand for extended periods, normal manual dexterity and eye-hand coordination, the ability to lift and move objects weighing up to 50 pounds, hearing and vision corrected to normal range, verbal communication skills, and the ability to properly use medical and office equipment, including computer, telephone, calculator, copiers, and fax machines.

SALARY ESTIMATES

Salary levels for public health nurses depend in part on academic degrees, credentialing, experience, as well as on market conditions related to the shortage of nurses in the area. At the lower end of these criteria, salaries of $10–$12 an hour are not uncommon. At the higher levels of these criteria, salaries may be in the $35–$40 per hour range. It is common for public health nurses to move up into unit and agency leadership positions and higher salaries. It is not uncommon for the public health agency director of a small agency to be an experienced public health nurse.

Registered nurses in the United States have a mean salary of $55,000, with 50% earning between $44,000 and $64,000. As indicated in Table 9–3, registered nurses working for federal agencies have higher average salaries than those working for state or local governmental agencies ($65,000 federal, $50,500 state, $53,000 local) but far lower than those working in acute care settings.

Licensed practical/vocational nurses have an average annual salary of $35,000, with 50% earning between $29,000 and $41,000. Mean salaries are similar for LPNs or LVNs working for the different levels of government ($37,000 federal, $34,000 state, $34,500 local).

CAREER PROSPECTS

Nurses remain in short supply throughout the health sector, making the recruitment and retention of public health nurses an issue for potential employers, both public and private. Public-sector agencies, such as local and state health departments as well as community and national not-for-profit organizations, often are not able to match salary and benefit

TABLE 9-3 Number and Mean Salary for Nurses in Federal, State, and Local Governmental Agencies, May 2004

Occupational Category	Federal Workers	Federal Worker Mean Salary	State Workers	State Worker Mean Salary	Local Workers	Local Worker Mean Salary	Total Federal, State, and Local Workers	Adjusted PH Enum. 2000 Workers
Registered Nurses	48,490	$64,780	35,540	$50,520	51,320	$53,200	135,350	63,753
Licensed Vocational/ Practical Nurses	12,690	$37,060	13,170	$34,240	16,620	$34,310	42,480	(est) 25,000

Source: Data for federal, state, and local governmental agency workers from Bureau of Labor Statistics. May 2004 national, state, and metropolitan area occupational employment and wage estimates. Available at: http://www.bls.gov. Accessed August 20, 2005. See Chapter 6 for adjusted number of public health workers from *The Public Health Workforce Enumeration 2000.*

levels available through private employers (such as hospitals, clinics, and health plans). Competition with private-sector employers has increased nursing salaries to some extent, although public health agencies generally are not able to match the salaries and benefits (including signing bonuses) available within the acute care and primary care sectors.

As the largest professional category employed by public health agencies, and due to the growing shortage of registered nurses, there are many opportunities for all levels of nurses within the public health workforce. Working hours and conditions for nurses working in public health agencies can be attractive, and many nurses appreciate the importance and impact of working in public health. Still, public health nurses are the number one worker category identified as needed now and in the future for public health agencies. The *Public Health Workforce Enumeration 2000* found 50,000 public health nurses, nearly all of whom worked in state and local public health agencies.

The number of undergraduate and graduate students entering nursing training programs has been increasing steadily in recent years. As noted earlier, the demand for public health nurses is also increasing, probably even faster than the supply.

ADDITIONAL INFORMATION

There are many good sources of information on public health nursing. Several sources of information are available on educational programs for these occupations as well as for continuing education and leadership development for public health nurses.

The Public Health Nursing section of the APHA Web site (http://www.apha.org) is a great source of information on public health nursing. The Public Health Nursing section has a long history and currently has many members, making it one of APHA's largest and most active sections.

Schools of public health are among the institutions offering master's and doctoral degrees in public health for nurses. The Association of Schools of Public Health Web site (http://www.asph.org) provides information on accredited schools of public health and on the characteristics of public health students and degree concentrations.

State licensing boards (which license registered nurses), schools of nursing, the American Nurses Association (ANA) and its many state affiliates are rich sources for additional information on public health nurses. The American Nursing Credentialing Center (ANCC) is the credentialing arm of the ANA (http://www.nursingworld.org/ancc/cert/eligibility/CommHealth.html) and awards a RN, BC (registered nurse, board certified) certification. ANCC certifies community health nurses who meet all the following requirements:

- Active registered nurse license in the United States
- Two full years of public health nursing practice in the United States
- Bachelor or higher degree in nursing
- Two thousand or more hours of clinical practice within the past 3 years (can include nursing administration, education, client care, and research)
- Thirty contact hours of continuing education within the past 3 years

The Quad Council of Public Health Nursing Organizations is an alliance of the four national nursing organizations that address public health nursing issues: the Association of

Community Health Nurse Educators (ACHNE), the ANA's Congress on Nursing Practice and Economics, the APHA's Public Health Nursing Section, and the Association of State and Territorial Directors of Nursing (ASTDN). The *Quad Council PHN Competencies* is designed for use with others documents. It complements the *Definition of Public Health Nursing* adopted by the APHA's Public Health Nursing Section in 1996 and the ANA's *Scope and Standards of Public Health Nursing Practice.*[3]

In developing the competencies, the Quad Council members concurred that the generalist level would reflect preparation at the bachelor level. Although recognizing that in many states much of the public health nursing workforce does not have a bachelor degree, the Quad Council believes that those nurses may require job descriptions that reflect a different level of practice or may require extensive orientation and education to achieve the competencies identified. Further, the specialist-level competencies described in this document reflect preparation at the master's level in community/public health nursing or public health. Again, while recognizing that there may be other public health nurses who are promoted or appointed to managerial or consultant positions that require specialist competencies, a master's degree prepares public health nurses for the specialist-level competencies identified in this document. At both levels, it is expected that on-the-job training and continuing education for nurses hired for these positions who have less than a bachelor or master's degree (as appropriate to the level) will assure that these competencies are attained.

TABLE 9–4 American Nurses Association Public Health Nursing Standards of Practice and Professional Performance

Standards of Practice

1. Assessment: The public health nurse assesses the health status of populations using data, community resource identification, input from the population, and professional judgment.
2. Population diagnosis and priorities: The public health nurse analyzes the assessment data to determine population diagnoses or priorities.
3. Outcomes identification: The public health nurse identifies expected outcomes for a plan that is based on population diagnoses or priorities.
4. Planning: The public health nurse develops a plan that identifies strategies, action plans, and alternatives to attain expected outcomes.
5. Implementation: The public health nurse implements the identified plan by partnering with others.
   a. Coordination: The public health nurse coordinates programs, services, and other activities in implementing the identified plan.
   b. Health education and health promotion: The public health nurse employs educational strategies to promote health, prevent disease, and ensure a safer environment for populations.
   c. Consultation: The public health nurse provides consultation to various community groups and officials to facilitate the implementation of programs and services.
   d. Regulatory activities: The public health nurse identifies, interprets, and implements public health laws, regulations, and policies.
6. Evaluation: The public health nurse evaluates the health status of the population.

Standards of Professional Performance

7. Quality of practice: The public health nurse systematically enhances the quality and effectiveness of nursing practice.
8. Education: The public health nurse attains knowledge and competency that reflects current nursing and public health practice.
9. Professional practice evaluation: The public health nurse evaluates one's own nursing practiced in relation to professional practice standards and guidelines, relevant statutes, rules, and regulations.
10. Collegiality and professional relationships: The public health nurse establishes collegial partnerships while interacting with representatives of the population, organizations, and health and human services professionals, and contributes to the professional development of peers, colleagues, and others.
11. Research: The public health nurse puts research findings into practice.
12. Resource utilization: The public health nurse considers factors related to safety, effectiveness, cost, and impact on practice and on the population in the planning and delivery of nursing and public health programs, policies, and services.
13. Leadership: The public health nurse provides leadership in nursing and public health.
14. Advocacy: The public health nurse advocates and strives to protect the health, safety, and rights of the population.

Source: American Nurses Association. Public health nursing: scope and standards of practice. Available at: http://www.nursingworld.org/practice/ publichealthnursing.pdf. Accessed September 20, 2005.

The Quad Council based its competency framework on several relevant assumptions. Public health nurses must first possess the competencies common to all nurses with bachelor degrees and then demonstrate additional competencies specific to their roles in public health. The progression from awareness to knowledge to proficiency is a continuum, and there are no discrete boundaries between those levels of competence. Both levels reflect competencies for a reasonably prudent public health nurse who has experience in the role (i.e., not a novice and not in a specialized or limited focus role). Defined competencies are intended to reflect the standard for public health nursing practice, not necessarily what is occurring in practice today. Importantly, in any practice setting, the job descriptions may reflect components from each level, depending on the agency's structure, size, leadership, and services. Table 9–4 outlines the ANA's *Scope and Standards of Public Health Nursing Practice*. Detailed information on core public health nursing competencies are available at http://www.nursingworld.org/anp/palpha.cfm, in various ANA publications, and in documents with the full scope and standards of public health nursing practice.

CONCLUSION

Public health nurses are the largest category of health professionals in the public health workforce. They are active in community as well as clinical services and at all levels of public health organizations, including serving as public health managers and administrators. Although there are more than 2 million nurses in the United States, only an estimated 75,000 work for governmental public health organizations, and relatively few of those have formal training in public health. The national nursing shortage, particularly acute for nursing positions in hospitals and long-term care facilities, also affects the ability of public health organizations to attract and retain qualified nurses. Recruitment and retention initiatives are widely discussed within the public health community, a testimony to the continuing importance of public health nurses if public health goals and objectives are to be achieved.

Discussion Questions and Exercises

1. What are the most important contributions to improving the health of the public that public health nursing makes today?

2. What features make public health nursing a career worth pursuing?

3. Using a scale from 1 to 10, how important to the effectiveness of the overall public health system is the need for more and better prepared public health nurses? How did you arrive at this rating?

4. What do you think are the most important new or expanded roles for public health nurses in the 21st century?

5. In which organizations and geographic regions will the need for public health nursing expand most rapidly in the next 2 decades?

REFERENCES

1. Bureau of Labor Statistics, U.S. Department of Labor. May 2004 national, state, and metropolitan area occupational employment and wage estimates. Available at: http://www.bls.gov/oes/current/oes_nat.htm. Accessed August 20, 2005.

2. Health Resources and Services Administration (HRSA), Bureau of Health Professions, National Center for Health Workforce Information and Analysis and Center for Health Policy, Columbia School of Nursing. *The Public Health Workforce Enumeration 2000.* Washington, DC: HRSA; 2000.

3. American Nurses Association. Scope and standards of public health nursing practice. Available at: http://www.nursingworld.org/practice/publichealthnursing.pdf. Accessed September 20, 2005.

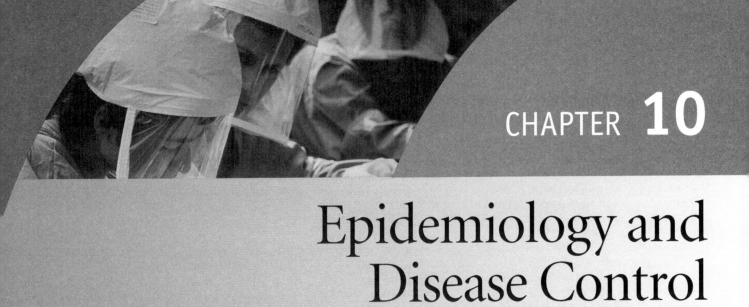

CHAPTER 10

Epidemiology and Disease Control

LEARNING OBJECTIVES

After completing Chapter 10, learners will be proficient in describing key features of occupations and careers in epidemiology and disease control and how these contribute to carrying out public health's core functions and essential services. Key aspects of this competency expectation include

- Describing several different occupational titles in this category
- Identifying several essential public health services that are critical for positions in this category
- Describing important and essential duties for several job titles in this category
- Identifying minimum qualifications and describing general workplace considerations, salary expectations, and career prospects for positions in this category

Epidemiology is often called the mother science of public health practice. Epidemiologists investigate and describe the determinants and distribution of disease, disability, and other health outcomes and help develop the means for their prevention and control. Epidemiology works hand in hand with biostatistics and field investigations to provide information and insights into factors that contribute to health and disease in a population. John Snow's methods of examining cholera outbreaks in 1854 demonstrated the usefulness of epidemiologic methods even when little was known about the microorganism causing these outbreaks. Epidemiology and biostatistics are essential tools for research and evaluation into causative factors as well as into the effectiveness of clinical and community interventions.

Recent concerns over bioterrorism threats and events have raised awareness of the important role played by epidemiologists and related occupations. One of the major objectives of increased funding for bioterrorism preparedness and response is to rapidly increase the number of epidemiologists working in state and local public health agencies. Table 10–1 provides a snapshot of an average day in the life of an epidemiologist.

OCCUPATIONAL CLASSIFICATION

Two standard occupational categories used for public health workers (epidemiologist and statistician) are addressed in this chapter. Epidemiologist is a standard occupational category that is commonly found in public health organizations. Biostatisticians are a subset of statisticians. Both categories are professional white-collar categories. Another important and related occupational category, disease investigators, is not included among the standard occupational titles but will also be described in this chapter, as their work complements that of epidemiologists and biostatisticians.

- The role of epidemiologist encompasses positions that investigate, describe, and analyze the distribution and determinants of disease, disability, and other health outcomes, and develop the means for their prevention and control. Epidemiologists also describe and analyze the efficacy of programs and interventions. This category includes individuals specifically trained as epidemiologists as well as those trained in another discipline (such as medicine, nursing, or environmental health) working as epidemiologists under such job titles as nurse epidemiologist. Bureau of Labor Statistics data indicate that in 2004 there were 4,600 epidemiologists in the United States, with state and local governments employing 1,800 of these positions.[1] *The Public Health*

TABLE 10–1 A Typical Day for an Epidemiologist

7:30 a.m.	Phone discussion from home with state epidemiologist regarding current status of West Nile Virus and follow-up on last week's foodborne illness outbreak involving local fast-food establishment
8:30 a.m.	Meeting with public health student completing internship project analyzing childhood asthma morbidity
9:00 a.m.	Staff meeting to review priorities for week
10:15 a.m.	Meet with agency director, health education, and planning staff regarding completion of community health assessment
10:45 a.m.	Meet with communicable disease control and public health nursing staff regarding community concerns over West Nile Virus threat
11:45 a.m.	Interview candidates for vacant entry-level epidemiologist position
12:15 p.m.	Lunch at desk while catching up with e-mail and phone messages
1:00 p.m.	Grand Rounds presentation at community hospital on nosocomial infections
2:30 p.m.	Office time to respond to e-mail and phone messages
3:00 p.m.	Conference call with epidemiologists and environmental health staff of neighboring jurisdictions and state health department regarding current status of West Nile Virus
4:00 p.m.	Review information suggested by staff for tonight's community meeting on West Nile Virus
4:30 p.m.	Brief agency director on West Nile Virus
5:15 p.m.	Complete final report on last week's foodborne illness outbreak involving local fast-food establishment
7:00 p.m.	Represent agency at community meeting regarding West Nile Virus concerns

Workforce Enumeration 2000 identified 1,400 epidemiologists working in federal, state, and local governmental public health agencies.[2] Data from these two sources are used throughout this chapter. Hospitals, scientific research and development companies, and educational institutions are also important sources of employment for epidemiologists. A 2004 survey conducted by the Council of State and Territorial Epidemiologists identified 2,600 epidemiologists working in state and local public health agencies, although it is likely that this number included some disease investigator positions.[3]

- The role of infection control/disease investigator includes positions that assist in identifying and locating individuals or groups at risk of specified health problems and incorporating those people into appropriate health promotion and disease prevention programs. This category includes public health investigators or sexually transmitted infection investigators without reference to educational preparation. Disease investigators may be undercounted if individuals with specific professional preparation (such as nursing, environmental health, or laboratory science) are primarily performing investigations but are employed under another professional title. As this title is not one of the standard occupational categories tracked by the Bureau of Labor Statistics, it is not clear how many disease investigator positions exist.

The Public Health Workforce Enumeration 2000 identified 1,200 infection control and disease investigator positions in governmental public health agencies.[2] It is likely that there is some overlap between these positions and those designated as epidemiologists or general program specialists (see Chapter 13).

- Biostatisticians apply statistical reasoning and methods in addressing, analyzing, and solving problems in public health; health care; and biomedical, clinical, and population-based research. The precise number of biostatisticians is not known. Bureau of Labor Statistics data indicates that in 2004 there were 17,000 statisticians in the United States, with nearly 6,000 working for governmental agencies.[1] The federal government alone employs over 3,500 statisticians. *The Public Health Workforce Enumeration 2000* identified 1,800 biostatisticians in governmental public health agencies, the majority working for federal and state agencies.[2]

PUBLIC HEALTH PRACTICE PROFILE

Epidemiologists, biostatisticians, and disease investigators primarily address public health responsibilities for preventing disease and injury and protecting against environmental hazards. These occupational groups may also be involved in emergency preparedness and response and, not infrequently, with assessing the impact and quality of health services within a community.

Among the 10 essential public health services, epidemiologists and related occupations are especially important for four: monitoring health status, diagnosing and investigating health events and threats in the community, assessing the impact and quality of services, and researching innovative solutions to health problems. Table 10–2 summarizes public health purposes and essential public health services at the core of positions for epidemiologists and disease control professionals.

IMPORTANT AND ESSENTIAL DUTIES

There are many job titles and positions in the public health workforce that investigate and analyze health problems and risks. The focus in this chapter will be on four positions: communicable disease investigator, entry-level epidemiologist, senior-level epidemiologist, and biostatistician. Each of these positions and a representative panel of their important and essential duties are described in this section.

Communicable Disease Investigator

This position investigates confirmed or suspected cases of communicable diseases to ensure patient treatment and follow-up. Duties are often characterized by the responsibility to implement key aspects of a communicable disease control program. This position performs communicable disease investigative work, bringing to treatment those patients with positive lab-oratory tests and providing information on sexually transmitted and other communicable diseases. Communicable disease investigator titles may include higher-level titles responsible for supervising the work of communicable disease investigators and providing the more difficult and sensitive pretest and posttest counseling to patients and families. Entry-level and midlevel communicable disease investigators exercise no supervision over other workers.

Operational duties related to identifying and obtaining treatment for carriers of communicable diseases include identifying target populations, conducting epidemiologic investigations, testing patients, and making referrals for social or community services. This position administers tuberculin skin tests, obtains laboratory samples, and performs epidemiologic investigations. Many personnel systems have several levels for disease investigators.

Important and essential duties of a communicable disease investigator include

- Interviews clients and contacts; performs risk assessment and counseling; performs disease testing; performs partner counseling and referral service to contacts of infected persons; counsels patients diagnosed as having a communicable disease regarding the disease process (such as the sequence of symptoms), appropriate medications,

---

TABLE 10–2 Public Health Practice Profile for Epidemiology and Disease Control

Epidemiology and Disease Control Professionals Make a Difference by:

Public Health Purposes
  Preventing epidemics and the spread of disease √
  Protecting against environmental hazards √
  Preventing injuries √
  Promoting and encouraging healthy behaviors
  Responding to disasters and assisting communities in recovery
  Assuring the quality and accessibility of health services

Essential Public Health Services
  Monitoring health status to identify community health problems √
  Diagnosing and investigating health problems and health hazards in the community √
  Informing, educating, and empowering people about health issues
  Mobilizing community partnerships to identify and solve health problems
  Developing policies and plans that support individual and community health efforts
  Enforcing laws and regulations that protect health and ensure safety
  Linking people with needed personal health services and assuring the provision of health care when otherwise unavailable
  Assuring a competent public health and personal health care workforce
  Evaluating effectiveness, accessibility, and quality of personal and population-based health services √
  Researching new insights and innovative solutions to health problems √

complications, and prevention so that they will be encouraged to be treated and give names, addresses, and phone numbers of contacts who have been exposed when this is appropriate

- Provides referrals to service providers
- Provides transportation for infected clients and their partners to get appropriate medical care
- Manages cases to closure including successful treatment or failure to comply
- Locates contacts by phone or field visits and informs contacts of infected persons of possible exposure to a sexually transmitted or other communicable disease; maintains confidentiality of information
- Reviews information (such as epidemiologic reports) from other jurisdictions regarding persons exposed to sexually transmitted and other communicable disease; initiates and provides such information for use by other agencies; consults with medical providers regarding specific clients' diagnosis, treatment plan, infection history, and location; consults with laboratory microbiologist regarding complex test results
- Attends meetings and in-service training on identification, testing, and treatment protocols for sexually transmitted and other communicable diseases; may serve as an agency resource or act on behalf of the program coordinator in that person's absence in an assigned program area
- Maintains professional knowledge in applicable areas and keeps abreast of changes in job-related rules, statutes, laws, and new business trends; makes recommendations for the implementation of changes; reads and interprets professional literature; attends training programs, workshops, and seminars as appropriate
- Identifies, contacts, and recruits high-risk patients for participation in communicable disease education and prevention programs
- Provides health education to community organizations, schools, and groups about risky lifestyles and contracting communicable diseases
- Maintains epidemiologic control record of patients, contacts, and suspects
- Maintains a central record file on communicable diseases
- Maintains records of locations where high-risk activity occurs
- Participates as member of a multidisciplinary team on disease surveillance and investigations with epidemiologists, biostatisticians, health care professionals, environmental health practitioners, health information specialists, and staff of regulated industries (such as restaurants, hospitals, and nursing homes)

- Maintains cooperative relationships with officials of the armed forces, state department of public health, and local police departments

Epidemiologist (Entry Level)

This position performs epidemiologic investigations of human morbidity and mortality; compiles, maintains, and analyzes health data and reports; identifies causative agents resulting in adverse health conditions and proposes corrective actions; and provides public health information and consultative services. This is the entry-level professional epidemiologist performing duties under the direct supervision of a higher-level epidemiologist.

Entry-level epidemiologists work in the investigation, analysis, prevention, and control of injuries or communicable, chronic, or environmentally induced diseases. An entry-level epidemiologist is responsible for conducting ongoing epidemiologic studies in order to investigate, identify, and analyze incidence, prevalence, trends, and causes of injuries or communicable, chronic, or environmentally induced diseases. An entry-level epidemiologist is also responsible for assisting with the development of intervention strategies, policies, and procedures and the evaluation of new and existing prevention and control programs based on epidemiologic findings. Work involves communicating with health care providers; social service agencies; schools; federal, state, and local officials; the media; and others concerning disease and injury investigation, prevention, and control. This position may supervise subordinate staff, such as communicable disease investigators. Work is subject to general review and direction by a higher-level epidemiologist, program administrator, or other designated superior; however, an entry-level epidemiologist works with considerable independence within established policies and procedures.

Important and essential duties of an entry-level epidemiologist include

- Assists in the design of or conducts epidemiologic studies of disease or injury occurrence, including evaluation of behavioral and clinical interventions
- Reviews and evaluates disease or injury reporting and surveillance systems and advises program administrators of important incidence or prevalence changes within reporting areas
- Conducts or assists in in-depth investigations of disease clusters using epidemiologic methods, including gathering information and biologic specimens
- Conducts field interviews of case subjects, potential case and control subjects, government officials, and others to ascertain disease incidence and prevalence

- Maintains contact with community physicians, hospital staff, and other health care professionals to encourage proper reporting of injuries and communicable, chronic, or environmentally induced diseases and conditions
- Participates as member of a multidisciplinary team on disease surveillance and investigations with disease investigators, biostatisticians, health care professionals, environmental health practitioners, health information specialists, and staff of regulated industries (such as restaurants, hospitals, and nursing homes)
- Communicates with health care providers; social service agencies; schools; federal, state, and local officials; the media; and others concerning disease and injury investigation, prevention, and control
- Conducts epidemiologic investigations, surveys, and special studies relating to public health, including assessment of risk behaviors or continuing risk of exposure to specific agents
- Conducts evaluations of control measures related to communicable, chronic, or environmentally induced diseases or injuries
- Prepares investigation reports, statistical analyses, and summaries on completed epidemiologic studies and evaluations
- Participates in preparing grant applications, research reports, and other public health documents

Epidemiologist (Senior Level)

This position coordinates, conducts, analyzes, interprets, and reports the findings from public health surveillance systems and advanced epidemiologic studies that identify the causes of morbidity and mortality; designs and coordinates appropriate preventive health measures based upon investigative results; and determines which specific public health issues require further epidemiologic studies. Medical epidemiologists (such as physicians, veterinarians, dentists, and nurses) provide professional medical consultation in the performance of these duties. This is the highest-level position in the series. Incumbents at this level independently propose and direct epidemiologic investigations or act as the principal investigator on local, state, or federal health research grants. Positions at this level may supervise or lead lower-level epidemiologists or other research staff.

Important and essential duties of senior-level epidemiologists include

- Conducts case control, cohort, or cross-sectional studies to identify the incidence, prevalence, or causes of human morbidity or mortality; prepares formal written reports of findings, including a description of the methods used, the findings, and the interpretation of the findings
- Conducts disease outbreak investigations to identify causative agents and environmental conditions resulting in disease outbreaks
- Performs statistical analyses of health data, such as analysis of variance, trend analysis, multiple logistic regression, survival analysis, and so on
- Trains interviewers and clerical staff in project-specific tasks as necessary
- Obtains, as necessary, approval from human subject review boards to conduct investigations or research
- Interacts during the course of investigations with health providers or other persons performing clinical or health research
- Collects surveillance information of reportable human morbidity and mortality as required by state law
- Compiles, maintains, and analyzes health data and reports using statistical methods
- Identifies corrective actions to environmental conditions resulting in adverse health conditions
- Independently proposes and supervises epidemiologic investigations of human morbidity or mortality
- Participates as member of a multidisciplinary team on disease surveillance and investigations with disease investigators, biostatisticians, health care professionals, environmental health practitioners, health information specialists, and staff of regulated industries (such as restaurants, hospitals, and nursing homes)
- Collaborates with a broad spectrum of public health constituents and participants including federal, state, and local public health officials, as well as government officials, private individuals, and senior researchers in academic settings
- Communicates health risks to public officials, the media, and the public
- Coordinates local, state, and federal health research programs
- Serves as principal investigator on local, state, and federal health research grants
- Supervises the work of lower-level epidemiologists

Biostatistician

This position conducts statistical analyses of morbidity and mortality data, quality assurance, clinical data, surveillance and other data, and serves as a resource for epidemiology and other agency staff.

Important and essential duties of a biostatistician include

- Provides usable reports to epidemiology, program, and clinical staff
- Advises and assists epidemiology staff with research design, statistical design, and statistical analysis of quantitative research projects and databases
- Designs research protocols
- Provides direction on sample size and distribution
- Directs appropriate measures for proper data handling and cleaning
- Analyzes statistical databases, such as birth, death, or disease records, for proper organization and treatment of data
- Suggests revisions based on statistical and research implications
- Writes research design and statistical portions of proposals and papers
- Works closely with epidemiologists to appropriately frame information for reports or papers
- Cultivates sources of population-based data and information available from other public and private agencies
- Participates as member of a multidisciplinary team on disease surveillance and investigations with epidemiologists, disease investigators, health care professionals, environmental health practitioners, health information specialists, and staff of regulated industries (such as restaurants, hospitals, and nursing homes)
- Assists with outbreak investigations, when needed; in unusual instances, such as a bioterrorism event or disease outbreak, the biostatistician may need to assist with interviewing victims, analyzing data, arranging sample collection, and so on, as directed by the agency leadership team

MINIMUM QUALIFICATIONS

Epidemiologists come from a variety of professional and experiential backgrounds. Among 2,500 positions in state health agencies, 12% are physicians, another 12% have some other doctoral degree (such as PhD, DrPH, DVM, or DDS), 42% have a master's degree, 23% have a bachelor degree, and 5% have less than a bachelor degree.[3]

Epidemiologists and communicable disease investigators work together in investigations of disease patterns and outbreaks. Epidemiologists often have graduate degrees, and some have other professional credentials such as an RN, MD, DDS, or DVM degree. Biostatistics is a specialized field in which master's and doctoral degrees are common. Communicable disease investigators may or may not have education and

training equivalent to a bachelor degree. Typical minimum qualifications for communicable disease investigators, entry-level and midlevel epidemiologists, and biostatisticians are detailed below.

Typical Minimum Qualifications for Communicable Disease Investigator

Knowledge, Skills, and Abilities

A typical communicable disease investigator generally has knowledge of

- Transmission, diagnosis, and treatment of sexually transmitted and other communicable disease
- Symptoms of sexually transmitted and other communicable diseases
- Methods and techniques used to conduct disease investigations
- Methods of infection control
- Laws and legal issues related to the control of communicable diseases
- Diagnostic and therapeutic problems involved in the control of communicable diseases
- Basic medical terminology, clinical practices, and medical procedures
- Principles and practices of customer service
- Available community and social service agencies
- Diverse cultural practices and customs
- Personal computers and related software

A typical communicable disease investigator generally has the skills and ability to

- Understand, interpret, and apply laws, regulations, policies, and procedures relating to communicable disease reporting
- Interview tactfully and effectively, and work cooperatively with other agencies involved in the control of sexually transmitted and other communicable diseases
- Deal firmly and fairly with clients of various socioeconomic backgrounds and temperaments
- Maintain accurate records and document actions
- Make referrals to local and regional providers of social, medical, and other specialized services
- Maintain confidentiality of information; recognize and respect limit of authority and responsibility
- Conduct interviews of a highly personal nature
- Exercise initiative and tact in tracing contacts and bringing them in to seek treatment
- Gain the confidence of many varied personalities

- Communicate and work effectively with coworkers, supervisors, and the general public sufficient to exchange or convey information and to receive work direction
- Communicate effectively both verbally and in writing
- Understand program objectives in relation to departmental goals and procedures
- Establish and maintain effective working relationships with officials, the general public, and personnel from other government agencies
- Operate personal computers, including spreadsheet database, word processing, presentation, and other related software

Experience and Education

Any combination of training and experience that provides the required knowledge and abilities will qualify an individual for this position. A typical way to obtain the required knowledge and experience is through 1 year of experience in a clinical or other health care setting requiring contact with the general public, and at least an associate degree or trade school diploma, preferably as a medical assistant or a closely related field with college-level course work in psychology, health education, or social work. Another path to these qualifications is through an associate degree in allied health or a related field and 2 years of experience providing emergency medical treatment as an emergency medical technician (EMT), medical technician, military corpsman, or related experience; or an equivalent interchange of related education and experience sufficient to successfully perform the essential duties of the job. Still another path is through graduation from an accredited college with a degree in biologic or behavioral sciences or a related field and 1 year of professional experience in public health, hospital services, or a related field. Qualifying experiences may substitute for the required education on a year-for-year basis.

Special requirements often necessary for this position include a valid driver's license, ability to travel independently, bilingual skills, and the ability to work in an environment that may include exposure to communicable diseases. Disease investigators may be required to work outside normal business hours and sign a statement agreeing to comply with state laws and regulations relating to child abuse reporting.

Typical Minimum Qualifications for Entry-Level Epidemiologists

Knowledge, Skills, and Abilities

A typical entry-level epidemiologist generally has knowledge of

- Modern epidemiologic principles and practices, including the symptoms, causes, means of transmission, and methods of control of communicable and chronic diseases
- Microbiology and pathophysiology
- Basic medical terminology
- Modern research procedures including biostatistic methodology
- Computers and programming in database management and statistical software
- Community organizations and resources related to the field of public health and epidemiology
- Epidemiologic techniques, methods, and surveillance systems, particularly those related to communicable, chronic, or environmentally induced diseases or injury control
- Current research and analytical methods related to public health and epidemiology
- Scientific methods and the pathobiology of disease or injury occurrence
- Nature and objectives of statewide public health programs addressing individual and community health problems
- Organization and operation of federal, state, and local governmental agencies relating to public health

A typical entry-level epidemiologist generally has the skills and ability to

- Apply laws, rules, and regulations to problems of disease control
- Communicate clearly and concisely orally and in writing on both technical and nontechnical levels
- Prepare grant proposals and budgets
- Implement and evaluate program activities relating to the prevention and control of injuries and communicable, chronic, or environmentally induced diseases
- Analyze and interpret epidemiologic data
- Assess a disease outbreak situation and make appropriate decisions
- Prepare or assist in preparing scientific articles, making presentations to professional groups, and clearly communicating the findings of epidemiologic studies
- Establish and maintain effective working relationships with other employees, health care providers, social service agencies, schools, the media, the public, and federal, state, and local officials

Experience and Education

Any combination of training and experience that provides the required knowledge and abilities will qualify an individual for this position. A typical way to obtain the required knowledge and experience is through a master's degree in epidemiology or a master's degree in public health (MPH) with specialization in epidemiology and 1 year of experience in epidemiology research and analysis. Another path is through 1 year of professional experience in chronic disease, communicable disease, human nutrition, injury control, environmental epidemiology, or infection control, which includes disease or injury investigation and risk assessment, and a master's degree from an accredited college or university in nursing, nutrition/dietetics, health care administration, biostatistics, sociology, psychology, anthropology, or a biological, physical, or environmental science. Another pathway is through 2 years of professional experience above the entry level in chronic disease, communicable disease, human nutrition, injury control, environmental epidemiology, or infection control, which includes disease or injury investigation and risk assessment, such as a position as a research analyst, program specialist, environmental specialist, nutritionist, community health nurse, or health educator.

Typical Minimum Qualifications for Senior-Level Epidemiologists

Knowledge, Skills, and Abilities

In addition to the knowledge and abilities required for the entry-level epidemiologist just listed, this position requires knowledge of disease control methods, recent developments in the field of epidemiology, and basic management skills. It also requires the skill and ability to supervise and lead lower-level staff and develop grant proposals.

Experience and Education

Any combination of training and experience that provides the required knowledge and abilities will qualify an individual for this position. A typical way to obtain the required knowledge and experience is through a doctoral degree in epidemiology or biostatistics and 2 years of experience in epidemiology research and analysis. Another pathway is through a doctoral degree in a health science field, with a master's degree in epidemiology or an MPH with specialization in epidemiology and 2 years of experience in epidemiology research and analysis. A third pathway is through a master's degree in epidemiology, or an MPH with specialization in epidemiology and 6 years of experience in epidemiology research and analysis. Yet another pathway is through a medical degree with a master's degree in epidemiology or an MPH with specialization in epidemiology and 2 years of experience in epidemiology research and analysis. It is possible that completion of related training or experience such as with the Centers for Disease Control or the National Institutes of Health could substitute for the MPH degree. When an MD is selected, a license to practice medicine in the state is necessary.

Biostatistician

Knowledge, Skills, and Abilities

A typical biostatician generally has knowledge of

- Biostatistics and statistics with basic knowledge of medicine and epidemiology, including research designs, probability, distributions, rates, proportions, odds, categorical variable analyses, regression, logistic regression, survival analysis, sample size calculations, and power analysis essentials
- Modern, high-level database management and statistical languages such as SAS and SPSS (and possibly S-Plus, StatXact and SigmaPlot), in addition to Microsoft Office software including Excel and Access
- Both parametric and nonparametric statistics
- Sample survey design and analysis including the survey software SUDAAN, FoxPro 2000, Dbase, Oracle, SQL, Visual Basic languages, and database formats

A typical biostatician generally has the skills and ability to

- Effectively interact with multidisciplinary teams and outside investigators
- Develop novel approaches for new situations and exhibit the leadership skills needed for successful implementation
- Prioritize conflicting tasks in a fast-paced environment with minimal supervision
- Communicate easily and successfully, both verbally and in writing, remain calm under pressure, work as part of a team, and meet deadlines while paying meticulous attention to detail
- Relate well with others and be flexible in unpredictable, ever-changing work environments

Experience and Education

Any combination of training and experience that provides the required knowledge and abilities will qualify an individual for this position. A typical way to obtain the required knowledge and experience is through a master's degree in biostatistics, epidemiology, or a related field and 4 years of experience in research analysis and database management, either as part of an educational process or as paid employment. Experience should be in a science, social science, or community-based research setting and involve extensive use of statistical methodologies.

WORKPLACE CONSIDERATIONS

Physical requirements for positions in this occupational category are similar to those for many other public health occupations. Most epidemiologist, biostatistician, and communicable disease investigator positions call for workers to be able to sit for extended periods and to frequently stand and walk short distances. Normal manual dexterity and eye-hand coordination and hearing and vision corrected to within the normal range are also important considerations. Normally, public health professionals must be able to communicate verbally and be able to use office equipment including computers, telephones, calculators, copiers, and fax machines. Although much of the work is performed in an office environment, frequent or continuous contact with staff and the public is also necessary. In some situations, a valid driver's license may be required.

Physical abilities necessary for most public health occupations include the ability to exert light physical effort in sedentary to light work, which may involve some lifting, carrying, pushing, and pulling of objects and materials of light weight (5–10 pounds). Tasks may involve extended periods of time at a keyboard or workstation. When epidemiologists and communicable disease investigators work outside the office, they must have the ability to work under conditions in which exposure to communicable disease risks and environmental factors poses a risk of moderate injury or illness.

SALARY ESTIMATES

Based on information from current job postings, salaries for communicable disease investigators fall in the $33,000–$53,000 range (see Table 10–3).

The average annual salary for an epidemiologist is $58,000, with the middle 50% earning between $46,000 and $68,000. The mean salary for epidemiologists working for local governmental agencies is greater than that for epidemiologists working for state agencies ($54,000 local versus $49,500 state). Entry-level epidemiologists can expect salaries in the $35,000–$45,000 range. Many small and medium-sized local public health agencies do not employ an epidemiologist. Larger local public health agencies and state health departments often have several. Larger governmental public health agencies can often offer salaries somewhat competitive to those found in the private and voluntary sectors ($65,000–$85,000 range). Epidemiologists with professional credentials, especially physicians, dentists, veterinarians, epidemiologists, and nurses, may be able to attract salaries in the six-figure category.

The 2004 Council of State and Territorial Epidemiologists (CSTE) survey found the highest ratios of epidemiologists to population on the East Coast and West Coast (1 per 10,000). The South and the Midwest lag behind, with 0.7 and 0.8 epidemiologists per 100,000 population, respectively.

Salary information for biostatisticians is not very straightforward, as biostatisticians are lumped with other types of statisticians in employment and wage surveys. Mean salaries for statisticians working for federal agencies are much higher than mean salaries of statisticians working for state and local governmental agencies ($79,500 federal, $43,500 state, $53,500 local).

CAREER PROSPECTS

According to a recent survey of state and territorial health agencies, epidemiologic capacity needs to be increased by 50%.[3]

TABLE 10–3 Number and Mean Salary for Epidemiologists and Statisticians in Federal, State, and Local Governmental Agencies, May 2004

Occupational Category	Federal Workers	Federal Worker Mean Salary	State Workers	State Worker Mean Salary	Local Workers	Local Worker Mean Salary	Total Federal, State, and Local Workers	Adjusted PH Enum. 2000 Workers
Epidemiologists	NA	NA	1,170	$49,390	650	$54,140	1,820	1,433
Statisticians	3,550	$79,680	1,500	$43,660	590	$53,330	5,640	1,800
Disease Investigators	NA	NA	NA	NA	NA	NA	NA	1,211

Source: Data for federal, state, and local governmental agency workers from Bureau of Labor Statistics. May 2004 national, state, and metropolitan area occupational employment and wage estimates. Available at: http://www.bls.gov. Accessed August 20, 2005. See Chapter 6 for adjusted number of public health workers from *The Public Health Workforce Enumeration 2000.*

Recent increases in epidemiologists have largely benefited bioterrorism preparedness and response efforts, often at the expense of communicable disease, chronic disease, injury, and environmental epidemiologic capacity. As a result, there is consensus that additional epidemiologists are needed, especially infectious disease, chronic disease, and terrorism-related epidemiologists. The Bureau of Labor Statistics also identifies epidemiologists as an occupation that will grow more rapidly than the average for all occupations over the next 10 years.

ADDITIONAL INFORMATION

There are many good sources of information on epidemiologists, disease investigators, and biostatisticians. Several sources are available for information on educational programs for these occupations as well as for continuing education and leadership development for practitioners.

The CSTE Web site (http://www.cste.org) and the CDC Epidemiologic Intelligence Service (EIS) Web site (http://www.cdc.gov/eis/) head the list of useful information sources. CSTE has nearly 1,000 members working in state and local public health agencies. The EIS is an elite unit of CDC that provides technical assistance and manpower to state and local governments during unusual or large outbreaks.

Schools of public health are among the institutions offering graduate degrees in health administration. The Association of Schools of Public Health (http://www.asph.org) has identified a battery of core epidemiology and biostatistics competencies appropriate for all students receiving the MPH degree. These competencies provide a useful baseline for professional practice and summarize what an MPH graduate should be able to do (see Table 10–4).

The epidemiology section and statistics section of the American Public Health Association's (APHA) Web site (http://www.apha.org) are also good sources of information for epidemiologists and biostatisticians. The epidemiology section has a long history and currently has 3,000 members, making it one of APHA's largest and most active sections.

Additional sources of relevant information include the American College of Preventive Medicine (http://www.acpm.org), the American College of Epidemiology (http://www.acepidemiology2.org), the American Epidemiology Society (http://www.acepidemiology.org), the Association for

---

TABLE 10–4 Epidemiology and Biostatistics Competency Expectations for Graduates of MPH Degree Programs

1. Explain the importance of epidemiology for informing scientific, ethical, economic, and political discussion of health issues.
2. Describe a public health problem in terms of magnitude, population affected, time, and place.
3. Apply the basic terminology and definitions of epidemiology.
4. Identify key sources of data for epidemiologic purposes.
5. Calculate basic epidemiology measures.
6. Evaluate the strengths and limitations of epidemiologic reports.
7. Draw appropriate inferences from epidemiologic data.
8. Communicate epidemiologic information to lay and professional audiences.
9. Comprehend basic ethical and legal principles pertaining to the collection, maintenance, use, and dissemination of epidemiologic data.
10. Identify the principles and limitations of public health screening programs.
11. Describe the role biostatistics serves in the discipline of public health.
12. Distinguish among the different measurement scales and the implications for selection of statistical methods to be used based on these distinctions.
13. Apply descriptive techniques commonly used to summarize public health data.
14. Describe basic concepts of probability, random variation, and commonly used statistical probability distributions.
15. Apply common statistical methods for inference.
16. Describe preferred methodological alternatives to commonly used statistical methods when assumptions are not met.
17. Apply descriptive and inferential methodologies according to the type of study design for answering a particular research question.
18. Interpret results of statistical analyses found in public health studies.
19. Develop written and oral presentations based on statistical analyses for both public health professionals and educated lay audiences.
20. Apply basic informatics techniques with vital statistics and public health records in the description of public health characteristics and in public health research and evaluation.

Source: Association of Schools of Public Health MPH core competency development process, version 2. Available at: http://www.asph.org. Accessed June 20, 2006.

Professionals in Infection Control and Epidemiology (http://www.apic.org), the International Epidemiological Association (http://www.dundee.ac.uk/iea/), and the Society for Epidemiologic Research (http://www.epiresearch.org).

CONCLUSION

Epidemiology is the virtual operating system of public health practice, and epidemiologists are in great demand. Although recent events have emphasized bioterrorism threats and events, epidemiologists, biostatisticians, and disease investigators work across the entire spectrum of diseases, conditions, and health risks. As the spotlight has focused on epidemiology, its visibility as a public health career has grown. As disease investigators acquire practical skills in the field, they often seek to complement their experience with additional education and training, establishing an effective partnership with public health epidemiologists in disease prevention and control efforts.

Discussion Questions and Exercises

1. What are the most important contributions to improving the health of the public that epidemiology and disease control makes today?

2. What features make epidemiology and disease control a career worth pursuing?

3. Using a scale from 1 to 10, how important to the effectiveness of the overall public health system is the need for more and better prepared epidemiology and disease control workers? How did you arrive at this rating?

4. What do you think are the most important new or expanded roles for epidemiology and disease control workers in the 21st century?

5. In which organizations and geographic regions will the need for epidemiology and disease control workers expand most rapidly in the next 2 decades?

REFERENCES

1. Bureau of Labor Statistics, U.S. Department of Labor. May 2004 national, state, and metropolitan area occupational employment and wage estimates. Available at: http://www.bls.gov/oes/current/oes_nat.htm. Accessed August 20, 2005.

2. Health Resources and Services Administration, Bureau of Health Professions, National Center for Health Workforce Information and Analysis and Center for Health Policy, Columbia School of Nursing. *The Public Health Workforce Enumeration 2000*. Washington, DC: HRSA; 2000.

3. Council of State and Territorial Epidemiologists. *2004 National Assessment of Epidemiologic Capacity: Findings and Recommendations*. Washington, DC: CSTE; 2004. Available at: http://www.cste.org/Assessment/ECA/pdffiles/ECAfinal05.pdf. Accessed August 20, 2005.

Public Health Education and Information

Public health education is one of the fastest growing public health professions. Public health educators play important roles in a variety of public health programs and in community relations in general. Chronic disease prevention programs, in-jury prevention and control activities, and community health planning and community health improvement initiatives all rely heavily on the expertise of health educators. Recent con-cerns over bioterrorism threats and events have raised aware-ness as to the importance of risk communication and public information skills within the public health workforce. Table 11–1 provides a snapshot of an average day in the life of a pub-lic health educator.

OCCUPATIONAL CLASSIFICATION

Two standard occupational categories for public health work-ers are addressed in this chapter—health educators and pub-lic information specialists.

A health educator is a white collar, professional category encompassing positions that promote, maintain, and improve individual and community health by assisting individuals and communities to adopt healthy behaviors. Health educators col-lect and analyze data to identify community needs prior to planning, implementing, monitoring, and evaluating programs designed to encourage healthy lifestyles, policies, and envi-ronments. Health educators serve as resources to individuals, other professionals, and the community, and may administer fiscal resources for health education programs. Bureau of Labor statistics indicate that in 2004 there were 47,000 health edu-cators working in the United States.[1] Federal, state, and local governmental agencies are among the biggest employers of health educators; these agencies employ 13,000 health educa-tors. The *Public Health Workforce Enumeration 2000* identified 3,500 public health educator positions in governmental public health agencies.[2] Data from these two sources are used through-out this chapter. At the state and local level, less than one half of the public health educators are professionally certified.

Public information specialist is somewhat similar to the standard occupational classification public relations specialist, which includes positions that engage in promoting or creating goodwill for individuals, groups, or organizations by writing or selecting material and releasing it through various communi-cations media. Public relations and media specialists present public health issues to the media and the public, often serving as spokespersons for public health agencies. These positions may prepare and arrange displays and make speeches and other presentations. There are more than 16,000 public relations and public information positions in federal, state, and local gov-ernmental agencies. The *Public Health Workforce Enumeration*

TABLE 11–1 A Typical Day for a Public Health Educator

7:30 a.m.	Breakfast meeting with steering committee of community health coalition for community health improvement plan
8:30 a.m.	Office time for phone messages and e-mail
9:00 a.m.	Staff meeting to review priorities for week
10:15 a.m.	Meeting with agency director, epidemiology, and planning staff on community health assessment
10:45 a.m.	Set up conference room for satellite downlink program
11:00 a.m.	Satellite downlink program on establishing a medical reserve corps unit, followed by staff discussion
12:15 p.m.	Lunch at desk revising presentation slides for staff orientation
1:00 p.m.	Staff orientation presentation on "What Is Public Health, and Where Do I Fit In?"
2:00 p.m.	Review draft for agency press release if West Nile Virus outbreak occurs
3:00 p.m.	Conference call meeting with technical program committee for state public health association annual meeting
4:00 p.m.	Review information to be distributed at tonight's community meeting on West Nile Virus threat
4:30 p.m.	Review and analyze participant evaluations from today's orientation program for new employees; revise presentation materials for next month's orientation
5:15 p.m.	Prepare remarks for tonight's community meeting
7:00 p.m.	Represent agency at community meeting regarding West Nile Virus concerns

2000 identified 900 public information positions in governmental public health agencies. [2]

PUBLIC HEALTH PRACTICE PROFILE

Health educators and public information officers are primarily involved with addressing public health responsibilities for promoting healthy behaviors and preventing disease and injury. These occupational categories may also be involved in emergency preparedness and response and sometimes in assessing the impact and quality of health services within a community.

Among the 10 essential public health services, public health education and information professionals are especially important for four—informing and educating the public, mobilizing community partnerships, developing policies and plans that support community health improvement, and assuring a competent workforce. Table 11–2 summarizes public health purposes and essential public health services at the core of positions for public health educators.

IMPORTANT AND ESSENTIAL DUTIES

There are several job titles and positions in the public health workforce that specialize in public health education and information services. The focus in this chapter will be on three positions: (1) entry-level public health educator, (2) senior-level public health educator, and (3) public information specialist/coordinator. Each of these positions and a representative panel of their important and essential duties are described in this section.

Public Health Educator (Entry Level)

This position encompasses entry-level professional work in the development and coordination of public health education and health promotion activities. Public health educators assist in the formulation of the health education plan and in the development and implementation of health promotion programs. Work includes providing technical assistance and training to local health professionals, schools, community organizations, government agencies, businesses, and individuals. Supervision is received from a higher-level health educator or other designated administrative superior; however, the employee is expected to work with considerable independence within established policies and procedural guidelines.

Essential and important duties for an entry-level public health educator include

- Assists in the development and implementation of health education, behavioral risk reduction, and health promotion programs for schools, worksites, communities, and individuals; provides healthy intervention strategies that meet specified and measurable objectives
- Collects, analyzes, and disseminates information regarding major health problems, behavioral risk factors, and health attitudes and knowledge using epidemiologic procedures; assists in the formulation of disease prevention and health promotion strategies
- Develops various educational materials, such as brochures, exhibits, videotapes, and slides; employs mass

TABLE 11–2 Public Health Practice Profile for Public Health Education and Information Professionals

Public Health Education and Information Professionals Make a Difference by:	
Public Health Purposes	
Preventing epidemics and the spread of disease	√
Protecting against environmental hazards	
Preventing injuries	√
Promoting and encouraging healthy behaviors	√
Responding to disasters and assisting communities in recovery	
Assuring the quality and accessibility of health services	
Essential Public Health Services	
Monitoring health status to identify community health problems	
Diagnosing and investigating health problems and health hazards in the community	
Informing, educating, and empowering people about health issues	√
Mobilizing community partnerships to identify and solve health problems	√
Developing policies and plans that support individual and community health efforts	√
Enforcing laws and regulations that protect health and ensure safety	
Linking people with needed personal health services and assuring the provision of health care when otherwise unavailable	
Assuring a competent public health and personal health care workforce	√
Evaluating effectiveness, accessibility, and quality of personal and population-based health services	
Researching new insights and innovative solutions to health problems	

media, group process, and counseling techniques in health education, health promotion, and behavioral risk reduction program activities

- Assists in development of training programs and works with others to plan and implement health promotion programs, policies, and legislation
- Maintains knowledge and skills in health education and health promotion research through review of professional literature, participation in conferences, and continuing education
- Provides assistance in the submission of applications for health education, behavioral risk reduction, and health promotion program funds; monitors existing programs for compliance with federal and state regulations

Public Health Educator (Senior Level)

Under direction, this position plans, develops, supervises, evaluates, and monitors specific health education program(s) for the agency. Senior-level public health educators are distinguished from lower-level public health educators by their responsibility for the preparation, administration, and evaluation of specific public health education programs, grant contracts, and budgets. In addition, a senior public health educator supervises staff assigned to specific programs. This position is

distinguished from the health education program manager in that the latter manages the overall agency public health education program, but this position is responsible for the preparation, administration, and evaluation of the public health education efforts of specific programs.

Essential and important duties of senior-level public health educators include

- Plans, implements, and evaluates specific public health education programs
- Assesses and identifies community needs for educational services in specific program areas
- Plans, organizes, designs, develops, and evaluates public health education activities; carries out or directs others to carry out public health education activities, including educational presentations and workshops
- Assists in the development and adaptation of data collection instruments and designs for assessment and evaluation activities
- Develops educational literature and flyers and provides information to the community
- Selects, trains, directs, evaluates, and handles disciplinary problems of subordinate staff
- Seeks funding sources for specific public health education programs

- Prepares grant proposals
- Develops memoranda of understanding and budgets
- Negotiates and monitors contracts with funding agencies and other subcontractors
- Develops and maintains contact with state and local public health agencies, community organizations, and the media
- Serves as the community leader of public health education efforts for specific programs
- Inputs, accesses, and analyzes data in a computer database

Public Information Specialist/Coordinator

This position is a midlevel informational and public relations professional for a public health organization. Public information specialists prepare and disseminate informational materials to support and promote the programs and services of their agency. Work includes composing and editing copy for press releases, articles, bulletins, newsletters, pamphlets, and other publications. Work may involve interpreting and communicating agency programs to employees, special interest groups, and the general public. Supervision is received from an administrative superior who reviews work in progress and upon completion.

Public health information coordinators perform more advanced duties in the coordination of informational and public relations activities in an agency or specialized program and serve as assistants to a public information administrator, or perform a comparable level of work. Work involves collecting, preparing, and disseminating informational material to support and promote agency programs and services, including composing and editing text and producing graphic and photographic illustrations for publication or distribution to the news media and other groups. Work includes interpreting and communicating agency programs to employees, special interest groups, and the general public. Supervision may be exercised over professional, technical, or clerical staff. General supervision is received from a public information administrator or other administrative superior; consequently, the employee is expected to work with considerable independence and technical skill in the area of communication and public relations.

Essential and important duties of public information specialists/coordinators include

- Gathers, compiles, and verifies information; composes and edits copy for newsletters, brochures, Web pages, and other publications

- Prepares news releases to inform and educate the public concerning agency programs and services
- Composes or edits articles for internal agency news bulletins; edits articles or correspondence for staff members
- Develops spot announcements and scripts for radio and television
- Answers requests for literature and information; maintains files of photographs, clippings, and agency publications
- Meets with agency officials and attends staff meetings for the purpose of discussing activities and securing newsworthy information
- Researches available material to assist in the preparation of speeches for agency officials
- Operates still and video cameras
- Creates illustrations and does layout work
- Assists with agency-sponsored and interagency public relations activities and special events
- Coordinates informational and public relations activities in a specialized program, serves as an assistant to a public information administrator, or performs work of comparable level and scope
- Provides assistance to higher-level management on matters pertaining to public relations and informational policy
- Develops and maintains working relationships with media representatives and public, private, labor, business, and civic organizations to ensure the effective dissemination of informational material
- Estimates costs, develops specifications, and makes recommendations on securing and accepting bids for printing; maintains contact with printing contractors to assure quality control; reviews and corrects printers' galley proofs
- Arranges public appearances and media engagements for agency officials; prepares or edits the material to be presented
- Makes presentations and serves as a spokesperson for assigned agency programs to special interest groups, employee groups, and the general public
- Informs management of public reaction to programs, suggests strategies for future communications, and makes recommendations for modified or new programs
- Coordinates special events and develops materials, displays, and programs to promote agency services, missions, and goals and to enhance consistency and accuracy in those efforts

- Provides training to improve the techniques of supervisory and professional staff in furthering public understanding of the services offered by the agency
- Supervises, trains, and evaluates subordinate staff

MINIMUM QUALIFICATIONS

Public health educators and public information staff work in professional positions often supported by administrative support and clerical positions. There are generally several steps in the health educator and public information series that allow for advancement and career development. Comparable positions exist in local public health agencies of all sizes, making career advancement from a small to larger employer not uncommon for these workers.

Public health training programs in schools of public health and other academic institutions produce health educators and other communications specialists. The vast majority of current workers in these titles, however, do not have a public health degree. This allows for variability in the types of experience and training that agencies require when filling these positions. As with virtually all public health positions, both experience and education are important considerations for hiring and promotion. Experience and education both contribute to necessary knowledge, skills, and abilities required for workers in this field. Typical minimum qualifications for entry-level and senior-level health educators and public information specialists/coordinators are detailed in this section.

Typical Minimum Qualifications for Entry-Level Public Health Educator

Knowledge, Skills, and Abilities

A typical entry-level public health educator generally has knowledge of

- Current principles, practices, and processes employed in the health education and health promotion component of a public health program
- Principles, techniques, and application of behavioral epidemiology as related to health education and health promotion
- The psychological, social, economic, and cultural determinants of behavior and methods to promote healthy lifestyles
- Educational methods and techniques of developing and presenting health education to individuals and groups
- Community organization principles and resources, and community health needs

- Current trends and developments in public health, medical sciences, and health care
- Research methods as applied to health education and health promotion

A typical entry-level public health educator has the skills and ability to

- Assist in the planning, development, implementation, and evaluation of effective health education and health promotion programs for various populations
- Perform statistical computations
- Explain complex medical information to civic and community groups and to public officials, and present ideas effectively
- Establish and maintain effective working relationships with other employees, community groups, and the public

Experience and Education

Any combination of training and experience that provides the required knowledge and abilities will qualify an individual for this position. A typical way to obtain these knowledge and abilities is through graduation from an accredited 4-year college or university with a bachelor degree with major specialization in health education or health promotion, or a master's degree in health education, health promotion, or public health with specialization in health education.

Typical Minimum Qualifications for Senior-Level Public Health Educator

Knowledge, Skills, and Abilities

A typical senior-level public health educator generally has knowledge of

- The principles of public health education, including program planning and evaluation
- Public health education methods and materials, including teaching methods and curriculum design
- Assessment techniques to identify community health problems in specific program areas
- Existing methods of intervention and control and the health education needs of various target groups
- Principles and practices of community organization for enhancing public health
- The philosophy, concepts, and principles of public health
- The functions and services of local community health agencies and community organizations
- Publicity and media practices and procedures

- Grant proposal writing and budgeting techniques
- Principles and practices of staff supervision and training

A typical senior-level public health educator has the skills and ability to

- Plan, organize, implement, and evaluate public health education services
- Design, effectively use, and evaluate public health education methods and materials
- Provide public health education consultation, and develop cooperative relationships with a wide range of individuals and representatives of organizations and the news media
- Prepare and present a variety of clear and concise written and oral reports
- Develop and nurture funding sources
- Analyze and prepare grant proposals, contracts, and related budgets
- Negotiate and monitor contracts
- Originate, prepare, and distribute informational and publicity materials
- Plan, assign, direct, and evaluate the work of staff
- Interpret legislation regulations, administrative policies, and procedures
- Input, access, and analyze data in a computer database

Experience and Education

Any combination of training and experience that provides the required knowledge and abilities will qualify an individual for this position. A typical way to obtain such knowledge and abilities is through 2 years of experience in public health education, promotion, or a related field that provides the knowledge and abilities previously identified. Some agencies may require a master's degree in health education from an accredited college and a valid driver's license.

Typical Minimum Qualifications for Public Information Specialist/Coordinator

Knowledge, Skills, and Abilities

A typical public information specialist/coordinator generally has knowledge of

- Journalism, photography, film/video production, graphic arts, publication, and printing
- News media operation and its proper utilization for dissemination of information
- Principles and methods of establishing and maintaining good public relations
- Community resources and organizations

- Commercial art methods and the general principles of layout and design
- Marketing and advertising practices and techniques
- Journalistic principles and practices, including techniques of planning, composing, and editing informational materials
- Use of methods and techniques of disseminating information to the public
- Public relations techniques and procedures
- Agency organizational structure, including programs, administrative rules and regulations, and staff
- Operation of still and video cameras and developing, processing, and editing the film or video

A typical public information specialist/coordinator generally has the skills and ability to

- Compose and produce a variety of informational materials
- Use a variety of desktop publishing software packages and Web formatting languages
- Establish and maintain working relationships with media representatives, agency officials, other employees, and the general public
- Communicate with special interest groups, employee groups, and the general public
- Produce graphic art, photographs, and other materials
- Interpret and explain agency policies, laws, and operations
- Stimulate public interest and gain support for agency programs
- Compose and produce a variety of informational materials for release to the media or other publications
- Conduct research to find pertinent and newsworthy information
- Advise and train agency staff in public relations methods and techniques

Experience and Education

Any combination of experience and training that results in the acquisition of the knowledge and skills described above will qualify an individual for this position. A typical way to acquire these qualifications is through graduation from an accredited 4-year college or university with specialization in journalism, communications, English, public relations, advertising, marketing, or closely related areas. Professional experience in the areas of journalism, advertising, marketing, film/video production, or public relations and information may be substituted on a year-for-year basis for the required education. For a public information coordinator, requirements may include

1 year as public information specialist or 2 years of professional experience in public relations, advertising, or journalism; and graduation from an accredited 4-year college or university with specialization in journalism, communications, English, public relations, advertising, marketing, or closely related areas. Professional experience in the areas of journalism, advertising, marketing, film/video production, or public relations and information may be substituted on a year-for-year basis for the stated education. Graduate work in the educational areas previously listed may be substituted on a year-for-year basis for 1 or more years of the stated experience.

WORKPLACE CONSIDERATIONS

State and local governmental agencies employ more than 11,000 health educators, and there is every indication that even greater numbers will be employed by these agencies over the next decade.

Physical requirements for positions in this occupational category are similar to those for other professional public health positions. Most health educator and public information positions call for workers to be able to sit for extended periods and to frequently stand and walk short distances. Normal manual dexterity and eye-hand coordination and hearing and vision corrected to within the normal range are also important considerations. Normally, public health educators and public information staff will be able to communicate verbally and be able to use office equipment including computers, telephones, calculators, copiers, and fax machines. Although much of the work is performed in an office environment, frequent or continuous contact with staff and the public is also necessary. In many situations, people filling these positions may be required to possess a valid driver's license.

SALARY ESTIMATES

The average annual salary for a health educator is $43,000, with the middle 50% earning between $30,000 and $53,000. Entry-level salaries for public health educators employed by public health agencies in the $25,000–$30,000 range are common. As indicated in Table 11–3, average salaries for health educators working for federal agencies are considerably higher than mean salaries for health educators employed by state and local governmental agencies ($79,000 federal, $42,500 state, $41,000 local).

The average salary for public relations specialists is $50,000, with the middle 50% earning between $33,000 and $60,000. Governmental agencies employ a relatively small number of public relations and public information officers. Entry-level salaries for public information specialists employed by public health agencies are often in the $25,000–$35,000 range; public information coordinator salaries are often in the $32,000–$47,000 range. Average salaries for public relations/public information specialists working for federal agencies are notably higher than average salaries at state and local governmental agencies ($70,000 federal, $45,500 state, $47,000 local).

CAREER PROSPECTS

As is the case with several other public health occupations, health educators and public information specialists can advance from entry-level to midlevel to senior-level positions in their specialty. But in view of their strong communication and

TABLE 11–3 Number and Mean Salary for Health Educators and Public Relations/Public Information Workers in Federal, State, and Local Governmental Agencies, May 2004

Occupational Category	Federal Workers	Federal Worker Mean Salary	State Workers	State Worker Mean Salary	Local Workers	Local Worker Mean Salary	Total Federal, State, and Local Workers	Adjusted PH Enum. 2000 Workers
Health Educators	1,990	$79,170	4,680	$42,600	6,660	$40,780	13,330	3,448
Public Relations/Public Information Specialists	3,830	$69,890	4,280	$45,690	8,100	$46,770	16,210	871

Source: Data for federal, state, and local governmental agency workers from Bureau of Labor Statistics. May 2004 national, state, and metropolitan area occupational employment and wage estimates. Available at: http://www.bls.gov. Accessed August 20, 2005. See Chapter 6 for adjusted number of public health workers from the *Public Health Workforce Enumeration 2000.*

information skills, these workers may be used by agencies for both program-specific work (i.e., as program staff for an assigned program) and at the agency level to deal with community and other public interactions. For example, health educators play a major role in organizing and coordinating community health planning efforts that lead to community health needs assessments, community health report cards, and ultimately to community health improvement initiatives. As community health improvement efforts have become a central role of local and state public health agencies, and as they continue to grow over the next decade, the need for health educators will continue to grow in comparison with other public health occupations. This greater emphasis on community planning and partnerships, as well as the need for more effective risk communication capabilities for bioterrorism and other threats, also increases the need and demand for public information specialists and coordinators.

Public health education, an increasingly recognized and important occupational category within the public health workforce, has developed a credential for highly skilled health educators. Certified health education specialists (CHES) illustrate the movement toward credentialing as a means of increasing the professional stature of an occupation. Many public health workers currently providing health education services, however, do not qualify to sit for the CHES exam because they have not completed a degree program in health education at the bachelor or master's level. For either group, however, ongoing continuing education initiatives will be important to

strengthen the corps of workers providing health education services to the public.

ADDITIONAL INFORMATION

There are many good sources of information on health education and public information as careers. Several sources are available for information on educational programs for health education as well as for continuing education and leadership development for practicing health educators seeking a professional credential.

Schools of public health are among the institutions offering graduate degrees in health administration. The Association of Schools of Public Health (http://www.asph.org) has identified a battery of behavioral science competencies appropriate for all students receiving the master's of public health (MPH) degree. These competencies provide a useful baseline for professional practice and summarize what an MPH graduate should be able to do (Table 11–4).

Additional sources of information on health education include the Web sites of several other organizations, including the American Association of Health Education (http://www. aahperd.org/aahe/template.cfm?template;eq main.html), the American College Health Association (http://www.acha.org), the American School Health Association (http://www.asha web.org), the Association of State and Territorial Directors of Health Promotion and Public Health Education (http:// www.astdhpphe.org), the Center for the Advancement of Community-based Public Health (http://www.cbph.org), the

---

TABLE 11–4 Social and Behavioral Science Competency Expectations for Graduates of MPH Degree Programs

1. Describe the role of social and community factors in both the onset and solution of public health problems.
2. Identify the causes of social and behavioral factors that affect the health of individuals and populations.
3. Identify basic theories, concepts, and models from a range of social and behavioral disciplines that are used in public health research and practice.
4. Apply ethical principles to public health program planning, implementation, and evaluation.
5. Specify multiple targets and levels of intervention for social and behavioral science programs and/or policies.
6. Identify individual, organizational, and community concerns, assets, resources, and deficits for social and behavioral science interventions.
7. Apply evidence-based approaches in the development and evaluation of social and behavioral science interventions.
8. Describe the merits of social and behavioral science interventions and policies.
9. Describe steps and procedures for the planning, implementing, and evaluating of public health programs, policies, and interventions.
10. Identify critical stakeholders for the planning, implementation, and evaluation of public health programs, policies, and interventions.

Source: Association of Schools of Public Health MPH core competency development process, version 2. Available at: http://www.asph.org. Accessed June 20, 2006.

International Union for Health Promotion and Education (http://www.iuhpe.org), and the Coalition of National Health Education Organizations (http://www.hsc.usf.edu/cfh/cnheo/). The coalition, for example, has as its primary mission the mobilization of the resources of the health education profession in order to expand and improve health education, regardless of the setting.

The American Public Health Association Web site (http://www.apha.org) has several sections active in health education issues, including the public health education and health promotion section and the school health education section.

Another useful resource for health education and information is the *Healthy People 2010 Toolkit: A Field Guide to Health Planning* (http://www. Health.gov/healthypeople/state/toolkit/). This toolkit contains practical guidance, technical tools, and resources for states, territories, tribes, and others involved in healthy people planning. Additional sources of information include the *National Heart, Lung, and Blood Institute Educational Materials Catalog* (http://www.nhlbi.nih.gov) and the Web site of the Society of State Directors of Health and Physical Education and Recreation (http://www.thesociety.org).

Central to making health education a profession are the efforts of the Society of Public Health Educators (SOPHE) and the National Commission for Health Education Credentialing (http://www.nchec.org) with its competency-based credentialing program for professional health educators (certified health education specialist, or CHES). CHES competencies are detailed in Table 11–5.

CONCLUSION

In an age of communications and information technology, it is no wonder that public health educators and public information professionals play key roles in public health practice. Public health agencies are increasingly adding staff with these capabilities and utilizing existing staff across programs to address community-wide concerns and issues. Public health educators have led the way in establishing a credential that is based on relevant practice competencies and respected in practice settings. It is expected that opportunities will continue to grow for public health educators and public information specialists over the next decade.

TABLE 11–5 Certified Health Education Specialist Competency Expectations

Responsibility I
Assessing Individual and Community Needs for Health Education
A. Obtain health-related data about social and cultural environments, growth and development factors, needs, and interests.
  • Select valid sources of information about health needs and interests.
  • Utilize computerized sources of health-related information.
  • Employ or develop appropriate data-gathering instruments.
  • Apply survey techniques to acquire health data.
B. Distinguish between behaviors that foster and those that hinder well-being.
  • Investigate physical, social, emotional, and intellectual factors influencing health behaviors.
  • Identify behaviors that tend to promote or compromise health.
  • Recognize the role of learning and affective experience in shaping patterns of health behavior.
C. Infer needs for health education on the basis of obtained data.
  • Analyze needs assessment data.
  • Determine priority areas of need for health education.

Responsibility II
Planning Effective Health Education Programs
A. Recruit community organizations, resource people, and potential participants for support and assistance in program planning.
  • Communicate need for the program to those who will be involved.
  • Obtain commitments from personnel and decision makers who will be involved in the program.
  • Seek ideas and opinions of those who will affect, or be affected by, the program.
  • Incorporate feasible ideas and recommendations into the planning process.
B. Develop a logical scope and sequence plan for a health education program.
  • Determine the range of health information requisite to a given program of instruction.
  • Organize the subject areas composing the scope of a program in logical sequence.

(continued)

TABLE 11–5 Certified Health Education Specialist Competency Expectations (*continued*)

C. Formulate appropriate and measurable program objectives.
- Infer educational objectives that facilitate achievement of specified competencies.
- Develop a framework of broadly stated, operational objectives relevant to the proposed health education program.

D. Design educational programs consistent with specified program objectives.
- Match proposed learning activities with those implicit in the stated objectives.
- Formulate a wide variety of the alternative educational methods.
- Select strategies best suited to implement educational objectives in a given setting.
- Plan a sequence of learning opportunities building upon, and reinforcing mastery of, preceding objectives.

Responsibility III

Implementing Health Education Programs

A. Exhibit competence in carrying out planned educational programs.
- Employ a wide range of educational methods and techniques.
- Apply individual or group process methods as appropriate to given learning situations.
- Utilize instructional equipment and other instructional media.
- Select methods that best facilitate the practice of program objectives.

B. Infer enabling objectives as needed to implement instructional programs in specified settings.
- Pretest learners to ascertain present abilities and knowledge relative to proposed program objectives.
- Develop subordinate measurable objectives as needed for instruction.

C. Select methods and media best suited to implement program plans for specific learners.
- Analyze learner characteristics, legal aspects, feasibility, and other considerations influencing choices among methods.
- Evaluate the efficacy of alternative methods and techniques capable of facilitating program objectives.
- Determine the availability of information, personnel, time, and equipment needed to implement the program for a given audience.

D. Monitor educational programs, adjusting objectives and activities as necessary.
- Compare actual program activities with the stated objectives.
- Assess the relevance of existing program objectives to current needs.
- Revise program activities and objectives as necessitated by changes in learner needs.
- Appraise applicability of resources and materials relative to given educational objectives.

Responsibility IV

Evaluating Effectiveness of Health Education Programs

A. Develop plans to assess achievement of program objectives.
- Determine standards of performance to be applied as criteria of effectiveness.
- Establish a realistic scope of evaluation efforts.
- Develop an inventory of existing valid and reliable tests and instruments.
- Select appropriate methods for evaluating program effectiveness.

B. Carry out evaluation plans.
- Facilitate administration of the tests and activities specified in the plan.
- Utilize data-collecting methods appropriate to the objectives.
- Analyze resulting evaluation data.

C. Interpret results of program evaluation.
- Apply criteria of effectiveness to obtained results of a program.
- Translate evaluation results into terms easily understood by others.
- Report effectiveness of educational programs in achieving proposed objectives.

D. Infer implication from findings for future program planning.
- Explore possible explanations for important evaluation findings.
- Recommend strategies for implementing results of evaluation.

Responsibility V

Coordinating Provision of Health Education Services

A. Develop a plan for coordinating health education services.
- Determine the extent of available health education services.
- Match health education services to proposed program activities.
- Identify gaps and overlaps in the provision of collaborative health services.

TABLE 11–5 Certified Health Education Specialist Competency Expectations (*continued*)

B. Facilitate cooperation between and among levels of program personnel.
   • Promote cooperation and feedback among personnel related to the program.
   • Apply various methods of conflict reduction as needed.
   • Analyze the role of health educator as liaison between program staff and outside groups and organizations.
C. Formulate practical modes of collaboration among health agencies and organizations.
   • Stimulate development of cooperation among personnel responsible for community health education programs.
   • Suggest approaches for integrating health education within existing health programs.
   • Develop plans for promoting collaborative efforts among health agencies and organizations with mutual interests.
D. Organize in-service training programs for teachers, volunteers, and other interested personnel.
   • Plan an operational, competency-oriented training program.
   • Utilize instructional resources that meet a variety of in-service training needs.
   • Demonstrate a wide range of strategies for conducting in-service training programs.

Responsibility VI
Acting as a Resource Person in Health Education
A. Utilize computerized health information retrieval systems effectively.
   • Match an information need with the appropriate retrieval system.
   • Access principal online and other database health information resources.
B. Establish effective consultative relationships with those requesting assistance in solving health-related problems.
   • Analyze parameters of effective consultative relationships.
   • Describe special skills and abilities needed by health educators for consultation activities.
   • Formulate a plan for providing consultation to other health professionals.
   • Explain the process of marketing health education consultative services.
C. Interpret and respond to requests for health information.
   • Analyze general processes for identifying the information needed to satisfy a request.
   • Employ a wide range of approaches in referring requests to valid sources of health information.
D. Select effective educational resource materials for dissemination.
   • Assemble educational material of value to the health of individuals and community groups.
   • Evaluate the worth and applicability of resource materials for given audiences.
   • Apply various processes in the acquisition of resource materials.
   • Compare different methods for distributing educational materials.

Responsibility VII
Communicating Health and Health Education Needs, Concerns, and Resources
A. Interpret concepts, purposes, and theories of health education.
   • Evaluate the state-of-the-art of health education.
   • Analyze the foundations of the discipline of health education.
   • Describe major responsibilities of the health educator in the practice of health education.
B. Predict the impact of societal value systems on health education programs.
   • Investigate social forces causing opposing viewpoints regarding health education needs and concerns.
   • Employ a wide range of strategies for dealing with controversial health issues.
C. Select a variety of communication methods and techniques in providing health information.
   • Utilize a wide range of techniques for communicating health and health education information.
   • Demonstrate proficiency in communicating health information and health education needs.
D. Foster communication between health care providers and consumers.
   • Interpret the significance and implications of health care providers' messages to consumers.
   • Act as liaison between consumer groups and individuals and health care provider organizations.

Source: National Commission for Health Education Credentialing. Responsibilities and competencies for CHES credentialing. Available at: http://www.nchec.org/aboutnchec/rc.htm. Accessed August 20, 2005.

Discussion Questions and Exercises

1. What are the most important contributions to improving the health of the public that health education and information makes today?

2. What features make public health education and information a career worth pursuing?

3. Using a scale from 1 to 10, how important to the effectiveness of the overall public health system is the need for more and better prepared public health education and information workers? How did you arrive at this rating?

4. What do you think are the most important new or expanded roles for public health education and information workers in the 21st century?

5. In which organizations and geographic regions will the need for public health education and information workers expand most rapidly in the next 2 decades?

REFERENCES

1. Bureau of Labor Statistics, U.S. Department of Labor. May 2004 national, state, and metropolitan area occupational employment and wage estimates. Available at: http://www.bls.gov/oes/current/oes_nat.htm. Accessed August 20, 2005.

2. Health Resources and Services Administration, Bureau of Health Professions, National Center for Health Workforce Information and Analysis and Center for Health Policy, Columbia School of Nursing. *The Public Health Workforce Enumeration 2000.* Washington, DC: HRSA; 2000.

CHAPTER 12

Other Public Health Professional Occupations

LEARNING OBJECTIVES

After completing Chapter 12, learners will be proficient in describing key features of various professional occupations in public health and how these contribute to carrying out public health's core functions and essential services. Key aspects of this competency expectation include

- Describing several different occupational titles in this category
- Identifying several essential public health services that are critical for positions in this category
- Describing important and essential duties for several job titles in this category
- Identifying minimum qualifications and describing general workplace considerations, salary expectations, and career prospects for positions in this category

This and the following chapter are organized somewhat differently than Chapters 7 through 11. This chapter highlights selected professional public health occupations within the public health workforce. These professional occupational categories and related technical occupational categories are addressed separately, as the career links are not as clear for these occupations as for those addressed in earlier chapters.

Many standard occupational categories carry out professional roles or perform technical duties in support of professionals. Within the public health workforce these include nutritionists and dieticians, dietetic technicians, medical and public health social workers, mental health and substance abuse social workers, substance abuse and behavioral disorder counselors, medical and clinical laboratory technologists and technicians, physicians, veterinarians, pharmacists, dental health professionals, and administrative judges/hearing officers.

Nutritionists and dieticians work in a variety of settings for governmental public health agencies, voluntary organizations, and health care providers. Public health social workers often have positions in maternal and child health programs or in mental health services offered by public agencies. Mental health substance abuse social workers and substance abuse and behavioral disorder counselors work with psychologists and other mental health providers in programs that offer mental health services.

Not all public health agencies have laboratories, but those that provide public health and clinical laboratory services employ medical and clinical laboratory technologists and technicians. Those labs also employ public health laboratory scientists with special expertise in microbiology, chemistry, and physics.

Physicians were once the largest and most active professional occupational category in the public health workforce. Today, however, they represent only a small percentage of the public health workforce. Veterinarians play key roles in animal control and communicable disease control programs, and pharmacists are increasingly involved in clinical and emergency preparedness and response roles. Dental health professionals, including dentists and dental hygienists, coordinate oral health programs within public health agencies. Finally, administrative law judges/hearing officers are important personnel in the wide variety of administrative and regulatory processes of governmental public health agencies. Together, these varied professional categories demonstrate the multidisciplinary and interdisciplinary nature of modern public health practice.

This chapter focuses on the following public health professional and supporting technical occupations that make up key subsets of the overall public health workforce: (1) nutritionists and dieticians; (2) public health social, behavioral, and mental health workers; (3) public health laboratory workers; (4) public health physicians, veterinarians, and pharmacists; (5) public health dental workers; and (6) administrative judges/hearing officers. Data from several sources are used throughout this chapter, including the Bureau of Labor Statistics[1] and the *Public Health Workforce Enumeration 2000*.[2] Table 12–1 provides a public health practice profile for each of these occupational categories, pointing out the prime public health purposes and essential public health services addressed by each category.

NUTRITIONISTS AND DIETICIANS

Nutritionists, dieticians, and dietetic technicians primarily work toward preventing the spread of diseases and conditions related to diet and exercise (see Table 12–1). These categories monitor health status to identify community health problems; inform, educate, and empower people about health issues; and link people with needed personal health services. They may also be involved in research activities.

Nutritionists and dieticians may supervise the activities of a program or unit providing nutrition or food services, counsel individuals, or conduct nutritional research. Nutritionists, dieticians, and dietetic technicians work in community-oriented programs such as the federally funded WIC program or state and locally funded maternal and child health programs, as well as in clinical settings, such as prenatal and well child clinics.

The Bureau of Labor Statistics indicates that there are 47,000 nutritionists and dieticians in the United States and 25,000 dietetic technicians. Most nutritionists, dieticians, and dietetic technicians work for hospitals, long-term care facilities, and community care facilities for the elderly. Only 7,300 nutritionists and dieticians and 1,000 dietetic technicians work for federal, state, and local governmental agencies, primarily public health departments. The *Public Health Workforce Enumeration 2000* identified 6,700 public health nutritionists in governmental public health agencies, largely based on information provided by the Association of State and Territorial Public Health Nutrition Directors.

The adjusted estimate of government-employed nutritionists (adjusted for underreporting of occupational categories in the year 2000 public health enumeration study) likely overestimates the number of government-employed nutritionists, because the year 2000 public health enumeration included national data from a comprehensive independent enumeration of nutritionists compiled by the Association of State and Territorial Public Health Nutrition Directors. As a re-

sult, it is likely that the actual number of nutritionist positions in state and local public health agencies is close to the 6,700 figure. Within state and local health agencies, most nutritionists work in WIC programs. WIC is short for Supplemental Foods Program for Women, Infants, and Children, which is funded by the U.S. Department of Agriculture. Nutrition positions are also found in regulatory programs for hospitals, nursing homes, day care centers, and other facilities as well as in Child and Adult Care Food Program (food stamps) and state Medicaid and school lunch programs.

Entry-level public health nutritionists plan and conduct nutritional programs that assist in the promotion of health and control of disease. Midlevel and senior-level nutritionists may supervise activities of a program or unit of an agency providing quality food services, counsel individuals, or conduct nutritional research. Many nutritionists and dietetic technicians seek the registered dietician (RD) and registered dietetic technician (DTR) credential.

Entry-level professional public health nutritionists are responsible for participating in the implementation of nutrition programs and services. Work involves providing nutrition program services to local health units or health and human services professionals. General supervision is received from an administrative superior, with professional supervision received from a higher-level nutritionist.

Essential and important duties of an entry-level public health nutritionist include

- Carries out program policies and procedures in implementing nutritional components of general or specialized public health programs
- Coordinates nutrition program services with other nutrition or public health programs within an assigned area
- Confers with public health personnel on food and nutrition related to health programs or problems
- Participates in conducting studies and surveys of the relationships of dietary factors to health and disease, including compilation of data and interpretation of results
- Conducts formal training using educational materials and visual aids in the education of students and public health staff, and assists in the evaluation and recommendation for improvement of such materials
- Participates and works with higher-level nutritionists or consultants in in-service training of health personnel
- Prepares reports, records, and other data related to nutritional services
- Assists in monitoring local health units for compliance with federal or state regulations related to nutrition programs or grant projects

TABLE 12–1 Public Health Practice Profile for Selected Public Health Professional Occupations

	Nutr	Soc Beh MH	PH Lab	MD DVM Phar	Dent Wkrs	Adm Law Jdg
Selected Public Health Professional Occupations Make a Difference by:						
Public Health Purposes						
Preventing epidemics and the spread of disease	✓		✓	✓	✓	✓
Protecting against environmental hazards		✓				✓
Preventing injuries						
Promoting and encouraging healthy behaviors	✓	✓		✓	✓	
Responding to disasters and assisting communities in recovery		✓				
Assuring the quality and accessibility of health services	✓	✓	✓	✓	✓	✓
Essential Public Health Services						
Monitoring health status to identify community health problems	✓		✓	✓	✓	
Diagnosing and investigating health problems and health hazards in the community			✓	✓		
Informing, educating, and empowering people about health issues	✓	✓			✓	
Mobilizing community partnerships to identify and solve health problems		✓				
Developing policies and plans that support individual and community health efforts		✓				✓
Enforcing laws and regulations that protect health and ensure safety			✓			✓
Linking people with needed personal health services and assuring the provision of health care when otherwise unavailable	✓	✓		✓	✓	
Assuring a competent public health and personal health care workforce						✓
Evaluating effectiveness, accessibility, and quality of personal and population-based health services	✓	✓	✓	✓	✓	✓
Researching new insights and innovative solutions to health problems	✓		✓	✓		✓

Key knowledge, skills, and abilities for entry-level public health nutritionists include

- Working knowledge of the principles and practices of nutrition and food, particularly in relation to health and disease
- Knowledge of current developments in public health nutrition and their application to statewide and/or local nutrition programs
- Knowledge of social, cultural, and economic problems and their impact on public health nutrition
- Knowledge of the general organization and function of public health agencies
- Ability to effectively use educational materials for the nutrition education of individuals and groups
- Ability to gather, interpret, evaluate, and use statistical data
- Ability to present ideas clearly and concisely

• Ability to establish and maintain working relationships with professional and lay groups, other employees, and the general public

Minimum qualifications, in terms of experience and training, for entry-level public health nutrition positions may call for graduation from an accredited 4-year college or university with a bachelor degree, including or supplemented by at least 15 semester hours in foods and nutrition including at least one course in diet therapy and one course in community nutrition or nutrition in life cycle; or completion of an undergraduate curriculum accredited or approved by the American Dietetic Association. Registration or current eligibility for registration by the Commission on Dietetic Registration may be accepted in lieu of other specified qualifications. A registered dietician is identified as an *RD*.

Salaries for nutritionists and dieticians average $45,000, with the middle 50% earning between $36,000 and $54,000. In general, nutritionists working for state and local governmental agencies earn less than those working for hospitals and other health care providers. Mean salaries for nutritionists employed by state and local governmental agencies are $43,000 and $40,500 respectively (see Table 12–2). Starting salaries for entry-level nutritionists in a public health agency setting may be in the $26,000–$36,000 range. The average salary for nutritionists employed by federal agencies, on the other hand, is nearly $60,000, well above the overall average for all nutritionists. Nutritionists working for federal health agencies work primarily as resources and consultants. Table 12–2 presents information on government employment and salaries for each of the public health professional occupations examined in this chapter.

PUBLIC HEALTH SOCIAL, BEHAVIORAL, AND MENTAL HEALTH WORKERS

Public health social workers, mental health and substance abuse social workers, and substance abuse and behavioral disorder counselors promote and encourage healthy behaviors and often participate in responses to disasters and public health emergencies (see Table 12–1). They diagnose and investigate health problems; inform, educate, and empower people about issues; mobilize community partnerships; and link people with needed personal health services.

Medical and Public Health Social Workers

Medical and public health social workers provide persons, families, or vulnerable populations with psychosocial support needed to cope with chronic, acute, or terminal illnesses, such as AIDS, cancer, or Alzheimer's disease. Public health social workers identify, plan, develop, implement, and evaluate social work interventions on the basis of social and interpersonal needs of total populations or populations at risk in order to improve the health of a community and promote and protect the health of individuals and families.

There are 104,000 medical and public health social workers in the United States. The majority work for hospitals, long-term care facilities, and nongovernmental home health care service agencies. Nearly 11,000 work for local governmental agencies, including local public health agencies. The *Public Health Workforce Enumeration 2000* identified 3,400 medical and public health social work positions in governmental public health agencies.

Entry-level professional social workers may provide basic protective services with, or on behalf of, children, families, or aged, blind, or disabled clients in instances of abuse, neglect, or exploitation. Responsibilities may also include foster care, unmarried parent services, adoption, and services for character disorders and serious physical, mental, or emotional handicaps. Work is performed under close supervision as part of a training process to develop the worker's understanding and skill. Workers receive close supervision from a social service supervisor or higher-level social service worker within the framework of agency rules, regulations, and procedures.

Essential and important duties of an entry-level public health social worker include

• Plans and conducts programs to combat social problems, prevent substance abuse, or improve community health and counseling services
• Collaborates with other professionals to evaluate patients' medical or physical condition and to assess client needs
• Serves as the primary case manager when families are served by more than one health agency resource
• Investigates child abuse or neglect cases and takes authorized protective action when necessary
• Refers patient, client, or family to community resources to assist in recovery from mental or physical illness and to provide access to services such as financial assistance, legal aid, housing, job placement, or education
• Counsels clients and patients in individual and group sessions to help them overcome dependencies, recover from illness, and adjust to life
• Organizes support groups or counsels family members to assist them in understanding, dealing with, and supporting the client or patient
• Advocates for clients or patients to resolve crises
• Identifies environmental impediments to client or patient progress through interviews and review of patient records

TABLE 12–2 Number and Mean Salary for Selected Public Health Professional Occupations in Federal, State, and Local Governmental Agencies, May 2004

Occupational Category	Federal Workers	Federal Worker Mean Salary	State Workers	State Worker Mean Salary	Local Workers	Local Worker Mean Salary	Total Federal, State, and Local Workers	Adjusted PH Enum. 2000 Workers
Nutritionists/dieticians	1,360	$59,340	2,480	$43,020	3,490	$40,560	7,330	10,330
Public health social workers	NA	NA	5,190	$38,180	10,130	$40,530	15,320	3,364
Microbiologists	2,200	$79,570	1,250	$44,890	510	$55,520	3,960	
Biochemists	410	$81,030	290	$43,870	30	$64,840	730	
Laboratory specialists	4,870	$53,330	930	$43,070	760	$51,760	6,560	21,785
Laboratory technicians	2,310	$35,220	1,150	$31,840	1,290	$31,390	4,750	8,182
Public health physicians	19,250	$101,920	1,270	$126,730	1,580	$118,220	22,100	9,290
Public health veterinarians	1,070	$78,210	520	$62,190	140	$71,690	1,730	3,150
Public health pharmacists	5,510	$82,310	1,090	$70,600	820	$79,810	7,420	2,313
Public health dentists	1,240	$84,090	270	$53,260	60	$55,840	1,570	
Public health dental hygienists	390	$44,680	320	$42,430	320	$46,240	1,030	3,142
Admin law judges/ hearing officers	4,160	$104,750	7,670	$60,910	3,000	$63,160	14,830	929

Source: Data for federal, state, and local governmental agency workers from Bureau of Labor Statistics. May 2004 national, state, and metropolitan area occupational employment and wage estimates. Available at: http://www.bls.gov. Accessed August 20, 2005. See Chapter 6 for Adjusted Number of Public Health Workers from *The Public Health Workforce Enumeration 2000*.

- Utilizes consultation data and social work experience to plan and coordinate client or patient care and rehabilitation, following through to ensure service efficacy
- Modifies treatment plans to comply with changes in clients' status
- Monitors, evaluates, and records client progress according to measurable goals described in treatment and care plan
- Supervises and directs other workers providing services to clients or patients
- Develops or advises on social policy and assists in community development
- Conducts social research to advance knowledge in the social work field

Relevant knowledge, skills, and abilities for entry-level public health social workers may include

- Knowledge of human behavior and performance; individual differences in ability, personality, and interests; learning and motivation; psychological research methods; and the assessment and treatment of behavioral and affective disorders

- Knowledge of principles and processes for providing customer and personal services, including assessment of customer needs, meeting quality standards for services, and evaluation of customer satisfaction
- Knowledge of principles, methods, and procedures for diagnosis, treatment, and rehabilitation of physical and mental dysfunctions, and for career counseling and guidance
- Knowledge of group behavior and dynamics, societal trends and influences, human migrations, ethnicity, and cultures and their history and origins
- Knowledge of the principles and methods of interviewing
- Knowledge of the general provisions, objectives, and philosophy of social welfare programs
- Knowledge of current social, economic, and community health problems
- Ability to plan and organize working time effectively
- Ability to work under a variety of situations and in all types of community environments
- Ability to provide protective services to clients following established rules and procedures

- Ability to work harmoniously with applicants, recipients, the general public, and other employees
- Ability to exercise good judgment in evaluating situations and in making decisions
- Ability to express ideas clearly, both orally and in writing, and to interpret laws and regulations

Minimum qualifications, in terms of experience and training, may call for graduation from an accredited 4-year college or university with major specialization (24 semester hours) in such areas as social work, family and child development, special education, psychology, sociology, gerontology, or related behavioral sciences. Professional employment in a public or private agency involving a substantial amount of time (over 50% of time) in the delivery of protective services to families, adults, children, or the aged may be substituted on a year-for-year basis for the required education.

The average salary for medical and public health social workers is $42,000, with the middle 50% earning between $32,000 and $50,000. Social workers employed by local governmental agencies have a lower average salary ($40,500) than those working for private organizations and schools.

Behavioral and Mental Health Workers

Public health organizations increasingly employ a variety of behavioral and mental health workers, including mental health and substance abuse social workers, substance abuse and behavioral disorder counselors, and psychologists and other mental health providers.

Mental health and substance abuse social workers assess and treat individuals with mental, emotional, or substance abuse problems, including abuse of alcohol, tobacco, and/or other drugs. Duties may include individual and group therapy, crisis intervention, case management, client advocacy, prevention, and education. There are 109,000 mental health and substance abuse social workers in the United States, with 22,000 employed by state and local governmental agencies.

Mental health counselors counsel and advise individuals with an emphasis on prevention. They work with individuals and groups to promote optimal mental health and may help individuals deal with addictions and substance abuse; family, parenting, and marital problems; suicide; stress management; problems with self-esteem; and issues associated with aging and mental and emotional health. Of the 90,000 mental health counselors in the United States, 11,000 work for local government agencies and another 2,000 work for state agencies.

Substance abuse and behavioral disorder counselors counsel and advise individuals with alcohol, drug, or other problems, such as gambling and eating disorders. They may counsel individuals, families, or groups or engage in prevention programs. Of the 69,000 substance abuse and behavioral disorder counselors, only 10,000 work for state and local governmental agencies (7,000 work for local government agencies).

Only a small number (2,400) of the government-employed behavioral and mental health personnel work in public health agencies. The average salary for mental health and substance abuse social workers is $36,000, with the middle 50% earning between $27,000 and $44,000. Mental health counselors have an average salary of $36,000, with the middle 50% earning between $26,000 and $44,000. Substance abuse and behavioral disorder counselors have a slightly lower average salary ($35,000), with the middle 50% earning between $26,000 and $41,000.

PUBLIC HEALTH LABORATORY WORKERS

Public health laboratory workers prevent the spread of disease, protect against environmental hazards, and assure the quality of services (see Table 12–1). Lab workers diagnose and investigate health problems and disasters, evaluate the effectiveness and quality of services, and research new insights and innovative solutions to health problems.

Public health laboratories require a variety of professional and technical workers, including public health scientists and laboratory technologists and technicians. Public health scientists are not one of the standard occupational categories tracked by the Bureau of Labor Statistics, although there are several other standard occupational categories that work in this capacity (such as microbiologists and biochemists). Technologists and technicians working in medical and clinical labs, including public health labs, are among the occupations for which national data are compiled.

Public Health Laboratory Scientists

Public health laboratory scientists are laboratory professionals who plan, design, and implement laboratory procedures to identify and quantify agents in the environment that may be hazardous to human health; biologic agents believed to be involved in the etiology of diseases in animals or humans, such as bacteria, viruses, and parasites; or other physical, chemical, and biologic hazards. Titles include microbiologist, chemist, toxicologist, physicist, and entomologist.

Public health laboratory scientists perform both professional and technical work in the public health laboratory. These include a variety of chemical, serologic, viral, or bacteriologic analyses of clinical or environmental specimens according to established procedures. Work involves performing complex tests under general supervision, assuring the accuracy of the tests through quality control procedures, notifying appropriate scientific and supervisory staff when a test system is not functioning, and, in consultation with appropriate authorities, implementing and documenting appropriate remedial and corrective actions. Work may also involve communicating with health professionals in other agencies regarding routine questions concerning specimen requirements and tests offered. Work is performed under general supervision; however, public health laboratory scientists are expected to exercise independent judgment within the framework of established procedures and policies.

Public health laboratory scientists include microbiologists, biochemists, and biophysicists. Microbiologists investigate the growth, structure, development, and other characteristics of microscopic organisms, such as bacteria, algae, or fungi. Biochemists and biophysicists study the chemical composition and physical principles of living cells and organisms, their electrical and mechanical energy, and related phenomena. They may conduct research to further understanding of the complex chemical combinations and reactions involved in metabolism, reproduction, growth, and heredity. Biochemists may also determine the effects of foods, drugs, serums, hormones, and other substances on tissues and vital processes of living organisms.

There are 14,000 microbiologists and 16,000 biochemists and biophysicists in the United States. Five thousand microbiologists work for federal, state, and local health agencies; federal agencies employ about one half of these scientists. Fewer biochemists and biophysicists, an estimated 1,000, work for governmental agencies. The *Public Health Workforce Enumeration 2000* identified 22,000 public health laboratory professionals working in governmental public health agencies.

Essential and important duties of a public health laboratory scientist include

- Performs routine serologic tests for the presence of antibodies or antigens to various disease agents
- Performs a variety of bacteriologic examinations for the presence of disease agents or contaminants in clinical or other specimens, such as feces, urine, sputum, spinal fluid, blood cultures, water specimens, dairy products, foods, and beverages
- Performs microscopic examinations of animal heads for rabies
- Performs microscopic examinations for tissue and intestinal protozoans, helminths, and nematodes
- Performs cultural and microscopic examinations for gonorrhea, and cultural, biochemical, and serologic examinations for various species of bacteria

- Performs analytic chemical analysis on clinical and environmental samples using a variety of methodologies and instrumentation
- Evaluates methods and instruments for determination of blood alcohol content in breath, blood, urine, or saliva; periodically performs quality assurance checks of field units; testifies in court as required
- Performs screening and confirmatory tests to detect inborn errors of metabolism and sickle cell disease
- Performs, records, and reviews quality control results to determine the validity, accuracy, or precision of tests performed and to ascertain the quality of reagents, chemicals, or media used for analysis
- Participates in sample accessioning and record keeping to ensure that all specimens are accounted for, appropriately handled, and properly and completely tested
- Records and reports results in the proper manner for the technical area of analysis; checks reports for accuracy; maintains confidentiality of reports
- Consults with public health personnel, physicians, other laboratorians, and health care professionals regarding the interpretation of results, collection of specimens, and the applicability of tests to particular circumstances

Knowledge, skills, and abilities relevant for public health laboratory scientists include

- Knowledge of the principles and practices of microbiology or analytic chemistry
- Knowledge of accepted analytic techniques
- Knowledge of laboratory methods, materials, techniques, and safety procedures
- Knowledge of the principles, practices, and methods of a public health, medical, or other health-related analytic laboratory
- Knowledge of common laboratory equipment and apparatus, and when appropriate, some knowledge of the operation, maintenance, and repair of specific instruments, such as gas chromatographs, atomic absorption units, fluorescent microscopes, and spectrophotometer readers
- Working knowledge of statistics, the metric system, and mathematics for interpreting data and reporting results
- Ability to perceive colors and, when applicable, eyesight sufficiently strong to permit extended microscopic work
- Ability to perform assigned tasks exactly according to prescribed procedures, to accurately observe and interpret results, and to make reports
- Ability to communicate effectively

- Ability to establish and maintain working relationships with staff members, public health personnel, physicians, other laboratories, and the public
- Ability to effectively organize work

Minimum qualifications for public health laboratory scientists often call for 2 years of professional experience as a chemist, microbiologist, medical technologist, or associate public health laboratory scientist, and graduation from an accredited 4-year college or university with a bachelor degree with major specialization in a biologic or chemical science, or medical technology. In some instances, possession of Clinical Laboratory Improvement Amendments of 1988 (CLIA '88) certification will substitute for the educational requirements. Graduate education in the above areas may substitute on a year-for-year basis for the stated experience.

Microbiologists have an average salary of $62,000, with the middle 50% earning between $41,000 and $75,000. Mean salaries for microbiologists working for federal agencies are well above the mean salaries at state and local governmental agencies ($79,500 federal, $45,000 state, $55,500 local).

Biochemists and biophysicists have an average salary of $72,000 with the middle 50% earning between $50,000 and $89,000. Mean salaries for biochemists working for federal agencies are well above the mean salaries at state and local governmental agencies ($81,000 federal, $44,000 state, $65,000 local).

Public Health Laboratory Technologists

Medical and clinical laboratory technologists perform complex medical laboratory tests for diagnosis, treatment, and prevention of disease. This involves technical work in the preparation of samples for analysis and the performance of routine medical and public health laboratory tests. Technologists may train and/or supervise other laboratory staff. Medical and clinical laboratory technicians perform routine medical laboratory tests for diagnosis, treatment, and prevention of disease. Lab technicians may work under the direction of a technologist.

Medical and clinical laboratory technologists number 152,000. The vast majority work for hospitals, nonhospital-based laboratories, physician offices, and universities. Federal health agencies employ 5,000 lab technologists; state and local health agencies employ another 5,000. There are 143,000 medical and clinical laboratory technicians employed by the same types of organizations as for lab technologists. The *Public Health Workforce Enumeration 2000* identified 8,000 public health laboratory technicians working in governmental public health agencies.

Essential and important duties for a public health laboratory technologist include

- Receives, counts, logs, and labels samples submitted by field staff and individuals for testing
- Prepares samples for analysis by racking, centrifuging, filtering, weighing, and so on, and distributes prepared samples to appropriate testing areas
- Pipettes serum samples onto testing plates and adds antigen or reagents in accordance with standard laboratory procedures; stirs, rocks, shakes, and incubates mixture for specified time; reads test results in accordance with established parameters
- Draws blood and collects urine, stool, sputum, and other samples for analysis as ordered by physicians; performs routine analyses of specimens
- Maintains basic records consistent with assigned responsibilities
- Prepares sample specimen kits and shipping boxes for mailing
- Cleans and maintains sample containers, laboratory equipment, and work areas

Key knowledge, skills, and abilities for public health laboratory technologists include

- Knowledge of basic science terminology, concepts, and principles
- Knowledge of laboratory procedures, techniques, and equipment
- Knowledge of blood-drawing techniques
- Ability to properly operate microscopes, centrifuges, autoclaves, sterilizers, or other laboratory equipment
- Ability to apply proper methods of handling and disposing of chemicals and infectious materials
- Ability to perform assigned tasks according to specific instructions and clearly prescribed procedures
- Ability to read, compare, identify, and record laboratory data accurately, such as names, numbers, sample descriptions, and so on
- Ability to perform basic mathematics and make accurate measurements
- Ability to make accurate observations and prepare accurate records of laboratory tests
- Ability to work with other employees, laboratory staff, health professionals, and the general public

Minimum qualifications for these positions may call for 1 year of experience in a medical or public health laboratory performing routine laboratory tests under the direction of a physician or qualified laboratory technician, and possession of a high school diploma or a GED certificate. College coursework with specialization in the chemical, physical, or biologic sciences may substitute on a year-for-year basis for deficiencies in the required experience.

The average salary for laboratory technologists is $47,000, with the middle 50% earning between $39,000 and $55,000. Lab technicians have an average salary of $33,000, with the middle 50% earning between $25,000 and $38,000. Mean salaries for laboratory technicians working for federal, state, and local governmental agencies are similar ($35,000 federal, $32,000 state, $31,500 local).

PUBLIC HEALTH PHYSICIANS, VETERINARIANS, AND PHARMACISTS

Public health physicians identify persons or groups at risk of illness or disability, and develop, implement, and evaluate programs or interventions designed to prevent, treat, or ameliorate such risks. Public health physicians may provide direct medical services within the context of such programs and include physicians with MD and DO degrees working as either generalists or specialists. Only a small proportion of the total number of active physicians (800,000) in the United States work in public health settings, and only a small number of those public health physicians have training in public health or preventive medicine. For example, the number of physicians who are board certified in preventive medicine with a specialization in public health decreased from 2,300 in 1980 to 1,800 in 2000. Those with specializations in general preventive medicine increased from 800 to 1,700, and those specializing in occupational medicine increased from 2,400 to 3,000 during that same period.

There are 22,000 physicians working for federal, state, and local governmental agencies; more than 19,000 work for federal agencies, however, mainly providing clinical care services. Only 3,000 physicians work for state and local governmental agencies. The *Public Health Workforce Enumeration 2000* identified more than 9,000 public health physicians working in federal, state, and local public health agencies. This total for public health physicians undercounts the actual number of physicians working in public health, as many physicians functioning under other titles (e.g., agency administrators, epidemiologists, occupational health specialists) are not counted as public health physicians. A reasonable estimate of the actual number of public health physicians is in the 10,000–12,000 range.

Public health veterinarians/animal control specialists identify and assess health risks to humans from animals; they plan, manage, and evaluate programs to reduce these risks. There are 1,700 veterinarians working for governmental agencies, with more than one half employed by federal agencies. The *Public Health Workforce Enumeration 2000* identified more than 3,100 veterinarians and animal control specialists working in governmental public health agencies, indicating that professionals other than veterinarians coordinate and manage animal control programs at the local level.

Public health pharmacists combine pharmacy and public health skills to plan, organize, and perform drug-related activities with a specific public health focus or within a public health setting. Public health pharmacists may work in agency-run pharmacies or serve as the liaison between private pharmacies and the public health agency in regards to standards, procedures, and education. They also dispense drugs prescribed by physicians and other health practitioners and provide information to patients about medications and their use. Pharmacists advise physicians and other health practitioners on the selection, dosage, interactions, and side effects of medications and are increasingly involved in Strategic National Stockpile planning and operations. The *Public Health Workforce Enumeration 2000* identified 2,300 public health pharmacists working in federal, state, and local public health agencies. There are 7,500 pharmacists working for federal, state, and local governmental agencies; more than 5,500 work for federal agencies, however, mainly providing clinical pharmacy services. Only 2,000 pharmacists work for state and local governmental agencies.

PUBLIC HEALTH DENTAL WORKERS

Public health dental workers, a category limited to workers formally trained in dentistry or dental health, plan, develop, implement, and evaluate dental health programs to promote and maintain optimum oral health of the public. Public health dentists may provide comprehensive dental care; dental hygienists provide limited dental services under professional supervisions. There are 1,600 dentists and 1,000 dental hygienists working for governmental agencies in the United States. Many provide clinical rather than public health dental services, especially those working for federal agencies. The *Public Health Workforce Enumeration 2000* identified 3,100 dental workers (both dentists and hygienists) in federal, state, and local public health agencies.

ADMINISTRATIVE JUDGES AND HEARING OFFICERS

Administrative judges and hearing officers provide legal advice to public health agencies, provide legal representation of public health officials in courts and administrative law proceedings, and preside over administrative law hearings of various kinds. The *Public Health Workforce Enumeration 2000* identified 900 administrative judges/hearing officers working in federal, state, and local public health agencies. There are 15,000 hearing officers in the United States; nearly all work for federal, state, and local governmental agencies.

ADDITIONAL INFORMATION

Many sources provide additional and more detailed information for the occupational categories addressed in Chapter 12.

The American Public Health Association (APHA, http://www.apha.org) has sections that focus on issues important to each of these occupational categories, including food and nutrition; social work; mental health; alcohol, tobacco, and other drugs; medical care; and oral health. APHA also has a laboratory special interest group, veterinary public health special interest group, and public health law forum.

The Association of State and Territorial Public Health Nutrition Directors (ASTPHND, http://www.astphnd.org/) provides information on and resources for public health nutrition professionals. For example, ASTPHND's Web site provides access to their most recent survey of the public health nutrition workforce (http://www.astphnd.org/resource_files/1/1_resource_file1.pdf). Another resource for nutritionists is the American Dietetic Association (ADA, http://www.eatright.org/Public/), which has 65,000 members and works in concert with the Commission on Dietetic Registration (CDR, http://www.cdrnet.org/). More than 76,000 dietitians and dietetic technicians across the country and the world have taken CDR exams over the past several decades. CDR currently awards four separate and distinct credentials: Registered Dietitian (RD); Dietetic Technician, Registered (DTR); Board Certified Specialist in Renal Nutrition (CSR); and Board Certified Specialist in Pediatric Nutrition (CSP). The commission's certification programs are fully accredited by the National Commission for Certifying Agencies (NCCA), the accrediting arm of the National Organization for Competency Assurance (NOCA).

Web sites of the National Association of Social Workers (http://www.socialworkers.org) and the Council on Social Work Education (http://www.cswe.org) provide information on accredited social work programs. The Association of Social Work Boards (http://www.aswb.org) is a good source of information on licensing requirements and testing procedures used for state licensing purposes.

Information on public health laboratory workers is available from the Association for Public Health Laboratories (http://www.aphl.org) and the National Center for Public Health Laboratory Leadership (http://www.aphl.org/national_center_for_phl_leadership/). The American College of Preventive Medicine (http://www.acpm.org) and American Medical Association (http://www.amaassn.org/) Web sites provide information on public health physicians.

CONCLUSION

Professionals comprise the major share of the public health workforce, although public health professionals are quite diverse in terms of their professional background and experience. Nutritionists are valuable resources for public health agencies and the communities they serve, although most nutritionist positions work within the massive federally funded WIC program. More local public health agencies than state public health agencies provide social, mental, and behavioral health services, as these programs may be funded by and relate to state agencies other than the state health agency in many states. Public health laboratory expertise is essential for disease and threat detection, and one of the major impacts of increased federal spending for terrorism preparedness is resulting in upgraded lab capabilities for state and local public health agencies. Recruiting and retaining the many levels of laboratory professionals and technicians necessary for lab operations has emerged as an important priority for public health as well as national security concerns. Physicians once dominated the field of public health. Today they represent one of many important professions within the public health workforce, standing beside veterinarians, pharmacists, and dental health workers. The regulatory and administrative processes within governmental public health agencies now requires a level of legal expertise beyond that called for in the past. These many and varied professional categories provide public health with the multidisciplinary and interdisciplinary muscle needed to battle modern public health threats and issues.

Discussion Questions and Exercises

1. What are the most important contributions to improving the health of the public that public health professional occupations make today?

2. What features make public health professional occupations a career worth pursuing?

3. Using a scale from 1 to 10, how important to the effectiveness of the overall public health system is the need for more and better prepared public health professional occupations? How did you arrive at this rating?

4. What do you think are the most important new or expanded roles for public health professional occupations in the 21st century?

5. In which organizations and geographic regions will the need for public health professional occupations expand most rapidly in the next 2 decades?

REFERENCES

1. Bureau of Labor Statistics, U.S. Department of Labor. May 2004 national, state, and metropolitan area occupational employment and wage estimates. Available at: http://www.bls.gov/oes/current/oes_nat.htm. Accessed August 20, 2005.

2. Health Resources and Services Administration, Bureau of Health Professions, National Center for Health Workforce Information and Analysis and Center for Health Policy, Columbia School of Nursing. *The Public Health Workforce Enumeration 2000.* Washington, DC: HRSA; 2000.

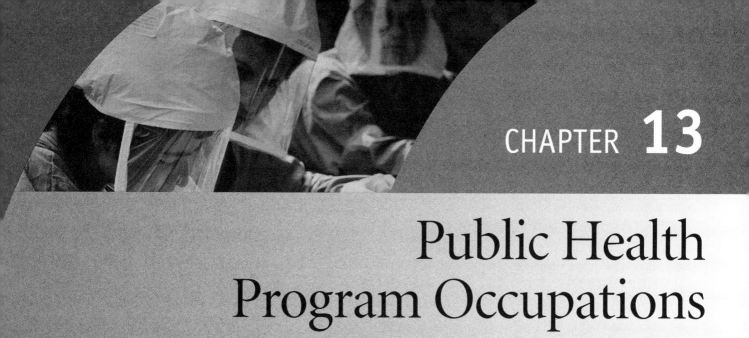

CHAPTER 13

Public Health Program Occupations

LEARNING OBJECTIVES

After completing Chapter 13, learners will be proficient in describing key features of various program occupations in public health and how these contribute to carrying out public health's core functions and essential services. Key aspects of this competency expectation include

- Describing several different occupational titles in this category
- Identifying several essential public health services that are critical for positions in this category
- Describing important and essential duties for several job titles in this category
- Identifying minimum qualifications and describing general workplace considerations, salary expectations, and career prospects for positions in this category

This and the previous chapter are organized somewhat differently than Chapters 7 through 11. This chapter highlights professional and technical public health occupations that are largely defined by the program in which they function. Each occupational category is addressed separately, as the career links are not as clear for these occupations as for those addressed in earlier chapters.

The public health roles attributed to these various professional and technical occupation categories vary enormously. As the programs in which they work have a narrower focus than either their agency as a whole or a broad agency division such as environmental health or nursing, many of these occupations focus on only one or a few public health responsibilities and essential public health services.

Unlike many of the public health occupations described in previous chapters, some positions work in public health program units using titles that are not tracked by the Bureau of

Labor Statistics as standard occupational categories. Some of these positions are generic titles, such as program specialist or program coordinator. Others are very specific titles, such as public health emergency response coordinator, a position that has increased in attention since 2001. As public health agencies increase their emphasis on policy development activities, policy analysts, health planners, and health economists are increasingly being hired by public agencies. The same can be said for health information specialists and data and computer analysts.

This chapter focuses on five public health occupations that make up key subsets of the overall public health workforce: (1) public health program specialists and coordinators; (2) public health emergency response coordinators; (3) public health policy analysts; (4) public health information specialists; and (5) community outreach and other technical occupations. Data from several sources are used throughout this chapter, including the *Public Health Workforce Enumeration 2000*[1] and Bureau of Labor Statistics data.[2] Table 13–1 provides a public health practice profile for each of these occupational categories with information as to the prime public health purposes and essential public health services addressed by each category. Table 13–2 presents information on government employment and salaries for each category.

PUBLIC HEALTH PROGRAM SPECIALISTS AND COORDINATORS

Public health program specialists plan, develop, implement, and evaluate programs or interventions designed to identify persons at risk of specified health problems and to prevent, treat, or ameliorate such problems. This includes public health workers reported as public health program specialists

TABLE 13–1 Public Health Practice Profile for Selected Public Health Program Occupations

	Selected Public Health Program Occupations Make a Difference by:				
	PH Prog Spec	ERC	PH Pol An	Hlth Info	Out Wkrs
Public Health Purposes					
Preventing epidemics and the spread of disease		✓	✓	✓	✓
Protecting against environmental hazards	✓		✓		
Preventing injuries	✓	✓			✓
Promoting and encouraging healthy behaviors	✓				✓
Responding to disasters and assisting communities in recovery		✓			
Assuring the quality and accessibility of health services			✓	✓	
Essential Public Health Services					
Monitoring health status to identify community health problems	✓			✓	
Diagnosing and investigating health problems and health hazards in the community	✓	✓			
Informing, educating, and empowering people about health issues			✓	✓	✓
Mobilizing community partnerships to identify and solve health problems		✓	✓		✓
Developing policies and plans that support individual and community health efforts	✓	✓	✓	✓	
Enforcing laws and regulations that protect health and ensure safety	✓				
Linking people with needed personal health services and assuring the provision of health care when otherwise unavailable		✓			✓
Assuring a competent public health and personal health care workforce					
Evaluating effectiveness, accessibility, and quality of personal and population-based health services	✓	✓	✓	✓	
Researching new insights and innovative solutions to health problems			✓	✓	

without specific designation of a program, as well as those reported as specialists working in a specific program (e.g., maternal and child health, AIDS awareness, immunization, retail food inspection programs). Public health program specialists have a wide range of educational preparation, including many individuals who have preparation in a specific occupational category or profession (e.g., dental health, environmental health, nutrition, nursing). The *Public Health Workforce Enumeration 2000* identified 12,000 public health program specialists.

A large number of public health program specialists work in licensing and regulatory programs performing various types of inspections. Many different titles are used, such as licen-

sure, inspection, and regulatory specialist. These positions audit, inspect, and survey programs, institutions, equipment, products, and personnel, using approved standards for design or performance. This title includes workers who perform regular inspections of a specified class of sites or facilities, such as restaurants, nursing homes, and hospitals whose personnel and materials present constant and predictable threats to the public, without specification of educational preparation. This classification also includes a number of individuals with preparation in environmental health, nursing, and other health fields. The *Public Health Workforce Enumeration 2000* identified 21,000 licensure/inspection/regulatory specialists working in federal, state, and local public health agencies.

TABLE 13-2 Number and Mean Salary for Selected Public Health Program Occupations in Federal, State, and Local Governmental Agencies, May 2004

Occupational Category	Federal, State, and Local Worker Estimated Mean Salary	Adjusted PH Enum. 2000 Workers
Public Health Specialists	$45,000	33,401
Emergency Response Coordinators	$45,500	NA
Public Health Policy Analysts	NA	5,687
Public Health Information Specialists	$44,000	7,078
Community Outreach Workers	$31,000	902
Other Technical Occupations	NA	(est) 13,500
Other Paraprofessional Occupations	NA	26,129

See Chapter 6 for Adjusted Number of Public Health Workers from *Public Health Workforce Enumeration 2000*.

Public health specialists carry responsibility for planning, performing, or supervising technical and professional work involving public health and consumer protection services. This includes performing inspections, surveys, and investigations to identify and eliminate conditions hazardous to life and health, providing consultative services and assistance in assigned areas of responsibility, ensuring corrective actions are taken to eliminate public health or other hazards, and ensuring compliance with applicable statutes and regulations.

The functions within this job family vary by level and from program to program, but may include the following:

- Develops, implements, and manages projects and initiatives for an assigned program or unit
- Develops and implements activities to ensure effective operations and compliance with established standards and/or contracted goals and objectives
- Serves as a team leader on specific projects
- Coordinates program activities that may include fiscal monitoring; grant writing; monitoring of funded programs or agencies to ensure compliance; report preparation and writing; and assisting with developing and distributing communications, brochures, and educational materials
- Coordinates/oversees activities that may include health education; training; development and oversight of requests for proposals and grants; and developing and distributing communications, brochures, and educational materials
- Collaborates and meets with management staff to determine program requirements, standards, and goals
- Evaluates projects or initiatives to determine effectiveness and to recommend changes and improvements

- Supervises employees; trains and evaluates staff; and reviews the work of subordinates for completeness, accuracy, and content
- Assists in overseeing specialized research and evaluation projects
- Delivers services according to established program protocols
- Conducts inspections, surveys, and investigations of food establishments, lodging facilities, barber shops, public bathing places, schools, day care centers, nursing homes, hospitals, and other regulated facilities to identify public health hazards or environmental conditions that are detrimental to life and health
- Monitors state food supplies and products; provides training and technical assistance; ensures compliance with applicable laws, rules, and regulations; and assists in the implementation of Hazard Analysis Critical Control Point (HACCP) systems in food establishments and in verifying implementation
- Responds to complaints concerning foodborne illnesses, adulterated foods, food tampering, recalls, insect or rodent infestation, or other issues related to food establishments or the sale of food and food products
- Reviews and acts on various epidemiologic reports and complaints, including animal bites, rabies, and disease outbreaks; conducts environmental assessments and other surveys related to lodging, public bathing, and barber services; and performs inspections for lead contamination and other public health hazards or nuisances
- Provides emergency response services for complaints concerning foodborne illnesses, fires in food establishments, accidents involving the transportation of food,

incidents concerning food or water contamination, and power outages or natural disasters involving food products; conducts inspections or investigations on an as-needed basis, including on weekends and at night

- Directs the embargo and disposal of food products found unfit for human consumption; conducts evaluations to determine imminent hazards to life or health that warrant the closure of a facility
- Prepares records, reports, and correspondence concerning regulatory actions as needed; conducts follow-up inspections and surveys to ensure corrective actions have been taken and that public health hazards are eliminated; and testifies at hearings and court proceedings concerning regulatory actions as required

The public health specialist series within a personnel system may include three or more levels that are distinguished by the level of complexity of specific job assignments, the extent of responsibility assigned for specific tasks, the level of expertise required for completion of the assigned work, and the responsibility assigned for providing leadership to others.

For public health program specialists working in an inspection or regulatory program, for example, the entry level of the series involves assigned duties and responsibilities in a training status to build skills in conducting inspections and investigations, performing basic professional analysis, and interpreting state and federal laws. Entry-level public health specialists perform tasks involving the evaluation of inspection or survey data and the preparation of technical records and reports, and assist in making recommendations concerning remedial actions to correct public health hazards and provide for consumer protection.

Knowledge, skills, and abilities required at the entry level include knowledge of the causes, impact, and prevention of public health problems in regulated establishments; food microbiology as it applies to preventing foodborne illness; basic epidemiology and chemistry; mathematical concepts, including basic statistical analysis; food processing techniques such as modified atmospheric packaging; and rules and regulations governing food establishments, public bathing places, nursing homes, schools, day care facilities, or other licensed establishments. Abilities required include the ability to conduct inspections and investigations of regulated facilities; identify the causes of foodborne illnesses and related health hazards; analyze and evaluate environmental and sanitary conditions; organize work and work independently; communicate effectively, both orally and in writing; and use computers to organize data and generate reports.

Experience and education requirements at this level consist of a bachelor degree with at least 30 semester hours in a biologic, medical, or physical science; food science or technology; and chemistry, nutrition, engineering, epidemiology, or closely related scientific field.

Midlevel public health specialist positions involve more advanced assigned duties for inspections, surveys, and investigations related to public health services, consumer protection, and the enforcement of applicable state and federal laws in the assigned area of responsibility. Midlevel public health specialists evaluate inspection and survey data, prepare technical records and reports, make recommendations concerning required remedial actions, and provide technical assistance and training as needed to correct public health or consumer protection problems. Some responsibility may also be assigned for providing limited guidance and training to entry-level employees in performing various consumer protection program duties. In addition, midlevel public health specialist positions may involve a clear specialization in a consumer protection or public health discipline and recognition as an expert in the specialty along with a high degree of technical and administrative freedom to plan, develop, organize, and conduct all phases of the work necessary for completion within broad program guidelines.

Knowledge, skills, and abilities required at this middle level include those identified in the entry level plus the ability to make recommendations concerning the implementation of HAACP systems and verify implementation; conduct preoperational inspections to determine compliance with approved plans; assist in planning and presenting education and training programs; plan and conduct field investigations; ensure that corrective action has been completed to eliminate health hazards; analyze and interpret engineering plans and specifications; and assist in developing HACCP plans for the regulated food industry.

Experience and education requirements at this level consist of those identified for entry-level positions plus 2 years professional work experience in public health or consumer protection or a master's degree in a listed field and successful completion of training in conducting food establishment inspections plus 2 additional years of qualifying experience.

Salary scales vary greatly from agency to agency, although entry-level positions may be in the $25,000–$30,000 range, with midlevel positions in the $35,000–$45,000 range. Higher-level public health specialist positions that oversee several program areas or units can expect salaries equivalent to other midlevel managers in these organizations. Job growth for public health specialists is expected to be about average for all positions in the health field.

PUBLIC HEALTH EMERGENCY RESPONSE COORDINATORS

Public health emergency response coordinators perform planning functions for a local public health agency, ensuring compliance with federal and state planning guidelines and regulations. These positions coordinate response plans with the state health department as well as other federal, state, and local government entities; perform all hazard, bioterrorism, and emergency planning; and coordinate plans with various response agencies, volunteer organizations, businesses, and private industries.

Massive federal bioterrorism preparedness funding for state and local public health agencies stimulated a rapid increase in the number of emergency response positions in the United States, making this title one of the fastest growing within the public health workforce. There was no information on public health emergency response coordinators available in the *Public Health Workforce Enumeration 2000*.

Important and essential duties for a public health emergency response coordinator include

- Performs administrative, technical, and planning duties to integrate bioterrorism and emergency response plans with response activities for other emergency management programs
- Develops and maintains the local public health agency's emergency operations plan (EOP)
- Reviews and maintains bioterrorism response appendices to meet Centers for Disease Control and Prevention (CDC) planning guidance and local standard operating guidelines
- Assists with coordination, integration, and implementation of emergency response plans and procedures from various jurisdictions, governmental entities, private industries, utility companies, and so on
- Reviews specialized studies and reports, formulates comments and summarizes content, and provides emergency planning recommendations
- Coordinates with the local jurisdiction's emergency management agency and the state health department in continual development and review of effective emergency preparedness and response activities
- Identifies unique planning considerations for bioterrorism threats
- Assists the public health community in developing jurisdictional emergency plans by attending meetings and facilitating discussions, reviewing concepts and procedures, and coordinating emergency response efforts of various agency units

- Acts as a resource for the public health community and the local public health agency in documenting their standard operating guidelines and operational checklists
- Coordinates overall emergency planning activities
- Conducts regular review of local, state, federal, and private industry emergency response plans, employing standard emergency management concepts and strategic methodologies
- Works in conjunction with the executive director, environmental health supervisor, risk communicator, epidemiologist, and public information officer to promote awareness of local public health agency emergency response plans and procedures
- Provides requisite planning activity reports, budget submissions, and other required documentation for federal and state emergency response funding sources
- Assists with the development of operational drills and exercise scenarios designed to train, test, and evaluate emergency response concepts or standard operating guidelines
- Adjusts emergency plans, procedures, or protocols to reflect changes and improve efficiency as appropriate
- Demonstrates continuous effort to improve operations, decrease turnaround times, streamline work processes, and work cooperatively and jointly to provide quality seamless customer service

Relevant knowledge, skills, and abilities for public health emergency response coordinators include

- Skill in organization and planning techniques
- Skill in public relations and public speaking
- Skill in computer and communication equipment operation
- Knowledge of basic budget development and fiscal management
- Knowledge of public health and epidemiology
- Ability to establish and maintain effective working relationships with other government and public health officials, employees, agencies, volunteers, and the public
- Ability to communicate effectively, verbally and in writing
- Ability to learn the principles, practices, and techniques involved in emergency management
- Knowledge of principles and practices of governmental and public health agency structures and resources

Special requirements for public health emergency response coordinator positions may include the ability to travel and to be on call 24 hours a day, 7 days a week. Emergency response coordinators may be required to complete training courses as recommended and made available through federal or state public health and emergency management agencies. In some instances, emergency response coordinators may be required to complete the Certified Emergency Manager (CEM) program through the National Coordinating Council on Emergency Management within some specified period of time.

Working conditions for this position include most work being performed in an office, library, computer room, or other environmentally controlled room. Emergency response activities may require work in a full-body protective suit with respirator protection from potential biologic, chemical, or nuclear material hazards.

Minimum qualifications call for the equivalent of a master's degree in public health, biologic sciences, community health, emergency management, planning, hazard assessment, business or public administration, or other related field; and 2 years of emergency management, community planning, or other related work experience. Selected applicants are subject to, and must pass, a full background check. In addition, emergency response coordinators generally are required to possess a valid state driver's license. Other organizations may require 5 years of responsible experience in public administration, research and finance, including 3 years of emergency management experience and a master's degree in public or business administration, government management, industrial engineering, or a related field. Other combinations of experience and education that meet the minimum requirements may be substituted.

Bureau of Labor Statistics data identify 920 emergency management specialists working for state governmental agencies and 5,080 working for local governmental agencies in 2004. The mean salary for these positions was $45,500.

PUBLIC HEALTH POLICY ANALYSTS

Public policy is one of the tools used by public health to promote conditions in which individuals and communities can be healthy. Public health policy analysts analyze needs and plans for the development of public health and other programs, facilities and resources, and/or analyze and evaluate the implications of alternative policies relating to public health and health care for a defined population. Public health analysts determine the questions that such policies will raise, answer those questions, and help shape policies that make our society a better place to live.

Public health policy analysts function under many different titles, including health planners, researchers, and health economists. Health economists conduct research, prepare reports, or formulate plans to aid in the solution of economic problems arising from the production and distribution of goods and services related to public health and health care. Health economists may collect and process economic and statistical data using econometric and sampling techniques.

Public health policy analysts must be able to dissect a problem, analyze and interpret data, and evaluate and create alternative courses of action. They provide information to government officials and the public about which policies will be most effective in meeting society's public health goals.

Public health policy analysts work in national, state, and local governments, nonprofit agencies, "think tanks," consulting firms, community action groups, and direct service organizations. International health and development organizations also employ public health policy analysts. The *Public Health Workforce Enumeration 2000* identified nearly 6,000 public health policy analysts, planners, researchers, and economists. Because of the wide variation in titles used for this function, it is likely that there are actually many more public health analyst positions in the public health workforce.

Important and essential duties of a public health policy analyst include

- Conducts site visits to assess the operations and costs of state, federal, and local health care programs
- Conducts literature reviews
- Performs quantitative analyses with large databases to determine program outcomes or conduct policy simulations
- Writes chapters of analytic reports and proposals for new projects
- Tracks financial progress of projects using computerized spreadsheets, prepares reports for monthly project reviews, and assists with budget revisions and contract proposals

Key knowledge, skills, and abilities for public health policy analyst positions include

- Knowledge of current policy issues in one or more of the following areas: managed care, public health infrastructure, state health policy, health care reimbursement issues, mental health/substance abuse, maternal and child health, disability, long-term care, or other relevant areas
- Knowledge of health care policy issues related to employer-based coverage, managed care, Medicaid, Medicare, and the uninsured
- Knowledge of how to use data to affect policy and systemic changes
- Ability to establish collaborative working relationships with diverse interest groups and stakeholders
- Excellent writing and verbal skills, particularly in presenting complex information in a clear, comprehensible format

Minimum qualifications for public health policy analyst positions vary greatly but generally require a master's degree in public policy, public health, economics, statistics, or a related field, or equivalent experience in a clinical field, and extensive knowledge of quantitative and qualitative research methods. In some instances, a bachelor degree and a minimum of 5 years of experience, preferably in health care advocacy or policy analysis, may be acceptable. Invariably, work experience with state or federal government, a foundation, a policy research organization, or a health care program is desirable.

Salaries for public health analysts vary considerably based on education, experience, and specific duties within an organization. With little information available on employment trends for these positions, it is difficult to assess future job prospects, although the number of such positions does not appear to be declining.

PUBLIC HEALTH INFORMATION SPECIALISTS AND ANALYSTS

Public health information systems and data analysts plan, direct, or coordinate activities in areas such as electronic data processing, information systems, systems analysis, and computer programming. They often work with computer specialists who manage the specialized technical aspects of computer operation, applications, operating systems, and hardware. Common titles include computing consultant, applications programmer, computer service technician, data entry technician, data processing specialist, network technician, information technology specialist, and vital records support specialist. Not included are titles that operate computers as part of administrative or professional tasks.

Important and essential duties of a public health information specialist include

- Plans and coordinates the collection, analysis, and dissemination of complex disease and other health data and information
- Performs health risk and community needs appraisals
- Monitors and evaluates programs for effectiveness and quality
- Collaborates with other agencies, organizations, and stakeholders in the identification and monitoring of community health needs
- Exercises independent judgment in analyzing problems, issues and situations; develops and implements recommendations
- Plans and conducts meetings
- Presents information and represents the agency at public and other meetings

- Complies with legal standards and requirements
- Collects, researches, verifies, enters, updates, analyzes, summarizes, and presents complex disease and other health information and data
- Records information and data accurately following procedures; prepares complete reports on time with supporting conclusions and recommendations, such as the health status report
- Communicates changes and progress and completes projects on time and within budget
- Formulates recommendations anticipating possible ramifications and appropriately communicates significance of findings

Public health information specialist positions require a bachelor degree in public health or a related field and 5 years of progressively responsible experience in public health evaluation or a related health field. A master's degree in public health is preferred. These positions require knowledge of core public health functions; epidemiologic principles and practices, including symptoms, causes, means of transmission, and methods of control of communicable, chronic, and complex disease; principles of disease investigation, control, and prevention; and emergency response principles and practices. These positions also require familiarity with the operation of computers and a variety of office software including word processing, spreadsheet, database, geographical information systems (GIS), mapping, statistical, and other applications related to the area of assignment.

The *Public Health Workforce Enumeration 2000* identified 900 health information specialists and 6,000 computer specialists working for governmental public health agencies. Salaries for health information specialists are often in the $40,000–$50,000 range. Health information specialist jobs are projected to be among the fastest growing in the health sector.

COMMUNITY OUTREACH WORKERS AND OTHER TECHNICAL OCCUPATIONS

Community outreach workers assist public health professionals in community contacts, referrals, or program development. This category includes individuals with on-the-job training in specific program areas but who generally lack postsecondary education or credentials. Community outreach workers provide health advising, provide information and referrals, carry out client orientation and intakes, and advocate for clients and communities. They work under dozens of different titles, such as community health advisor; health worker; public health aide; community health outreach worker; community health aide; immunization outreach worker; Early Periodic Screening,

Diagnosis, and Treatment (EPSDT) outreach worker; maternal and infant advocate; and school health aide.

Other technician titles are also widely used by public health agencies. This includes safety, research, hearing and vision, and health promotion technicians, as well as emergency service personnel. The *Public Health Workforce Enumeration 2000* identified 900 outreach workers and between 10,000 and 15,000 other technicians.

The starting salary for a community outreach worker at some metropolitan health agencies is in the $28,000–$34,000 range. Several institutions offer certificate programs for community outreach workers that are accepted as a minimum qualification for the civil service health worker positions. Community health workers (CHWs) who work for community-based organizations generally make somewhat less. Minimum qualifications may require an associate degree with 18 credits in health science/education, or an associate degree and 1 year of experience in a health or human service agency providing referral assistance to the public. In some instances, a high school diploma or GED and 3 years of experience may be sufficient.

ADDITIONAL INFORMATION

Many sources provide additional and more detailed information for the occupational categories addressed in Chapter 13. For example, the Federal Emergency Management Agency (FEMA) is a rich source of information for public health emergency response coordinators, and the Community Health Planning and Policy Development section of the American Public Health Association (APHA) Web site (http://www.apha.org) provides useful information for public health policy analysts.

Similarly, the American Health Information Management Association (AHIMA, http://www.ahima.org) is the premier association of health information management professionals, with 50,000 members committed to advancing the health information management profession. AHIMA focuses on advocacy, education, certification, and lifelong learning and works

through the Commission on Accreditation for Health Informatics and Information Management Education (CAHIM) to accredit degree-granting programs in health informatics and information management. CAHIM establishes quality standards for the educational preparation of future health information management professionals.

Useful information and resources for community outreach workers are available through the American Public Health Association and its Community Health Workers Special Interest Group. Another source for information on innovative training and certification programs for community outreach is Community Health Works (http://www.communityhealthworks.org/chwcertificate/).

CONCLUSION

Public health organizations use many different titles for public health program staff. Indeed, most public health workers function within a defined program or program-related unit such as environmental health, maternal and child health, Supplemental Food Program for Women, Infants, and Children (WIC), or immunization program. Program specialists work on all aspects of program planning, implementation, and evaluation in concert with professionals, technicians, and administrative support personnel. Because the programs in which they work often have specific goals and objectives, program specialists are at risk of operating in an isolated environment. This contributes to the critique that programs operate as silos within an agency, often unrelated to the operation of the many other silos housed within that same agency. Because of their generalist skills, program specialists may move from one program to another as a means of career and salary advancement. Their crosscutting, core, generalist public health practice skills are generally acquired through work experiences rather than academic preparation. The size and impact of this corps of public health program specialists argue that development and enhancement of these crosscutting competencies should be a central strategy of public health workforce development efforts.

Discussion Questions and Exercises

1. What are the most important contributions to improving the health of the public that public health program occupations make today?

2. What features make public health program occupations a career worth pursuing?

3. Using a scale from 1 to 10, how important to the effectiveness of the overall public health system is the need for more and better prepared public health program occupations? How did you arrive at this rating?

4. What do you think are the most important new or expanded roles for public health program occupations in the 21st century?

5. In which organizations and geographic regions will the need for public health program occupations expand most rapidly in the next 2 decades?

REFERENCES

1. Health Resources and Services Administration, Bureau of Health Professions, National Center for Health Workforce Information and Analysis and Center for Health Policy, Columbia School of Nursing. *The Public Health Workforce Enumeration 2000.* Washington, DC: HRSA; 2000.

2. Bureau of Labor Statistics, U.S. Department of Labor. May 2004 national, state, and metropolitan area occupational employment and wage estimates. Available at: http://www.bls.gov/oes/current/oes_nat.htm. Accessed August 20, 2005.

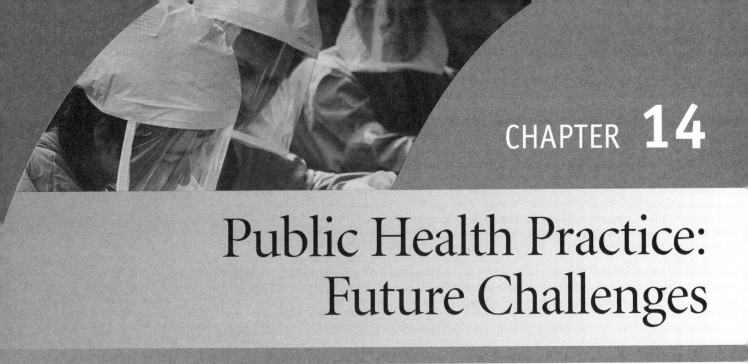

CHAPTER 14

Public Health Practice: Future Challenges

LEARNING OBJECTIVES

After completing Chapter 14, learners will be proficient in identifying and describing key challenges facing public health workers in the early 21st century. Key aspects of this competency expectation include

- Identifying at least three issues that will impact the growth of the public health workforce
- Describing how these issues will affect the distribution and composition of the public health workforce of the future
- Discussing the role of competency frameworks in public health workforce development efforts
- Identifying and discussing at least three lessons from public health's achievements in the 20th century

For too long too little attention has been directed to the public health workforce and its needs. Despite ample warnings in the 1988 Institute of Medicine (IOM) report,[1] there were few efforts between 1980, when Health Resources and Services Administration (HRSA) produced crude estimates of the size and composition for the U.S. Congress,[2] and 2000, when Kristine Gebbie and colleagues completed their landmark enumeration report on the public health workforce at the turn of the century for HRSA.[3] Two decades of inattention provide eloquent testimony to the low priority given to the public health system's most important asset—its workforce.

Beginning in the year 2002, funding for workforce preparedness and training increased dramatically. This influx of funding also brought increased expectations for positive change and greater accountability for results. As a result, the public health system is now under the microscope, with federal, state, and local governments needing to show that the vital signs of the public health infrastructure, including its work-

force, are improving. But decades of inattention left little information to serve as a basis for comparison.

A central challenge for public health workforce development efforts over the next decade is to provide more and better information about key dimensions of the public health workforce in terms of its size, distribution, composition, and competency, as well as its impact on public health goals and community health. This book, like the *Public Health Workforce Enumeration 2000*, seeks to advance this important agenda. This final chapter addresses several critical questions important to current and future public health workers:

- Will the public health workforce increase or decrease in size over the next 10 years? What trends in the overall economy, the health sector, or the public sector will impact public health jobs and career opportunities over this period?
- Where will job opportunities be most abundant, and which occupational categories are likely to grow most rapidly and be in greatest demand?
- What core competencies and skills will require the greatest attention, and what training and education opportunities are available to prepare workers for jobs and careers in public health?

The sections that follow examine each of these questions and associated challenges.

PUBLIC HEALTH WORKFORCE GROWTH

Will the public health workforce increase or decrease in size over the next 10 years? There should be little controversy over this question, but there is. One reason for controversy derives from the lack of accurate information on the size of the public health workforce between 1980 and 2000. Another relates to the many complex forces within public health and the broader economy that influence the number of public health workers needed.

In hindsight, it is clear that the frequently cited figure that the workforce numbered 500,000 in 1980 lacked precision in terms of what was included and how it was generated. This is unfortunate, as the 500,000 figure from 1980 is frequently cited as documentation that the public health workforce must be shrinking because only 450,000 public health workers were enumerated in 2000. As noted in Chapter 6, the HRSA 1980 estimate actually indicated that only 250,000 of the 500,000 public health workers were in the primary public health workforce consisting of federal, state, and local public health agency workers and selected others who devoted most of their work efforts on public health activities.[2] Within this 250,000 figure, there were faculty and researchers at academic institutions; occupational health physicians and nurses working for various private companies; health educators teaching in schools; and administrators working in hospitals, nursing homes, and other medical care settings. The actual number of public health professionals working for federal, state, and local public health agencies in 1980, after adjusting for these inclusions, was closer to 140,000. The total for the comparable categories from the *Public Health Workforce Enumeration 2000* was 260,000, a figure that indicates the public health workforce is growing rather than shrinking. Data from the employment census of governmental agencies support this conclusion, showing there has been a steady increase in full-time equivalent (FTE) workers of governmental health agencies over the past decade (see Table 14–1, as well as Table 6–3 and Figure 6–1 in Chapter 6).[4]

These findings indicate that the public health workforce has been increasing since 1980, throughout the 1990s, and into the early years of the current decade. This is consistent with the documented expansion of the health sector within the overall economy, which continues to grow at a more rapid rate than the rest of the economy. If public health activities continue to maintain their small share of total health spending, funding for public health activities and public health workers will grow commensurately. It is conceivable that public health activities could even increase their share of overall health spending, fostering even more rapid growth of employment opportunities.

There is evidence, however, that the growth of the public health workforce may be slowing or even reversing. The number of FTE workers for federal, state, and local health agencies climbed steadily through 2001, reaching its peak of nearly 556,000 in 2003 before declining by about 6,000 by 2005 (see Table 6–3 in Chapter 6). Interestingly, federal health agency

TABLE 14–1 Average Annual Change in the Number of Public Health Workers, Selected Sources and Years, 1980–2004

Time Period	Average Annual Change (+/−)
1980[a]–2000[b]	+6,000
1994–1999[c]	+5,400
2000–2003[c]	+8,700
2003–2005[c]	−3,000

[a]Health Resources and Services Administration. *Public Health Personnel in the United States, 1980: Second Report to Congress*. Rockville, MD: HRSA; 1982.
[b]Health Resources and Services Administration, Bureau of Health Professions, National Center for Health Workforce Information and Analysis and Center for Health Policy, Columbia School of Nursing. *The Public Health Workforce Enumeration 2000*. Washington, DC: HRSA; 2000.
[c]U.S. Bureau of the Census. Federal, state, and local governments, public employment and payroll data. Available at: http://www.census.gov/govs/www/apes.html. Accessed June 20, 2006.

workers actually increased slightly, while state and local workers fell by more than 6,000. Bioterrorism funding for federal health agencies largely explains the increase in the number of federal health workers. However, the number of FTE state and local public health workers fell by 6,000 even while federal bioterrorism funding for state and local public health agencies was being used to support more than 6,000 positions (about 2,000 in state agencies and 4,000 in local agencies). It appears that state and local governments moved existing staff onto the federal bioterrorism grants in response to fiscal pressures on state and local government budgets. Rather than a net increase of 6,000 new positions, there was a net reduction of 6,000 positions, indicating that funding sources other than the federal bioterrorism grants were supporting 12,000 fewer positions.

This scenario illustrates how federal funding to states and localities for bioterrorism preparedness serves as a temptation to replace or supplant state and local support for public health with federal money. The funding of epidemiologists further illustrates this phenomenon. In 2004, federal bioterrorism funds paid the salaries of 460 epidemiologists; among 390 epidemiologists working on bioterrorism and emergency response activities, 62% were funded by the federal government. Infectious disease epidemiologists did not increase between 2001 and 2004, but in 2004 nearly 20% were paid through federal bioterrorism funds.[5] This scenario may also be true for several other public health occupational categories, such as laboratory workers and emergency response coordinators. It underscores the important role of the underlying financial health of state and local governments in determining the size of the public health workforce.

Two additional modern forces affect public health workforce size. These are the expansion of information technology and the resulting increase in worker productivity. Public health practice, by its very nature, is information dependent and information driven. Enhanced information technology tools and increased individual worker productivity mean fewer workers are needed to support the work of administrators, professionals, and technical staff. This trend would tend to increase the proportion of professionals within the public health workforce; however, these trends also mean fewer professionals are needed to perform the same volume of work. The net effect is therefore difficult to predict in terms of the number and types of workers needed.

The influence of these trends will be affected by events and forces within the overall economy, the health system, and the public sector in general. Public health workers and public health agencies are key components of the public health system, but it is important to consider the larger context in which they operate. This larger environment is in constant flux, undergoing changes that impact the public health system and its components. For example, information and communication technologies advance continuously. These developments enable public health agencies and workers to carry out their duties in a more efficient and effective manner. The work of public health is especially information dependent. The speed at which information is accessed and communicated significantly affects how well public health achieves its mission and objectives. Advances in information and communications technology improve public health practice and public health outcomes. There is every reason to believe that these advances will continue at least at levels achieved in recent decades. The net effect is to make public health workers more effective and productive. The challenge is to assure that public health workers have access to the education and training resources that assure this happens.

Trends within the health sector will also continue to affect public health workers. Health is highly valued both as a personal and societal goal. The economic value placed on health exceeds $2.0 trillion annually, or about $6,000 per person for every man, woman, and child in the United States. There is no indication that health will assume a lower priority within the American social value system. In recent years, for example, expenditures for health purposes have grown faster than the rate for the overall economy. In effect, health is becoming an even greater priority. Between the two general strategies to achieve health—preventive and therapeutic approaches—the balance

may be slowly shifting toward more prevention. There is still a notable imbalance, with a 25 to 1 ratio; however, this shift is likely to continue. Taken together with an increased priority on health itself, public health activities, including those carried out by public health agencies and workers, should continue to increase in size, importance, and value to society.

The value placed on public health activities can be measured in economic terms, such as funding levels for programs, services, and the workers who implement public health programs and services. To sustain or even enhance public health funding, national leadership is necessary. Federal health agencies such as the Centers for Disease Control and Prevention (CDC) and HRSA within the Department of Health and Human Services (DHHS) are especially important in the area of public health workforce development. In addition to national leadership, state and local governments must remain committed to and invested in public health objectives. However, states and local governments face difficult economic circumstances and tough choices across the United States and are looking to cut back services that are either low priority or that have other funding sources. If state and local governments supplant their own funding with the new federal funds, the overall effort will be less than it should be.

Beyond funding, administrative and bureaucratic obstacles challenge public health workforce development efforts in the public sector. State and local agencies are often the source of some of the most significant recruitment and retention problems facing the public health workforce. These include slow hiring by governmental agencies, civil service systems, hiring freezes, budget crises affecting state and local government, and the lack of career ladders, competitive salary structures, and other forms of recognition that value workers for their skill and performance.

Despite the uncertainties inherent in these influences, past trends and current forces suggest that professional and administrative jobs and careers in public health are likely to grow over the next decade. Unfortunately, it will be difficult to measure the progress that has been made without deployment of a standard taxonomy for public health occupations and more comprehensive enumeration strategies and tools that provide better information on the key dimensions of the public health workforce, including its size and distribution in official agencies and private and voluntary organizations.

PUBLIC HEALTH WORKFORCE DISTRIBUTION AND COMPOSITION

In addition to the size of the public health workforce, its distribution and composition are important to current and future public health workers. Key questions include: (1) Where will public health job opportunities be most abundant? and (2) Which occupational categories are likely to grow most rapidly and be in greatest demand?

Job opportunities generally track with population density and demographic shifts. Within the health sector, job opportunities cluster around metropolitan areas. Public health positions also follow this pattern. There are more positions, and therefore more opportunities, in metropolitan areas than there are in rural areas. General demographic trends indicate a continuing shift of population from the Northeast and Midwest regions of the United States to the South, Southwest, and West Coast. It is likely that health sector jobs and public health positions will also follow this pattern.

The ratio of positions to population, however, can be higher in rural areas (and states that have higher proportions of their population living in nonmetropolitan areas). This occurs because there is a basic core staffing that must be present regardless of the size of the population and because rural and remote communities often lack other public health resources and assets. For example, local public health agencies in small as well as large communities will have an agency administrator, director of nursing, and environmental director. Public health agencies serving larger communities may have more total workers, but the ratio of workers to population is often lower due to the effect of core (or overhead) staffing. In addition, nongovernmental resources are often lacking in rural communities. Governmental agencies may constitute a larger proportion of a rural community's overall resources than for urban or suburban communities. A higher public health worker to population ratio in rural areas raises issues of efficiency in terms of scarce resources, including public health professionals, and can be used as an argument for con-

TABLE 14–2 Composite Public Health Practice Profile for Public Health Occupations and Titles Addressed in Chapters 7–13

	PH Adm	Env Hlth	PH Nurs	Epi	PH Ed	Nutr	Soc Beh MH	PH Lab	MD DVM Phar	Dent Wkrs	Adm Law Jdg	PH Prog Spec	ERC	PH Pol An	Hlth Info	Out Wkrs
Public Health Purposes																
Preventing epidemics and the spread of disease	√	√	√	√	√		√	√	√	√	√			√	√	√
Protecting against environmental hazards		√	√						√		√	√	√	√		
Preventing injuries		√		√	√							√	√			√
Promoting and encouraging healthy behaviors		√			√	√	√		√	√		√				√
Responding to disasters and assisting communities in recovery	√						√						√			
Assuring the quality and accessibility of health services	√		√			√	√	√	√	√	√			√	√	
Essential Public Health Services																
Monitoring health status to identify community health problems		√	√		√		√	√	√			√		√		
Diagnosing and investigating health problems and health hazards in the community		√	√	√				√	√			√	√			
Informing, educating, and empowering people about health issues		√			√	√	√			√				√	√	√
Mobilizing community partnerships to identify and solve health problems	√				√		√							√	√	√

solidation of several small local public health agencies into one large agency.

Table 14–2 provides a snapshot describing the distribution and composition of the public health workforce from a different perspective by aggregating the public health practice profiles from Chapters 7 through 13. This composite profile illustrates the breadth of roles in addressing public health's broad purposes and essential services as well as the contribution of the various public health occupational categories and titles.

This composite highlights the importance of preventing the spread of disease and assuring the quality of health services as public health purposes. The majority of public health occupations place significant emphasis on these purposes. Only a few public health occupations and titles focus on emergency response as a primary duty. Virtually all, however, have roles in responding to public health emergencies as a secondary-level responsibility.

Among the 10 essential public health services, nearly all public health occupations and titles are actively involved in evaluating the effectiveness, accessibility, and quality of personal and population-based health services. Eight other essential public health services are widely distributed across the various occupational categories and titles. Only a few public health occupations focus extensively on assuring a competent workforce.

As noted in Chapter 6, some health sector occupations will grow more rapidly than others, even while the health sector grows more rapidly than the rest of the economy.[6] Among the many public health occupations, several appear to be growing rapidly and several others appear to be in danger of their supply not keeping pace with anticipated demand.

TABLE 14–2 Composite Public Health Practice Profile for Public Health Occupations and Titles Addressed in Chapters 7–13 (*continued*)

	PH Adm	Env Hlth	PH Nurs	Epi	PH Ed	Nutr	Soc Beh MH	PH Lab	MD DVM Phar	Dent Wkrs	Adm Law Jdg	PH Prog Spec	ERC	PH Pol An	Hlth Info	Out Wkrs
Essential Public Health Services																
Developing policies and plans that support individual and community health efforts	√				√		√				√	√	√	√	√	
Enforcing laws and regulations that protect health and ensure safety	√	√					√			√	√					
Linking people with needed personal health services and assuring the provision of health care when otherwise unavailable			√			√	√		√	√		√			√	
Assuring a competent public health and personal health care workforce	√				√							√				
Evaluating effectiveness, accessibility, and quality of personal and population-based health services	√	√	√	√		√	√	√	√	√	√	√	√	√	√	
Researching new insights and innovative solutions to health problems			√	√		√		√	√		√				√	√

Notes: PH Adm—Public Health Administrator; Env Hlth—Environmental Health Practitioner; PH Nurs—Public Health Nurse; EPI—Epidemiologist; PH Ed—Public Health Educator; Nutr—Nutritionist; Soc Beh MH—Public Health Social, Behavioral, and Mental Health Workers; PH Lab—Public Health Laboratory Worker; MD DVM Phar—Public Health Physicians, Veterinarians, and Pharmacists; Dent Wkrs—Dental Health Workers; Adm Law Jdg—Administrative Law Judge; PH Prog Spec—Public Health Program Specialist; ERC—Emergency Response Coordinator; PH Pol An—Public Health Policy Analyst; Hlth Info—Health Information Specialist; and Out Wkrs—Outreach Workers.

It is not surprising that public health nurses and environmental health practitioners are repeatedly identified as the positions in greatest demand. Indeed, these occupational categories are the largest in the public health workforce, and it is only natural that these categories undergo greater turnover than others. For registered nurses, there is substantial evidence of a current national shortage. For environmental health practitioners, this is not so clear.

The aftermath of terrorist events of 2001, including the series of anthrax spore attacks through the postal system, spotlighted the need for two professional positions. The first, emergency response coordinators, is new to the list of public health occupations; the second, epidemiologists, is one of the oldest public health professional occupations. State and local public health agencies are rapidly hiring emergency response coordinators. These people come to these new positions with a wide range of academic and experiential qualifications. Epidemiologists, on the other hand, have more restrictive qualifications in terms of academic preparation such as master's and doctoral degrees. Concerns over the past few decades that epidemiologists were in short supply and great demand are now heightened as agencies seek to quickly hire these specialists. The number of epidemiologists coming out of graduate programs does not appear to be keeping pace with the need, despite an increase in interest as measured by the number of applications for epidemiology training programs.

Prior to 2001, health educators and community health planners were steadily growing professional categories in the public health workforce. Expansion of health education and promotion services, and an increase in community health planning and community health improvement activities account for this trend. It is not clear whether this trend will continue in view of the current emphasis on bioterrorism and public health emergency preparedness.

PUBLIC HEALTH WORKFORCE SKILLS AND COMPETENCIES

Beyond workforce size, distribution, and composition are issues related to the core competencies and skills that will be most important in public health practice and how these skills are best acquired. Establishing and promoting competencies for public health workers is tricky business. For one thing, public health workers come from a variety of professional backgrounds, many of which have their own core competencies. For example, public health nursing has a set of core competencies (see Chapter 9), and health educators use a sophisticated competency framework for purposes of certification (see Chapter 11). The same can be said for public health physicians, administrators, epidemiologists, and several other

public health professional occupations. Identifying a common core for these various professional categories generally leads to a framework with very general and nonspecific competencies that are difficult to relate to a specific situation or problem. The Council on Linkages between Academia and Public Health Practice spent more than a decade grappling with this problem before arriving at a set of core competencies for public health professionals in 2001.

The national public health organizations endorsed and adopted these core competencies, which track to the essential public health services framework (see Table 14–3 for an example), as the basis for assessing and enhancing the skills of public health workers. Core public health practice competencies serve as a useful benchmark for competency frameworks developed to serve state or local public health systems or to guide the development of more focused skills, such as in public health law, informatics, genomics, and emergency preparedness.

There are several important and practical uses for competency frameworks. Core competencies can serve as models whenever an agency's job descriptions are developed, updated, or revised. As competency-oriented job descriptions become more widely used, core competencies can guide orientation and training activities for new employees. Core competencies are also useful in employee self-assessment activities as well as in personnel evaluation activities when supervisors review the past performance of employees and set performance expectations for the next cycle. The use of competencies within personnel and human resources systems is growing slowly within the public sector, although widespread implementation could take decades.

The identification of core competencies for public health practice and for emergency preparedness and response demonstrate the support for competency-based training among practice organizations. A companion effort to identify a panel of core competencies for graduates of master's of public health (MPH) programs in schools of public health is under development under the auspices of the Association of Schools of Public Health (ASPH). This panel of competencies addresses discipline-specific competencies for behavioral sciences, health administration, epidemiology, biostatistics, environmental health, and public health biology as well as crosscutting competencies in the areas of communication, informatics, cultural proficiency, ecologic determinants of health, leadership, policy development, professionalism, program development and evaluation, and systems thinking.

Despite this progress, formidable challenges lie ahead.[7,8] These include the establishment of mechanisms to support workforce planning and training in all states and local jurisdictions, and refinement and validation of public health practice competencies associated with each of the various disciplines that compose the workforce. Enhanced competencies are necessary to improve basic, advanced, and continuing education curricula for public health workers. Also needed are strategies to certify competencies among practitioners. In addition, large-scale assessments of current levels of workforce preparedness as measured by core competencies are lacking. For education and training of the public health workforce to be taken seriously, both academic and practice interests must view public health workforce development as an important priority.

Education and training opportunities for public health workers are widely available today and likely to expand even further over the next decade. The first school of public health was established in 1916 at the Johns Hopkins School of Hygiene and Public Health with the support of the Rockefeller Foundation. In 1969, there were only 12 schools of public health, but that number grew to 37 by mid-2005, with a half dozen new schools in the pipeline. The number of accredited programs offering the MPH and equivalent degrees is also increasing. Many unaccredited programs also exist.

Before 1970, students in public health training were primarily physicians or members of other disciplines with professional

---

TABLE 14–3 Core Public Health Competencies Related to Essential Public Health Service #2: "Diagnose and Investigate Health Problems and Health Hazards in the Community"

Analytic/Assessment Skills
- Defines a problem
- Determines appropriate uses and limitations of both quantitative and qualitative data
- Selects and defines variables relevant to defined public health problems
- Identifies relevant and appropriate data and information sources
- Evaluates the integrity and comparability of data and identifies gaps in data sources
- Applies ethical principles to the collection, maintenance, use, and dissemination of data and information
- Partners with communities to attach meaning to collected quantitative and qualitative data
- Makes relevant inferences from quantitative and qualitative data
- Obtains and interprets information regarding risks and benefits to the community
- Recognizes how the data illuminate ethical, political, scientific, economic, and overall public health issues

Policy Development/Program Planning Skills
- Collects, summarizes, and interprets information relevant to an issue
- States policy options and writes clear and concise policy statements
- Articulates the health, fiscal, administrative, legal, social, and political implications of each policy option
- States the feasibility and expected outcomes of each policy option
- Decides on the appropriate course of action
- Develops mechanisms to monitor and evaluate programs for their effectiveness and quality

Communication Skills
- Communicates effectively both in writing and orally, or in other ways; solicits input from individuals and organizations
- Leads and participates in groups to address specific issues
- Uses the media, advanced technologies, and community networks to communicate information
- Effectively presents accurate demographic, statistical, programmatic, and scientific information for professional and lay audiences
- Listens to others in an unbiased manner, respects points of view of others, and promotes the expression of diverse opinions and perspectives (attitude)

Cultural Competency Skills
- Utilizes appropriate methods for interacting sensitively, effectively, and professionally with persons from diverse cultural, socioeconomic, educational, racial, ethnic, and professional backgrounds, and persons of all ages and lifestyle preferences
- Understands the dynamic forces contributing to cultural diversity (attitude)

Community Dimensions of Practice Skills
- Accomplishes effective community engagements
- Identifies community assets and available resources
- Develops, implements, and evaluates a community public health assessment

(continued)

TABLE 14–3 Core Public Health Competencies Related to Essential Public Health Service #2: "Diagnose and Investigate Health Problems and Health Hazards in the Community" (*continued*)

Basic Public Health Sciences Skills
- Defines, assesses, and understands the health status of populations, determinants of health and illness, factors contributing to health promotion and disease prevention, and factors influencing the use of health services
- Identifies and applies basic research methods used in public health
- Applies the basic public health sciences, including behavioral and social sciences, biostatistics, epidemiology, environmental public health, and prevention of chronic and infectious diseases and injuries

Financial Planning and Management Skills
- Develops and presents a budget
- Manages programs within budget constraints
- Applies budget processes
- Develops strategies for determining budget priorities
- Monitors program performance
- Prepares proposals for funding from external sources
- Applies basic human relations skills to the management of organizations, motivation of personnel, and resolution of conflicts
- Manages information systems for collection, retrieval, and use of data for decision making Leadership and Systems Thinking Skills
- Creates a culture of ethical standards within organizations and communities
- Identifies internal and external issues that may impact delivery of essential public health services (i.e., strategic planning)

Source: Council on Linkage between Academia and Practice. Competency list by essential public health service. Available at: http://www.train.org/Competencies/essential.aspx#2. Accessed August 20, 2005.

degrees. In recent decades, however, more than two thirds of the students enter public health training in order to obtain their primary postgraduate degrees. Public health training evolved from a second degree for medical professionals to a primary health discipline. Schools of public health that initially emphasized the study of hygiene and sanitation have expanded their curricula to address five core disciplines—biostatistics, epidemiology, health services administration, health education/behavioral science, and environmental science.

The number of individuals earning graduate degrees in public health doubled between 1975 and 2005, from 3,000 to more than 6,000.[9] Surprisingly, this increase has not had a significant impact on the number and proportion of professionals trained in public health in the primary public health workforce. In the 1970s, about one half of MPH graduates took jobs with governmental public health agencies, the primary public health workforce. Currently, only about one in five MPH graduates take jobs with governmental public health agencies.

Despite this impressive growth of public health schools and programs, most public health workers continue to receive their professional preparation elsewhere. This is not surprising in view of the number of training programs for key occupational categories in the public health workforce. There are more than 1,500 basic RN training programs at the bachelor, associate, or diploma level; well in excess of 1,000 LPN training

programs; more than 150 programs in health administration; and several hundred programs offering training in environmental health sciences.

In sum, educational resources contribute to a national network of nearly 40 accredited schools of public health, another 90 graduate training programs in public health, and as many as 500 other graduate-level education programs in areas related to public health, such as health administration, public health nursing, and environmental engineering. Sources for additional information on discipline-specific education and training are provided in Chapters 7 through 13.

Training activities that focus on public health workers rather than students are also extensive. HRSA has long been the primary federal health agency supporting development of the various health professions, although the public health workforce has never been a priority for that agency. Because many public health workers come from other health disciplines, however, HRSA support for training other health professionals also benefits the public health workforce. Throughout the 1990s, HRSA training activities for public health focused increasingly on strengthening links between schools of public health (SPH) and public health agencies. Early in the 1990s, HRSA initiated support for the Council on Linkages between Academia and Public Health Practice, which has grown to include representation from many prominent public health academic and practice organizations. Since 1999, HRSA has funded Public Health

Training Centers, which are multistate training collaborations involving SPHs and health agencies, with 14 such centers (with approximately $5 million in annual funding) operating in late 2003. Beginning in 2002, HRSA also funded states and several large cities to support hospital bioterrorism planning and provided funds for curriculum development and training for health care professionals and for community-wide planning related to bioterrorism and other public health emergencies.

During the 1990s, the CDC became increasingly engaged in supporting capacity development and improving state-based public health systems through the establishment of national and regional leadership development projects in the early 1990s. CDC also provided direct financial assistance to state public health systems for emergency preparedness later in that decade. CDC encouraged states and large cities to utilize this funding to improve the capacity of their public health infrastructures in order to respond to a wide range of both emergency and routine threats, including bioterrorism preparedness. CDC increasingly emphasized and supported public health workforce development as the cornerstone of infrastructure improvement. Between October 2000 and October 2002, through its cooperative agreement with the ASPH, CDC awarded substantial grants (approximately $1 million per center per year) to more than two dozen academic Centers for Public Health Preparedness.

Since 1998, funding for public health workforce development through SPHs has increased dramatically, from under $1 million (primarily from HRSA) in 1997 to more than $30 million (mainly from CDC) in 2005. Approximately another $70–$80 million for public health training is available in the bioterrorism grants awarded to states and several large cities, an estimated 10% of those grants. A total of more than $100 million is being programmed specifically for public health workforce development in 2005 in addition to resources that prepare other health professionals to participate in responses to public health emergencies.[7]

The extent of organized workforce development activities within state and local health departments and other public health organizations is unknown. Nonetheless, virtually all public health organizations provide some form of orientation, training, and support of continuing education for their workers. Costs for these activities are often buried in agency budgets as human resources, administrative support, and employee travel expenditures encompassing both direct and indirect, or opportunity costs for time spent away from performing official duties. Aggregating these costs would likely represent a significant pool of resources.

Efforts to forge links between academic and training partners and public health practice agencies at all levels of gov-ernment are advancing, although unevenly from state to state. Comprehensive approaches that serve the entire public health workforce with an extensive menu of options for workers at varying stages of career development are lacking. More limited approaches that increase the number of workers who can acquire formal public health training through degree programs or that provide advanced skills to specific categories of workers within the public health workforce are useful but not sufficient. These efforts serve a relatively small portion of the overall public health workforce. More comprehensive and systems-based approaches are needed.

PUBLIC HEALTH WORKFORCE DEVELOPMENT

Although education and training are key components of public health workforce strategies, they are not by themselves sufficient. Comprehensive public health workforce development efforts assess and promote competencies in addition to enhancing them. Efforts to promote the acquisition of public health competencies focus on several fronts but necessarily emphasize the workplace and the organizations that employ workers. Critical skills and core competencies are promoted in the workplace through job descriptions and performance appraisals that are organized around those skills and competencies. Managers and supervisors work with their employees to manage the professional development of workers and build skills that are necessary for career advancement. These administrative and personnel policies and practice create a culture that values competent performance and the acquisition of new skills.

A complementary approach to promote competencies relies on external bodies to validate and recognize skill levels through credentialing programs. Previous chapters identify many different forms of credentials for various categories of public health workers. For example, nutritionists may earn the RD (registered dietician) credential, health educators may become CHES (Certified Health Education Specialists), physicians may achieve board certification in preventive medicine and public health, and many different credentials are available to environmental health practitioners. With discipline-specific credentials available to so many different public health worker occupational categories, it should come as no surprise that there are now efforts to develop credentials specific to public health.

The intent of any credential is to distinguish someone who is eligible for some status from others who are not. Identifying individuals who have demonstrated practice-relevant competencies at a specified level (from frontline workers to senior professionals, specialists, and leaders) provides an incentive for individuals to enhance their skills. Health professions have taken various approaches to credentialing that include licensing (for physicians and nurses), certification (for health education specialists), and registration (for dieticians and sanitarians). These examples suggest that credentialing is already widely used for public health workers; examples include board-certified preventive medicine physicians, certified community health nurses and health education specialists, and certified, registered environmental health practitioners. There is still a need for credentials for those who would not fit into these specialty-specific credentials, such as public health physicians not certified in preventive medicine, or health educators who are not certified health education specialists. Because many, indeed most, workers will not be able to meet the specific requirements for specialty credentialing, such as the 3-year residency for physicians or completion of a health education degree at the undergraduate or graduate level for certified health educators, a midlevel public health-specific credential could be attractive to many public health disciplines. Fledgling competency-based credentialing programs for public health managers and for public health emergency response coordinators exist in one state using an independent certification board.[10] ASPH is planning for a credential for graduates of MPH degree programs based on a national test. These and other models focus more on public health practice competencies rather than on a worker's core discipline, making them fertile ground for turf battles with professional organizations. Considerable input from these professional organizations and from professionals in practice will be needed, however, for any framework to be valued and widely used. A three-prong credentialing strategy emerged from the National Public Health Workforce Development Conference in early 2003 calling for recognition of public health competency at a basic or Public Health 101 level and at a leadership level as well as expansion of existing credentialing activities for public health disciplines to cover those not now included.[11]

For workers to value credentials and the competencies upon which they are based, employers and health agencies must find value in them as well and base decisions about hiring, promotion, salaries, and the like on an individual worker's demonstration of those competencies. Improving workers' ability to perform their functions competently relies on both worker training and work management strategies.[7] As performance standards for public health organizations and public health systems gain headway through initiatives such as the National Public Health Performance Standards Program and the National Association of County and City Health Officials' (NACCHO's) Mobilizing for Action through Planning and Partnerships (MAPP) process, competency-based performance standards for workers will increasingly be viewed as key ingredients of organizational and system performance.

An innovative NACCHO program, Public Health Ready, holds great promise for promoting public health workforce preparedness. Public Health Ready recognizes public health agencies that meet standards for worker competency, agency preparedness plans, and regular exercises of those plans.[12] Workers can demonstrate preparedness competencies during those drills and simulations, furthering the ability of the agency to verify and document the preparedness levels of the organization and its staff. As this approach is deployed beyond several dozen pilot sites certified in 2004 and 2005, it could serve to focus public health workforce development efforts through its emphasis on the work, workers, and work organizations that constitute the governmental public health enterprise.

Although several forms of incentives are slowly advancing, one key element of a system of incentives remains lacking—there is no common currency in the form of a public health continuing-education unit (CEU) that assures quality and consistency of training activities nationally. Neither CDC, nor any of the national public health organizations, has sought to serve in this capacity. A common currency that has credibility in the practice sector and is linked with organized workforce development strategies and funding from recent bioterrorism preparedness legislation would provide a considerable incentive for competency-based approaches to public health workforce development. Nonetheless, the obstacles and inertia that have accrued over several decades remain formidable challenges for the public health system.

LESSONS FROM A CENTURY OF PROGRESS IN PUBLIC HEALTH

The remarkable achievements of the 20th century did not completely eradicate the public health problems faced in 1900. Many of these continue to threaten the health of Americans and impede progress toward realizing the life span projections presented in Figure 14–1. New faces for old enemies have appeared in the form of challenges and obstacles to be overcome in the early decades of the 21st century. Infectious diseases, tobacco, maternal and infant mortality, unintentional injuries, cardiovascular diseases, food safety, oral health, and occupational health remain high on the list of leading threats to the public's health. Each presents special challenges.

Infectious Diseases

The continuing battle against infectious diseases will be fought on several fronts due to the emergence of new infectious diseases and the reemergence of old enemies, often in drug-resistant forms. Infections due to *Escherichia coli* O157:H7 have emerged as a frequent and frightening risk to the public. Initially identified as the cause of hemorrhagic conditions in the early

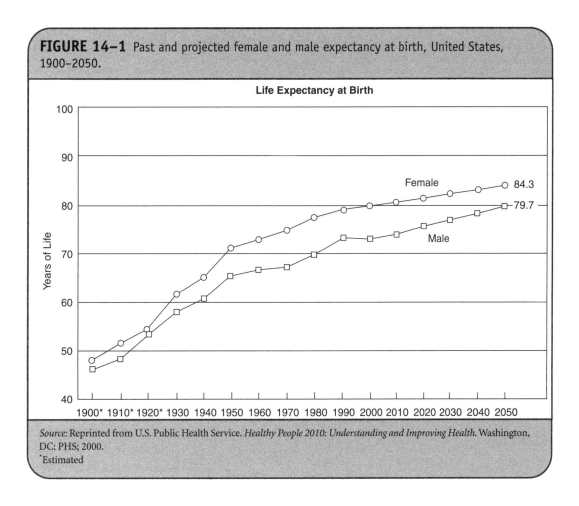

FIGURE 14–1 Past and projected female and male expectancy at birth, United States, 1900–2050.

Source: Reprinted from U.S. Public Health Service. *Healthy People 2010: Understanding and Improving Health.* Washington, DC: PHS; 2000.
*Estimated

1980s, this pathogen was increasingly associated with foodborne illness outbreaks in the 1990s, including a major outbreak in the Pacific Northwest related to *E. coli*-contaminated hamburgers distributed through a national fast food chain.[13] The source of the *E. coli* was cattle. Other outbreaks of this pathogen involved swimmers in lake water contaminated by bathers infected with the organism (Figure 14–2). Because many of the illnesses are minor and both medical and public health practitioners fail to perform the tests necessary to diagnose *E. coli* infections properly, current surveillance efforts greatly underreport the extent of this condition.

Multi-drug-resistant pathogens represent another emerging infectious disease problem for the public health system. The widespread and, at times, indiscriminate use of antibiotics in agricultural and health care settings produces strains of bacteria that are resistant to these drugs. Antimicrobial agents have been increasingly deployed throughout the second half of the 20th century. Slowly, over this period, the consequences of these "miracle drugs" have been experienced in the community, as well as in health facilities. The emergence of drug-resistant strains has reduced the effectiveness of treatment for several common infections, including tuberculosis, gonorrhea, pneumococcal infections, and hospital-acquired staphylococcal and enterococcal infections. For tuberculosis, drug resistance played a substantial role in its resurgence in the early 1990s.

Pathogens, both old and new, have devised ingenious ways of adapting to and thwarting the weapons used to control them. Many factors in society, the environment, and global interconnectedness continue to increase the risk of emergence and spread of infectious diseases. Heightened concerns over the risk of acts of bioterrorism add a new dimension to the threats posed by infectious diseases. As noted in Chapter 5, these concerns have raised expectations for public health to serve both national security and personal safety roles.

The role of infectious diseases in the development of chronic diseases such as diabetes, heart disease, and some cancers further argues that infectious diseases will continue as important health risks in the new century. To battle infectious diseases, the development and deployment of new methods, both in laboratory and epidemiologic sciences, are needed to better understand the interactions among environmental

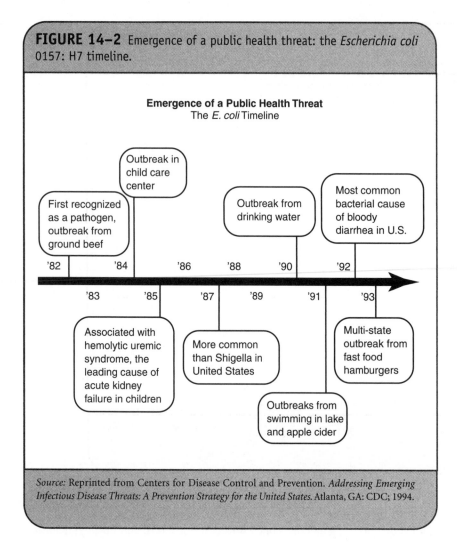

FIGURE 14–2 Emergence of a public health threat: the *Escherichia coli* 0157: H7 timeline.

Emergence of a Public Health Threat
The *E. coli* Timeline

Outbreak in child care center

First recognized as a pathogen, outbreak from ground beef

Outbreak from drinking water

Most common bacterial cause of bloody diarrhea in U.S.

'82   '84   '86   '88   '90   '92

'83   '85   '87   '89   '91   '93

Associated with hemolytic uremic syndrome, the leading cause of acute kidney failure in children

More common than Shigella in United States

Multi-state outbreak from fast food hamburgers

Outbreaks from swimming in lake and apple cider

Source: Reprinted from Centers for Disease Control and Prevention. *Addressing Emerging Infectious Disease Threats: A Prevention Strategy for the United States.* Atlanta, GA: CDC; 1994.

factors as contributors to the emergence and reemergence of infectious disease processes. Also, despite the successes realized in the development and use of vaccines over the past century, substantial gaps persist in the infrastructure of the vaccine delivery system, including the roles played by parents, providers, information technology, and biotech and pharmaceutical companies. Improving the coordination of these elements holds the promise of reducing the toll from infectious diseases in the 21st century.

Tobacco Use

The potential gains to be realized from further reduction of tobacco usage are also apparent. Despite the overall decline in tobacco use among adults over the second half of the 20th century, an alarmingly high prevalence of tobacco use among teens persists, and rates among adults are no longer declining, as they did prior to 1980. These trends suggest that concerns over risks related to exposure to environmental tobacco smoke will continue for many years to come. Disparities in tobacco

use by race and ethnicity, together with the growth of demographic groups with high use rates, add yet another dimension to the war against tobacco. New approaches and new products will raise new issues of safety, whereas the increase in tobacco use across the globe will transport old and new challenges around the world.

Maternal and Child Health

Even as maternal and child health outcomes have improved dramatically, there has been little change in the prime determinants of perinatal outcomes—the rate of low birth weight and preterm deliveries. This situation must be addressed to even partially replicate the gains realized in the 20th century. Another important risk factor moving in the wrong direction is the rate of unintended pregnancies. Together, these challenges call for improved understanding of the biologic, social, economic, psychological, and environmental factors that influence maternal and infant health outcomes and in the effectiveness of intervention strategies designed to address these causative factors.

Motor Vehicle Injuries

The impressive gains realized in reducing motor vehicle injuries have uncovered gaps in our understanding of comprehensive prevention. Challenges include expanding surveillance to monitor nonfatal injuries, detect new problems, and set priorities. Greater research into emerging and priority problems, as well as intervention effectiveness, is also needed, as are more effective collaborations and interagency partnerships. Injuries to pedestrians from vehicles other than automobiles will also challenge public health in the 21st century. The effects of age, alcohol use, seat belt use, and interventions targeting these risks will require greater attention for progress to continue in the battle against motor vehicle injuries.

Cardiovascular Disease

An aging population less threatened by infectious disease and injury will place even more people at risk of ill health related to cardiovascular diseases. Greater attention to research to understand the various social, psychological, environmental, physiologic, and genetic determinants of cardiovascular diseases is needed in the new century. Reducing disparities that exist in terms of burden of disease, prevalence of risk factors, and ability to reach high-risk populations represents another mega challenge. Identifying new and emerging risk factors and their relationships, including genetic and infectious disease factors, will be necessary in both developed and developing parts of the world.

Food Safety

Our understanding of food safety and nutrition made great strides in the 1900s, but both old and new risks will need to be addressed in the new century. Iron and folate deficiencies continue, and many of the advantages related to breastfeeding remain unrealized. The emergence of obesity as an increasingly prevalent condition throughout the population is one of the most startling developments of the late 20th century. Persistent challenges include applying new information about nutrition, dietary patterns, and behavior that promote health and reduce the risk of chronic diseases.

Oral Health

One of the most overlooked achievements of public health in the 20th century was the dramatic decline in dental caries due to fluoridation of drinking water supplies. Ironically, these advances in oral health have contributed to the perception that dental caries are no longer a significant public health problem and that fluoridation is no longer needed. These battles are likely to be fought in political, rather than scientific, arenas, presenting a substantial challenge to public health in the 21st century.

Workplace Safety

Workplaces are now safer than ever before, yet challenges remain on this front, as well. Improved surveillance of work-related injuries and illnesses and better methods of conducting field investigations in high-risk occupations and industries remain formidable challenges. Applying new methods of risk assessment to improve assessment of injury exposures and intervention outcomes, as well as improved research into intervention effectiveness, surveillance methods, and organization of work represent additional challenges for public health practice in the 21st century.

Unfinished Agenda

It is clear that much remains to be done. *Healthy People 2010* articulates this unfinished agenda by identifying important targets and leading indicators of health status for the United States.[14] Various chapters of this text identify some of these leading indicators and targets, including tobacco use, access to care, physical activity, and immunizations. Targets for other leading indicators have also been established, including sub-

stance abuse (Figure 14–3), obesity, sexual behavior, mental health, environmental quality, and injuries/violence (Table 14–4). Many of these represent health problems that are new to the public health agenda. In recent decades, medical care issues, substance abuse, mental health, long-term care, and, today, violence have been categorized as public health problems and have taken their rightful place on the public health agenda. Applying the lessons learned from the recent century of progress in public health to both new and persisting health threats will be necessary to increase the span of healthy life and eliminate the huge disparities in health outcomes that are the overarching goals of the year 2010 national health objectives. The public health challenges of both centuries call for the application of sound science in an environment that supports social justice in health. This remains the most formidable challenge facing public health practice in the 21st century.

LIMITATIONS OF 21ST-CENTURY PUBLIC HEALTH

Despite the remarkable achievements of the 20th century, there is much for public health to do in the early years of the new century. Continued progress is by no means assured due to a new constellation of problems and important limitations of conventional public health efforts. Global environmental threats, the disruption of vital ecosystems, global population overload, persistent and widening social injustice and health inequalities, and lack of access to effective care add to the list of health problems left over from the 20th century.[15] Consider, for example, the implications of Figure 14–4, in terms of the link between income and health, and a nation growing more and more diverse, with a disproportionate burden of poverty falling on children, minorities, and one-parent families. Further gains in health status may be less related to science than to social policies. For some public health professionals, the limitations of conventional public health are difficult to accept because, in large part, they represent the supporting pillars of the public health enterprise. This reluctance to critically self-assess makes future progress less certain. It is useful to examine these limitations in terms of their relationship to the two major forces shaping public health responses—science and social values.

Among the limitations affecting the science of public health is an undue emphasis on reductionist thinking that seeks molecular-level explanations for social and structural phenomena. Identification of risk factors has been useful for public health efforts, but the emphasis on individual risk factors often obscures patterns that call for multilevel responses. The persistent identification of the association of social deprivation with many of the important health problems of the last century is a case in point. Approaches for reducing coronary heart disease provide another example. Health interventions targeting a

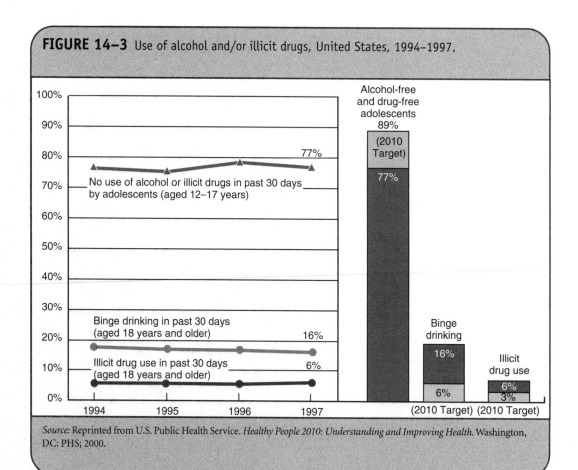

FIGURE 14–3 Use of alcohol and/or illicit drugs, United States, 1994–1997.

Source: Reprinted from U.S. Public Health Service. *Healthy People 2010: Understanding and Improving Health.* Washington, DC: PHS; 2000.

TABLE 14–4 Year 2010 Targets for Selected Health Indicators

Indicator	Reference Year	Reference Level	Year 2010 Target
Overweight or obese children & adolescents	1988–94	11%	5%
Obese adults >20 years of age	1988–94	23%	15%
Motor vehicle death rate (per 100,000)	1997	15.8	9
Homicide death rate (per 100,000)	1995	7.2	3.2
Exposed to ozone above EPA standard	1997	43%	0%
Exposed to environmental tobacco smoke	1988–94	65%	45%
Sexually active unmarried women ages 18–44 who use condoms	1995	23%	50%
Adolescents in grades 9–12 not sexually active or sexually active who use condoms	1997	85%	95%
Adults with depression who receive treatment	1997	23%	50%

Source: Adapted from U.S. Public Health Service. *Healthy People 2010: Understanding and Improving Health.* Washington, DC: PHS; 2000.

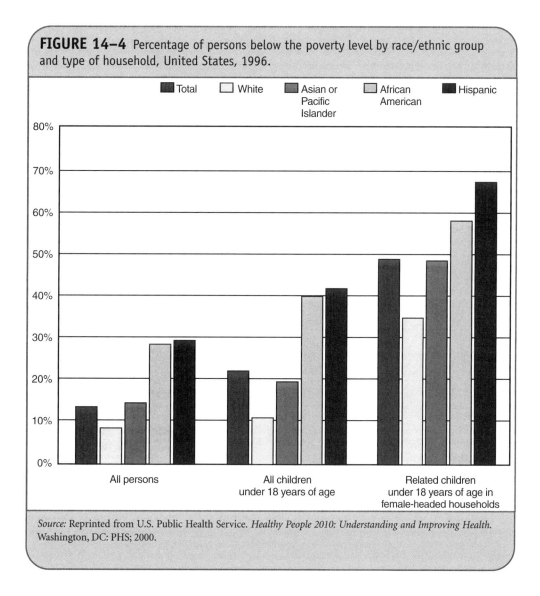

FIGURE 14–4 Percentage of persons below the poverty level by race/ethnic group and type of household, United States, 1996.

Source: Reprinted from U.S. Public Health Service. *Healthy People 2010: Understanding and Improving Health.* Washington, DC: PHS; 2000.

reduction in coronary heart disease frequently focus on risk factors at the physiologic level, such as blood pressure control, cholesterol, and obesity and on lifestyle factors at the individual level, including smoking, nutrition, physical activity, and psychosocial factors. However, there are also environmental influences, such as geographic location, housing conditions, occupational risks, and social structure influences, such as social class, age, gender, and race/ethnicity. In this multilevel view of coronary heart disease, interventions that focus on primary and secondary prevention (those addressing the physiologic and individual levels) need to be supplemented by organization-level and community-level interventions (addressing environmental influences) and healthy public policy (addressing the social structure level).

Another limitation of public health's scientific heritage is the penchant for dichotomous thinking and the failure to view

health phenomena as continuous. Using coronary heart disease as an example, dichotomous thinking draws attention to individual and physiologic level factors, whereas viewing this condition as continuous encourages a population-wide view and development of interventions that reduce overall incidence and prevalence by affecting frequency distributions in the entire population. A view of health problems as continuous phenomena suggests that efforts be made throughout the population to move the entire frequency distribution for coronary heart disease "to the left," rather than to reduce disease burden only among those groups most heavily impacted. Here it is apparent that science and social values are not pure and mutually exclusive forces.

Discussion and debate over scientific approaches to public health problems are not, however, purely scientific in nature. At the heart of collective actions are collective values as to whether issues affecting individuals are more important than issues affecting communities of individuals and as to the meaning of health itself. Should public health emphasize the health of individuals or the health of communities? In part, these reflect the different perspectives of health described in Chapters 2 and 3. On one hand is a mechanistic view of health as the absence of disease, promoting health interventions that emphasize curative treatment for afflicted individuals. On the other hand is a more holistic view of health that sees health as a complex equilibrium of forces and factors necessary for optimal functioning of that individual. This latter view emphasizes health maintenance and health promotion, often through broad social policies affecting the entire community. Differences in public health systems among societies are largely described by these differences. Some societies, like the United States, focus on individuals using a largely medical treatment approach. Others are more heavily influenced by collectivism and a holistic view of health. At the core of what can be accomplished under either view, however, are basic values and social philosophies that guide the use of the scientific knowledge available at any point in time. These differences in social values also affect perceptions as to what is expected of government and, as a result, the form and leadership of public health efforts. To a large extent, these forces have hastened the development of community public health practice and career opportunities in public health in the United States, a phenomenon described in previous chapters.

CONCLUSION

Concerns over the future of the public health workforce are mounting. Sources point to the aging of the public health workforce, current shortages of public health nurses and epidemiologists, and the imminent retirement of many public health professionals. Legislative proposals in Congress would authorize more than $200 million for scholarships and loan repayment programs to push more public health professionals through the pipeline and into positions in state and local agencies.[16–18]

Responses to these concerns, however, reflect a view that public health workforce development strategies must produce more public health workers. Strategies that focus on the pipeline are useful, but they will never be sufficient to assure an effective public health workforce over the long term. Strategies that focus on the workforce itself are also needed.[7]

The public health workforce is growing and will continue to grow for years to come. Many public health occupational categories will see a steady increase; others will grow even more rapidly. As a population-based enterprise, public health jobs should mirror demographic changes in terms of both location of job opportunities and the diversity and cultural proficiency of workers. Core public health practice competencies will increasingly influence education and training programs and find their way into the human resource activities and personnel systems of governmental public health agencies. Worker recognition initiatives based on relevant competencies, such as credentialing and certification programs, will also grow in order to address the need for both heightened accountability and expanded career pathways. The recent influx of resources to support public health workforce development will continue only if measurable progress and impact can be demonstrated. Without those resources, however, the progress of public health workforce development efforts could stall. In the end, the most important asset of the public health system remains its workforce.

The job description of public health has never been clear. As a result, public health has become quite proficient in delivering specific services, with less attention paid to mobilizing action toward those factors that most seriously affect community health status. Among traditional health-related factors, tobacco, alcohol, and diet are factors responsible for much of modern America's mortality and morbidity. Nonetheless, the resources supporting interventions directed toward these factors are minuscule. Similarly, the primary cause of America's relatively poor health outcomes, in comparison with other developed nations, as well as the most likely source for further health gains in the United States, resides in the huge and increasing gaps between racial and ethnic groups. The public health system, from national to state and local levels, must recognize these circumstances and move beyond them to advocate and build constituencies aggressively for efforts that target the most important of the traditional health risk factors and that promote social policies that will both minimize and equalize risks throughout the population. The task is as simple as following the Golden Rule and doing for others what we want done for ourselves, because efforts to improve the health of others make everyone healthier. This does not constitute a new job description for public health in the United States, but rather a recommitment to an old, successful, and necessary one.

Discussion Questions and Exercises

1. What was the most important achievement of public health in the 20th century? Why?

2. What will be the most important achievement of public health in the 21st century? Why?

3. Using a scale from 1 to 10, how effective is the public health system in the United States? How did you arrive at this rating?

4. What do you think are the most important new or expanded roles for public health in the 21st century?

5. Which public health occupations and careers are most likely to expand to meet the challenges of public health practice in the 21st century?

REFERENCES

1. Institute of Medicine, National Academy of Sciences. *The Future of Public Health.* Washington, DC: National Academy Press; 1988.

2. Health Resources and Services Administration, U.S. Department of Health and Human Services. *Public Health Personnel in the United States, 1980: Second Report to Congress.* Washington, DC: U.S. Public Health Service; 1982.

3. Health Resources and Services Administration, Bureau of Health Professions, National Center for Health Workforce Information and Analysis and Center for Health Policy, Columbia School of Nursing. *The Public Health Workforce Enumeration 2000.* Washington, DC: HRSA; 2000. Available at: http://www.phppo.cdc.gov/owpp/docs/library/2000/Public%20Health%20Wo rkforce%20Enumeration%202000.pdf. Accessed August 20, 2005.

4. U.S. Bureau of the Census. Federal, state, and local governments, public employment and payroll data. Available at: http://www.census.gov/govs/www/apes.html. Accessed August 20, 2005.

5. Council of State and Territorial Epidemiologists. *2004 National Assessment of Epidemiologic Capacity: Findings and Recommendations.* Washington, DC: CSTE; 2004. Available at: http://www.cste.org/Assessment/ECA/pdffiles/ECAfinal05.pdf. Accessed August 20, 2005.

6. Bureau of Labor Statistics, U.S. Department of Labor. *Occupational Outlook Handbook, 2004–2005 Edition.* Available at: http://www.bls.gov/oco/. Accessed August 20, 2005.

7. Turnock BJ. Public health workforce preparedness roadmap. *J Public Health Manage Pract.* 2003;9:471–480.

8. Tilson H, Gebbie KM. The public health workforce. *Ann Rev Pub Health.* 2004;25:341–356. Available at: http://arjournals.annualreviews.org/doi/full/10.1146/annurev.publhealth.25.102802.124357. Accessed August 20, 2005.

9. National Center for Health Statistics. *Health, United States, 2004.* Washington, DC: NCHS; 2004.

10. Turnock BJ. Competency-based credentialing of public health administrators in Illinois. *J Public Health Manage Pract.* 2001;7:74–82.

11. Cioffi JP, Lichtveld MY, Thielen L, Miner K. Credentialing the public health workforce: an idea whose time has come. *J Public Health Manage Pract.* 2003;6:451–458.

12. National Association of County and City Health Officials. Project Public Health Ready. Available at: http://www.naccho.org/topics/emergency/pphr.cfm. Accessed August 20, 2005.

13. Centers for Disease Control and Prevention. *Addressing Emerging Infectious Disease Threats: A Prevention Strategy for the United States.* Atlanta, GA: CDC; 1994.

14. U.S. Public Health Service. *Healthy People 2010: Understanding and Improving Health.* Washington, DC: PHS; 2000.

15. McKinlay JB, Marceau LD. To boldly go . . . *Am J Public Health.* 2000;90:25–33.

16. Association of State and Territorial Health Officials, Council of State Governments, and National Association of State Personnel Executives. State public health employee worker shortage report: a civil service recruitment and retention crisis. Available at: http://www.astho.org/pubs/Workforce-Survey-Report-2.pdf. Accessed August 20, 2005.

17. Health Resources and Services Administration, National Center for Health Workforce Analysis. Public health workforce study. Available at: http://www.bhpr.hrsa.gov/healthworkforce/reports/publichealth/. Accessed August 20, 2005.

18. Health Resources and Services Administration, Bureau of Health Professions. The key ingredient of the national prevention agenda: workforce development. Available at: ftp://ftp.hrsa.gov/bhpr/nationalcenter/hp2010.pdf. Accessed August 20, 2005.

Glossary

TERM	DEFINITION (*NOTE: Some definitions are quoted from other sources; refer to text for citations.)
Access	The potential for or actual entry of a population into the health system. Entry is dependent on the wants, resources, and needs that individuals bring to the care-seeking process. Ability to obtain wanted or needed services may be influenced by many factors, including travel distance, waiting time, available financial resources, and availability of a regular source of care.
Actual Cause of Death	A primary determinant or risk factor associated with a pathologic or diagnosed cause of death. For example, tobacco use would be the actual cause for deaths from many lung cancers.
Adjusted Rate	The adjustment or standardization of rates is a statistical procedure that removes the effect of differences in the composition of populations. Because of its marked effect on mortality and morbidity, age is the variable for adjustment used most commonly. For example, an age-adjusted death rate for any cause permits a better comparison between different populations and at different times because it accounts for differences in the distribution of age.
Administrative Law	Rules and regulations promulgated by administrative agencies within the executive branch of government that carry the force of law. Administrative law represents a unique situation in which legislative, executive, and judicial powers are carried out by one agency in the development, implementation, and enforcement of rules and regulations.
Age-Adjusted Mortality Rate	The expected number of deaths that would occur if a population had the same age distribution as a standard population, expressed in terms of deaths per 1,000 or 100,000 persons.
Appropriateness	Health interventions for which the expected health benefit exceeds the expected negative consequences by a wide enough margin to justify the intervention.
Assessment	One of public health's three core functions. Assessment calls for regularly and systematically collecting, analyzing, and making available information on the health of a community, including statistics on health status, community health needs, and epidemiologic and other studies of health problems.
Assets	Resources available to achieve a specific end, such as community resources that can contribute to community health improvement efforts or emergency response resources, including human, to respond to a public health emergency.

Association
The relationship between two or more events or variables. Events are said to be associated when they occur more frequently together than one would expect by chance. Association does not necessarily imply a causal relationship.

Assurance
One of public health's three core functions. It involves assuring constituents that services necessary to achieve agreed-upon goals are provided by encouraging actions on the part of others, by requiring action through regulation, or by providing services directly.

Attributable Risk
The theoretical reduction in the rate or number of cases of an adverse outcome that can be achieved by elimination of a risk factor. For example, if tobacco use is responsible for 75% of all lung cancers, the elimination of tobacco use will reduce lung cancer mortality rates by 75% in a population over time.

Behavioral Risk Factors Surveillance System
A national data collection system funded by the Centers for Disease Control and Prevention (CDC) to assess the prevalence of behaviors that affect health status. Through individual state efforts, CDC staff coordinate the collection, analysis, and distribution of survey data on seat belt use, hypertension, physical activity, smoking, weight control, alcohol use, mammography screening, cervical cancer screening, and AIDS, as well as other health-related information.

Bioterrorism
The threatened or intentional release of biologic agents (viruses, bacteria, or their toxins) for the purpose of influencing the conduct of government or intimidating or coercing a civilian population to further political or social objectives. These agents can be released by way of the air (as aerosols), food, water, or insects.

Capacity
The capability to carry out the core functions of public health. Also see *infrastructure*.

Capitation
A method of payment for health services in which a provider is paid a fixed amount for each person served, without regard to the actual number or nature of services provided to each person in a set period of time. Capitation is the characteristic payment method in health maintenance organizations.

Case Definition
Standardized criteria for determining whether a person has a particular disease or health-related condition. Criteria often include clinical and laboratory findings, as well personal characteristics (e.g., age, sex, location, time period). Case definitions are often used in investigations and for comparing potential cases.

Case Management
The monitoring and coordinating of services rendered to individuals with specific problems or who require high-cost or extensive services.

Casualty
Any person suffering physical and/or psychological damage that leads to death, injury, or material loss.

Causality
The relationship of causes to the effects they produce; several types of causes can be distinguished. A cause is termed necessary when a particular variable must always precede an effect. This effect need not be the sole result of the one variable. A cause is termed sufficient when a particular variable inevitably initiates or produces an effect. Any given cause may be necessary, sufficient, neither, or both.

Cause of Death
For the purpose of national mortality statistics, every death is attributed to one underlying condition, based on the information reported on the death certificate and utilizing the international rules for selecting the underlying cause of death from the reported conditions.

Centers for Disease Control and Prevention (CDC)
The Centers for Disease Control and Prevention, based in Atlanta, Georgia, is the federal agency charged with protecting the nation's public health by providing direction in the prevention and control of communicable and other diseases and responding to public health emergencies. CDC's responsibilities as the nation's prevention agency have expanded over the years and will continue to evolve as the agency addresses contemporary threats to health, such as injury, environmental and occupational hazards, behavioral risks, and chronic diseases; and emerging communicable diseases, such as the Ebola virus.

Certification
A process by which an agency or association grants recognition to another party who has met certain predetermined qualifications specified by the agency or association.

Chronic Disease	A disease that has one or more of the following characteristics: (1) it is permanent, (2) it leaves residual disability, (3) it is caused by a nonreversible pathologic alteration, (4) it requires special training of the patient for rehabilitation, or (5) it may be expected to require a long period of supervision, observation, or care.
Clinical Practice Guidelines	Systematically developed statements that assist practitioner and patient decisions about appropriate health services for specific clinical conditions.
Clinical Preventive Services	Clinical services provided to patients to reduce or prevent disease, injury, or disability. These are preventive measures (including screening tests, immunizations, counseling, and periodic physical examinations) provided by a health professional to an individual patient.
Community	A group of people who have common characteristics; communities can be defined by location, race, ethnicity, age, occupation, interest in particular problems or outcomes, or other common bonds. Ideally, there should be available assets and resources, as well as collective discussion, decision making, and action.
Community Health Improvement Process	A systematic effort that assesses community needs and assets, prioritizes health-related problems and issues, analyzes problems for their causative factors, develops evidence-based intervention strategies based on those analyses, links stakeholders to implementation efforts through performance monitoring, and evaluates the effect of interventions in the community.
Community Health Needs Assessment	A formal approach to identifying health needs and health problems in the community. A variety of tools or instruments may be used; the essential ingredient is community engagement and collaborative participation.
Community Preventive Services	Population-based interventions to reduce or prevent disease, injury, or disability. These are preventive interventions targeting the entire population rather than individuals.
Comprehensive Emergency Management	A broad style of emergency management, encompassing prevention, preparedness, response, and recovery.
Condition	A health condition is a departure from a state of physical or mental well-being. An impairment is a health condition that includes chronic or permanent health defects resulting from disease, injury, or congenital malformations. All health conditions except impairments are coded according to an international classification system. Based on duration, there are two types of conditions—acute and chronic.
Consequence Management	An emergency management function that includes measures to protect public health and safety, restore essential government services, and provide emergency relief to governments in the event of terrorism.
Contamination	An accidental release of hazardous chemicals or nuclear materials that pollute the environment and place humans at risk.
Contributing Factor	A risk factor (causative factor) that is associated with the level of a determinant. Direct contributing factors are linked with the level of determinants; indirect contributing factors are linked with the level of direct contributing factors.
Core Functions	Three basic roles for public health for assuring conditions in which people can be healthy. As identified in the Institute of Medicine's landmark report, *The Future of Public Health*, these are assessment, policy development, and assurance.
Cost-Benefit Analysis	An economic analysis in which all costs and benefits are converted into monetary (dollar) values, and results are expressed as dollars of benefit per dollars expended.
Cost-Effectiveness Analysis	An economic analysis assessed as a health outcome per cost expended.

Cost-Utility Analysis	An economic analysis assessed as a quality-adjusted outcome per net cost expended.
Covert Releases	For biologic agents, an unannounced release of a biologic agent that causes illness or other effects. If undetected, a covert release has the potential to spread widely before it is detected.
Crisis Management	Administrative measures that identify, acquire, and plan the use of resources needed to anticipate, prevent, and/or resolve a threat to public safety (such as terrorism).
Crude Mortality Rate	The total number of deaths per unit of population reported during a given time interval, often expressed as the number of deaths per 1,000 or 100,000 persons.
Cultural Competence	The ability to communicate with and provide services to an individual or a group with full respect for the culturally associated values, preferences, language, and experiences of the group.
Decision Analysis	An analytic technique in which probability theory is used to obtain a quantitative approach to decision making.
Decontamination	The removal of hazardous chemicals or nuclear substances from the skin and/or mucous membranes by showering or washing the affected area with water or by rinsing with a sterile solution.
Demographics	Characteristic data, such as size, growth, density, distribution, and vital statistics, which are used to study human populations.
Demonstration Settings	A population-based or clinic-based environment in which prevention strategies are field-tested.
Determinant	A primary risk factor (causative factor) associated with the level of health problem (i.e., the level of the determinant influences the level of the health problem).
Disability Limitation	An intervention strategy that seeks to arrest or eradicate disease and/or limit disability and prevent death.
Disaster	Any event, typically occurring suddenly, that causes damage, ecologic disruption, loss of human life, or deterioration of health and health services and which exceeds the capacity of the affected community on a scale sufficient to require outside assistance.
Disaster Severity Scale	A scale that classifies disasters by the following parameters: (1) the radius of the disaster site, (2) the number of dead, (3) the number of wounded, (4) the average severity of the injuries sustained, (5) the impact time, and (6) the rescue time. By attributing a numeric score to each of the variables from 0 to 2, with 0 being the least severe and 2 the most severe, a scale with a range of 0 to 18 can be created.
Discounting	A method for adjusting the value of future costs and benefits. Expressed as a present dollar value, discounting is based on the time value of money (i.e., a dollar today is worth more than it will be a year from now, even if inflation is not considered).
Distributional Effects	The manner in which the costs and benefits of a strategy affect different groups of people in terms of demographics, geographic location, and other descriptive factors.
Early Case Finding and Treatment	An intervention strategy that seeks to identify disease or illness at an early stage so that prompt treatment will reduce the effects of the process.
Effectiveness	The improvement in health outcome that a strategy can produce in typical community-based settings. Also, the degree to which objectives are achieved.
Efficacy	The improvement in health outcome effect that a strategy can produce in expert hands under ideal circumstances.
Emergency	Any natural or manmade situation that results in severe injury, harm, or loss to humans or property.
Emergency Management Agency	The agency, under the authority of the governor's office, that coordinates the efforts of the state's health department, housing and social service agencies, and public safety agencies (such as state police) during an emergency or disaster. The emergency management agency also coordinates federal resources made available to the states, such as the National Guard, Centers for Disease Control and Prevention, and the Public Health Service.

Emergency Medical Services (EMS) System	The coordination of the prehospital system (including public access, 911 dispatch, paramedics, and ambulance services) and the in-hospital system (including emergency departments, hospitals, and other definitive care facilities and personnel) to provide emergency medical care.
Emergency Operations Center (EOC)	The site from which civil governmental officials (such as municipal, county, state, or federal) direct emergency operations in a disaster.
Epidemic	The occurrence of a disease or condition at higher than normal levels in a population.
Epidemiology	The study of the distribution of determinants and antecedents of health and disease in human populations, the ultimate goal of which is to identify the underlying causes of a disease, then apply findings to disease prevention and health promotion.
Escherichia coli (*E. coli*) O57:H7	A bacterial pathogen that can infect humans and cause severe bloody diarrhea (hemorrhagic colitis) and serious renal disease (hemolytic uremic syndrome).
Essential Public Health Services	A formulation of the processes used in public health to prevent epidemics and injuries, protect against environmental hazards, promote healthy behaviors, respond to disasters, and ensure quality and accessibility of health services. Ten essential services have been identified:

1. Monitoring health status to identify community health problems
2. Diagnosing and investigating health problems and health hazards in the community
3. Informing, educating, and empowering people about health issues
4. Mobilizing community partnerships to identify and solve health problems
5. Developing policies and plans that support individual and community health efforts
6. Enforcing laws and regulations that protect health and ensure safety
7. Linking people to needed personal health services and ensuring the provision of health care when otherwise unavailable
8. Ensuring a competent public health and personal health care work force
9. Evaluating effectiveness, accessibility, and quality of personal and population-based health services
10. Conducting research for new insights and innovative solutions to health problems

Evacuation	The organized removal of civilians from a dangerous or potentially dangerous area.
Federal Response Plan	The plan that coordinates federal resources in disaster and emergency situations in order to address the consequences when there is need for federal assistance under the authorities of the Stafford Disaster Relief and Emergency Assistance Act.
Federally Funded Community Health Center	An ambulatory health care program (defined under Section 330 of the Public Health Service Act), usually serving a catchment area that has scarce or nonexistent health services or a population with special health needs; sometimes known as a neighborhood health center. Community health centers attempt to coordinate federal, state, and local resources in a single organization capable of delivering both health and related social services to a defined population. Although such a center may not directly provide all types of health care, it usually takes responsibility to arrange all medical services for its patient population.
Field Model	A framework for identifying factors that influence health status in populations. Initially, four fields were identified: (1) biology, (2) lifestyle, (3) environment, and (4) health services. Extensions of this approach have also identified genetic, social, and cultural factors and have related these factors to a variety of outcomes, including disease, normal functioning, well-being, and prosperity.

Foodborne Illness	Illness caused by the transfer of disease organisms or toxins from food to humans.
General Welfare Provisions	Specific language in the Constitution of the United States that empowers the federal government to provide for the general welfare of the population. Over time, these provisions have been used as a basis for federal health policies and programs.
Goals	For public health programs, general statements expressing a program's aspirations or intended effect on one or more health problems, often stated without time limits.
Governmental Presence at the Local Level	A concept that calls for the assurance that necessary services and minimum standards are provided to address priority community health problems. This responsibility ultimately falls to local government, which may utilize local public health agencies or other means for its execution.
Harm Reduction	A set of practical strategies reflecting individual and community needs that meet individuals with risk behaviors where they are to help them reduce any harms associated with their risk behaviors.
Hazard	A possible source of harm or injury.
Health	The state of complete physical, mental, and social well-being and not merely the absence of disease or infirmity. It is recognized, however, that health has many dimensions (anatomic, physiologic, and mental) and is largely culturally defined. The relative importance of various disabilities will differ, depending on the cultural milieu and on the role of the affected individual in that culture. Most attempts at measurement have been assessed in terms of morbidity and mortality.
Health Disparity	Difference in health status between two groups, such as the health disparity in mortality between men and women, or the health disparity in infant mortality between African-American and white infants.
Health Education	Any combination of learning opportunities designed to facilitate voluntary adaptations of behavior (in individuals, groups, or communities) conducive to good health. Health education encourages positive health behavior.
Health Maintenance Organizations	Entities that manage both the financing and provision of health services to enrolled members. Fees are generally based on capitation, and health providers are managed to reduce costs through controls on utilization of covered services.
Health Planning	Planning concerned with improving health, whether undertaken comprehensively for an entire community or for a particular population, type of health services, institution, or health program. The components of health planning include data assembly and analysis, goal determination, action recommendation, and implementation strategy.
Health Policy	Social policy concerned with the process whereby public health agencies evaluate and determine health needs and the best ways to address them, including the identification of appropriate resources and funding mechanisms.
Health Problem	A situation or condition of people (expressed in health outcome measures such as mortality, morbidity, or disability) that is considered undesirable and is likely to exist in the future.
Health Problem Analysis	A framework for analyzing health problems to identify their determinants and contributing factors so that interventions can be targeted rationally toward those factors most likely to reduce the level of the health problem.
Health Promotion	An intervention strategy that seeks to eliminate or reduce exposures to harmful factors by modifying human behaviors. Any combination of health education and related organizational, political, and economic interventions designed to facilitate behavioral and environmental adaptations that will improve or protect health. This process enables individuals and communities to control and improve their own health. Health promotion approaches provide opportunities for people to identify problems, develop solutions, and work in partnerships that build on existing skills and strengths.
Health Protection	An intervention strategy that seeks to provide individuals with resistance to harmful factors, often by modifying the environment to decrease potentially harmful interactions. Those population-based services and programs control and reduce the exposure of the population to environmental

or personal hazards, conditions, or factors that may cause disease, disability, injury, or death. Health protection also includes programs that ensure that public health services are available on a 24-hour basis to respond to public health emergencies and coordinate responses of local, state, and federal organizations.

Health Regulation   Monitoring and maintaining the quality of public health services through licensing and discipline of health professionals, licensing of health facilities, and enforcement of standards and regulations.

Health Status Indicators   Measurements of the state of health of a specified individual, group, or population. Health status may be measured by proxies such as people's subjective assessments of their health; by one or more indicators of mortality and morbidity in the population, such as longevity or maternal and infant mortality; or by the incidence or prevalence of major diseases (communicable, chronic, or nutritional). Conceptually, health status is the proper outcome measure for the effectiveness of a specific population's health system, although attempts to relate effects of available medical care to variations in health status have proved difficult.

Health System   As used in this text, the sum total of the strategies designed to prevent or treat disease, injury, and other health problems. The health system includes population-based preventive services, clinical preventive and other primary medical care services, and all levels of more sophisticated treatment and chronic care services.

Healthy Communities 2010   A framework for developing and tailoring community health objectives so that these can be tracked as part of the initiative to achieve the year 2010 national health objectives included in *Healthy People 2010*.

Healthy People 2010   The national disease prevention and health promotion agenda that includes 476 national health objectives to be achieved by the year 2010, addressing improved health status, risk reduction, and utilization of preventive health services.

Incidence   A measure of the disease or injury in the population, generally the number of new cases occurring during a specified time period.

Incident Command System (ICS)   The model for command, control, and coordination of a response to an emergency providing the means to coordinate the efforts of multiple agencies and organizations.

Indicator   A measure of health status or a health outcome.

Infant Mortality Rate   The number of live-born infants who die before their first birthday per 1,000 live births; often broken into two components, neonatal mortality (deaths before 28 days per 1,000 live births) and postneonatal mortality (deaths from 28 days through the rest of the first year of life per 1,000 live births).

Infectious Disease   A disease caused by the entrance into the body of organisms (such as bacteria, protozoans, fungi, or viruses) that then grow and multiply there (often used synonymously with communicable disease).

Infrastructure   The systems, competencies, relationships, and resources that enable performance of public health's core functions and essential services in every community. Categories include human, organizational, informational, and fiscal resources.

Inputs   Human resources, fiscal and physical resources, information resources, and system organizational resources necessary to carry out the core functions of public health (sometimes referred to as capacities).

Intervention   A generic term used in public health to describe a program or policy designed to have an impact on a health problem. For example, a mandatory seat belt law is an intervention designed to reduce the incidence of automobile-related fatalities. Five categories of heath interventions are: (1) health promotion, (2) specific protection, (3) early case finding and prompt treatment, (4) disability limitation, and (5) rehabilitation.

Leading Causes of Death   Those diagnostic classifications of disease that are most frequently responsible for deaths (often used in conjunction with the top 10 causes of death).

Leading Health Indicators   A panel of health-related measures that reflect the major public health concerns in the United States. They were selected to track progress toward achievement of *Healthy People 2010* goals and objectives. They address 10 public health concerns: (1) physical activity, (2) overweight and obesity, (3) tobacco use, (4) substance abuse, (5) responsible sexual behavior, (6) mental health, (7) injury and violence, (8) environmental quality, (9) immunizations, and (10) access to health care.

Life Expectancy   The number of additional years of life expected at a specified point in time, such as at birth or at age 45.

Local Health Jurisdiction (LHJ)   A unit of local government (county, multicounty, municipal, town, other), often with oversight and direction from a local board of health and with an identifiable local health department, that carries out public health's core functions throughout a defined geographic area.

Local Public Health Agency (LPHA)   Functionally, a local (county, multicounty, municipal, town, other) health agency, operated by local government, often with oversight and direction from a local board of health, that carries out public health's core functions throughout a defined geographic area. A more traditional definition is an agency serving less than an entire state that carries some responsibility for health and has at least one full-time employee and a specific budget.

Local Public Health Authority   The agency charged with responsibility for meeting the health needs of the community. Usually this is the policy/governing body and its administrative arm, the local health department. The authority may rest with the policy/governing body, may be a city/county/regional authority, or may consist of a legislative mandate from the state. Some local public health authorities have independence from all other governmental entities, whereas others do not.

Local Public Health System   The collection of public and private organizations having a stake in and contributing to public health at the local level. It involves far more than the local public health agency.

Managed Care   A system of administrative controls intended to reduce costs through managing the utilization of services. Managed care can also mean an integrated system of health insurance, financing, and service delivery that focuses on the appropriate and cost-effective use of health services delivered through defined networks of providers and with allocation of financial risk.

Measure   An indicator of health status or a health outcome, used synonymously with *indicator* in this text.

Medicaid   A federally aided, state-operated and administered program that provides basic medical services to eligible low-income populations, established through amendments as Title XIX of the Social Security Act in 1965. It does not cover all of the poor, however, but only persons who meet specified eligibility criteria. Subject to broad federal guidelines, states determine the benefits covered, program eligibility, rates of payment for providers, and methods of administering the program.

Medical Reserve Corps   Locally based teams of health professionals and other personnel who provide surge capacity for emergencies.

Medicare   A national health insurance program for elderly persons established through amendments to the Social Security Act in 1965 that were included in Title XVIII of that act.

Midlevel Practitioners   Nonphysician health care providers, such as nurse practitioners and physician assistants.

Mission   For public health, assuring conditions in which people can be healthy.

Mitigation   Measures taken to reduce the harmful effects of a disaster or emergency by attempting to limit the impact on human health and economic infrastructure.

Mobilizing for Action through Planning and Partnerships (MAPP)	A voluntary process for organizational and community self-assessment, planned improvements, and continuing evaluation and reassessment. The process focuses on community-wide public health practice, including a health department's role in its community and the community's actual and perceived problems. It provides for a community health improvement process to assess health needs, sets priorities, develops policy, and ensures that health needs are met.
Morbidity	A measure of disease incidence or prevalence in a given population, location, or other grouping of interest.
Mortality	Expresses the number of deaths in a population within a prescribed time. Mortality rates may be expressed as crude death rates (total deaths in relation to total population during a year) or as death rates specific for diseases and sometimes for age, sex, or other attributes (e.g., the number of deaths from cancer in white males in relation to the white male population during a given year).
National Health Expenditures	The amount spent for all health services and supplies and health-related research and construction activities in the United States during the calendar year.
Objectives	Targets for achievement through interventions. Objectives are time-limited and measurable in all cases. Various levels of objectives for an intervention include outcome, impact, and process objectives.
Outcomes	Indicators of health status, risk reduction, and quality-of-life enhancement (sometimes referred to as results of the health system). Outcomes are long-term objectives that define optimal, measurable future levels of health status; maximum acceptable levels of disease, injury, or dysfunction; or prevalence of risk factors.
Outputs	Health programs and services intended to prevent death, disease, and disability, and to promote quality of life.
Personal Health Services	Diagnosis and treatment of disease or provision of clinical preventive services to individuals or families in order to improve individual health status.
Police Power	A basic power of government that allows for restriction of individual rights to protect the safety and interests of the entire population.
Policy Development	One of public health's three core functions. Policy development involves serving the public interest by leading in developing comprehensive public health policy and promoting the use of the scientific knowledge base in decision making.
Population-Based Public Health Services	Interventions aimed at disease prevention and health promotion that affect an entire population and extend beyond medical treatment by targeting underlying risks, such as tobacco, drug, and alcohol use; diet and sedentary lifestyles; and environmental factors.
Postponement	A form of prevention in which the time of onset of a disease or injury is delayed to reduce the prevalence of a condition in the population.
Preparedness	All measures and policies taken before an event occurs that allow for prevention, mitigation, and readiness.
Prevalence	A measure of the burden of disease or injury in a population, generally the number of cases of a disease or injury at a particular point in time or during a specified time period. Prevalence is affected by both the incidence and the duration of disease in a population.
Prevented Fraction	The proportion of an adverse health outcome that has been eliminated as a result of a prevention strategy.
Prevention	Anticipatory action taken to prevent the occurrence of an event or to minimize its effects after it has occurred. Prevention aims to minimize the occurrence of disease or

its consequences. It includes actions that reduce susceptibility or exposure to health threats (primary prevention), detect and treat disease in early stages (secondary prevention), and alleviate the effects of disease and injury (tertiary prevention). Examples of prevention include immunizations, emergency response to epidemics, health education, modification of risk-prone behavior and physical hazards, safety training, workplace hazard elimination, and industrial process change.

Preventive Strategies

Frameworks for categorizing prevention programs, based on how the prevention technology is delivered—provider to patient (clinical preventive services), individual responsibility (behavioral prevention), or alteration in an individual's surroundings (environmental prevention)—or on the stage of the natural history of a disease or injury (primary, secondary, tertiary).

Primary Medical Care

Clinical preventive services, first-contact treatment services, and ongoing care for commonly encountered medical conditions. Basic or general health care focuses on the point at which a patient ideally seeks assistance from the medical care system. Primary care is considered comprehensive when the primary provider takes responsibility for the overall coordination of the care of the patient's health problems, whether these are medical, behavioral, or social. The appropriate use of consultants and community resources is an important part of effective primary health care. Such care is generally provided by physicians but can also be provided by other personnel, such as nurse practitioners or physician assistants.

Primary Prevention

Prevention strategies that seek to prevent the occurrence of disease or injury, generally through reducing exposure or risk factor levels. These strategies can reduce or eliminate causative risk factors (risk reduction).

Public Health

Activities that society undertakes to assure the conditions in which people can be healthy. These include organized community efforts to prevent, identify, and counter threats to the health of the public.

Public Health Agency

A unit of government (federal, state, local, or regional) charged with preserving, protecting, and promoting the health of the population through assuring delivery of essential public health services.

Public Health in America

A document developed by the Core Functions Project that characterizes the vision, mission, outcome aspirations, and essential services of public health. Also see *essential public health services* and Table 1–5.

Public Health Organization

A nongovernmental entity (e.g., not-for-profit agency, association, corporation) participating in activities designed to improve the health status of a community or population.

Public Health Practice

The development and application of preventive strategies and interventions to promote and protect the health of populations.

Public Health Practice Guidelines

Systematically developed statements that assist public health practitioner decisions about interventions at the community level.

Public Health Processes

Those collective practices or processes that are necessary and sufficient to assure that the core functions and essential services of public health are being carried out effectively, including the key processes that identify and address health problems and their causative factors and the interventions intended to prevent death, disease, and disability, and to promote quality of life.

Public Health Service

U.S. Public Health Service, as reorganized in 1996, which now includes the Office of Public Health and Science (which is headed by the Assistant Secretary for Health and includes the Office of the Surgeon General), eight operating agencies (Health Resources and Services Administration; Indian Health Service; Centers for Disease Control and Prevention; National Institutes of Health; Food and Drug Administration; Substance Abuse and Mental Health Services Administration; Agency for Toxic Substances and Disease Registry; and Agency for Health Care Policy and Research); and the Regional Health Administrators for the 10 federal regions of the country.

Public Health System

That part of the larger health system that seeks to assure conditions in which people can be healthy by carrying out public health's three core functions. The system can be further described by its inputs, practices, outputs, and outcomes.

Public Health Workforce   The public health workforce includes individuals

- Employed by an organization engaged in an organized effort to promote, protect, and preserve the health of a defined population group. The group may be public or private, and the effort may be secondary or subsidiary to the principal objectives of the organization
- Performing work made up of one or more specific public health services or activities
- Occupying positions that conventionally require at least 1 year of postsecondary specialized public health training and that are (or can be) assigned a professional occupational title

Quality-Adjusted Life Years (QALYs)   A measure of health status that assigns to each period of time a weight, ranging from 0 to 1, corresponding to the health-related quality of life during that period. These are then summed across time periods to calculate QALYs. For each period, a weight of 1 corresponds to optimal health, and a weight of 0 corresponds to a health state equivalent to death.

Quality of Care   The degree to which health services for individuals increase the likelihood of desired health outcomes and are consistent with established professional standards and judgments of value to the consumer. Quality also may be seen as the degree to which actions taken or not taken maximize the probability of beneficial health outcomes and minimize risk and other undesired outcomes, given the existing state of medical science and art.

Rapid Needs Assessment   A variety of epidemiologic, statistic, anthropologic techniques designed to provide information about an affected community's needs following a disaster or other public health emergency.

Rate   A mathematical expression for the relation between the numerator (e.g., number of deaths, diseases, disabilities, services) and denominator (population at risk), together with specification of time. Rates make possible a comparison of the number of events between populations and at different times. Rates may be crude, specific, or adjusted.

Recovery   Actions of responders, government, and victims that help return an affected community to normal by stimulating community cohesiveness and governmental involvement. The recovery period falls between the onset of an emergency and the reconstruction period.

Rehabilitation   An intervention strategy that seeks to return individuals to the maximum level of functioning possible.

Response   The phase in a disaster or public health emergency when relief, recovery, and rehabilitation occur.

Risk   The probability that exposure to a hazard will lead to a negative consequence.

Risk Assessment   A determination of the likelihood of adverse health effects to a population after exposure to a hazard.

Risk Factor   A behavior or condition that, on the basis of scientific evidence or theory, is thought to influence susceptibility to a specific health problem.

Risk Ratio/Relative Risk   The ratio of the risk or likelihood of the occurrence of specific health outcomes or events in one group to that of another. Risk ratios provide a measure of the relative difference in risk between the two groups. Relative risk is an example of a risk ratio in which the incidence of disease in the exposed group is divided by the incidence of disease in an unexposed group.

Screening   The use of technology and procedures to differentiate those individuals with signs or symptoms of disease from those less likely to have the disease. Then, if necessary, further diagnosis and, if indicated, early intervention and treatment can be provided.

Secondary Medical Care   Specialized attention and ongoing management for common and less frequently encountered medical conditions, including support services for people with special challenges due to chronic or long-term conditions. Services are provided by medical specialists who generally do not have their first contact with patients (e.g., cardiologists, urologists, dermatologists). In the United States, however, there has been a trend toward self-referral by patients for these services rather than referral by primary care providers.

Secondary Prevention   Prevention strategies that seek to identify and control disease processes in their early stages before signs and symptoms develop (screening and treatment).

Span of Healthy Life   A measure of health status that combines life expectancy with self-reported health status and functional disabilities to calculate the number of years in which an individual is likely to function normally.

Specific Rate   Rates vary greatly by race, sex, and age. A rate can be made specific for sex, age, race, cause of death, or a combination of these.

State Health Agency   The unit of state government that has leading responsibility for identifying and meeting the health needs of the state's citizens. State health agencies can be freestanding or units of multipurpose health and human service agencies.

Strategic National Stockpile   A collection of pharmaceuticals, medical supplies, and equipment that can be immediately deployed to meet state and local needs during a public health emergency (formerly known as the National Pharmaceutical Stockpile).

Strategic Planning   A disciplined process aimed at producing fundamental decisions and actions that will shape and guide what an organization is, what it does, and why it does what it does. The process involves assessing a changing environment to create a vision of the future; determining how the organization fits into the anticipated environment, based on its mission, strengths, and weaknesses; and then setting in motion a plan of action to position the organization.

Surveillance   Systematic monitoring of the health status of a population through collection, analysis, and interpretation of health data in order to plan, implement, and evaluate public health programs, including determining the need for public health action.

Tertiary Medical Care   Subspecialty referral care requiring highly specialized personnel and facilities. Services are provided by highly specialized providers (e.g., neurologists, neurosurgeons, thoracic surgeons, intensive care units). Such services frequently require highly sophisticated equipment and support facilities. The development of these services has largely been a function of diagnostic and therapeutic advances attained through basic and clinical biomedical research.

Tertiary Prevention   Prevention strategies that prevent disability by restoring individuals to their optimal level of functioning after a disease or injury is established and damage is done.

Triage   The selection and categorization of victims of a disaster or other public health emergency as to their need for medical treatment according to the degree of severity of illness or injury as well as the availability of medical and transport facilities.

Vulnerability   The susceptibility of a population to a specific type of event, generally associated with the degree of possible or potential loss from a risk that results from a hazard at a given intensity. Vulnerability can be influenced by demographics, the age and resilience of the environment, technology, social differentiation and diversity, as well as regional and global economics and politics.

Weapons of Mass Destruction   Any device, material, or substance used in a manner, in a quantity or type, or under circumstances evidencing intent to cause death or serious injury to persons or significant damage of property.

Years of Potential Life Lost (YPLL)   A measure of the impact of disease or injury in a population that calculates years of life lost before a specific age (often age 65 or age 75). This approach places additional value on deaths that occur at earlier ages.

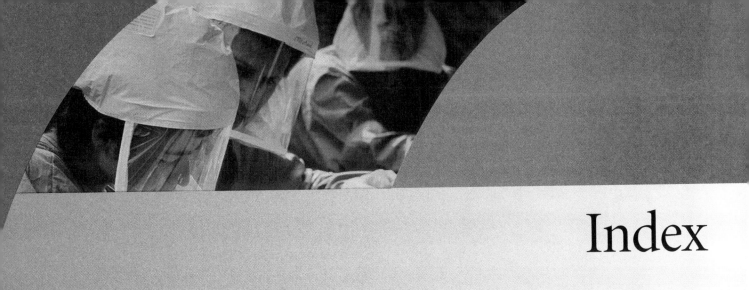

Index

A

AAEE (American Academy of Environment Engineers), 165

ABIH (American Board of Industrial Hygiene), 165

access to health services, 30, 62–64, 67. *See also* risk factors
    universal, 69

accreditation of health administration programs, 149

administration
    guidelines for emergency response, 112
    obstacles to building workforce, 233

administrative law, 76–77

administrators and administrative occupations, 131–132, 141–150
    important and essential duties, 142–145
    judges and hearing officers, 209, 217–218
    minimum qualifications, 145–148
    salary and career prospects, 148–149
    workplace considerations, 148

advisory system (homeland security), 105, 111–112

African-American populations. *See* racial differences

agencies. *See* public health agencies

Agency for Health Care Research and Quality (AHRQ), 81

agenda of public health. *See* scope of public health

age-specific mortality rates, 26–27

AHIMA (American Health Information Management Association), 228

AHRQ (Agency for Health Care Research and Quality), 81

air pollution, 31–32. *See also* environmental and occupational health

alcohol use, 244

analysis of causation. *See* causation analysis

analysis of emergencies, 100–101, 114

ANCC (American Nursing Credentialing Center), 176

animal control. *See* veterinarians

antecedent causes, identifying. *See* causation analysis

antimicrobial agents, 241

APHA (American Public Health Association), 149–150

assessment, as core function, 6, 8

assurance, as core function, 6, 8

ATSDR (Agency for Toxic Substances and Disease Registry), 81

AUPHA (Association of University Programs in Health Administration), 149

avoidance, as health tactic, 3

B

behavior (health), 29, 32–33. *See also* risk factors
    interventions, 55
    during public health emergencies, 101

behavioral disorder counselors, 209, 214, 218

behavioral science competencies, 202

biochemists, salaries for, 216

biologic risk factors, 30. *See also* risk factors

biological agents with bioterrorism potential, 103, 114

biophysicians, salaries for, 216

biostatisticians, 181, 182, 185–186, 188

bioterrorism, 102–103
    emergency response coordinators, 225–226
    epidemiology and, 181
    federal money at state and local levels, 232
    state and local grants, 113–117

birth rates, 36. *See also* fertility rates

black populations. *See* racial differences

boards of health, 3, 84, 89–90

breadth of public health, 11. *See also* core functions of public health

budgeting health care costs. *See* funding government programs

bureaucratic obstacles to building workforce, 233

C

cardiovascular disease, 242–243

career development, 129, 136–137

career prospects, 136–137, 234

 environmental and occupational health, 162–164

 epidemiology and disease control, 189–190

 public health administrators, 148–149

 public health education and information, 201–202

 public health nursing, 175–176

case finding, 54, 57

causation analysis, 32–33, 36–39

 emergency investigation and analysis, 100–101, 114

causes of death, 22–24, 28, 32–33, 68

 motor vehicle–related, 94

 racial and gender differences, 22, 24

 reduction contributions, 59

CCHEST (Council on Certification of Health, Environmental, and Safety Technologies), 165

CDC (Centers for Disease Control and Prevention), 80, 82, 239

 EIS (Epidemiologic Intelligence Service), 190

 emergency preparedness and response, 106

 public health infrastructure funding, 108, 114, 117

CEHTs (certified environmental health technicians), 164

Centers for Disease Control and Prevention. *See* CDC

certifications for environmental health professions, 164

certified health education specialist (CHES), 202–205

CEUs. *See* continuing education

CFSPs (certified food safety professionals), 164

Chardwick, Edwin, 3

chemical agents with bioterrorism potential, 104, 114

CHES (certified health education specialist), 202–205

child health, 242

childhood disease, 28–29

cholera, 3

cigarettes. *See* tobacco use

city health agencies, 75, 89. *See also* local government

classifications, occupational. *See* standard occupational categories for public health

clinical interventions, 55

clinical laboratory technicians and scientists, 209, 214–217, 218

CMS. *See* Medicare and Medicaid

collaboration. *See* multidisciplinary approach to public health

command-and-control approach to public health, 12

common law, 77

communicable disease investigators, 181–182, 183–184, 186. *See also* epidemiology and disease control

communication of public information, 195–205

communication of risk in emergencies, 101, 111–112, 114–115. *See also* public health education and information

communication skills, 237

community dimensions of practice skills, 237

community health nurses. *See* public health nursing

community health profiles (proposed), 45

community outreach workers, 227–228

community-oriented primary care, 57

community-wide emergency response, 101–102

competencies. *See also* credentialing

 changes in, 236–239

 cultural, 62–63, 237

 emergency preparedness, 115

 environmental health professions, 165

 epidemiology and biostatistics, 190

 health administration, 149–150

 public health nursing, 177

 public health workforce, 129

 social and behavioral science, 202

composition of public health workforce, 124–126, 133–134, 233–236

compression of morbidity, 55

constitutional law, 76

content of public health work. *See* practice of public health

continuing education, 240. *See also* education

 health administration, 149

 public health education, 202

 public health workforce, 129

contributing factors. *See* risk factors

core competencies. *See* competencies

core functions of public health, 6, 8. *See also* public health practice

 workforce and, 123–124

core values of public health, 6

cost-benefit analyses, 39

cost-effectiveness analyses, 39

costs of public health, 39–41, 57. *See also* economics of public health; resources of public health

 funding. *See* funding government programs

 opportunity costs, 40

 U.S. health system, 59–62, 79–80

cost-utility analyses, 39

county government, role of, 75, 89. *See also* local government

credentialing, 239–240
    environmental health professions, 164
    public health administrators, 149
    public health education, 202–205
    public health nursing, 176

credibility. *See* public perception

crude mortality rate, 26–27

CTE (Council of State and Territorial Epidemiologists), 190

cultural competencies, 62–63, 237. *See also* competencies

cultural differences, 13

cultural influences on health, 33–35

D

DALY (disability-adjusted life year), 27–28

days lost, 28–29

death rate. *See* mortality rate

definitions of public health, 5–7, 258

degree programs. *See* education

delivery systems for health care, 64–66

demographic trends (U.S.), 62–64

dental health workers, 209, 217, 243

Department of Homeland Security. *See* DHS

determinants. *See* causation analysis

development of policy, 6, 8, 237

development of public health workforce, 231, 239–240

DHHS (Department of Health and Human Services), 78–79, 81–83
    emergency preparedness and response, 105–106

DHS (Department of Homeland Security), 104–107
    advisory system, 105
    guidelines for LPHAs, 111–112

dichotomous thinking, 245

dieticians and nutritionists, 209, 210–212, 218

diphtheria, 15, 16

direct contributing factors, 36–38. *See also* risk factors

directors, LPHAs, 144, 147

disabilities
    defining, 25
    levels of, 22
    limiting, 54
    measures of, 27–29

disability-adjusted life year (DALY), 27–28

discrimination. *See* social justice

disease control. *See* epidemiology and disease control

disease, defining, 25

disease investigators, 181–182, 183–184, 186. *See also* epidemiology and disease control

disease management, 56

disease surveillance, 100, 112, 114. *See also* biostatisticians

disparities. *See* equality (equity)

dissemination of information in emergencies, 101, 111–112, 114–115. *See also* public health education and information

distribution of public health workforce, 124–126, 133–134, 233–236

district government, role of, 75. *See also* local government

diversity of U.S. population, 62

DMATs (Disaster Medical Assistance Teams), 107–108

DMORTs (Disaster Mortuary Teams), 107–108

drug-resistant pathogens, 241

E

E. coli, 240–241

early detection, 54

economic development, 3, 35

economic risk factors. *See* socioeconomic status

economics of public health, 59. *See also* costs of public health; funding government programs
    prevention, 39–41
    U.S. health system, 59–62, 79–80

education, 237–239. *See also* continuing education
    emergency preparedness and response, 111, 115–116
    public health workforce, 129
    requirements. *See* minimum qualifications for public health jobs

educators (public information), 195–205

EIS (Epidemiologic Intelligence Service), 190

emergency operations center (EOC), 109

emergency preparedness and response, 99–119
    coordination, national, 104–108
    coordination, state and local, 108–113
    public health roles, 99–104
    state and local bioterrorism grants, 113–117

emergency response coordinators, 225–226, 236

employees. *See* workforce

environmental and occupational health, 153–165, 236
    health statutes, 87
    important and essential duties, 155–159
    interventions, 55
    minimum qualifications, 159–162
    occupational categories, 153–155
    risk factors, 30, 31–32. *See also* risk factors
    salary and career prospects, 162–164
    workplace considerations, 162

environmental engineering technicians, 154, 162–164

environmental engineers, 154, 155–156, 159–160, 162

Environmental Protection Agency (EPA), 164

environmental science and protection technicians, 154, 163
environmental specialists, 154, 156–158, 160–161, 163
EOC (emergency operations center), 109
EPA (Environmental Protection Agency), 164
epidemic diseases, 3
Epidemiologic Intelligence Service (EIS), 190
epidemiologists, 181–182, 184–185
epidemiology and disease control, 13, 177, 181–191, 236
    emergency preparedness and response, 100, 114
    important and essential duties, 183–186
    minimum qualifications, 186–188
    salary and career prospects, 189–190
    workplace considerations, 188
equality (equity), 22
    access to health services, 63, 67
    social justice, 9–11, 12
eras in public health history, 5
Escherichia coli, 240–241
essential duties for specific professions, 134–135, 234–235
    emergency response coordinators, 225
    environmental and occupational health, 155–159
    epidemiology and disease control, 183–186
    information specialists and analysts, 227
    nutritionists and dieticians, 210–211
    policy analysts, 226
    public health administrators, 142–145
    public health education and information, 196–198
    public health laboratory scientists, 215–216
    public health laboratory technicians, 216
    public health nursing, 171–173
    social workers, 212–214
essential public health services, 8, 10, 123–124. *See also* public health practice
ethics in public health workforce, 128–129
ethnic differences. *See also* equality (equity)
    causes of death, 22
    demographic trends (U.S.), 62–64
    mortality rates, 27
    socioeconomic status, 34
    years of healthy life, 27
expenses for public health, 39–41, 57. *See also* economics of public health; resources of public health
    funding. *See* funding government programs
    opportunity costs, 40
    U.S. health system, 59–62, 79–80
extension of morbidity, 55

F

family structure, changes in, 63
FDA (Food and Drug Administration), 81, 106

federal government. *See also* law; politics of public health
    emergency preparedness and coordination, 104–108
    funding. *See* funding government programs
    grants, 5, 74–75, 82–83. *See also* funding government programs
    health administrators, 149
    health agencies, 78–83. *See also* public health agencies
    health objectives. *See Healthy People 2010*
    health system of, 49–70
        changes and reform, 66–70
        demographics and utilization, 62–64
        economic dimensions, 59–62
        prevention and health services, 50–59
        resources, 64–66
    intergovernmental relationships, 77, 92–96
    public health activities. *See* government programs
    role in public health, 11–12, 75
    role of, 74
    SNS (Strategic National Stockpile), 102, 108
FEMA (Federal Emergency Management Agency), 106
fertility rates, 52
financial planning skills, 238
food safety, 164, 243. *See also* FDA
FTE workers. *See* size of public health workforce
functions of public health, 6, 8. *See also* public health practice
    workforce and, 123–124
funding government programs, 79–81, 93. *See also* expenses for public health
    bioterrorism grants (state and local), 113–117
    cost control, 66–69
    federal money at state and local levels, 232
    local, 86, 90–91
    public health infrastructure, 108, 114, 117
    state-level, 83–86
    workforce development, 239
future challenges in public health, 231–246
    competencies, 236–239
    current limitations, 243–246
    lessons learned, 240–243
    workforce development, 239–240
    workforce distribution and composition, 233–236
    workforce growth, 231–233
future costs, 39–40

G

GDP, health care services and, 60
gender differences, 22, 27. *See also* demographic trends (U.S.)
global influences on health, 35

goals of public health, 6, 8, 123–124. *See also* public health practice
government employment, 126. *See also* workforce
government health agencies. *See* public health agencies
government policy, 11–12, 67
    analysts, 226–227
    development of, 6, 8, 237
    national health objectives. *See Healthy People 2010*
    obstacles to building workforce, 233
    unfinished public health agenda, 243
government programs, 4–5, 11–12. *See also* public health agencies
    debate over, 67
    funding. *See* funding government programs
    national health objectives. *See Healthy People 2010*
government, role of, 73–76. *See also* law
    obstacles to building workforce, 233
    state government, 83–86
grant programs, federal, 5, 74–75, 82–83. *See also* funding government programs
    performance measures, 82
group-model HMOs, 66
growth of public health workforce, 231–233

H

hazardous substances professionals, 164
HCFA (Health Care Financing Administration), 81
health agencies. *See* public health agencies
health behavior, 29, 32–33. *See also* risk factors
    interventions, 55
    during public health emergencies, 101
health care delivery systems, 64–66
health, defining, 25, 254
health educators, 195–202
health expenditures, 39–41, 57. *See also* economics of public health; resources of public health
    funding. *See* funding government programs
    opportunity costs, 40
    U.S. health system, 59–62, 79–80
health indicators, 26–29, 244
    community health profiles (proposed), 45
    economic dimensions, 39–41
    Healthy People 2010 program, 44
    morbidity-based (quality of life), 27–29, 45
    mortality-based, 26–27
health insurance, 61, 63–66. *See also* access to health services
health measurement, 25–28
    causation analysis, 32–33, 36–39
    economic dimensions, 39–41
    indicators. *See* health indicators

influences on, 29–36
    national health objectives, 41–44
    performance measures for public agencies, 82
health officers, 89, 145, 147–148
health problem analysis worksheet, 38. *See also* causation analysis
health promotion, 50–53
    role of government, 74–75
health protection, specific, 51–53
health reform, 66–70
health sector trends, 233
health services administrators, 141
health services managers, 143–144, 146
health status indicators, 26–29, 244
    community health profiles (proposed), 45
    economic dimensions, 39–41
    Healthy People 2010 program, 44
    morbidity-based (quality of life), 27–29, 45
    mortality-based, 26–27
Healthy People 2010, 41–44, 203, 243
hearing officers, 209, 217–218
heart disease, 242–243
Hispanic origin. *See* racial differences
history of public health (U.S.), 3–5
HIV antibody testing, 58
HMOs. *See* managed care
home health nurses. *See* public health nursing
homeland security. *See* DHS
homicide rates, 22
hospital preparedness, 115, 117
hospital-based resources, 64, 69
hospitals, collaborations with public health, 58–59
household income level, 29, 30, 245. *See also* poverty; social influences on health
HP2010. *See Healthy People 2010*
HRSA (Health Resources and Services Administration), 80, 82
    emergency preparedness and response, 106

I

ICS (incident command systems), 109–110
identification of emergency situations, 100, 112, 114. *See also* biostatisticians
IHS (Indian Health Service), 80
illness, defining, 25
immunizations, public health law and, 77
important duties for specific professions, 134–135, 234–235
    emergency response coordinators, 225
    environmental and occupational health, 155–159
    epidemiology and disease control, 183–186

information specialists and analysts, 227
nutritionists and dieticians, 210–211
policy analysts, 226
public health administrators, 142–145
public health education and information, 196–198
public health laboratory scientists, 215–216
public health laboratory technicians, 216
public health nursing, 171–173
social workers, 212–214
incidence prevention, 54
incident command systems (ICS), 109–110
income level, 29, 30, 245. *See also* poverty; social influences on health
indicators of health status, 244
community health profiles (proposed), 45
economic dimensions, 39–41
Healthy People 2010 program, 44
morbidity-based (quality of life), 27–29, 45
mortality-based, 26–27
indicators of public health, 21–24
indirect contributing factors, 36–38. *See also* risk factors
individual rights (legal), 77
industrialism, 3. *See also* economic development
inequality, 22
access to health services, 63, 67
social justice, 9–11, 12
infant mortality, 1–2, 26–27
poverty (socioeconomic status) and, 34
20th-century reduction, 50–52
infection control investigators. *See* disease investigators
infectious diseases, 3, 240–242
death rate (1900–1996), 16
influences on health, 29–36
information dissemination. *See* dissemination of information in emergencies; public health education and information
information specialists and analysts, 227
information technology, workforce productivity and, 233
infrastructure for public health, 108, 114, 117
injuries, 25, 41
inputs to public health system, 7–8
insurance, 61, 63–66. *See also* access to health services
interdisciplinary approach to public health, 13
Medical Reserve Corps, 110
medicine vs. public health, 58–59
public health workforce, 126–129
intergovernmental relationships, 77, 92–96
intervention. *See also* prevention
economic considerations, 39–40

emergency, 101
policy. *See* policy
investigation of emergencies, 100–101
IOM (Institute of Medicine), definition of public health, 6

J

Jenner, Edward, 3
job opportunities, 136–137, 234
environmental and occupational health, 162–164
epidemiology and disease control, 189–190
public health administrators, 148–149
public health education and information, 201–202
public health nursing, 175–176
jobs in public health. *See* workforce
judicial law, 77
justice (social). *See* social justice

L

labor force participation, 63
laboratory investigation and analysis, 100–101, 114
laboratory technicians and scientists, 209, 214–217, 218
law, 76–78
environmental health statutes, 87
medical oversight and regulation enforcement, 145
purposes of, 77–78
legislatively-based law, 76
licensed vocational nurses (LVNs), 170, 173, 175
life expectancy, 1–2, 26–27, 241. *See also* indicators of public health
poverty (socioeconomic status) and, 34
racial and gender differences, 27, 28
life quality, 27–29, 45
lifestyle risk factors, 30, 32–33. *See also* health behavior; risk factors
behavioral interventions, 55
during public health emergencies, 101
local agencies. *See* LPHAs
local boards of health, 89–90
local government. *See also* law; politics of public health
demands on state government, 83
emergency preparedness and coordination, 110–113
bioterrorism grants, 113–117
employment in. *See* workforce
funding. *See* funding government programs
health administrators, 149
intergovernmental relationships, 77, 92–96
public health activities. *See* government programs

public health organizations, 88–92. *See also* LPHAs;
    public health agencies
    role in public health, 11–12, 75
local workforce, 125, 127–128. *See also* workforce
long-term care, 56–57
LPHAs (local public health agencies), 82, 88–92, 94–95. *See also* local government
    directors of, 144, 147
    emergency preparedness and coordination, 110–113
        bioterrorism grants, 113–117
    employment in, 125, 127. *See* workforce
LPNs (licensed practical nurses), 170, 173, 175
LVNs (licensed vocational nurses), 170, 173, 175

M

managed care, 64–66, 68. *See also* health insurance
management skills, 238
Marine Hospital Service, 74
market justice, 9
master's degree programs. *See* education
maternal mortality rates, 52, 242
measles, 16
measurement of health, 25–28
    causation analysis, 32–33, 36–39
    economic dimensions, 39–41
    indicators of health status, 26–29, 244
        community health profiles (proposed), 45
        economic dimensions, 39–41
        Healthy People 2010 program, 44
        morbidity-based (quality of life), 27–29, 45
        mortality-based, 26–27
    influences on, 29–36
    national health objectives, 41–44
    performance measures for public agencies, 82
measuring value of public health, 13–15
medical insurance, 61, 63–66. *See also* access to health services
medical laboratory technicians and scientists, 209, 214–217, 218
medical practice, role of, 56–59
Medical Reserve Corps, 110
Medicare and Medicaid, 67, 69, 80
Medicine/Public Health Initiative (1994), 58
mental health social workers, 209, 214, 218
Metropolitan Medical Response System (MMRS), 108
minimum qualifications for public health jobs, 135
    administrators, 145–148
    emergency response coordinators, 226
    environmental and occupational health, 159–162

    epidemiology and disease control, 186–188
    information specialists and analysts, 227
    laboratory scientists, 216
    laboratory technicians, 216–217
    nursing, 173–175
    nutritionists and dieticians, 211–212
    policy analysts, 227
    public education and information, 198–201
    public health program specialists, 224
    social workers, 214
mixed-model HMOs, 66
MMRS (Metropolitan Medical Response System), 108
Model Public Health Emergency Powers Act, 108
morbidity postponement, 54–55
morbidity-based indicators of health status, 27–29, 45
mortality rates, 16, 26–27. *See also* indicators of public health
    infant mortality, 1–2, 26–27, 50–52
    maternal, 52
    poverty (socioeconomic status) and, 34
mortality-based indicators of health status, 26–27
motivation of government, 12
motor vehicle safety, 93–94, 242
movement, public health as, 7–8
multidisciplinary approach to public health, 13
    Medical Reserve Corps, 110
    medicine vs. public health, 58–59
    public health workforce, 126–129
multi-drug-resistant pathogens, 241
mumps, 16, 17

N

national expenditures. *See* costs of public health
national government. *See* federal government
NEDSS (National Electronic Disease Surveillance System), 114
NEHA (National Environmental Health Association), 164
neonatal mortality. *See* infant mortality
NIH (National Institutes of Health), 80–82, 106
NIMS (National Incident Management System), 107
nongovernmental employment in public health, 125–126
nursing. *See* public health nursing
nutritionists and dieticians, 209, 210–212, 218

O

occupational categories (SOCs), 130, 133, 134
    environmental health, 153–155
    public health administration, 141–142

occupational health. *See* environmental and occupational health
occupational health and safety specialists, 155, 158–159, 161–162, 163
occupational health and safety technicians, 155, 163
occupational health nurses. *See* public health nursing
occupations. *See* jobs in public health; workforce
Office of Health Promotion and Disease Prevention, 82
OHSTs (Occupational Health and Safety Technologists), 165
on-the-job training, 129
OPHEP (Office of Public Health Emergency Preparedness), 106
OPHS (Office of Public Health and Science), 78
opportunity costs, 40
oral health. *See* dental health workers
organizing responses to emergencies. *See* emergency preparedness and response
outcome displacement, 70
outcomes, economics of, 39–41
outputs of public health system, 7–8

P

perception, public, 113, 117
performance measures for public agencies, 82
periodic physical exams, 54
personnel. *See* workforce
pertussis, 16
pharmacists, 217
PHS (U.S. Public Health Service), 78–79, 81–82
physical exams, 54
physical requirements for professions. *See* work setting for public health
physicians, 64, 209, 217. *See also* health officers
planning
    emergency preparedness, 101. *See also* emergency preparedness and response
    policy development, 6, 8. *See also* policy
police powers, 74, 77
policy, 11–12, 67
    analysts, 226–227
    development of, 6, 8, 237
    national health objectives. *See Healthy People 2010*
    obstacles to building workforce, 233
    unfinished public health agenda, 243
polio (1950s), 14–15
poliomyelitis, 16
politics of public health, 11, 67
    funding. *See* funding government programs
    medical care vs. public health, 57–59

role of government, 73–76
    social justice, 9–11, 12
pollution, 31–32. *See also* environmental and occupational health
population rates, 36, 62. *See also* demographic trends (U.S.); fertility rates
population-based public health services, 56–57, 61–62
postneonatal mortality rate. *See* infant mortality
postponement of morbidity, 54–55
poverty, 4, 34–36, 244
    neonatal mortality, 34
PR specialists. *See* public information specialists
practice of public health, 55–57, 124, 133–134, 211, 234–235. *See also* essential duties for specific professionals
    environmental and occupational health, 155–156
    epidemiology and disease control, 182–183
    future of. *See* future challenges in public health
    public health administrators, 142–143
    public health education and information, 196–197
    public health nursing, 170–171
    in public health programs, 222
    public nursing, 169–171
preparedness planning, 101. *See also* emergency preparedness and response
prevalence prevention, 54
prevention, 13
    agencies and organizations, 53
    cultural influences and, 35
    economics of, 39–41
    national expenditures on, 61–62
    U.S. health system, 50–59
primary medical care, 56–57
primary prevention, 54–55, 61–62
private health care providers, 113
private health insurance. *See* insurance
process of public health system, 8
productivity from information technology, 233
professional occupations, 131. *See also* workforce
program specialists and coordinators, 221–224
program-based occupations, 221–228
programs. *See* government programs
promotion of health, 50–53, 74–75
prompt treatment, 54
protection, specific, 51–53
psychosocial risk factors, 30. *See also* risk factors
public education, 195–205
public health, as system, 7–8. *See also* U.S. health system
public health, definitions of, 5–7, 258

public health, history of, 3–5
public health, value of, 13–15
public health activities, 12
public health administrators, 141–150
    important and essential duties, 142–145
    minimum qualifications, 145–148
    salary and career prospects, 148–149
    workplace considerations, 148
public health agencies, 4, 92–96
    federal agencies, 78–83
    funding and cost control. *See* funding government
        programs
    intergovernmental relationships, 92–96
    local organizations, 88–92
    performance measures, 82
    prevention, 53
    role of government, 73–76
    salaries in. *See* salaries for public health jobs
    state agencies, 83–88
public health costs, 39–41, 57. *See also* economics of public
        health; resources of public health
    funding. *See* funding government programs
    opportunity costs, 40
    U.S. health system, 59–62, 79–80
public health education and information, 195–205, 236–239
    important and essential duties, 196–198
    minimum qualifications, 198–201
    salary and career prospects, 201–202
    workplace considerations, 201
public health features, 8–13
public health indicators, 26–29, 244
    community health profiles (proposed), 45
    economic dimensions, 39–41
    Healthy People 2010 program, 44
    morbidity-based (quality of life), 27–29, 45
    mortality-based, 26–27
public health infrastructure funding, 108, 114, 117
public health law, 76–78
    environmental health statutes, 87
    medical oversight and regulation enforcement, 145
    purposes of, 77–78
Public Health Leadership Society, 150
public health nursing, 169–178
    important and essential duties, 171–173
    minimum qualifications, 173–175
    salary and career prospects, 175–176
    workplace considerations, 175
public health policy, 11–12, 67
    analysts, 226–227

development of, 6, 8, 237
national health objectives. *See Healthy People 2010*
obstacles to building workforce, 233
unfinished public health agenda, 243
public health practice, 55–57, 124, 133–134, 234–235. *See
        also* essential duties for specific professions
    environmental and occupational health, 155–156
    epidemiology and disease control, 182–183
    future challenges, 231–246
        competencies, 236–239
        current limitations, 243–246
        lessons learned, 240–243
        workforce development, 239–240
        workforce distribution and composition, 233–236
        workforce growth, 231–233
    public health administrators, 142–143
    public health education and information, 196–197
    public health nursing, 170–171
    in public health programs, 222
    public nursing, 169–171
public health program-based occupations, 221–228
Public Health Ready program, 240
public health surveillance, 100, 112, 114. *See also*
        biostatisticians
public health workforce, 123–137
    composition of, 126–128
    education. *See* education; training
    essential duties, 234–235. *See also* essential duties for
        specific professions
    ethical principles, 128
    future challenges, 231–240
    occupational classifications, 131–133
    in public health programs, 221–228
    size and distribution, 124–126, 133–134, 231–236
    skills and competencies, 129
    specific occupations, 209–218
        environmental and disease control, 236
        environmental and occupational health, 153–165
        epidemiology and disease control, 181–191, 236
        public education and information, 195–205, 236–239
        public health administrators, 141–150
        public health nursing, 169–178, 236
public information communication, 195–205
public information specialists, 195–196, 198, 200–201
public perception, 113, 117
public policy. *See* policy
public relations. *See* public information specialists
purchasers of health care, 66–67. *See also* U.S. health
        system

Q

Quad Council of Public Health Nursing Organizations, 176–178
qualifications for public health jobs, 135
   administrators, 145–148
   emergency response coordinators, 226
   environmental and occupational health, 159–162
   epidemiology and disease control, 186–188
   information specialists and analysts, 227
   laboratory scientists, 216
   laboratory technicians, 216–217
   nursing, 173–175
   nutritionists and dieticians, 211–212
   policy analysts, 227
   public education and information, 198–201
   public health program specialists, 224
   social workers, 214
quality of life, 27–29, 45

R

racial differences. *See also* equality (equity)
   causes of death, 22, 24
   demographic trends (U.S.), 62–64
   life expectancy, 28
   mortality rates, 27
   socioeconomic status, 34
   uninsured people, 63
   years of healthy life, 27
recognition of emergency situations, 100, 112, 114. *See also* biostatisticians
reductionist thinking, 243–245
referendum health agencies, 88
reform of health care system, 66–70
registered nurses (RNs), 170, 173, 175. *See also* public health nursing
regulation. *See* law
rehabilitation, 54
REHS/RS credential, 164
remediation. *See* intervention
resolution health agencies, 88
resources of public health, 57, 64–66, 69. *See also* costs of public health
   federal, 64–66
   management of (incident response), 109
   workforce composition, 126–128
   workforce size, 124–126, 133–134, 231–233
responding to emergencies. *See* emergency preparedness and response

responsibilities of public health work. *See* practice of public health
RETs (registered environmental technicians), 164
RHSPs (registered hazardous substances professionals), 164
RHSSs (registered hazardous substances specialists), 164
rights of individuals (legal), 77
risk communication in emergencies, 101, 111–112, 114–115
risk factors, 29–33
   causation analysis. *See* causation analysis
   social and cultural, 33–35
RNs (registered nurses), 170, 173, 175. *See also* public health nursing
Robert T. Stafford Relief and Emergency Assistance Act, 106
rubella, 16
rural opportunities. *See* distribution of public health workforce

S

salaries for public health jobs, 136
   administrators, 148–149
   community outreach workers, 213, 228
   emergency response coordinators, 213, 223, 226
   environmental and occupational health, 162–164
   epidemiology and disease control, 189–190
   information specialists and analysts, 213, 223, 227
   laboratory scientists, 213, 216
   laboratory technicians, 213, 217
   nursing, 175–176
   nutritionists and dieticians, 212, 213
   policy analysts, 223, 227
   public education and information, 201–202
   public health program specialists, 213, 223–224
   social workers, 213, 214
SAMHSA (Substance Abuse and Mental Health Services Administration), 81
sanitary movement (19th–20th century), 5
Satcher, David, 6
school nurses. *See* public health nursing
science of public health, 12–13
scientific approaches to public health, 243–246
scope of public health, 11. *See also* core functions of public health
screening tests, 54, 57
secondary medical care, 56–57
secondary prevention, 54–55, 61–62
self-reported health status, 28–29
setting for public health work, 124–126, 135–136
   administrators, 148
   education and information, 201

emergency response coordinators, 226
environmental and occupational health, 162
epidemiology and disease control, 188
nursing, 175
sex. *See* gender differences
Shattuck, Lemuel, 4
size of public health workforce, 124–126, 133–134, 231–233. *See also* workforce
smallpox, 3, 16
smoking. *See* tobacco use
Snow, John, 3
SNS (Strategic National Stockpile), 102, 108
social class. *See* socioeconomic status
social enterprise, public health as, 7–8
social influences on health, 33–35
social justice, 9–11, 12. *See also* politics of public health
social policies. *See* policy
social sciences, 12–13, 243–245
    competencies in, 202
social workers, 209, 212–214, 218
socioeconomic status, 29, 30, 245. *See also* demographic trends (U.S.); social influences on health
    poverty, 4, 34–36, 244
    uninsured people, 66
SOCs (standard occupational categories), 130, 133, 134
    environmental health, 153–155
    public health administration, 141–142
specific protection activities, 51–53
spending. *See* costs of public health; funding government programs
staffing. *See* workforce
standard occupational categories for public health, 130, 133, 134
    environmental health, 153–155
    public health administration, 141–142
state boards of health, 84
state constitutions, 76
state government, 108. *See also* law; politics of public health
    emergency preparedness and coordination, 108–110
        bioterrorism grants, 113–117
    employment in. *See* workforce
    funding. *See* funding government programs
    health administrators, 149
    health agencies, 83–88. *See also* public health agencies
    intergovernmental relationships, 77, 92–96
    local agencies, 88
    public health activities. *See* government programs
    role in public health, 11–12, 74–75

state public health workforce, 125, 127–128. *See also* workforce
statisticians. *See* biostatisticians
status, health. *See* indicators of health status
statutory law, 76
Strategic National Stockpile (SNS), 102, 108
substance abuse social workers, 209, 214, 218
supply of health care resources. *See* resources of public health
surveillance of public health, 100, 112, 114. *See also* biostatisticians
system of public health, understanding, 7–8

T

targets for preventative strategies, 57
technicians, 132, 227–228
    environmental engineering technicians, 154, 162–163
    environmental science and protection technicians, 154, 163
    laboratory technicians and scientists, 209, 214–217, 218
    occupational health and safety technicians, 155, 163
terrorism. *See* bioterrorism
tertiary medical care, 56–57
tertiary prevention, 54–55
tetanus, 16
tobacco use, 29–32, 43, 242
town agencies. *See* local government
training, 237–239
    emergency preparedness and response, 111, 115–116
    public health workforce, 129
    requirements. *See* minimum qualifications
travel requirements for jobs. *See* work setting for public health
trends of public health, 5. *See also* future challenges in public health
    health sector, 233

U

unfinished public health agenda, 243
unified command structure, ICS, 109
uninsured people, 63–64. *See also* access to health services
universal access to health care, 69. *See also* access to health services
urban opportunities. *See* distribution of public health workforce
urbanization, 35
U.S. Department of Homeland Security (DHS), 104–107
    advisory system, 105
    guidelines for LPHAs, 111–112

U.S. Environmental Protection Agency (EPA), 164
U.S. government. *See* federal government
U.S. health system, 49–70
　changes and reform, 66–70
　demographics and utilization, 62–64
　economic dimensions, 59–62, 79–80
　prevention and health services, 50–59
　resources, 64–66
　structural framework, 78–96
　　federal agencies, 78–83
　　local agencies, 88–92
　　state agencies, 83–88
U.S. Public Health Service (PHS), 78–79, 81–82
use of health services, 62–64. *See also* access to health
　　services

V

vaccination, 3–4
　mortality rate change, 16
　public health law and, 77
value of public health, measuring, 13–15
veterinarians, 209, 217
Vickers, Geoffrey, 7

W

water pollution. *See* environmental and occupational health
water-related diseases, 37
wellness, 25, 45
white population. *See* ethnic differences; racial differences
Winslow, C. E. A., 1, 6–7
work experience, 129

work setting for public health, 124–126, 135–136
　administrators, 148
　education and information, 201
　emergency response coordinators, 226
　environmental and occupational health, 162
　epidemiology and disease control, 188
　nursing, 175
workforce, 123–137
　composition of, 126–128
　education. *See* education; training
　essential duties, 234–235. *See also* essential duties for
　　specific professions
　ethical principles, 128
　future challenges, 231–240
　occupational classifications, 131–133
　in public health programs, 221–228
　size and distribution, 124–126, 133–134, 231–236
　skills and competencies, 129
　specific occupations, 209–218
　　environmental and disease control, 236
　　environmental and occupational health, 153–165
　　epidemiology and disease control, 181–191, 236
　　public education and information, 195–205, 236–239
　　public health administrators, 141–150
　　public health nursing, 169–178, 236
workplace emergency preparedness, 103
workplace safety, 243

Y

years of health life (YHL), 27–28
years of potential life lost (YPLL), 26–27